CHRISTIAN and JEW

Bronze bust by George Henry Paulin R.S.A., 1933

FREDERICK LEVISON

CHRISTIAN and JEW
The Life of
LEON LEVISON 1881 – 1936

"The Lord said to Abraham, 'Leave your own country, your kinsmen and your father's house, and go to a country that I will show you."

Genesis 12.1

"Nothing worth doing is completed in our lifetime; therefore, we must be saved by hope."

Reinhold Niebuhr

The Pentland Press Ltd.,
EDINBURGH

© Frederick Levison 1989
First published in 1989 by
The Pentland Press
Kippielaw, by Haddington,
East Lothian, Scotland.

All rights reserved
Unauthorised duplication
contravenes applicable laws.

Jacket design by Ann Ross Paterson

ISBN   0 946270 69 4

Typeset by Print Origination (NW) Ltd.
Formby Industrial Estate, Liverpool L37 8EG
Printed and bound by Holmes McDougall Ltd.

For Charles
Ann, Elspeth and Freda,
David, Elizabeth and Christopher,
the grandchildren who never knew him.

Family Tree

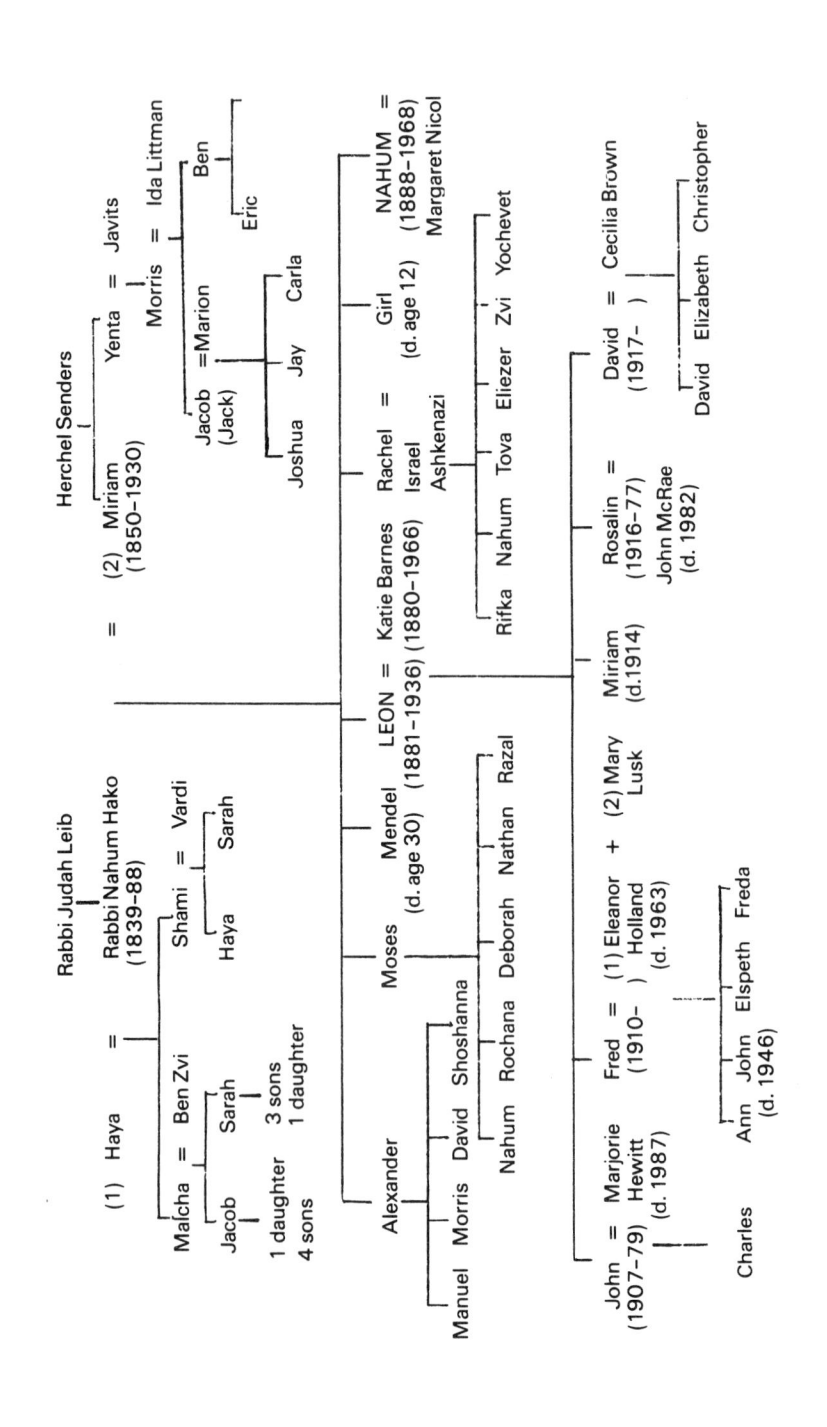

Rabbi Judah Leib = **Herchel Senders**

Rabbi Nahum Hako (1839–88) — (2) Miriam (1850–1930)

(1) Haya

- Yenta = Javits
- Morris = Ida Littman
  - Jacob (Jack) = Marion
    - Joshua
    - Jay
    - Carla
  - Ben
  - Eric

Shami = Vardi
- Haya
- Sarah

Malcha = Ben Zvi
- Jacob
- Sarah
- 1 daughter
- 3 sons
- 4 sons
- 1 daughter

Children of Rabbi Nahum Hako line:
- Alexander
- Moses
- Mendel (d. age 30)
- **LEON** (1881–1936) = **Katie Barnes** (1880–1966)
- Miriam (d. 1914)
- **NAHUM** (1888–1968) = Margaret Nicol

Children of Mendel:
- Manuel
- Morris
- Nahum
- David
- Rochana
- Shoshanna
- Deborah
- Nathan
- Razal

Children of Leon & Katie:
- Fred (1910–) = (1) Eleanor Holland (d. 1963) + (2) Mary Lusk
  - Ann
  - John (d. 1946)
  - Elspeth
  - Freda
- John (1907–79) = Marjorie Hewitt (d. 1987)
  - Charles
- Rifka
- Nahum
- Tova
- Eliezer
- Zvi
- Yochevet
- Rachel = Israel Ashkenazi
- Girl (d. age 12)
- Rosalin (1916–77) = John McRae (d. 1982)
- David (1917–) = Cecilia Brown
  - David
  - Elizabeth
  - Christopher

CONTENTS

	Introduction	ix
	Acknowledgements	xi
PART ONE	01. Rabbi's Son	1
Forebears and	02. Paris Interlude	21
Formative Years.	03. Edinburgh: Early Days	24
Up to 1913.	04. Younger Brother	42
	05. Safed Revisited	50
	06. The Girl Next Door	56
	07. Missionary and Student: 1907 – 14	64
PART TWO	08. The War Years	77
Author, Fund-raiser,	09. The Zionist Dream	93
Missionary, Patriot.	10. "St Paul"	103
1914 – 23.	11. "The Menace of Socialism"	115
	12. Re-enter Nahum	124
	13. Family Affairs	131
	14. Disputatious Rabbi	144
PART THREE	15. Islington to Hamburg	163
The Hebrew Christians.	16. Hamburg to High Leigh	186
1924 – 33.	17. The Year of High Leigh	208
	18. Domestic Interlude	224
	19. Sundry Matters	231
	20. Forebodings	244
	21. Tangier to Mildmay	256
PART FOUR	22. 1934 – 35	275
Advocate for the Oppressed.	23. "A drawing-down of blinds"	295
1934 – 36.	24. "In all their affliction..."	310
	25. The After Years: Katie, Nahum and the Alliance	321
	26. Leon	338
	Appendices A and B	349

LIST OF ILLUSTRATIONS

Bronze bust by George Henry Paulin R.S.A., 1933	Frontispiece
Rabbi Nahum	5
Miriam	10
Rabbi Nahum's synagogue (photo 1972)	13
Leon's exit visa	20
Fred and Julia Sawkins	34
Jewish Medical Mission, 46 Lauriston Place, 1907	34
The young missionary	40
Nahum, c. 1925	49
The remains of the family house in Safed (Photo 1972)	53
Kitty Robinson	63
Katie with John 1909	63
Leon, 1911	69
"Admiral Jellicoe" and "Admiral Sturdee"	133
Leon, 1928	185
The Insignia of the Order of the Knight Grand Cross and Star of the Church of the Holy Sepulchre	207
Ben Rohold	209
The family in 1932	225
Polish Alliance, Warsaw, April 1933	249
Harcourt Samuel	282
Hugh Schonfield	282
Jacob Peltz	282
Leon: the last snapshot	313
The opening of Memorial House	322
Harcourt Samuel: elder statesman	325
Katie: the middle years	326
Nahum and Margaret, 1939	329
Nahum at 72	335
Sir Leon	338

INTRODUCTION

One day, when I was about twelve, the form-master left the room. When he was out of earshot a boy began banging the lid of his desk to the chant,
> "Son of the tribe of Levi,
> Son of the tribe of Levi."

Soon the whole class was at it. There was no malevolence, and we all thought it extremely funny. But that was when I realised for the first time that there was something not quite Scottish about my family.

Some years earlier when my brother John and I were very young we were told that in some far-off land we had an Uncle Moses. We were convulsed with mirth and rolled about on the carpet, gurgling "Is there an Uncle Abraham as well?" No such luck! But no one else in Morningside, Edinburgh, as far as we knew, could boast an Uncle Moses. That, too, set us apart.

I knew, of course, when I was twelve, that my father was a missionary to the Jews; and that he had been brought up as a Jew, in Palestine. But that did not seem to impinge on his children's lives. Our lot was in no way like that of Rabbi Daiches' sons Lionel and David, at the same school, who were excused School Prayers and could not join the literary or dramatic clubs because these met on Friday evenings, nor in any sports, to which Saturdays were dedicated. No, we were thoroughly assimilated and had never thought of ourselves as anything but Scots.

And that, many a patriotic Jew would say, is the trouble. When a Jew becomes a Christian he ceases to be a Jew and within a generation all traces of his Jewish birthright are lost.

My father was well aware that he had joined the despised

meshunadim — the turncoats and renegades. He could not, however, deny his Christian faith, nor would he deny his Jewish identity. His wife was not Jewish and he would not impose Jewish traditions or customs on her (although she became interested in them), still less on his children. But he never ceased to call himself "a Jew by race and a Christian by grace"; and to those who said it was impossible to be both he would have replied as did St Paul, who also looked on himself as no less a Jew for being a Christian: "Are they Hebrews? So am I. Are they Israelites? So am I. Are they the seed of Abraham? So am I." (2 Corinthians 11:22)

I have for the most part written in the third person in order to attain a greater objectivity. For a filial biography is peculiarly difficult. Emotionally involved, one may make it either a sentimental act of pious adulation or, if one's childhood has been unhappy, a perverse one of denigration. Since more than fifty years have elapsed since my father's death, however, age and time have sufficiently dimmed the past, I hope, for my feelings, deeply affectionate though they are, not to intrude unduly. I am also encouraged by Dr Johnson's assertion that "Nobody can write the life of a man but those who have ate and drunk and lived in social intercourse with him."

My father's life was closely bound with those of his fellow Hebrew Christians, and especially of his brother Nahum; and this is their story too. It is also the story of the Edinburgh Jewish Medical Mission, of the International Hebrew Christian Alliance, and *inter alia* of his family life, his public service in peace and war, his writings and his travels. And rather than bring the biography to an abrupt end with his death I have, as I suspect many readers would wish, followed through the subsequent development of some of these themes.

The term 'Hebrew Christian' might equally be 'Jewish Christian' or 'Messianic Jew' and the last two are perhaps more frequently used today. But my father and his associates preferred the prefix 'Hebrew' because it referred unambiguously to their race. 'Jewish' connotes both race and religion and Judaism and Christianity are two religions not one, even if, as Christians aver, the Old and New Testaments belong together. "We are Christians", wrote one of his colleagues, "but . . . retaining what we had before we became Christians we use the term 'Hebrew Christian', a term which looks right back to Abraham the Hebrew."

The invisible hand, a biographer declared, is more powerful than the manipulative hand. Having shared in many of the events I have described in the later chapters, I cannot remain invisible. And because most of my father's friends are long dead, his papers lost and letters destroyed, biography has sometimes turned into memoir. But with the help of the *Hebrew Christian Quarterly* which he edited and various church reports, and having consulted my brother David and a number of friends, I have tried to reconstruct a jigsaw of which not too many pieces are missing.

ACKNOWLEDGEMENTS

My principal sources have been family papers, the Minutes of the Edinburgh Jewish Medical Mission up to 1907 and the *Hebrew Christian Quarterly* from 1928 to 1938.

I am indebted to the following for information and photographs: the Rev. Harcourt Samuel, the late Dr Hugh J Schonfield and his daughters, Mrs Molly and Miss Ann Davidson Kelly, the late Mrs Charlotte Davidson, Mr Nahum Ashkenazi, Mr Robertson Sutherland, Mr R Forbes Ridland, Mrs Diana Herdman-Newton, Mrs Rose, Mrs Withers, Dr Alex King and Miss May Slidders. Also to my brother David, my nephew Charles and particularly his secretaries, Kirsty Eastwood and Colleen Hue, who typed the manuscript; and to my wife Mary for her constant encouragement and helpful advice.

The graciousness of Dr David Daiches in allowing me to quote the passage on page 146 and to express my disagreement is especially appreciated.

Mr Douglas Law of the Pentland Press has been unfailingly helpful.

My cordial thanks to the Drummond Trust, 3 Pitt Terrace, Stirling for financial assistance.

PRONOUNCIATIONS

Leon is pronounced 'Lee-on' and not, as frequently in Britain, 'Lay-on'.
Rabbi Nahum was known as 'Naahoom'; but in Britain his son was 'Nay-um'.
In Schonfield the 'ch' is hard.

Forebears and Formative Years.
Up to 1913.

1. RABBI'S SON

Go and swim in the Sea of Galilee, north of Tiberias. Perhaps at the kibbutz hotel near Magdala. Lie on your back and gaze westwards. You will then see, on the crest of the far hills, over 3000 feet up, some ancient ramparts. They are Crusader remains and enclose a public garden known as the Citadel which affords a magnificent viewpoint for visitors to the town of Safed.

To devout Jews Safed is one of the four holy cities of Israel. The others are Jerusalem, the City of David; Hebron, with its Machpelah cave — the tomb of the Patriarchs; and Tiberias, the seat of the Sanhedrin after the destruction of the Temple, and burial place of Maimonides of Cordoba, the great 12th century physician, philosopher and Talmudic theologian.

Once, in this ancient and holy city of Safed, the rabbis of sixteen synagogues studied the mystic writings of the Cabbala; and the disciples of Luria, the 16th Century apostle of Hebrew mysticism, gathered yearly, as some still do, to honour him. Today it is a spa with sixteen hotels and a flourishing artists' colony; but the old huddled Jewish quarter to the north-west, where houses lean on one another across cobbled alleys, still stands, as does the small Ashkenazi synagogue, richly decorated in green and gold, where Leon's father ministered, and where he sat, an alert little boy with thick dark curly hair, among his brothers. His mother, Miriam, and his sister Rachel, both of whom he loved dearly, perforce sat elsewhere.

Round the corner from the synagogue, perched above the steep western slopes, are the remains of the rabbi's house. It was small and overcrowded for he brought up there the two children of his first marriage and six of his second. Leon, or Leib or Loeb as he was then called, came fourth among the latter. He was born in 1881 and was, in fact, named Judah Leib to signify the tribe of his descent. This imprecision of nomenclature, although shared by Shakespeare, whose surname is variously spelt, has long been a Jewish characteristic. Nobody cared whether Safed had priority over Safad, Sefad, or, more recently, Zvet or Zfat. Two of these would appear on the same official document.

Nor did Leon's grandfather, Rabbi Judah Leib, nor his father, Rabbi Nahum Hako, think it necessary to have a surname. It was only when Queen Victoria awarded the latter British citizenship that it became essential. Hitherto they were known simply as 'the Aaronic family'.

The surname chosen was that of Rabbi Nahum's maternal uncle, Isaac Baer Levinsohn (1788-1860). This admired member of the family was a citizen of Kishinev in the Ukraine, which had a large Jewish population.

Isaac Levinsohn was both distinguished and enlightened, and merits a place in the Jewish Encyclopaedia where it is said of him that "he lived in various Russian cities and had the ear of the Czar in matters concerning the Jews. He pleaded for their relief from persecution, especially the persecution of their children, and for the advancement of their education. He was also a leader of the reforming movement of Hassidism which advocated the loosening of the stricter rabbinic laws, the teaching of agriculture and practical trades, and a more tolerant attitude towards Christianity." He wrote two books of some repute, *Yalkut Ribal* and *Efes Damim*, the latter to refute an allegation, endorsed by the Czar, that the Jews drank blood at Passover.

His reforming spirit was shared by his nephew and later by Leon. But what brought the family to Palestine? It was from about 1830 that immigrants from many countries returned to their Holy Land; older men and women to lay their bones in ancestral dust, for they regarded their long sojourn in Europe and Russia as years of exile; young men, with their families, to escape conscription, especially in Russia.

From Kishinev in 1838 came the young Rabbi Judah and his wife because, it is said, she was infertile and they believed that in the Holy Land her prayers, like Hannah's of old, would be heard.

So indeed it was. For the following year Nahum was born. They had not gone to Safed, which had been devastated in 1837 by an earthquake which killed over 4,000 Jews — how many Arabs we are not told — but had settled in Jerusalem. They were joined there in 1841 by another relative, Rabbi Samuel Salant, a saintly and much loved figure in Jerusalem who became its Chief Rabbi and the acknowledged leader of the community. He was the confidant and mentor of Sir Moses Montefiore, that Grand Old Man of British Jewry, who crossed Europe seven times by coach — the final journey being in his ninetieth year — to perform works of philanthropy in 'Erez Israel'.[1] (The coach is preserved at his memorial in Jerusalem). Accompanied by Salant, often by Judah and later by Nahum, and conspicuous by his height, Sir Moses toured the country founding agricultural colonies, a textile factory, a hospital, a printing press and other institutions.

These were sadly needed, for Palestine was impoverished. The hills were barren, the valleys overgrown and often swampy and malarial, the roads unsurfaced and the cities bedevilled with slums. On each of his tours Sir Moses visited Safed and it was by him that its houses were rebuilt and its synagogues restored.

The 4,000 deaths at Safed indicate the rapid increase of the Jewish population; for at the beginning of the century there were scarcely 10,000 Jews in the whole land. A century later there were 90,000, 20,000 of whom had returned between 1850 and 1880, driven back by endless Russian pogroms. From this influx were born new hopes and the seeds of Zionism. By 1883 the first all-Jewish village, Petah Tikvah, 'The Gate of Hope', was established[2], and in 1897, at the first Jewish Congress, Theodor Herzl set forward the revival of Jewish national life.

In mid-century, however, it needed Montefiore, his in-laws the Rothschilds, and enlightened Palestinian Jews like Leon's forebears, to alleviate the social burdens of ignorance, disease and poverty, and to combat the lack of material resources and industrial skills.

Rabbi Nahum, like his father, was noted for good works. Having been appointed to Safed he ran a free pharmacy there, paying from his own pocket for medicines for Jews and Moslems alike. During one of the country's crop failures he went to Mesopotamia and bought up wheat. His brethren appointed him a Rabbin or Chief Rabbi and prevailed on him to give up a life of study in order to plead abroad the cause of the poor. This in fact he did, but not without hazard. In London he was arrested for trying to raise unauthorised sums for a hospital in Jerusalem and for the Russian immigrants. Imprisoned for his pains, he was able to communicate with Lord Montefiore (as he now was), who not only rescued him but presented him to the Queen, as Disraeli was to do on two other occasions.

Montefiore would probably remind Her Majesty that at the Indian Mutiny of 1857-58 Nahum had earned merit with the British when, during a prolonged stay in India, he had persuaded Indian Jewry not to join in the revolt. It does not sound like the work of a lad of barely 18, but one has to remember the precosity of well-educated Jews who were taught, as Leon was, to read the Torah from the age of two! Anyhow, it was either then or in the 1880s, when Nahum was working among the sizeable Jewish population of Calcutta, that the family was granted British Indian citizenship. Maybe it was in the benefactions associated with her Jubilee in 1881, the year of Leon's birth. It was around this time that Nahum was instrumental, at the Queen's behest, in ending a conflict between the *Baghdadis* (Sephardic Jews from Iraq who had settled in India) and the *Cochinis* (the black Jews of Cochin). It is an incident which prompts the question: how can a Jew assume the pigment of another race, be it Indian, Ethiopian or Chinese? It can only be that after centuries of intermarriage, through which the faith and traditions have been stubbornly preserved, the pigmentation has suffered change or, alternatively, it may have been through conversion.[3]

Not long after his return from India Rabbi Nahum again came to the Queen's notice. In May 1882 oppressive laws against the Jews were imposed in Russia, and there was a new exodus to Palestine. The subsequent distress prompted him to promote a hospital in Jerusalem — possibly the first Jewish hospital, *Bikur Cholim;* and for this he received a letter of appreciation possibly written, but certainly signed, in the Queen's own hand. About the same time he founded the Nissan Bank Synagogue and Rabbinical College in the Old City. The synagogue was for a community of poor Jews from Galicia. There was difficulty in completing the building, but help came from an unexpected quarter. The Emperor Franz Joseph on a visit asked the rabbi why the synagogue was roofless. "It took its hat off to the Kaiser!" was his reply; and this *bon mot,* hardly scintillating to modern ears, won from Franz Joseph a handsome donation.

A further example of the rabbi's altruism was the stand he took on behalf of those oppressed by their overlords the Turks, who robbed the immigrants ruthlessly both at the frontiers and after their settlement. He urged British protection for them and was backed by Disraeli and Montefiore. The Prince of Wales, who visited Safed at the time, lent a sympathetic ear; the petition was granted — to what effect is not known — but as a corollary other prominent citizens of Safed were given the protection of British citizenship.

Rabbi Nahum

Rabbi Nahum was President of Safed's Cabbalistic School. He was also the *Toen* or rabbinical advocate, without whom none of the religious disputes could be settled nor the laws administered. But his calling took him far beyond Safed. His son Alexander wrote, "He was also Rabbi in Gibraltar and in Morocco, in Tunis, Tripoli and Algeria, and in India. In all these places he was known as a 'holy man' and a 'Grand Rabbi'." Then in 1881, the year of Leon's birth, he was appointed Palestinian representative to Jewish communities in Italy, France, Austria, Great Britain, Northern and Southern Africa, Arabia, Egypt, Bosnia and America. The scroll of his appointment, signed at Beirut by the German and Austrian consuls, is still preserved.

Rabbi Nahum was unable to visit all these countries — certainly not America — but he was concerned, as his son was to be, for their poor and needy and, as Leon was also to do, made arduous journeys among them. His travels took him to Persia, where there was some disaffection owing to a decree of the Shah that the Jews must close their shops on Fridays. It is said that when the rabbi put the Jewish case to the Shah he spoke so perfectly in the Persian tongue that the law was annulled and the Jews enabled to observe their own Sabbath instead of the Moslem holy day, His linguistic ability also enabled him to speak fluent English, French, Arabic and Russian, in addition to Hebrew and Yiddish.

Nahum's first wife, Haya, came from Jerusalem and bore him two children, Malcha and Shami. Their descendants include a U.N. Representative, a concert pianist, and the Ben-Zvis, who are associated with the Central Press in Jerusalem and its publications. On Haya's death he married Miriam Hershel Senders (also given the surname of Hethinger) who was Safed-born and known as Baba. Senders is the equivalent of Alexander, which was the name they gave their first-born; there followed Moses, Mendel, Leon, Rachel, another daughter who died, and then Nahum. Although her parents were immigrants from Roumania, Miriam claimed that the vineyards she inherited near Safed had been her family's for many generations and were now repossessed; indeed, that her family had lived in Northern Galilee and owned property there since 300 A.D.

Leon too was convinced that he had a long-established Palestinian pedigree. The first words of a biographical note which he wrote in 1903 are these: "I was born in the year 1880 in Safed . . . . My parents can trace their descent as rabbis for thirteen generations and have all this time been natives of Palestine." Actually he was born in 1881 — exactitude was not his strong point — and although it is true that his forebears claimed a long rabbinic descent, they do not all appear to have lived in Palestine. Going back beyond these thirteen generations, there was Rashi an 11th century French Jew of Troyes who, says Professor David Daiches (who also claims him for an ancestor), "made the rabbinical schools of Champagne and northern France famous throughout Jewry." Other ancestors were the medieval Maharal of Prague and, in a later century, a rabbi of Frankfurt.

There is imprecision in these matters as in much else. Was Levinsohn, for instance, the maternal surname, or Levinshon or

Levison? Leon and his brothers opted for Levison and so it has remained; although it is frequently confused with the more widely known Levinson.

In 1887 when Leon was six, the family was in Calcutta. It was there, in the following year, that his brother Nahum was born. The destiny of both brothers lay in Scotland, but after living there for thirty years Nahum found it necessary, when India achieved independence in 1947, to take out naturalisation papers, having been classified as a British Indian subject. Leon's passport had the same classification, but whether he was also born in India, or the citizenship bestowed on the family included the word 'Indian', is not clear. His own words, "I was born in Safed", might only be his imprecise way of saying that it was his home town.

That their father served the Calcutta synagogue for considerable periods of time is apparent from a statement concerning his ministry in Safed.

"My father", wrote his eldest son Alexander, "would never accept monetary remuneration. He was not even paid for his services as Rabbi in the synagogue, owing to the poverty of the people. How then did he live? He had properties and was also well paid by the people in Calcutta. They used to send him money even after he had left Calcutta. He owned five houses and had an estate of vines and olive trees. Four houses and the estate were sold on his death and his widow occupied the fifth."

Nahum's affluence derived from Miriam's dowry, her father being a wealthy trader in wheat and oil. According to Leon, the four square miles of vineyards and arable land which lay across the north-west valley by the village of Ain Zitoun had been in the family's possession for generations; but that could only mean his mother's family.

These vineyards were to play a significant part in his life. Because of them he was to have an agricultural training and at the age of seventeen to become their manager. He was therefore a privileged young man, and not only in material things. He was privileged in being born into a highly educated as well as a loving home; privileged also in that it was not a claustrophobic Jewish family, but one open to the wider world, and especially to the idealistic side of Victorian life. He was also privileged to have travelled early, for India would have made an indelible impression on a precocious six year-old.

His parents loved him 'not wisely but too well.' He was doted upon as the favourite son. Since the days of Joseph and Benjamin, the Hebrews had preserved this to us reprehensible custom, and compelled the chosen one to wear a silver collar and gold earrings. "I was the pet of the household," wrote Leon, "I wore these ornaments till I had sense enough to take them off."

His status does not seem to have aroused any jealousy among his brothers, and with the local youth he was popular and, indeed, became their leader. Several stories are told to that effect. On one occasion when he found other boys tormenting a gypsy woman whom they had dubbed a witch, he sent them packing. The woman in her gratitude offered to teach him to read hands, and he acquired some knowledge of palmistry. His belief in it was fortified when one of her prognostications came true. She had said that someone he knew well would shortly be drowned. Drowning was a rare occurrence and the prophecy had seemed incredible; but a young man's horse stumbled, throwing him into a river swollen by recent storms, and he drowned.

Some thirty years later Leon still read palms, but then vowed he would cease doing so, not from any theological consideration, but because he foresaw too much that was dark and tragic in his friends' lives. If, however, he was asked how he could square this seeming dalliance with fatalism with his religious beliefs, he would reply that what palmistry predicts is not absolute. Both divine intervention and the human will have the freedom to alter one's destiny. What the palmist foretells are probabilities, not certainties.

The young Jews of Safed formed two camps, the Sephardic and the Ashkenazic, which had little to do with one another. Leon, however, brought them together, welding them, said his brother, into a group which served the community well. At thirteen he became *Bar Mitzvah* and responsible for his own actions according to the moral law; and he was barely fourteen when he decided to intervene in a quarrel between two sheiks, one of Ain Zitoun the other of Mairoun, villages adjoining the family vineyards. The Jews normally avoided such disputes among Arabs, which were apt to become blood-feuds, but Leon, accompanied by a courier called Herschel, dared to go to one of the sheiks, plead for peace and bring back an offer.

On another occasion he was riding into Acre when an Arab guard appeared and claimed that the horse had been stolen and was his.

Leon's companion turned tail as the guard drew his revolver and other Arabs arrived with drawn daggers. Leon, however, kept calm. "I am Leib," he told them, "the son of Rabbi Nahum of Safed. If you leave the horse in my keeping I promise that if the British Consul decides that it is yours you will get it back." Surprisingly, the Arab agreed: "I am assured of justice," he said.

Leon's parents could conceive no greater future for their sons than that they should become rabbinic scholars and ultimately rabbis. Their eldest, Alexander, was to fulfil their hopes and Moses too, after a diversion into agriculture, became a rabbi. Leon's youngest brother Nahum was set on the same course but, as we shall see, took a different one. As for Leon, he felt that the Torah was not a sufficient occupation. He had a brilliant but not an academic mind. He wanted to learn but also to do; so he persuaded his parents to let him acquire a trade. He chose tailoring, which he studied in his spare hours. "He was very proud, I remember" wrote his brother Nahum,[4] "when he was commended by the tailor for neatness of hand and straight-iron cutting. He persisted in that accomplishment until he was told that he could now do a suit himself. That seemed to satisfy him, and tailoring was given up for a more intense interest in agriculture."

This, however, was not before he had had a thorough grounding in the Jewish curriculum. First there was the small classroom still to be seen opposite the synagogue. Then tuition along with one of his brothers and some other boys by Rabbi Joshua of Acre, whom his father invited to Safed. Rabbi Joshua was one of the most eminent teachers in the land, and Leon was again privileged when he was accepted into his school. The rabbi, a saintly and unworldly man, kept the Sabbath so strictly that from Friday afternoon to Saturday night he was silent, uttering only such words as concerned the Sabbath itself. He was, says Nahum again, very fond of Leon "and sought to improve him not only with his learning but with his kindly and beautiful spirit, and Leon idolised him and would do for him what he would do for no one else."

In 1888, and only in his fiftieth year, Rabbi Nahum died. Five months later Miriam bore a son in Calcutta and gave him his father's name. He too, like Leon, was to have a chequered destiny, and their lives would be closely intertwined.

Seventy years later, recalling the influence of his mother, Nahum said, "My mother was very restless and travelled widely after my

Miriam

birth. By the time I was three she came back for a time and the first recollection I have of her was her teaching me to recite the 121st Psalm.". This psalm told him of a personal God who did not sleep, and this removed his fear of the dark. "She got up," he wrote, "before the other members of the family and recited the set portions of the Psalms. I often crept in beside her. . . I got to know the Psalter in Hebrew by heart. . . I still feel I have a strong bias for the Psalms, and cannot deal with them impersonally. They are my devotional life and will remain so to the end."

A mystery surrounds the rabbi's death. It occurred suddenly and far from home. While some believed that he had contracted pneumonia, others maintained that he was poisoned.

Having returned from India, he had been sent by Rabbi Salant on a mission to Kishinev, where two brothers were engaged in a bitter and prolonged dispute over the estate of their father, who had died intestate. Eventually they agreed to approach their rabbi, who in turn wrote to Rabbi Salant. Then Rabbi Nahum, expert in Jewish law and emissary, for various purposes, to the Jews of the Diaspora, was despatched to resolve the matter. However, in Odessa he fell ill. He struggled back to Kratia in the Ukraine, where, in the house of his birth, he died. Some hold that he was murdered. At the time he was also carrying a large sum of money with which he had been hoping to persuade the Tsarist officials to enable a number of elderly Jews to emigrate to Palestine. This money, it was suggested, had been taken by Tsarists to be proof of a political plot, and Nahum was poisoned because he was believed to be working on behalf of the dissident Russian Jews.

Whichever way it happened, it was an untimely end to a life richly endowed and prolifically used for the spiritual and material welfare both of his compatriots and of widely scattered fellow Jews; and Leon, equally endowed, was to be similarly used.

At the age of twelve, his schooling completed, Leon was sent to the agricultural college, *Mikvah de Israel,* near Jaffa. For it had been decided that the estate would best be managed not by strangers but by two of the rabbi's sons. Moses was despatched to Germany to learn the science of winemaking, in which Palestine carried out a large trade, while to Leon was allocated the culture of the fruit trees and vines.

In the college vacations Leon entered into the community life of his home-town where, again according to his brother, "the needy were his brothers and sisters, the fallen his care, and his greatest gift that of enlisting the sympathy of others in good causes. He was roused to indignation where others were concerned, and once he had taken up the cause of an individual or an ideal he fought for it not bitterly but with all the courage of his name, 'Lion'." He was also concerned with self-improvement, and persuaded his mother to provide him with a tutor in French. She was reluctant but he told her, "You must know what other people think." It was this determined search for knowledge that brought him, a few years later, to learn English, even though it meant clandestine visits to the Scottish Mission, which was out of bounds and held in general contempt.

When, at sixteen, he left the college, it is rumoured that he went abroad for further training in France or Germany; but there is no evidence of this. All we know is that having taken over the management of the estate he had no difficulty in handling its 200 Arab labourers. The vineyards were adjacent to Baron Edmund de Rothschild's colony at Rosh Pinnah with its imported staff of French vine growers, to whose factor Leon gave some assistance; at the same time, no doubt, he was practising his French.

Baron Rothschild introduced new plant species and, after further Russian pogroms in 1880, employed and instructed some of the settlers; but his system of patronage was unpopular, and in 1900 his settlements were transferred to the Jewish Colonization Association, most of them soon to become self-supporting. Nevertheless his was a major role in the development of the wine industry in Palestine.

Leon, not to be outdone, applied his college expertise and (Nahum again): "there were soon very few men in Palestine who could pick a better cane of wild olive or vine. He experimented with cross-grafting and ultimately produced an eating-grape that was appraised by some as the most luscious . . . ever produced in Palestine. The Governor of Beirut used to consider it a great treat to receive a basketful of grapes."

The course of Leon's life seemed now to be set. At seventeen he had a responsible job for which he was well qualified. His interest in European culture was growing and he longed to travel, but that could be achieved some day from his home base. Sophisticated pleasures were not to be found in Safed, but he was content to ride with his friends, sometimes down to the Lake — half a day's

Rabbi Nahum's synagogue   (photo 1972)

journey — to swim; and to learn to play the violin. He also wanted to study English and to visit Britain as his father had done. Not far ahead, for marriage was early, lay the prospect of a bride, and his mother may already have been looking around for one, apart from his own thoughts on the matter.

However, what the palmist, or anyone else, predicts is never a certainty. Divine intervention and the human will have the freedom to alter one's destiny. So it was to be.

One day when he was perhaps fourteen, his elder brothers, Alexander and Moses, had gone abroad. In their absence he had the chance, usually taken by them, to sing and read one of the six appointed passages in the synagogue. Two of these passages were read by officials and the third by someone nominated by the rabbi — as when Jesus read at Nazareth. The other three were reserved for families in the congregation who bought the privilege on a yearly basis, and thus subscribed to the upkeep of the synagogue. Along with his brothers, Leon held this privilege, and in their absence he sang and read the portion on succesive Sabbaths.

After one of these services a woman spoke to his mother. "Your son," she said, "reads well; but do you think he understands what he is reading?" "Of course he does," said Miriam; "he is an excellent Hebrew scholar," However, when she repeated the conversation to Leon she added that he ought to make a closer study of the Scriptures; and that if he did so he would put more meaning into the words he sang.

At first he rejected her advice, which would entail more hours indoors and less for his chief pleasure, which was riding. "But," he says, "she kept on at me and expressed to Father[5] her desire for me to read the Bible." He decided to give in, and told them he would read it; they, however, said "Not by yourself," and found a tutor who, says Leon, "was paid well to instruct me, and help me over the dangerous passages which might harm me or make me a Christian . . . . All went well till we had passed the Torah, but on beginning the Psalms and Prophets the tutor became more particular and wanted me to pass over certain portions. I asked him why. . . but he said 'Never mind, if we skip them we shall be done the sooner.' This aroused my curiosity. . . I told him I could not understand why those chapters had been put in if they were not worth reading. . . [He] still did not give me any reason, and would not allow me to read the portions dangerous to the Jewish faith. I noted [them] down secretly, and when my lesson was over I read them over and over, paying serious attention to prophecies of the Messiah. . .

"The prophecy of Daniel was specially instrumental in convincing me that the Messiah must have come long ago. I determined that I would find out more about this, and hearing that at the mission they were preaching and speaking of a Messiah having come, I paid a visit to the mission secretly one night. It was only about a hundred yards from our house, but to get there without suspicion I took a ride of four miles to Dr Wilson's door. . . [He] was much surprised when he saw me, but welcomed me most kindly. We had a long conversation together which led up to the Messiah. I thought to myself, 'This is just what I wanted to know. . .' We spent three hours talking, after which he presented me with a New Testament in Hebrew and asked me to come again. He would have Mr Friedenthal, the Jewish missionary, to meet me, a good Hebraist."

In high summer Safed was a haven from the stifling plain.[6] Even in Safed, however, the hot *sirocco* winds and the sand-laden *hamseen* from Arabia, brought discomfort and the sun blazed fiercely. At noon the shutters were drawn for the siesta. It was then that Leon, a *kaffiya* on his head but in European clothes, rode up from the estate, had a light meal with the family, and withdrew to his garden tent to rest. There he would read avidly. Scattered around there may well have been books in several languages on history, philosophy, literature, science and politics, as well as studies in rabbinics. It was there, in a cavity in the dusty soil underneath the rugs, that he hid the Hebrew Testament. "I dug it up daily" he said, "and read it through several times. I also visited Dr Wilson every night to ask questions. With his and Mr Friedenthal's kind help my difficulties gradually cleared and I saw, through God's holy Spirit, that the Old and New Testaments are but one.

"I gave my heart in secret to the Lord Jesus and tried to serve and follow Him. After several months of this concealed belief I came to the conclusion that I must make an open confession. . . Dr Wilson deeply sympathized with me as he knew all the sufferings and trials it would entail. He spoke most kindly to me, praying and giving me comforting texts to support me, knowing that when it came out I might have to leave home. I had been saving up some money to go away with, and asked the Lord to strengthen me for the struggle, as we were a most affectionate family."

Leon omits from this narrative that he had had previous contact with the mission, which had suffered the derision of the population since the Free Church of Scotland had set it up in 1889, and that he had met Dr George Wilson, who was surprised when he came alone to see him, because hitherto he had come with others to form an English class. The class was not taken by Dr Wilson, who was a medical missionary and spent much of his time assisting Dr Torrance at the hospital in Tiberias, but by a teacher in the mission school, one Masaud-el-Hadad. After the first winter Masaud invited Dr Wilson to come and see how his pupils were getting on. "Dr Wilson," wrote Nahum, "was a man of kindly disposition and before long his visits to the class became frequent and the youths took a great liking to him, and he, taking the opportunity offered to him, commended Christ to them. I am not sure how many of that class did ultimately accept Christianity, but I can think of four. As far as one can judge it was not only the influence, humanly speaking, of Dr Wilson that ultimately led these young men to accept Christ, but of their leader Leon,"

What happened to the other converts is not known. That it would be made hard for them is evident when one thinks of the experience of James Cohen, a convert in Tiberias who worked as a colporteur for the mission there. So great was the pressure brought on his Arab wife, that she and their children deserted him, and he had eventually to be moved from Tiberias to a less dangerous post at Constantinople.

Leon, being a son of the former Rabbi, and of a family highly respected in the community and beyond, was in the most vulnerable position. What he had done would not only bring disgrace to his family and break their hearts; it would also be looked upon as outrageous, the act of a traitor to his synagogue and people.

He had no illusions as to the cost of discipleship. Yet to remain a secret believer, a Nicodemus or Joseph of Arimathea, was impossible. It would mean living a lie. The other way was catastrophic, but there was no escape and the Lord would stand by him as he had stood by His apostle Paul.

In the event it proved both better and worse than he expected. Better, because his family did not immediately fling him out, but let him remain with them in the desperate hope that he would recant. It was only when their persuasions and inducements had failed, and the tension and stress were too great to bear, that exile became inevitable.

Yet it was also worse than he envisaged. For when he finally left home it was to reach Edinburgh in the chill of winter, to experience a life of drudging work, then of poverty and unemployment, and to battle with loneliness and ill-health. In his thoughts the fleshpots, as they must have seemed, of Safed, and the love of his close-knit family, would loom large.

He has described his confrontation with those who were at home. Young Nahum, for one, was absent, for when he returned from the rabbinical college in Jerusalem it was to be told, not that Leon had become a Christian, but that he had gone abroad and, later, that he had died.

It was at the supper table that he told them. It was the night after Dr Wilson's words and prayers of comfort. And it was his mother's solicitude that gave him his cue. "You look pale and ill," she said; "are you unwell? Or maybe," she added brightly, "you have fallen in love."

Yes, he had fallen in love. Yet because of that consuming love a sword must pierce her heart as once it had pierced Mary's, and as other mothers in Galilee must have been cut to the quick when their sons became Jesus' disciples. When He said, "A man must hate his father and mother for my sake," that, surely, was what He meant; not literal hatred, but acting as if it were so; ignoring a mother's pleas and bringing scandal on her head. "If only," Leon said later, "I could have broken my own heart instead of hers." To lose a comfortable and privileged home and the esteem of many friends was as nothing to this; for the bond with his mother was deep.

"Are you ill, or in love, or is it about money? What can we do to help you?" "While they were putting these questions," says Leon, "I was in an agony of heart and mind how to tell them . . . . So I lifted up my heart for strength and courage. And the Lord himself helped me to say, 'The Bible you wished me to study has opened my eyes to see that Christ who [sic] the missionaries preach is the Messiah of the Jews. I now believe in Him as my Saviour and my Lord,' As soon as I said this they cried out, and my mother fainted away. She especially was in a dreadful state that I should have become an apostate. When they had recovered from the shock they argued with me in every way to shake my faith . . . .

"My home life after this confession was very miserable, except for the joy and peace within. I suffered so much persecution that I was advised by the missionaries to leave home."

Rabbi Nahum's uncle in Kishinev had advocated a more tolerant attitude towards Christianity, and in Safed that may have meant letting the mission exist, even while ostracizing it; but when conversion in one's own family was the result the effect was cataclysmic. Their reaction shows the depth of their horror, devastation and grief, as well as of their love for the son who, without warning, seemed to have profaned and abandoned all that they held dear.

Leon's reference to the persecution he suffered requires comment. For the family observed a conspiracy of silence. They did not, as we have seen, even tell his brother Nahum, who took several years to discover what had happened. Had the news spread, and Leon been persecuted by the community, Nahum could not have failed to hear of his defection. The persecution, it appears, could only have been by his elder brothers and by the coldness or bitter reproaches of his parents.

Anyhow, he had to go. But where? It is not difficult to guess how Dr Wilson would advise him. "If you make for Edinburgh," he would say, "you will find friends. There is a mission to the Jews there — it was started in the same year as this one — and my uncle has some connection with it. He is a Hebrew scholar and loves the Jews. I will give you a letter to take to him. If you go to the church of which he is the minister, or to any Scottish Free Church, you will find a missionary spirit and a warm welcome. You will also find a simple form of worship, with preaching and teaching and much emphasis on the expounding of the Word — not unlike the synagogue. And you will love Edinburgh. It is full of history, and of beauty and of learning. You may not be able to be employed at the mission, but my uncle will advise you about finding work. And, as it happens, I myself will be on a furlough in six months' time and will be coming to Edinburgh." To one leaving the serene uplands of Galilee the doctor may well have added something about Scottish shepherds and the green Border hills.

With such a prospect before him, Leon set off undismayed although his heart was heavy, and would remain so during their lifetime at the parting from his family and the spiritual gulf between himself and those for whom the lighting of the Sabbath candles and the deep joys of the Sabbath table would never again be without a shadow of grief. He was never to see his guardian again; but with his mother, his brothers and sister there was, after some years, to be reconciliation if not the former rapport.

Leon's course in life was changed not only because his search for truth had brought him to recognise Jesus as the Messiah, but because he met Him and was converted. A great Scottish churchman, Dr John White, was asked in a broadcast to say what brought him into the ministry. "I met a Man" was his simple reply. Leon would have said the same. Sadly, few of his family's descendants in Israel today will accept this. A rabbi's son, they say stubbornly, can never be converted; there must have been some other motive for his going. There was hunger in Palestine then; perhaps he went to better himself, and in search of food!

The author's cousins — and he met nearly forty of them in Israel — are far from hostile, and no longer bear any grudge. They are gentle, warm and friendly. But this one blind spot remains. Their self-protective insularity can only be removed as they meet with, or become aware of, other Jews who, like Leon, have found their Messiah. That such Jewish Christians exist in their hundreds of thousands, is now widely recognised throughout the western hemisphere. The establishment, in five continents, of the Hebrew Christian Alliance, with which Leon's name was to be identified, is in itself irrefutable proof, as are the many religious books published in America and Europe in which converts have told their stories.

To acknowledge the fact of conversion from one faith to

another — and it need not be Christianity — should not, to the open-minded, be hard. What will always be difficult is to understand the inner process; what happens in a human soul. That, as Jesus told Nicodemus, is as mysterious as the wind. Neither Leon nor any other convert could adequately have described it. It is also as mysterious as falling in love, its closest analogy. "The love of Jack and herself," says a novelist, "was the force which had transmuted her life into something marvellous." What Leon had experienced was similar. He could only have said with St Paul, "For anyone who is in Christ there is a new creation; the old creation has gone, and now the new one is here." (2 Cor. 5:17 in the *Jerusalem Bible*.)

NOTES:
1. The term used by those who regarded Palestine as "The Promised Land." After World War I it was the official Hebrew designation for the area under the British Mandate.
2. Among its founders was Moses Zvi Levinson, a member of the family.
3. Arthur Koestler instanced the conversion of a whole tribe of the Khazars to Judaism. He designated them "The Thirteenth Tribe."
4. The quotations from Nahum in this chapter are taken from an article on "Early Days in Palestine" in the *Hebrew Christian Quarterly* of January 1937.
5. In the document of 1903 he refers more than once to his "father", who, he says, had died since his arrival in Scotland. This must refer to a guardian, perhaps an uncle, who had assumed the parental role, or possibly to a stepfather, although Miriam is not known to have married again.
6. In 1921, Sir Herbert Samuel, then High Commissioner, spent the summer months in 'the Simla of Palestine'. About the same time, the missionaries in Tiberias, which is 600 feet below sea-level, were ordered to do so.

CHRISTIAN AND JEW

No. 7

By John Dickson, Esquire,
Her Britannic Majesty's Consul for Palestine.

These are to request and require, in the Name of Her Majesty, all those whom it may concern, to allow *Leib Lewison, a British Indian Subject, proceeding to England via France* to pass freely without let or hindrance, and to afford *him* every assistance and protection of which *he* may stand in need.

Given at Jerusalem, the 14th day of November 1900

Signature of the Bearer.
Leib Lewison

Leon's exit visa

2. PARIS INTERLUDE

At the British Consulate in Jerusalem on 14th November, 1900, he applied for an exit visa. The single sheet, still preserved, was made out to 'Leib Levison, a British Indian subject, proceeding to England via France'. He was never to use 'Leib' again. It belonged to his past, and as 'Abram' became 'Abraham' and 'Saul' 'Paul' so he marked the change in his life by using, from then on, only the name of Leon.

He elected to go by France because, as he afterwards explained, he had heard of the Great Exhibition there. In truth it was an *annus mirabilis* in Paris, the locus for a succession of Exhibitions, for 1900 marked the centenary of the Exposition Universelle. It was an opportunity not to be missed. Yet he missed it, for on the 14th of November, when he was still in Jerusalem, it closed! Thus by the time he arrived in Paris, having taken ship to Marseilles and then walked part of the way, the displays were dismantled, the lights and banners lowered, and the crowds had gone home. The leafless December city was left comparatively bleak and desolate.

Yet only comparatively. For Paris is Paris, and its spacious *fin de siècle* beauty, preserved in the paintings of Pissaro, was there. The squares and boulevards, churches, bridges and public buildings which confronted the wide-eyed nineteen year-old from Safed were a breath-taking sight. Only as a small boy amid the imperial glories of Calcutta, or in Jerusalem, had he seen great artefacts. In Paris he must have been stunned at the sublime largesse, the magnificence of it all. At the Tuileries Gardens and the Louvre, Notre Dame and the Hôtel de Ville, the Luxembourg Palace and, if he reached it, Versailles, the genius and history of much of Europe was to be found, and in its architecture and monuments, the age-long growth

21

of a metropolis, was recorded. Finally, watching over the city from the heights of Montmartre, was the gleaming landmark of Sacré Coeur, built only twenty-five years before and pristinely white.

The Exhibitions had left a marvellous residue. An enduring monument to a previous one was the Tower that Gustave Eiffel had been commissioned to build for the World Fair of 1889. Another was the decorative Alexander III Bridge, newly built to link the Left Bank with the Exposition. Between it and the Champs Elysées there now stood two imposing pavilions of marble, stone and glass, the Grand Palais and the Petit Palais, relics akin to London's Crystal Palace and surpassed only by Seville's Plaza de España. There was also, marvel of marvels, the Métro, its first stages completed in time for the event of 1900. Leon may not have known much about European art, but he knew that this was a city of the arts. He may have been unaware of the Impressionists, but their day had dawned. Cézanne was now sixty, and with the younger painters had won recognition inasmuch as a room at the Exposition had been devoted to them; and they had been exhibiting at the Salon since 1874. As he lingered at art dealers' windows and visited galleries their influence would reach him.

The streets, too, were magical with their horse-drawn vehicles and occasional motor-cars; on wide boulevards some of the latter achieving the reckless speed of twelve miles an hour. The same is true of the variety of shops, the bookstalls on the Left Bank, the warmly glowing cafés, the smart hotels, the river-traffic, and glimpses of the *beau monde* — the men top-hatted and cloaked, the women in silks, jewels and furs being driven to the Comédie Française or to the Opéra. It was a never-ending pageant, and heady stuff.

He would explore the churches, hearing mighty organs and, perhaps, cathedral choirs, and it was his introduction to Roman Catholicism. Statues, images and ikons had played no part in his worship either as a Jew or as a fledgling Christian. Even the Christmas cribs, in many churches that December, were foreign to him. But if this was how millions worshipped he would want to know about it. He was never an iconoclast or one to inveigh against others' cherished beliefs, which he differentiated from their superstitions. Yet the authoritarianism and legalism of Rome, its emphasis on tradition, its lack at that time, of charismatic and Biblical forms of spirituality, reminded him too much of the kind of

Pharisaism from which evangelical Christianity had set him free.

French Protestants would have welcomed him, but in his brief stay he may not have discovered them; nor would he have found the Scots Kirk on the Rue Bayard unless Dr Wilson had visited it. Still, Leon would pursue his own devotions and, being gregarious, would not have sunk into depths of loneliness. Rather, no doubt, he would make contact, possibly in a students' café or hostel, with other young men. All we know for certain is that at a photographer on the Rue de Rivoli he had a print of his mother made from a negative he carried. (And this he was to enlarge later and hang on his wall.)

It was more than a pleasant interlude and recuperation from the tensions of home. It was a continuing self-discovery as he entered a new world, a cultural baptism and a time of enlightenment into both the riches of the past and the exuberant, teeming life, both rude and splendid, of a *belle époque* which would last until 1914.

How long, or where, he lodged we do not know. However, his money dwindling, he had to leave; nor was he able to stop in London. With £4 in his pocket he arrived in Edinburgh sometime in January 1901.

On January the 22nd Queen Victoria died, and the Empire mourned. The young immigrant who was her patriotic subject shared in that grief, which slowly dispelled as the Edwardian Age dawned. Leon, too, was shortly to know a period of darkness before entering a brighter stage in his pilgrimage.

3. EDINBURGH: EARLY DAYS

The last lap was by sea, and he disembarked at Leith early in 1901, if not before the Queen's demise then probably before her funeral on February 4th.

His family venerated the Queen and he would continue to share in her homage. Had she not, he would recall, made a famous promise in 1858, never forgotten in India, that race and colour should constitute no bar to admission to governmental posts? His own acceptance in Britain and the lack of anti-semitism there owed much to her enlightened attitudes, from which, however, Edward the Seventh, though a friend of the Jews, was to some extent to depart — opposing for instance the appointment of native Indians to the Viceroy's Council.

Later, when he became engaged to a girl from a well-to-do English family, Leon found that the British upper classes were not without racial prejudice, but on the whole (and apart from America) he could not have chosen a more tolerant country, nor, in Scotland, one whose religious atmosphere was more congenial. The simple austerity of the church buildings, the emphasis on teaching and preaching in Presbyterianism, the veneration for the Word and the attention paid to the Old Testament, the strong theological tradition, and the plain form of worship with its roots not only in Calvin but, as Calvin claimed, in the Early Church and therefore in the Synagogue — all this awakened resonances in a Jewish Christian. As the years passed Leon was to love his adopted country, Church and city with all his heart.

To begin with, however, the going was hard. £4, even then was not a princely sum, and shelter and employment were urgent needs. First he called on Dr Hood Wilson at 1, East Castle Road, the

EDINBURGH: EARLY DAYS

Barclay Church manse, with his letter of introduction. "I was kindly received by both the Doctor and Mrs Wilson," he wrote, "and through them I got a situation as under-gardener."

Dr Hood Wilson, who was to baptise him five months later, was then 72, and his ministry was drawing to its close. Mrs Wilson died suddenly in 1902, and the Doctor conducted his forenoon service for the last time in November 1903, his jubilee year, and died a fortnight later.

From him Leon would have learned at first hand about the Edinburgh Medical Mission to the Jews; for Dr Wilson had helped to found it in 1889. That was also the year when the Free Church had commenced its work in Safed. Dr Wilson knew Safed, for he had been for twelve years Convener or Joint-Convener of the Church's Jewish Mission Committee, and had visited all its stations. Moreover he had a love of Jewish lore and was fascinated by the steadily growing Christian work among the Jews. He was also a Hebrew scholar and "at his prayer meeting", it was said, "his knowledge of Hebrew often made the Psalms luminous".

An eminent Church leader, he had been Moderator in 1895 and his two charges, the Fountainbridge and Barclay Churches were, according to his biographer, "probably the two greatest nurseries of foreign missionaries in Scotland." The same writer observes that "three-fourths of the congregational monthly magazine is devoted to foreign missions." In being advised, even for a short period, and prepared for baptism by such a man Leon was extremely fortunate.

It may have been Dr Wilson who found him lodgings, for they were in Grove Street, in the vicinity of his former charge of Fountainbridge. If so, he would at least have had a good landlady; but the address itself conjures up overcrowded tenements, dimly lit stairs and all the trappings of poverty.

The dismal tenements of Fountainbridge have been described by Sean Connery, the actor, who was born in one of them thirty years later. The Connerys had two rooms, a large kitchen which doubled as living-room, a common lavatory, and no bathroom. People bathed at the public baths, where for a few pence they could get a hot bath. In 1976, seventy-five years after Leon's arrival, Connery revisited his birthplace. He described it, shortly before its demolition, as "still a dump with no hot water, four flats sharing two toilets, gas mantles on the landings." For Leon the dreariness of these lodgings was in the sharpest contrast with his home in Safed, while the massive Clydesdales, stabled in Fountainbridge and trundling milk-carts through the cobbled streets, would sharpen his longing for his own sprightlier horse.

The Edinburgh climate, especially in February when 'snell' winds blow in from the North Sea and the damp mist or 'haar' frequently descends, was not only a trial but a hazard. Thus a job in the open-air, though in theory it seemed a suitable choice for an expert vinegrower, and one who still stumbled in the English tongue, was not, after all, a wise one. As an under-gardener, pushing a barrow in the Botanic Gardens, Leon was subject to constant chills and colds; so much so that he was driven to go to a doctor, who advised him to seek indoor employment. For a pittance he washed bottles and did odd jobs for a chemist. Then a member of the Barclay Church, hearing of his predicament, approached one of the elders, Mr Simon Henderson, who had a biscuit factory in Grove Street, and he took him on. However, this work, too, was unsuitable though he stuck to it for two years. Still unaccustomed to manual labour, he found the humping of flour sacks exhausting. The furnaces hurt his eyes and he badly injured a hand in the machinery through his inability to understand the instructions.[1] In addition, his workmates were a rough lot, who bullied and ridiculed him because he was a foreigner and a Jew.

He became depressed. Then one night he dreamt that the Lord came to him and spoke the words in Isaiah chapter 41 verse 10: "Do not fear, for I am with you; do not be dismayed, for I am your God. I will strengthen you and help you." (He would hear these words as he knew them well, in Hebrew, which this plain modern version best conveys.) At that moment he knew that God wanted him for His service. "I went back to work refreshed", he said, "continuing on at the factory until my health gave way and I had to go to a convalescent home at Gilmerton. There I was very kindly treated and made several friends. I then returned and continued in the factory for eighteen months, working sixteen hours a day for fifteen shillings a week." (Sixteen hours was surely an exaggeration — one of his weaknesses — but it may well have been twelve).

On 16th June 1901 he was baptised. The ceremony had been postponed until Dr George Wilson, on furlough from Safed, could be present. Afterwards, many members of the congregation spoke to him. Among them was a white-bearded patriarch who thrust a scrap of paper into his hand. Leon never discovered who he was, but

EDINBURGH: EARLY DAYS

the words were these: "Go into all the world and preach the gospel to every creature beginning at Jerusalem."

"These words," he said, "kindled a great fire within me to be a missionary to Jews . . . . I longed to give my brethren also the Water of Life."

The factory work was still too arduous. He had a breakdown and was again sent to Gilmerton. There a doctor advised him (Leon says 'ordered') to leave the factory, which he did. Yet for six months neither he nor his friends could find other work for him. Though offered financial help, he was too proud to accept it, determined whatever the difficulties to stand on his own feet. But one wonders why, with his tailoring skill, he never found employment in the rag-trade. It was a trade largely in the hands of the Jews and it may be that doors were closed by his unwillingness to hide his Christian faith; or there may simply have been no openings. "All seemed against mē," he wrote, "and for days I went without food." At last, in answer to his prayers "the Lord sent me three true friends. Then the way was open for me to work in the Medical Mission to Jews."

Who these three friends were is not known; but since he had already been visiting the Jews and preaching to patients at the Mission's dispensary, they were probably workers at the Mission. One of these was Mrs Kennedy, whose husband was the librarian of New College, the United Free Church's College of Divinity. The Kennedys were among the first to help him; and they rescued him from Grove Street and took him to stay with them at Hartington Place until lodgings were found in Viewforth nearby.

It was not until 1904 that the Mission engaged him as their full-time missionary. However, since 1902, while still at the factory, he had been spending evenings and weekends there helping the young missionary, David Sandler (a Hebrew Christian from Constantinople), and himself being helped at the English classes. The mission hall and dispensary (where for many years Dr Macdonald Robertson and various colleagues worked on a part-time basis) were at 15, Spittal Street, a somewhat depressed locality half a mile from Grove Street.

The Report of the Mission for 1902 puts the number of Jewish families resident in Edinburgh "as certainly not less than 500, embracing 2,500 souls,[2] but it is known that besides these there are very many Jews who live here temporarily." The city at that time had three synagogues. In the English and Hebrew language class Mr

Sandler reported, "I have valuable help from Mr Levison, and while teaching them we do not neglect the opportunity to tell of Jesus, the Son of David, who is the Christ."

David Sandler was studying medicine and took his MB degree in April 1902. A year later he returned to Constantinople as the U.F. Church's Medical Missionary to the Jews. It took some time to fill the vacancy. Dr Sandler had suggested a medical student named Leo Levi, who expected to take his degree in June, and also Leon, thinking that the two young Jewish Christians might work in harness. This, however, was something the Committee could not afford, the Mission having been abruptly impoverished when the Free Kirk, (the 'Wee Frees') the remnant of the union with the United Presbyterians in 1900, won its case in the House of Lords for the retention of the former Free Kirk's property and funds. Until 1928, when it was taken over by the Church of Scotland, the Mission only survived by becoming undenominational, a step which was taken in this very year of 1903. Although Leo applied, Leon was appointed; Mrs McIntyre, who did sterling work among the women and girls had, along with her husband, spoken in his favour.

At first the Committee was cautious, employing him without status to visit among the Jews and teach the evening class at a salary of 15 shillings per week. Leon, in his enthusiasm, at once asked if he could visit Jewish patients in the Royal Infirmary. "All the Jews?" asked the hospital chaplain, "or only those who attended the mission?" The committee replied that they hoped Mr Levison (whom they sometimes called Levinsohn or Levinson) would be allowed to talk to any Jew willing to converse with him on Christianity. The Rev. Robert Henderson, however, replied that he could not be allowed to speak to any Jews whom he pleased; but that he would readily let him know of any who expressed a wish to see him.

Shortly afterwards the Rev. John McCarter, who had been asked to supervise the appointment, reported that he was "greatly pleased with the tact and gentleness of Mr Levison in his argument with them (the Jews), and that from his thorough knowledge of the scriptures, combined with the spirituality of mind manifest in Mr Levison, he believed that, with further experience in the work and instruction in the Word of God, Mr Levison would prove himself, by grace and the blessing of God, a very efficient missionary to the Jews." The gentleness of his approach was to characterise his ministry, in marked contrast to that strident evangelism which has so often proved counter-productive.

It was agreed that he should continue to be employed at 15 shillings under Mr McCarter's supervision, "but only as a temporary arrangement at present." On the 1st of July his salary was raised to 20 shillings and he was given permission to occupy as a resident one of the empty rooms at the dispensary, the ladies on the Committee undertaking to provide the furniture.

However, in November it was reported that the Sanitary Inspector had condemned 15, Spittal Street as unfit to be occupied as a dwelling place; and it was decided to call on the owner, Mr Inglis, to have it thoroughly repaired. When this proved unsatisfactory, it was agreed in January not to renew the lease but to seek other premises. By March they had failed to find anything suitable and the lease was renewed for twelve months. Nothing more was said of Leon residing there, and this probably never came off. His housing problem, in any case, was soon to be resolved.

In December a sub-committee had been set up to review the salary. Meanwhile the Treasurer was authorized to give him a Christmas gratuity of £5, towards which £4 had been received from one donor and £1 from another. Finally, in February 1904, he was engaged officially as Missionary at a salary of £70 per annum. He was not yet 23.

Meanwhile he was coming to grips with his task. In November 1903 he reported that a young Jew, with whom he had been dealing as an enquirer for some weeks, had asked for baptism and wished to become a member of a church. The Committee, ever cautious, asked three of its members to see the man and ascertain the reality of his conversion. They reported back two months later that Mr Levi should be baptised, and recommended that as he resided in a lodging house in the West Port near the Chalmers Territorial Church, the minister of that church, Mr Bowie, should be asked to baptise him. Mr Bowie, however, to Mr Levi's acute disappointment, had misgivings and was slow to move. Eventually he was persuaded of Mr Levi's credentials and took the matter to the Kirk Session, who in April gave a favourable decision. The baptism took place on 1st May.

A similar case was that of a Roumanian with an unpronounceable name, who had chosen to call himself Mr Primrose (an admirer of Disraeli?). In April 1904 Leon recommended him for baptism and he was referred to the Minister (no longer Dr Hood Wilson) and Kirk Session of the Barclay Church. In June the Session decided that he should be put on probation before being presented for baptism; but by October Mr Primrose had departed unbaptised to take up a job in Newcastle.

Such delays must have irked Leon's eager spirit. His instinct was to welcome the convert with open arms. Once he had met in a Jew the new light and love born of faith in Christ he would want to respond as Philip to the Ethiopian, "What hinders you from being baptised?" But his eagerness was not always well founded. He had another protégé that April, Mrs Hedge, the wife of a non-churchgoing Episcopalian, whom he deemed ready for baptism; and he had taken it upon himself to go to the Rector of St Thomas's Episcopal Church who, he claimed, had consented and was about to perform the sacrament. The Committee were dubious about Leon's initiative, and they got in touch with the the Rector, who said that Mr Levison had been wholly mistaken in stating that he would baptise the lady at once. He would certainly not do so, for he had found her exceedingly ignorant. It is possible that the Rector was asking her the wrong questions; but more likely that Leon had over-estimated her. He was predisposed to think the best of people, and sometimes turned geese into swans.

If the attitude of the Committee, and of some ministers, erred in being over-cautious, it at least provides a refutation of the assertion made, both then and now, by Orthodox Jewry that the Christians played the numbers game and were out to gain converts as quickly as possible.

The slow but steady stream of conversions through the patient work of the Mission in the half-century of its existence was due to the work of its doctors and voluntary helpers as well as of its full-time missionaries, and it has to be seen in the context of much medical, social, educational and pastoral work. To the Committee in October 1903, for instance, Leon reported that during the two months since his return to Edinburgh after a month's holiday he had visited 147 Jewish families. He also intimated that he intended to commence evening classes and meetings on Monday, Tuesday, Thursday and Friday evenings. There was also a report from Mrs McIntyre on her class for girls, which 16 young Jewesses attended.

A few months later Leon reported that the Jews at his evening classes wanted to establish a benefit fund to be maintained by a weekly payment of threepence by each member, for the relief of such of them as might fail to get work.

For indeed many were on the brink of destitution. As Chaim Bermant has pointed out (in an article on Jack Ronder's television serial "The Lost Tribe", which in 1980 portrayed the immigration of Russian Jews to Scotland at the turn of the century), they had come to Scotland to escape from anti-semitism, but only their children escaped from poverty. "In Lithuania", he wrote, "the Jew tended to regard everyone as an anti-semite except where he showed himself to be a friend; in Scotland he regarded everyone as a friend save where he showed himself to be an anti-semite, and the worst affliction which the newcomers had to face was poverty. If the Scots had it hard, the Jews had it harder."

With renewed Russian pogroms, notoriously at Kishinev at Easter 1903, there was a large increase of destitute immigrants, and in October 1904 Leon told the Committee a pathetic story and solicited their help. A young man had come to him, he said, in a state of malnutrition and he had given him two shillings to buy food. But he was told that the lad used it to pay some rent he owed, and the following morning he was found dead in the Meadows. Others, said Leon, were in dire straits and must be helped. The Committee took this to heart and the Secretary was instructed to write to *The Scotsman* with a general appeal. They also approached the Chief Constable, Mr Ross, and gave him some addresses supplied by Leon. Mr Ross, however, reported back that the policeman he had sent there saw no evidence of starvation, nor was there any knowledge of a body being found in the Meadows. Summoned by the committee, Leon maintained that the Jews had been afraid to tell the truth, and that they insisted that one of their people was found dead.

The Committee wisely did not dismiss Leon's version, but asked him to bring as many destitute refugees as he could muster to the hall at Spittal Street, and appointed a sub-committee to examine them. Leon produced 14 refugees who spoke very little English. They told their stories in Yiddish which he translated. Later the whole Committee heard the evidence which, says the minute, "was listened to with painful interest" and the Secretary was instructed to despatch the letter which he had not yet sent to *The Scotsman*. As a result £7.11 was received from eight donors — not as meagre an amount as it sounds now. Furthermore, a larger sum was raised by the Jewish Board of Guardians, who had been alerted and who are rarely wanting in generosity to their own people.

Leon was working hard, and he was still not in good health. However, new friends appeared. Mr and Mrs Frederick Sawkins, of whom we shall learn much more, had come to know and admire the young missionary. On 10th December 1904 they took him for two weeks to their home at Budleigh Salterton in Devonshire. (They had settled in Edinburgh but were Devonians). They paid his fare and also sent him to their doctor, who prescribed another two weeks sick leave because of a persistent cough.

When he went on holiday he had left several refugees in lodging houses at the expense of the Committee. They accepted this *fait accompli*, but on his return told him that "no more food or lodging shall be provided for such persons, as the funds will not admit of such expenditure." Leon was able, however, to counter this with the news that a number of wealthy Jews had been stirred by Mr Scott Moncrieff's letter to raise funds, and that they had already subscribed £40.

In January 1905 the Committee welcomed Leon back. "Now that Mr Levison has returned from the south . . . all were pleased to see him and in restored health." He reported that the Sawkinses had arranged several meetings for him in Devon, from which he handed over donations; and also that they had given him £25 in their great desire that he should have an assistant. He had in mind a young man named Eisenberg, and he asked the Committee to make up Mr Eisenberg's salary to £30. This, however, they were unable to do, for the kitty was empty. They also pointed out that Mr Eisenberg was not yet baptised, nor had they assessed his suitability.

In February Leon reported that Mr Eisenberg had left for the United States. He added that though unbaptised, he had given such a full and clear confession of his Christian faith at a meeting of Jews that it was impossible to doubt the reality of his conversion. Meanwhile a sub-committee report on his fitness (on the event of his baptism) to be an assistant missionary had been prepared but, in the event, was shelved. In fact the Sawkinses' wish was not fulfilled until, twenty years later, he was given a woman assistant.

At the Annual Meeting in 1905 it was reported that 1068 patients had been treated by Dr Macdonald Robertson and his colleagues at the dispensary (an increase of 216). Of the poorest of them, most were Russians who needed medical advice in Yiddish. "The Committee made no secret of the fact that the condition they imposed was that the Jews listened to the Word of God while they were awaiting attendance at the dispensary." That Word was given in Yiddish by Leon.

The annual report ends with a remark which was quoted, as was doubtless intended, in the Press. "The Committee expressed surprise and disappointment that only one minister in the city had permitted the cause of the mission to be placed by their missionary before his people in his church. Yet many of the churches made collections annually for missions to Jews in lands far away."

Leon was continuing to report conversions, and a sub-committee was set up "to examine such converts as Mr Levison may introduce to them, so that, if satisfied, the committee may recommend such converts to some minister."

That was in March, 1905. On the ninth of April, at St Mary's U.F. Church in Albany Street, the Rev. George Davidson baptised H.F. Schrieder and S. Levi at an evening service. There was a crowded congregation and Leon, at the special request of Mr Davidson, gave a brief address.

Here we observe that between 1903 and 1927, the period when the Mission was under the aegis of an undenominational (though largely U.F. Church) committee, there were no fewer than 125 baptisms; and that of those baptised seven became ordained ministers and six missionaries.

By May two more enquirers had been examined, one being approved. Five converts from elsewhere had also arrived in Edinburgh, making quite a caucus of Jewish Christians.

At the heart of it all stands the Rev. George Davidson, a saintly man, wise, scholarly and evangelical, whom Leon admired and loved. He took a personal interest in Mr Levi, whom he had baptised, and wanted to give him £5 to enable him to start in business. Being short of cash, he asked the Committee, through Leon, to advance the money, and this they did with the proviso that it was not a present.

Prior to this, and possibly as early as 1903, Leon had transferred his church membership from the Barclay to St Mary's, and it was there that he took his brother Nahum early in 1905. How Nahum, not yet seventeen, had found his way to Edinburgh will be explained in due course. Suffice it to say here that Mr Davidson took him under his wing, and by the end of the year (when he baptised him) was convinced that his future lay in the Christian ministry; it was a vocation which Nahum resisted for several years but came to in the end.

Meanwhile Leon's relationship with Fred and Julia Sawkins had deepened. His holidays with them were only the prelude to their becoming his surrogate parents. There was no formal adoption, but he became the son they had never had. When he left the Viewforth lodging it was to live with them, first at Forbes Road and then, until his marriage, at 8 Albert Terrace.

Fred and Julia Sawkins

Jewish Medical Mission, 46 Lauriston Place, 1907

EDINBURGH: EARLY DAYS

Fred Sawkins was an architect and looked the part. From a finely shaped head locks of hair hung loosely over his brow, and he gazed quietly from beneath craggy eyebrows. He had a drooping moustache, carried an eyeglass, and smoked a meerschaum pipe. He wore comfortable tweeds and sported a bow tie and a buttonhole. Gentle and soft spoken, he loved to play the flute, and to play chess with Leon.

As he grew older his mental faculties failed; and although he lived into the thirties, as early as the First World War he had spells in Craighouse, Edinburgh's mental hospital. My own last memory of "Grandpa Sawkins" is of seeing him entrapped high in the mulberry tree in his Devonshire garden, and the gardener being summoned to fetch him down! In his heyday he was the gentlest and most generous of men and was able to support Leon at one or two particularly difficult moments.

Julia, who was to outlive Leon, though sound in mind was more eccentric than her husband. She wrote romantic novels under her maiden name of Julia Edwards, dabbled in the occult — chiefly horoscopes in which she was expert, and palmistry — and banged out Beethoven's sonatas on the piano. More germane is the fact that she studied both Hebrew and Greek. She was also a cat-lover and fussed over them as if they were her children; as indeed they were until Leon came along. He too was cossetted, and given the health care he manifestly needed. Again I have my own memories of her, an eager, bird-like little woman, her round face puckered, her hair coiled in an untidy bun, her pince-nez dangling on a velvet ribbon. She found her 'grandchildren' amusing, kissed them fondly with wet lips, and encouraged them to play for hours on her harmonium.

How the Sawkinses, who were Episcopalians, discovered the Mission is not known. But in November 1905 Mrs McIntyre proposed that they be invited to join the Committee and this was agreed. It was fortunate that they did so for Leon was in deep trouble in a matter which surfaced in January when the Secretary reported the claim of a moneylender against him.

It transpired that Leon, still in material things naive, had signed his name endorsing a promissory note for £25. The note had been signed by a Jew named Isakoff and endorsed by another Jew as well as by Leon. Both Jews, however, had failed soon after receiving the £25, and in the previous January (1904) Leon had found himself called upon to reimburse the money with very heavy interest. He had offered to make an interim payment of £12.10 but this had been refused.

Called before the Committee, he gave a full account of the matter. Then Mr Sawkins arose and offered to pay the full amount without further question, and begged the Committee not to continue the discussion.

However, this was not the end. The moneylender had a year earlier, given a "notice of arrestment" of Leon's wages and this had never been acted upon. The Committee decided that this should now be carried into effect and that no salary in excess of 20 shillings per week would be paid to Leon. On being called in, Leon willingly accepted both penalty and blame.

He then went on to tell the Committee of two more baptisms which had been performed by Mr Davidson. The following month he reported that three more had confessed Christ at his meetings and that one of them had applied for baptism, which Mr Davidson would administer that very Sunday.

As well as baptisms, drawing-room meetings were on the increase, and he referred to three, one of which he and Mrs McIntyre had addressed at the house of a Mr and Mrs Harding, members of the Committee.

He had also, the previous April, addressed a meeting in Moffat "with the entire sympathy of the Ministers there." He had gone there for a brief holiday but without informing the secretary, and for this he was rapped over the knuckles; as on other occasions, he was reprimanded for acting independently or "jumping the gun." Yet the Committee never came down on him heavily. They realised, I am sure, that the whole experience of working with a committee was unfamiliar to him. He was an innocent abroad, and had no intention of being insubordinate. Yet he must have been difficult to handle, for he was impulsive and apt to embarrass his employers.

Mr Sawkins saw things from Leon's point of view. He knew that being the servant of a committee, and, for instance, having to wait in the anteroom before being summoned to give his written monthly report, chafed Leon. He tried to improve the situation by moving that the missionary be present at the committee meetings. At first this was resisted as a dangerous precedent, for what employee could at that time sit in council with his employers? But what is true for the world may not be true for the Church. Is not the very word 'employee' inappropriate of a full-time servant of Christ?

It says much for the Committee that having deferred the matter for two months, and Mr Sawkins having withdrawn his motion, they agreed to let Leon attend the meetings "not by right but only on invitation." They reserved the right to meet without him, and asked him to apprise the Secretary when he intended to be present.

Leon's Committee acted generously; but it was clear that he needed their wisdom and support no less than they needed him. For his own good they could not give him a free rein. Yet in the light of the Moffat episode, they agreed that he should have recognised holidays; and that the Mission should be closed from the first day of Passover, the Jewish holidays, for one week. They also decreed that he should not leave Edinburgh without having obtained permission from the Secretary. In later years as he grew in stature, and was involved in work far beyond the city, this rule was waived, or at least a blind eye was turned; while he, for his part, honoured his local obligations, regularly taking a sleeper on the London train to save being absent longer than was necessary.

The problem of the destitute did not go away. Consequently, although the Mission was run on a shoestring, Leon felt obliged to renew his appeals to the Committee for financial help. On one occasion they were willing to reimburse some money he had given in relief. As he had not referred to them when he gave it, however, he declined to take it back. At the same time he asked for more money for some families known to himself and Mrs McIntyre.

The acuteness of the need is illustrated by a case recounted by the Committee's Secretary, Mr Scott Moncrieff. A Jew had told him that he was harbouring in his back shop a Mr Reuter, with a pregnant wife and five children whom the shopkeeper could keep no longer. The Reuters had come from Canada to Aberdeen, someone having paid their fare. There being no prospects in Aberdeen, they had made for Edinburgh, but as they could not pay for their tickets the Railway Company had sequestered their luggage. Could the Committee prevent the break-up of the family and the taking of the children into care? Deeply moved, Mr Moncrieff helped them from his own pocket. Four months later, however, it transpired that Mr Reuter had obtained the addresses of a number of supporters of the Mission and was going round them one by one begging. The outcome is not known, nor whether Leon in compassion had provided the addresses, but the Mission withdrew its help.

In order to relieve destitution Leon devised a new system, and with some success. He persuaded the Jewish Board of Guardians to promise to help certain families on the basis that they would give as much as he had already given. The Mission also made more strenuous efforts to raise money both by an annual Sale of Work (the first, in 1905, raised £30) by an increase in drawing-room and public meetings, and by co-operation from the churches — the Women's Working Association of Mr Davidson's congregation, for instance, supplied a goodly amount of clothing.

There was also a large donation of £63 from a Palestine exhibition held in the Music Hall in June 1905. Leon had earned a black mark for not informing the Committee that he was participating in the exhibition and failing to give his monthly report. However, when they learned that he had been lecturing from four to seven times a day both on The Holy Land and on the history, ritual, feasts and customs of the Jews, and had continued to visit Jewish homes in the late evenings; that he had been drawing large audiences and receiving a number of invitations to address meetings; and that he had been promised a donation of not less than £60, all was forgiven. Later in life he was to participate in similar exhibitions, although not, as then, in native dress.

The costume he wore, being that of a biblical shepherd, became a standby in later years for many a Nativity play.

These exhibitions were the brain-child of the Reverend Samuel Schor, a Palestinian Jew who had become a clergyman in the Church of England. The first one, at Felixstowe in 1891, when it was not yet easy for tourists to visit the Holy Land, proved popular, and from it grew a huge London exhibition (two years after the Edinburgh one) which in three weeks drew 40,000 people to the Agricultural Hall in Islington. Mr Schor's name is one to remember, for in 1925 he was to play a fateful part in Leon's future.

The publicity meetings increased, and it is of interest that he addressed one in the home of Mr and Mrs John Lusk, a well attended meeting which raised £7. For, sixty years later, Leon's son Fred, then a widower, was to marry the Lusks' grand-daughter, who later, as the Rev. Mary Levison, made a distinctive contribution to the life and work of the Church, and in 1988-89 was Moderator of the Presbytery of Edinburgh. Her grandfather, who had earlier been the first to entertain Leon in an Edinburgh home, was on the Mission Committee, on occasion took the chair, and, on Mr Scott Moncrieff's retirement, acted for a period as Secretary and Treasurer.

EDINBURGH: EARLY DAYS

The Churches too were opening their doors. Between 17th June and 12th July 1905 Leon spoke in seven of them. By December 1906 it was recorded that "Mr Levinson's [sic] addresses at various meetings were highly commended as tending to widen and deepen the acquaintance of the Christian public in Edinburgh with the work of this Mission". This form of deputation work for the Committee became an ever-increasing feature of his life, extending eventually to churches in every corner of Scotland. There was to come a day when he even had to avoid attending the General Assembly or any gathering of ministers for fear of being pressed into more engagements than he could handle.

The work of the Mission and the capabilities and fortunes of its missionary were advancing steadily. That the work was growing is indicated by the attendances at the annual summer picnic. In 1905, 50 children and some 20 mothers went on what was known as The Treat; by 1907, when they went to the beach at Cramond, the number had risen to 150. At that time the average attendance at the Saturday afternoon services was 27. In the 1930's, when the Jewish population had declined, there were still almost as many.

In 1906 the Mission received its first legacy, of £300, and moved from Spittal Street to 46, Lauriston Place, closer to the city's Jewish area and nearer to the central synagogue (then in Graham Street).

After the Great War there would be a further move eastwards to 24, Nicolson Street at the heart of the Jewish quarter, and finally, in the thirties, to Buccleuch Place in the same area.

By 1909 there was a Ladies Auxiliary, which both created new interest and, from its sales of work, furnished an average annual sum of £100. The prime organiser of these was Mrs James Kennedy, who also for many years conducted a Mothers' Meeting, and was to bequeath the Mission £1,100. In 1910 a Miss Anderson gave £2,000 to the medical work, and later £1,500 for the new premises in Nicolson Street. By these and further legacies the future was assured.

As for Leon, his adoption by the Sawkinses had by 1905 opened up the possibility of further education. His first choice was a medical qualification, impressed as he had been with the work of medical missionaries in Safed and Tiberias, and also in Edinburgh. The Sawkinses were more than willing to see him through college. However, one whiff of the dissecting room scotched that notion. He discovered belatedly that he was squeamish at the sight of blood.

39

CHRISTIAN AND JEW

He turned therefore to the university's Arts Faculty and, enrolling as a non-regular student, took classes in Natural and Moral Philosophy and Political Economy, and also in History, of whose colourful Professor, 'Dickie' Lodge, he often spoke. He relished Professor Pringle-Pattison's lectures on Logic and Metaphysics, and his brother, Professor James Seth's on Ethical Principles, the title of his authoritative book. (Pringle-Pattison was a Seth, but, on inheriting an estate in the Borders, adopted a new surname). In Economics under Professor Shields Nicholson, he found a subject which both fascinated him and enlarged his understanding of public affairs.

Many years later, when Fred entered the same Faculty, his father gave him some enthusiastic advice. "Whatever you go in for," he said, "and especially if it is the ministry, you should study Political

The Young Missionary

EDINBURGH: EARLY DAYS

Economy." I was reminded of this when I read how Siegfried Sassoon's mentor, the psychiatrist Dr Rivers, gave him similar counsel. "Rivers considered that political economy would be a useful preparation for my participation in the Labour Movement, though for once he was mistaken in assuming that I could absorb economics." Believing that his father was equally mistaken, Fred did not, probably to his deprivation, take his advice. Yet it reflected Leon's belief that, as the familiar tag has it, Christians, and especially ministers, should not be so heavenly minded as to be of no earthly use.

At the university Leon joined the Diagnostic Society, where he made the acquaintance of some of the brightest of his fellow students. He struck up a friendship with one of them, Charlie Ridland, a law student and keen debater who played the violin and smoked a pipe. (I remember him dimly: his eyes twinkled above a large nose and small moustache and he wore a bow tie). But the demands of the Mission and its pastoral work restricted his participation in student activities. He did, however, find his way to John Kelman's popular student services in The Operetta House, which perhaps is why in 1911 he joined Kelman's congregation at Free St George's. He also found his way to Charlie Cotter's Gymnasium in Leith Street, a popular haunt of young men seeking physical fitness. The Indian clubs and dumb-bells which lay for years on top of his study cupboard testify to the gymnastics, and when he gave his sons boxing gloves he told them how he had learned what was then called 'the noble art of self-defence'. "Hit me if you can," he would say, but we found it impossible to break his classic defence. He also learned ju-jitsu (now judo), which enabled him, some years later, to rescue a woman whom he found, in a lonely street at night, being molested; he was so effective that he broke her assailant's arm!

These arduous activities of his youth, however, were not long maintained, and in after years the best he could do was to walk home instead of taking the tram, or to leave his study-chair for a half-mile excursion to the post-office or bank, and, of course, to climb many a tenement stair.

NOTES:
1. He was clumsy at times, and some years later broke his arm by letting his front door slam on it on a windy day.
2. Leon, in 1903, said 900 *families.*

4. YOUNGER BROTHER

Six years younger than Leon, Nahum was from an early age devoted to his brother. In 1900 when Leon left home Nahum was only twelve; yet he was already marked out for the rabbinate and was a student at Yesubath Etz Chaim, the Rabbinic College in Jerusalem. The régime was monastic and intense, and he was unaware of events at home. "Our hours," he wrote later, ". . . were from 7 a.m., with time for three daily prayers and meals, till 11 p.m., and sometimes we just slept in our seats, or found some corner of the Yashevah to sleep in. Three to four double pages of the Mishna and Talmudic comments had to be learned by heart each week."

The precocity which had first brought Nahum to Jerusalem to the college of his father's relative and mentor, Rabbi Salant, one of the greatest scholars in the land, also led him at fifteen to be the youngest graduate of Yesubath.

Meanwhile, on a visit home, he learned that Leon had gone to Paris, and was then told that he had died. "This was a great shock to me," he wrote, "for I was very fond of him; but there was nothing to be done. He had died, and that seemed to be the end of that." So he continued his studies, which were to lead him first to Heidelberg to grapple with Ancient Philosophy and Indo-European and Semitic Philology, then to the Sorbonne for Modern Philosophy and General Philology. He, too must have been overwhelmed by Paris. In 1904 a mild outbreak of cholera erupted in Safed and the town was placed in quarantine. Nahum was at home at the time and was assigned the task of keeping watch at the city's northern exit; ostensibly to see that no unauthorized person went in or out, but in reality to keep an eye on the Turkish officials who were only too ready to accept baksheesh. He expected the missionaries to be the first to turn up with bribes of gold. "Great was my surprise," he said, "to discover that while the local doctors tried. . . to get away, the missionary doctors stayed. . . and worked night and day with their staff to help the stricken. . . This behaviour. . . impressed me deeply."

The same year one of the missionaries, a Mr Friedman, bought wine for communion from the family vineyard. He sent a pound too much and Nahum went to return it to him. Now Ben Friedman, before his conversion, had been a friend of the family's but had suddenly disappeared, only to be heard of again when he returned as a missionary. The pious Jews in Safed could not, as was their wont, attribute his conversion to bribery or to any worldly ambition, for he cared for none of these things. Indeed, Nahum's mother went so far as to conclude that he must be one of the 'Hidden Saints'. The tradition was that there are thirty-six of this Messianic company scattered in the world, but unknown to one another; and that when they come together the Messiah will come. Ben Friedman had gone over to Christianity, she maintained, because he had to conceal his identity lest something dreadful would happen.

"I can still to this day feel some of the fear and trembling with which I made up my mind to return the extra pound," says Nahum (in the autobiographical article in *The Hebrew Christian Quarterly* of Spring 1968 from which much of this chapter is derived). "I stood at a distance and called to him to accept the pound which I threw to him." However, Mr Friedman persuaded him to come and talk, and discussed the Talmud with him. "I learned from him that he knew my mother, and had received great kindness from her family; and I was utterly thunderstruck when he asked me how my brother was. I told him he was dead, but he very seriously told me he was alive, that he was in Scotland, and that he was a Christian. I cannot express the grief that overtook me. First, that my mother had told me an untruth about my brother, and then that my brother was a Christian."

Nahum managed to verify Mr Friedman's statement. At the same time he enquired of a wise and gentle sage, the revered Gaon of Slutsk, who for six months tutored him in Safed, how the missionaries, who worshipped the hated Nazarene, could do such good. "He told me there were good people among all nations, but especially among the British people. . .[and] that they did not worship images and did not worship the Cross."

Nahum then started to read a New Testament which Mr

43

CHRISTIAN AND JEW

Friedman had given him. He began with the Gospel of Matthew. "But," he says, "I soon threw it away; it seemed to be a composition by some fanatic; too many miracles, too many impossible stories, too many quotations from our literature thrown together, and then at the end of the story the Nazarene is crucified! Well, they said, he rose again; but that was pure imagination! I gave it up. But the Holy Spirit was working in my heart. . . One day, passing the Gospels, I started to read Romans. That gripped me. I read and read it again; and when I had read it many times I resolved to go to Britain and hear what my brother had to say."

This explanation of his awakening to Christianity is supplemented in later accounts. In the course of a paper on *The Old and New Covenants and Baptism* he says, "On first reading the New Testament I found the Gospels unhelpful. My New Testament was discovered among my books by one of my brothers and burned. (It was a Hebrew translation). For a time I gave it up, but something within me urged me to go back to the book, and so I got a new copy and started with Acts. St Paul fascinated me, and I read on through Romans and Corinthians. The benediction in II Cor 13:13 brought me to a standstill. It seemed to me sheer blasphemy to put the grace of Christ before the love of God. . . St. Paul had won my heart but not my mind, and I tried to follow his reasoning in this grave departure. In time the answer came to me. God's love had not been enough to keep us true to his holy will; we had failed to maintain the laws or observe the covenants. So that grace (*chesed*) had to be manifested, and grace was of the Messiah. Love still remained, but grace became the bond between God and ourselves. . . Christ doing for us what we could not do for ourselves.

"Having found an adequate explanation, I went on to Galatians, and there found St Paul answering many of my questions and solving many of my problems. There was no alternative for me. Christ was the Messiah, the Son of God, and I must confess Him as such. The step, however, meant great pain to my family and a shame that would haunt them day by day. Yet there was no way out."

It was Leon, not Nahum, who published a *Life of St Paul*. But such was the debt that Nahum owed the apostle that he, too, wrote his life. The book was never published, and all but the preface and the first chapter are lost, but it was completed, for Professor Manson of Edinburgh is thanked for reading the manuscript. In the preface Nahum again recounts his initial reaction to the Gospels and his enlightenment through Paul.

"From 1908[2] when he left Edinburgh he has kept me in touch with all his movements; and since his return to Edinburgh we have met, generally once a week and mainly for the study of the O.T. prophecies. But I feel that our positions are now reversed for he is the teacher and I the learner.

"Indeed the conviction has grown upon me that God has been preparing Mr Levison in a special manner for the work of the ministry. He has, by the Divine Spirit, wrought in this young man a rare experimental knowledge of the truth as it is in Jesus.

"Mr Levison recently preached in St Mary's with more than ordinary acceptability. He *can* preach and preach to some purpose. It could not be otherwise with his deep convictions and clear intellectual grasp of truth.

"Personally I am convinced that his admission to our church will be the admission of a man of God and a man whom God has led to devote his life to the winning of souls."

The following year it was George Davidson who preached in the U.F. Church at the fishing village of Johnshaven, in Kincardineshire, at the induction of Nahum to his first Scottish charge. Nahum had a towering intellect, and in later life was a member of learned societies and contributor to scholarly magazines. In this he differed from Leon, who, though highly intelligent and the author of several well-researched books (for example, *The Jew in History*), would have laid no claim to scholarship.

In appearance they were equal in height — five foot nine or ten; but whereas Leon was frequently referred to as handsome, was wide-browed, thick-haired and had a moustache, at first long but later trim, Nahum was of stockier build with heavier features, a broader nose, a domed forehead, a sparse head of hair, and remained clean-shaven. Leon had a light tenor voice and sang; Nahum's intonation was guttural and he was unmusical.

In temperament, too, they differed. Leon was even-tempered and conciliatory, Nahum at times up in arms. Again, though both were frequently at odds with officialdom, Leon, as one who served in the Church's Jewish Department recalled, "would use the rapier, Nahum the bludgeon."

Nahum, indeed, was once to startle a Presbytery meeting by declaring "The Church will never prosper until '121' (the Church Offices) is burned to the ground and," he added for good measure, "not a soul be allowed to escape!" (Hebrew hyperbole again). Such outbursts, however, were rare, and he was known throughout his life as a man of deep humility, blazing sincerity and tenderness of heart.

To return to November 1905 when he was baptised. What then? Where was he to go and what to do? At first he sought work in Edinburgh but none was to be found. He then offered himself to the British Jews Society (which also worked in Safed) for training as a missionary, and was immediately dispatched to the American Mission College at Beirut with a view to working in the Middle East. In February 1906 he applied to the Consulate at Alexandria for a passport "for the Ottoman Dominions", and spent the rest of that year at the college. But, like Leon's, his heart was sore at the thought of their family's, and especially their mother's, grief and coldness towards them, and at the assumption that they had repudiated their Jewish people. The brothers therefore agreed that in the spring of 1907 they would try to go to Safed together and see what could be done.

Notes
1. Now The Presbyterian Theological Seminary.
2. However, it was somewhat earlier. Nahum was in Beirut by early 1906.

YOUNGER BROTHER

He came to the Gospels, he says, expecting a defence of the Christian position against the Jewish. However, he found little ethical teaching which was not in the rabbinical literature. "There was of course the story of Jesus Himself, but this, I was taught to believe, was pure invention and utter blasphemy, so that I put the Gospels down with some relief and said to myself I need trouble myself no more about these legends.

"I ought to make it quite clear that I was strictly forbidden to read the New Testament. It was a case of stolen waters; but they did not taste sweet. . . The reason that I felt constrained to disregard the strict injunctions not to read the New Testament was that I watched the lives of some Christian missionaries. Their exemplary lives made me feel that I ought to read the books that inspired them. . .but I came to the conclusion that it was not they that called forth the self-sacrificing life of the missionaries.

"Other acts of self-sacrifice brought the matter to the fore again. . .I must read again — but this time I started with the Epistle to the Romans. It gripped me. Here, I said, is a worthy defence of the Christian position, and it was thus that St Paul became my schoolmaster leading me to Christ. . . Of course I have learned to read the Gospels in quite a different way and St Paul receded as Christ grew upon me, till Christ became all in all. Yet during the thirty-odd years of my Christian life St Paul has been my chief commentator on the Gospels and my foremost exponent of Christianity."

There are, he adds, many far better books on St Paul than the one he has now written. He "deserves and has had, and will continue to have, more worthy exponents, but few who regard him in higher esteem and have learned more from him."

It was at the beginning of 1905 that Nahum set out for Britain. "I had to take the greatest care that no one should become aware of my purpose; and after many tribulations I reached Scotland where, influenced by the gentleness of some Christian friends of my brother's, the instruction of my brother and of that prince of men and preachers, George Davidson, of St Mary's Free Church, Edinburgh, I accepted Christ and was baptised in His Name."

The Christian friends referred to were no doubt the Sawkinses, and later he was to enshrine his love for Fred Sawkins on the flyleaf of one of his books: "To FILS (i.e. F.J.L.S.) THIS VOLUME IS AFFECTIONATELY DEDICATED." However, the first book he published is dedicated to the Rev. George Davidson, "BELOVED PASTOR, MINISTER, GUIDE AND FRIEND."

Mr Davidson's instruction lasted for six months, during which he elucidated the doctrine, polity and sacramental practices of his Church. For Nahum this was new ground. "I was seventeen" he said, "when I presented myself for membership of the Church. I had read the New Testament but knew nothing of the beliefs and practices of the Church. From observation I concluded that the Christian Church was divided in its practices, and that there was no love lost between Greek Orthodox and Latin, or Latin and Protestant."

In due course he was asked whether he was willing to be baptised in public. "I had nothing against the rite being performed at a diet of worship," he wrote, "but I questioned the necessity of the act. . . The Gentiles needed to be baptised to wash away all uncleanliness of idolatry, but I was not an idolator. . . This set my dear pastor quite a problem. He explained that in the Christian view baptism was engrafting into Christ. I knew something about grafting: I had grafted olive trees and vines. I asked him 'Is that like going into the Tabernacle over which the Shekinah dwelt, or like enveloping oneself in the Talith as in the Shekinah?' Yes, it was something like that. . . Was baptism in itself grace which the Church as representing Christ on earth bestowed, or was it a means of grace? We spent a few evenings thrashing out this question. Our conclusion was that it was accompanied by grace if there was faith. Again I turned to St Paul. Finding that he himself had been baptised, I had no difficulty about the omission of it from the defence before Agrippa. It would only have confused Agrippa. But the evidence was decisive, and I was ready to be baptised. . . Baptism was like twine with which the graft is bound into the trunk. I was baptised into Christ by this act and so became partaker of the grace which was in the Lord Messiah."

Almost at once he was urged by Mr Davidson to go into the ministry. However, he resisted the thought for several years. It was not until 1915 that he entered the McCormick Seminary[1] in Chicago. The following year he was ordained, and after the briefest of ministries in Arizona enlisted in the Canadian Army. When in 1921 he applied for admission to the ministry of the United Free Church of Scotland, it was to his 'father-in-God' that he applied for a testimonial, in the course of which Mr Davidson said this:-

Nahum, c. 1925

5. SAFED REVISITED

Having obtained permission for two months' leave, and subsidised by his adoptive parents, Leon set off at the end of March 1907 for Beirut where he joined Nahum. For the Mission the trip to Palestine was not without purpose, for he brought back 200 photographs to replace the now dated set of slides given by Mr Scott Moncrieff; and these, together with the Mission's new lantern, would encourage more speaking engagements.

But the main object was, along with Nahum, to see his family. Some time earlier his mother had written asking him if he was still so foolish as to continue as a Christian. He replied that nothing would shake his faith, and that he wished all Jews were as foolish as he was. To this she responded bitterly, saying that she had cut him out of her will; that he was no child of hers, nor a brother to her children; and that this would be the last letter she would write.

Leon, however, did not cease to write to her; and he accepted neither the obduracy of her will nor the inflexibility of her disaffection. As the years passed he hoped that she would mellow and at least be willing to speak to him. As for the language in which she had rejected him, so devastating and seemingly so irrevocable, he knew that it signified less than it said. This was first because it was the habitual and predictable Jewish reaction to apostasy and, second, because in many a passionate Jewish utterance there is hyperbole. When a Jew says, "May God strike you dead," or when the Psalmist says of his Babylonian captors "Happy is he who would take your children and dash them against the rocks", they are not to be taken literally. (This applies also to some of the more difficult sayings of Jesus). His mother's imprecations were less savage than those of other parents, which are exemplified in the following letter to a thirty-one year old rabbi who had become a Christian:-

"Philip,
You are no longer my son. We have buried you in effigy and now may the God of Abraham, Isaac, and Jacob strike you blind, deaf, and dumb, and damn your soul forever. You have left your father's religion and the synagogue for that impostor, Jesus, so now take your mother's curse.
Jane"

These harsh attitudes belong to a bygone age; but by rigid adherents of Judaism conversion is still regarded as a betrayal of faith and by many Zionists as an act of racial treachery.

As he crossed Anatolia by train Leon was in Pauline territory, and his thoughts turned to the apostle. Eleven years later, in his *Life of Paul* he wrote thus:-

"During our visit to Palestine and the Near East in the spring of 1907 we had the great happiness and privilege of going over almost all the routes traversed by St Paul. One of the most lasting impressions derived from these journeys. . . was our unspeakable amazement at the purely physical accomplishments of St Paul the traveller. . .

"With special passport and diplomatic recommendations in your pocket, you have taken your seat in the comfortable, up-to-date carriage of the Anatolia Railway. As the train carries you without exertion over the top of the pass, the last gleams of daylight show you far away below the ancient road, narrow and stony, winding its way up the pass, and on this road a few people on foot or on donkeys or horseback, are hurrying towards the dirty-looking inn. It must be reached before night has fallen, for the night is no man's friend. . .

"Or, leaving the modern Levant Hotel, with its lift and French menus, go into the miserable Shan at the top of the pass known as the Syrian Gates on the road to Antioch, and sleep for a single night on the hard boards of its unsavoury plank-beds tortured by bad air, cold and vermin. . . On that darkening road we have seen St Paul; on those hard boards St Paul sought repose. . ."

In Beirut they hired horses, but the joy, for Leon, of being back in the saddle after more than seven years, and heading for home, was overcast with anxiety. How were they to approach their mother; and would she receive them?

"We rode a whole day", says Nahum. "We sent the drivers of our baggage animals away, and every hour or so a new suggestion was made. 'It is terrible, it is unbearable. The worst of it is she thinks that we have come to hate our Jewish people. How shall we dissuade her?' Towards evening as we were coming towards Methulla we halted our horses. 'I am not going into any town,' said Leon, 'till we have decided what to do.' 'Will you go to father's synagogue and give some money for the poor?' 'Will that mean compromise?' 'Not at all,' was my answer. 'You stay an extra day with Rachel (our sister) at Yeshod Hamaala, and I will go on to Safed. I will meet Mother and tell her the only condition upon which you are ready to follow, and unless she sends for you we shall leave Palestine for as long as she lives.' "

So Leon waited in the farmhouse where Rachel, the brothers' sole sympathiser, though never a convert, lived with her husband Israel Ashkenazi and their three-year-old child. (That child, Nahum, still lives there and farms the land.) Leon would then, no doubt, have taken photos in the Tiberias area, which may explain why he did not visit the Tiberias Mission later.

Miriam did send for him. "The meeting," says Nahum, "showed the deep affection that bound them to each other, and her terrible anger at his acceptance of Christ. 'You must leave the Nazarene out of this house; you must not mention his name. Do you hear, both of you?' 'Yes, mother,' said Leon, 'but I cannot leave Him out; He and I are inseparable.' She kissed him, and just what that kiss meant I do not know to this day.

"The next day being Saturday we went to the synagogue. My uncle, who did not know of our arrangements with Mother, wanted Leon to come up to the reading of the Torah and to make a donation. He refused. He promised the donation, he was willing to stay till the prayers were over, but he would not in any sense compromise."

However, this visit to the synagogue had unforeseen and acute repercussions. To a bigoted observer it was as dire a betrayal as if today in Ireland a leader of the Orange Order had gone to Mass. Fifteen miles away in Tiberias, there was such an observer in the person of a United Free Church missionary, the Rev. Thomas Steele, who assumed the worst; that Leon had recanted and was, as an agent of the Church, an impostor.

Leon never flinched before the storm.

"If you want me to explain I will not do it. If you care to condemn

SAFED REVISITED

The remains of the family house in Safed   (Photo 1972)

me. . . I have a clear conscience before God and my Saviour." He could not turn to the Safed Mission for help. For it was in a period of transition and Dr George Wilson was no longer there. (The medical side of the Scottish work was being phased out, and by 1908 it was abandoned; for the Anglicans had erected a large hospital and dispensary in Safed. The Scots, however, had a well-managed boys' school, of which the Rev. S.H. Semple, who became a close friend of Leon's, was appointed Principal in 1909; and also a girls' school which was known as one of the best in Palestine.)

   Mr Steele at once wrote to Edinburgh to inform the Committee of their missionary's apostasy. He also accused him of having passed himself off as a graduate and a B.Sc., and reviled him in the pages of a magazine in which he wrote under the pseudonym "Nassud". That Mr Steele was a sick man who had to come home after only a year at Tiberias, may have affected his attitude. Leon's response again was, "If the cap fits I will wear it; but this cap simply does not fit"

   Had Mr Steele been in Safed, Leon might possibly have put him in the picture. But he was too hurt or proud to return to Tiberias to explain. Besides, Tiberias was, until the British built a road in 1921-22, a day's journey. The Scottish journalist W.P. Livingstone, coming in the other direction, described Safed as "almost inaccessible for want of a pathway. I rode up to it over stony ground and it took the best hours of the day."

Back in Edinburgh in June, an explanation was required; and there Leon expressed his desire that the allegations be investigated without delay. He was then brought before the Committee and told that Mr Steele's charges were twofold: that he had posed as a Jewish believer, thereby denying Christ, and that he had claimed to be a graduate and a B.Sc. of Edinburgh University. Before the Committee he was asked: Did you deny Christ; and did you represent yourself as a B.Sc.? To both questions he gave a categorical denial, and there the matter ended. He was told that the Committee had never wavered in their confidence in him, and the subsequent entry in the minutes was as follows:

"The Committee instructed the Chairman to explain to Mr Levison that the questions were put not so much for the satisfaction of the Committee as, in justice to himself, he ought to have an opportunity of categorically and solemnly denying the said allegations. When he did so, the Committee agreed to this motion: The Committee having had the letter before them. . . and having heard him and fully discussed the matter, express their sympathy with him in the charge of apostasy, confirm their entire confidence in his character, and that the letter referred to be destroyed."

When they parted at Beirut the brothers scarcely saw one another again until after the War; although they may have done so, fleetingly, when Nahum's army postings brought him to London. Leon returned to Edinburgh not only to resume his work and clear his name, but to enter the U.F. Church's New College, where in the words of John Baillie who began there in 1908, there were "excellent teachers, most of them well-known and highly honoured throughout the whole Christian world." These included, in Leon's time, Marcus Dods and Alexander Whyte as Principals, and H.A.A. Kennedy, A.R. MacEwen, H.R. Mackintosh, Alex Martin and J.Y. Simpson as Professors. The Librarian was his old mentor James Kennedy, and the Warden of the College Settlement (adjacent to the Jewish area) Harry Miller. Later there was a third Kennedy (A.R.S.), a lover of the Jews, who became Convener of the Established Church's Jewish Committee.

Leon's decision to remain a non-regular student was not due to his lack of qualifications. His modified university course, preceded by studies in Palestine, along with his missionary experience, might well have admitted him to a full course culminating in ordination. But since at the Mission neither the sacraments nor the ordinance of marriage were provided, ordination seemed unnecessary. He may also have shared the view of Henry Drummond, that great missioner among students, who was licensed but not ordained, and whose influence was still powerful in Edinburgh, that he could work more advantageously as a layman. To be called "Reverend" would create a barrier; it would obscure the fact that he was an emissary not merely of the Church but of the Messiah.

He entered the life of the College with relish, and among his contemporaries were John Baillie and the son, David, of Mr John Lusk of the Mission Committee. Baillie was to become one of the most distinguished churchmen and theologians of his time. In the 1930s he became my own teacher at New College, and in the 1940s taught David Lusk's daughter, Mary, who was to become my wife. Her father was a man greatly loved both as Chaplain to the London Scottish and, after the First War, as minister of St Columba's Oxford and Chaplain to the Presbyterian members of the University.

What with the removal of the Sawkinses, and himself, to Albert Terrace, the spring in Palestine, the autumn at New College, and the ongoing work at the Mission, 1907 was a full and exciting year. However, its best was yet to be: his engagement to the girl next door.

He began to throw roses over the wall!

6.THE GIRL NEXT DOOR

Her name was Katie Barnes, and she too had left her family home. From the country estate of Bunker's Hill, with its long low Georgian mansion, south-west of Carlisle, she had come to Edinburgh. Strong-willed and independent, and having claimed a substantial inheritance, she had at the age of twenty abandoned the comforts but also the disaffections and, as she saw them, the frivolities of Bunker's Hill for the sedate but by no means dull life of the Scottish capital. It was the decisive step that so many of Tchekov's young women, isolated and frustrated in similar circumstances, and whom she resembled also in dress and coiffure, failed to achieve.

Her grandfather, Dr Thomas Barnes, an eminent physician, was a co-founder of the Cumberland Infirmary. He had considerable means, for his wife, an Ismay, was the heiress of Tring in Buckinghamshire, the 17th century manor designed by Wren which Charles II had presented to Nell Gwynn, and which with its 3500 acres became one of the Rothschild estates.

Her father, John Barnes J.P., as a young man had also aspired to a medical career; but failing to qualify in Edinburgh, where he won minor notoriety by riding his horse up the steps of the Surgeons' Hall for a wager, he settled at Bunker's Hill in the role of squire or gentleman-farmer. A few years later he eloped to Gretna Green with the gamekeeper's young daughter. Her name was Catherine Miller, and she was regarded as flighty and of an inferior station. The legality of the marriage was questioned, and their eldest daughter Louise (called Louie) was considered illegitimate; but before the birth of their only son, Tom, they remarried. John, according to a later photograph, grew into a dignified figure with a grey top hat and a neat white beard. They had four more daughters, May, Ada, Annie and Kate. Thus while Leon had four brothers and one sister, Katie had four sisters and a brother.

Ada, who was slightly spastic, never married; and Tom was no sooner wed than he broke his neck in the hunting field. Louie married a landed proprietor named Jack Robinson. They had a daughter, Kitty, of whom Katie was very fond, and who, on her mother's early death, was to join her aunt, to whom she was devoted, in Edinburgh.

May married a ne'er-do-well who, in after years, would turn up in Edinburgh after either a drinking bout or a spell in prison, seeking financial help.

The sister with whom Katie had the closest affinity was Annie; but their relationship, as we shall see, came under a considerable and prolonged period of strain. The family rift, which involved their mother, was one of the causes of Katie's departure to Edinburgh.

However, it was not the only one. First and foremost she felt out of tune with the life-style and the Philistine values of the squirearchy. Not that the social mores were particularly raffish; but her family pursued a life of leisure and pleasure, with much hunting, shooting, and the giving of parties at which, as Katie, defending her strict teetotalism, was wont to declare, she had seen too many drink themselves under the table.

In the second place, she was dissatisfied with the family's casual and formal adherence to the Church of England. She herself had discovered a small Low Evangelical church in the nearby hamlet of Brough where she attended Evensong with one of the family servants. The rector, Canon Baines, was gentle and saintly (I met him in his old age and thought he had one of the most beautiful faces I had ever seen), and through his ministry Katie underwent an experience of conversion and was confirmed. The canon's daughter, Kathleen, also became a lifelong friend.

The third cause of her defection was engendered by Annie's runaway marriage and the events which surrounded it.

After John Barnes' death the family had continued to spend the summer months at their holiday residence, Birnock Lodge, in the Scottish Border town of Moffat. There they were highly respected, occupying a rented pew in the parish kirk and consorting with their close friends Willie Tate, the Town Clerk, and his wife. But there also lived in Moffat a young schoolmaster named John Davidson Kelly and, from time to time, his brother Andy who was a medical student.

The trouble began when Mrs Barnes, still young-looking and attractive, set her cap at John, while he, though not averse to a flirtation, preferred her daughter Annie. When Annie was wooed and won Mrs Barnes was furious. Annie was told either to give John up or to leave home. She chose the latter and earned her living as a nursery governess until illness forced her to seek refuge with an aunt (her father's sister), where she remained until the wedding, which took place very privately in 1898 at Weston-super-Mare.

The couple returned to John's private school at Moffat, where the Barneses one and all continued to cold-shoulder them. It is said that Mrs Barnes ostentatiously snubbed them from her carriage, and that Katie and Ada, obeying orders, cut Annie in the street. To avoid further unpleasantness the Kellys moved to Bridge of Allan, where John started a new school. Later their home was in Bonnybridge and finally in Glasgow.

It took several years for Katie and Annie to be reconciled. The death of their mother, early in the century, and the need to make provision for Ada, brought them together. (Ada went to the Kellys and later to a Glasgow flat under the care of a housekeeper). In addition Katie's growing friendship with John's brother, Andy, their subsequent engagement and the fact that she now lived within reach, in Edinburgh, must also have helped heal the rift.

However this was not for long; for John was outraged — and small wonder — when she jettisoned Andy in favour of a later suitor. The fact that that suitor appeared to be an almost penniless foreigner and a Jew, and had not known better than to approach a girl already plighted, added fuel to his rancour, and he refused to speak to Katie and Leon for several years. As for Andy, he must by then have qualified, and to be jilted at the eleventh hour would be a bitter blow. He departed to Newcastle, his native heath, and tried to mend his broken heart by marrying, disastrously it is said, on the rebound.

Eventually John, under Annie's benign influence — for her nature was warm and affectionate — agreed to let bygones be bygones. Amity was restored and there was to be much coming and going, in future years, between the two families.

The Davidson Kellys have left their mark in the world. Of their sons one, his father's namesake, became a patristic, liturgical and biblical scholar of the first rank and was for many years Principal of St Edmund Hall, Oxford. He was also the Archbishop's envoy in

Anglican-Roman Conversations. Nevill, a solicitor, became the foremost layman in the field of worship and liturgy in the Church of Scotland. Graeme was a parish minister, Marjory (McCracken) a much loved doctor and town councillor in Kelso, and Ann a Head Almoner in London. Their father regarded himself as a failure, for more than one of his preparatory schools went bankrupt; but it was to his personal tuition and drive that the family owed much of their success.

My own memory of my Uncle John is of one florid in appearance, bluff in manner and potentially peppery. Round-faced and with a handlebar moustache, he sported a fur coat and spats. These and the cigar in his hand gave him an air of bravado which, no doubt, masked, and was an antidote to, his anxieties. He died in 1929, and thereafter Katie kept in close touch with Annie, who died, to her great sorrow, less than a year after Leon.

Katie's choice of Edinburgh may have been determined by the city's romantic history and its beauty; or because in 1900 it had more to offer culturally than any other northern city. It may, of course, also have been where Andy was. Her books suggest that she studied literature: Ruskin, Pater and Carlyle, as well as Dickens and the Victorian poets. Lecture courses were then in vogue with young people of leisure, and she probably attended some; but she never attempted to enrol at the university.

From an address in the Craiglockhart area she and a companion, Mary McLeod, both Episcopalians, were in 1901 received into St Michael's, a congregation of the Established Church of Scotland. In 1903 Miss McLeod departed to Leith, and Katie bought 9 Albert Terrace, a house destined to play a major part in this narrative.

The move to a Presbyterian Church is indicative of her independence. Most Scottish Episcopal churches were High in comparison to the Low Church evangelicalism of Canon Baines. Nor were there any near Craiglockheart; and when she moved to the vicinity of Edinburgh's 'Holy Corner' she would regard the one there as 'high'. St Michael's, on the other hand, had a fine evangelical minister in Dr George Wilson (who was unrelated to the other Wilsons), and the building was more conducive to worship than many a Presbyterian kirk, including the one at Moffat. She continued there until Dr Wilson had married her to Leon and their older children had been baptised. Then in 1911, the mile-long trek with no direct route proving too difficult, they moved to Free St

George's which, though further, was more accessible.

In 1903 Louie Robinson, the eldest sister, died; and in 1904 Katie brought her daughter Kitty to live with her. Kitty Robinson was then a lively thirteen year-old, and Katie, *in loco parentis,* arranged for her further schooling at St Denis. However, each year the relationship became less parental and more that of companions. Thus when Leon came on the scene he may well have taken them for sisters. Kitty gave Katie some of the happiest days of her life, and to the end of her days whenever Kitty came back to Number Nine, the house was filled with laughter.

Number Nine was the last of the terraced houses; beyond were villas. Being at the end, it had the widest garden, which lay chiefly to the rear and extended seventy yards southwards. The main feature of the terrace, however, which surmounts one of the city's east-west ridges in the area known as Church Hill, is its southern aspect. From the upper windows one looks over the roofs of Morningside to the Blackford and Braid Hills and the panorama of the Pentlands. And from the drawing-room one steps through French windows on to an ample balcony, where many a tea-party was held and visitors contemplated the vista of hills and sky or looked down on the gardens below. It was from the next-door balcony that Leon would call across to Katie or observe her in her garden.

And what did Katie make of Leon? She had lived in a society insular in outlook and with a chauvinistic dislike of foreigners. The young man who had come to live next door was plainly foreign. His thick black hair rose in untidy curls, and below a fairly long moustache his strong teeth gleamed as most Westerners' teeth did not. The pallor of his skin gave him a semi-Indian look; while the easy confidence of his manner differentiated him from many of the awkward and buttoned-up young men whom she had known. She was a very private person, and his exuberant, demonstrative nature both contrasted with and compensated for her own reserve.

There is no record of how they met and fell in love — only the legend that Leon tossed roses over the wall. She remembered this because it marked her awareness of his love. And if they had not yet spoken, she must have been startled indeed. (To Kitty it would seem hilarious). Leon never hid his feelings from those he loved; and once she acknowledged his gesture it would not be long before he poured out his heart. She in turn would respond, not because he was glamorous and romantic, but because what she learnt of his faith and his struggles and, above all, of his missionary dreams awakened an eager response.

To discard Andy Kelly was not easy. By one who took life as seriously as Katie it could not be lightly done. Yet as she weighed up her two suitors and searched her heart, it was evident where her future lay: in sharing in a missionary vocation; in loving the Jews as Leon loved them; in creating a Christian and church-centred home; in sharing Leon's love of the Bible and his prayer-life. It was all so different from what poor Andy had to offer, for there is no indication that he shared in her religious interests.

It was 1906 or 1907 when Leon came to Albert Terrace, and they were married in 1908. Between these dates he was pursuing his studies at the University as well as his missionary work; and in the autumn of 1907 he entered New College. Earlier that year there had also been the visit to Safed. She, too, may have gone abroad. For at some point she went to South Africa for her friend Ruth Blaylock's wedding. Since she was absent from the January and March Communions in 1908, and Leon went alone to the latter, his first in St Michael's, it may have been then. Whenever it was, it was a brave enterprise for an unchaperoned young woman. That she was an intrepid traveller and of independent spirit would appeal greatly to Leon.

Incidentally there is a curious pencilled comment beside Leon's name in the St Michael's Communion Roll in March 1908: "after instruction. G.W." Why should a New College student, who had been for several years a communicant, require instruction? We can only assume that the Established Church held that a member of the U.F. Church needed further knowledge of its history, traditions and beliefs.

There was good reason for Leon to think carefully before he proposed. It seemed such a precarious union. In race and antecedents, socially, culturally, physically, the gap between them was so wide. Yet against all odds it turned out to be an almost ideal partnership. Not only were their backgrounds disparate, but so, too, were their incomes. Leon had no private means and would continue to receive a meagre salary (never above the minimum stipend of a minister). This must have worried him, for he would not wish to be beholden to the Sawkinses or to depend on Katie's ability to support him.

His anxiety was needless; because for Katie their incomes belonged neither to her nor to him. What they happened to have was their good fortune, and they would use it well. They had few wants and although, in accordance with the time, they employed a cook, a housemaid, and in due course a nannie, their tastes were far from extravagant. Katie, apart from two early forays abroad, spent all too little on herself. She was thrifty, whereas Leon was open-handed and apt to give too much away. Later, she became a shrewd investor and he a confident participator in large business deals — but never for personal enrichment.

Meanwhile what of the wedding? Katie's family disapproved and she was left to make her own arrangements. These were simplified in that Leon had only to move from next door into a ready-made home. (It was to be their home for the rest of his life). The wedding presents included a handsome revolving bookcase from the Mission and a Bible in several large India-paper volumes for family worship. The bridesmaid was almost certainly Kitty, now in her seventeenth year, and the best man was Charlie Ridland. They were to see much of the Ridlands in the years to come. During the War Leon sought the help of Charlie, now a solicitor, in his fund-raising efforts, and after it they were ordained to the eldership together in Free St George's. But in 1928, for the sake of Mrs Ridland's health, they emigrated to California.

On the marriage certificate C. Forbes Ridland is recorded as the second witness, the first being Dr James Kennedy, to whose seniority he would defer. The bridesmaid, normally a witness, was not so on this occasion; which would confirm that she was Kitty, who was under the statutory age requirement.

The wedding in St Michael's was on 30th June, and without their families (and apparently without a photographer either) was quiet indeed. After the celebrations, at which the Sawkinses, other supporters of the Mission, fellow-students and whatever friends Katie had acquired were the guests, the couple set off for the north, the banns being forwarded on 2nd July to c/o Mrs Smith, Turlundie, Banchory, Aberdeenshire.

They had attended a Quarterly Communion together for the first time on the Sunday before the wedding, but were not to do so again until the following March. This suggests that in October and January (the Communion seasons) they were out of town. In their early married life they visited Venice, and I recall talk of Mont Blanc and of funicular railways. One of these trips — a prolongation of their honeymoon — may well have been within this period. The other

THE GIRL NEXT DOOR

may have taken place a few years later, when the first two of their children were still infants, and when a capable nannie would have been left in charge.

Such absences indicate an indulgence both on the part of the Mission Committee and the New College authorities which might not be so readily shown today. The case of David Lusk, however, Leon's contemporary, is evidence that the continuity of a student's course could be broken; he was absent for a year, teaching in India. Similarly Leon was not at New College in 1909-10 but resumed for the 1910-11 Session.

On the 1st of May 1909 their first son, John, was born. This was Katie's father's name, while its association with "the disciple whom Jesus loved" made it a mutually desired choice. Fifteen months later came Fred, called after Frederick Sawkins. Then in 1914 Miriam arrived, named after Leon's mother. Her death in infancy caused a considerable age-gap between the two firstborn and the later children, Rosalin and David. It was said of Rosalin, born in 1916, that her mother, having chosen the name Rosalind for its beauty, learned too late that Leon, whose spelling was atrocious, had registered her without the 'd'! Finally, in 1917, there was Leon David. Although he was always to be known as David (and was Judah Leon not of the House of David rather than of Levi?), Katie had insisted on including 'Leon', which David, in his turn, has included in the names of one of his sons.

Such was the family. At its genesis, however, Leon was only beginning to launch out beyond the roles of local missionary and student into a wider world.

Kitty Robinson

Katie with John 1909

7. MISSIONARY AND STUDENT 1907—14

1907 was the year of his visit to Safed. In his absence the Sawkinses, together with Mrs McIntyre and Mrs Kennedy, were responsible for the meetings and activities of the Mission. Leon, having been offered his salary for April and May, had declined, preferring to receive it on his return; it was a clear indication that the Sawkinses were helping him. Before he set out, the new premises at 46, Lauriston Place were opened.[1] The Committee placed on record "their deep sense of obligation to Mr John Lusk for the great services he had rendered in securing, preparing, equipping and inaugurating the new home of the Jewish Medical Mission. They owe it to his able strenuous efforts and his unwearying zeal that all that was needed has been so admirably accomplished, and that in so short a time." Praise indeed!

In March 1907 the Annual Meeting noted that there were 500 Jewish families in Edinburgh and between 2,000 and 3,000 Jews. Lord Provost Gibson was the guest of honour, and in his address referred to the recent persecutions of Jews in many parts of the world, and the refugees who came to Britain.

That such persecution was rife in Russia is borne out by a memorandum which Lord Rothschild was moved to send to the King (Edward VII) in June of the following year. It was a plea to which the King was most sympathetic, even to the extent of raising the matter with Mr Stolypin, the Russian Prime Minister. He asked whether action would be taken to remove Jewish disabilities and to discourage pogroms. Mr Stolypin replied that legislation was contemplated for the amelioration of the lot of the Jews in Russia. Lord Rothschild, however, had little confidence in these assurances.[2]

Two weeks after the move to Lauriston Place, Leon reported that the meetings had been especially good and that he thought the difficulty of their close proximity to the synagogue had been overcome.

On that satisfactory note he went abroad. During his absence, however, exception was taken to a case cited in one of his reports. "It was agreed that Mr Levison be reminded that such cases should be remitted to the Committee appointed for that purpose." At the first meeting after his return, however, he deflected disapproval of his continuing impetuosity by presenting the mission with a desk — a token of gratitude from a Jew to whom, fifteen months ago, he had given 15/- to enable him to start in business as a joiner.

Shortly afterwards he reported that since his return he had been visiting some of the high-class Jews with very encouraging results; and that he hoped, probably with this new clientèle in mind, to lecture on Saturday afternoons on the life of St Paul.

Unfortunately the Committee's minute-book breaks off at the end of 1907, and no other volume has been discovered. So the fate of the lectures is not known. I am only certain that they would not have replaced the weekly service nor curtailed its social hour. They must have been an additional element crowded into these afternoons of the Jewish Sabbath.

The final pages of minutes contain one or two further sidelights. For instance, in June Mr Sawkins revealed that during Leon's absence abroad he had had to disburse more than the £5 given him by the Treasurer — a predicament Leon knew well — but asked for no repayment; and in November Leon reported that he had distributed a similar amount among twelve cases of need, there being much destitution. On a happier note, he added that on making 25 visits he had found the Jews more open to talk about Jesus Christ than hitherto.

In November it was announced that Dr Alexander Whyte would open the Sale of Work, and that Leon would give two lime-light lectures. But in December Leon was ill and Mr Sawkins read his report. The men's classes, it said, were the largest of the year. Mr Sawkins went on to say that he himself had been visiting the mission, and was pleased with the different meetings and classes — with one exception. When he went to the meeting for men on November 25th, in Mr Levison's absence they all vacated the room!

The lack of documentation in succeeding years does not conceal the fact that Leon continued to 'gang his ain gait,' as we say in Scotland. He would take risks and was frequently taken advantage of in his efforts to combine evangelism with practical help. It is known that he was taken in by a former synagogue cantor whom he tried to set up in a shop, and by a devious carpet-dealer. And Katie is said to have persuaded him, in the nick of time, to withdraw from a deal which would have landed them in financial disaster. So much for economics!

These events occurred over a long period; nevertheless they show his continued gullibility or perhaps that, like Nathaniel, he was 'a man without guile.' If it was a fault, it sprang from his generous, compassionate nature. He could not see a Jew in distress, apparent or real, without wanting to help. This was for him the clear implication of the Gospel. He would have said with St Paul: "I may have faith strong enough to remove mountains; but if I have no love, I am nothing."

In October 1907 he had entered New College. He attended during the sessions of 1907-8 and 1908-9, was absent in 1909-10, and completed his course in 1910-11 after his first two children were born.

His activities in 1909 are not on record, but in February of that year he received a letter from his eldest brother:-

Holy City of Jerusalem

"The Lord be blessed!
To my dear brother Leon Levison.

Dear Brother,
I came back today from the holy town, Safed, I am glad to inform you that our brother Moses Joseph has received the photo of our father which you sent to him and also the glass frame. I was also glad to see that the photo is very good: it will remain in our house for eternal memory of our father, blessed be his righteous memory. I have had then the intention to go abroad, and perhaps also to see you face to face.
We are all keeping well, thanks be to God. With much love and greetings from the mountains of Zion.
                    Alexander Levison."

Coming less than two years after the reconciliation with his mother, this affectionate letter must greatly have heartened him.

He also spoke that year to the annual meeting of the Edinburgh

Jewish Missionary Society and his words were reported. "Quietly, slowly, unmistakably the influence of missions has told, with the result that large bodies of Jews have been formed in Germany and in other Continental countries, and in America, which resolve to set forth Christ as the foremost of the Jewish race. . . We feel that 'a people are being prepared.' "

Such words reflect his growing powers as a public speaker, his characteristic optimism and his expanding awareness.

The phrase "Quietly, slowly, unmistakably, the influence. . . has told" would have been beyond him in earlier years. It is the kind of phrase familiar to politicians. One could imagine it on the lips of Lloyd George, whom he admired, and whom he may have heard in Edinburgh in May 1908 at a demonstration in the King's Theatre in favour of the English Licensing Bill.

At this stage it would appear that Leon wrote out his speeches, though not his less formal talks, in full. Later, his practice was simply to jot down headings on a postcard, even when addressing so formidable a body as the Church's General Assembly.

As for his optimism, the belief in a future for the Jewish people never left him, even through the dark days of Russian, Turkish and German oppression. And in Russia and Russian Poland, where half the population of the Jewish world resided, this was indeed a dark time, as we have seen. As Jeremiah, in similar days of darkness, saw an almond tree in early bloom as a sign of hope and of the continuing purpose of God, so Leon was for ever seeing signs of the fulfilment of the divine promises. Israel would one day be saved and become a light to the nations; she would return to her own land and the Messiah would yet be her King.

His awareness of the wider scene came not only from immigrants but also from his reading, which included *The Jewish Chronicle*, a journal richly informative on world-Jewry. It was also influenced by his friendship with Sabati Benjamin Rohold, whom he had first met in 1903. Ben Rohold, a Palestinian Jew, was then Missionary of the Bonar Memorial Mission in Glasgow. While in Edinburgh, attending the General Assembly of the United Free Church, he called on Leon and took him out to lunch. "From that moment," wrote Leon, "a friendship sprang up between us which grew in strength and confidence, and which led to our sharing in each other's work in a manner which I dare say was almost unique."

Rohold was on the verge of leaving for Canada, where he took charge of the missionary work in Toronto and built up a Christian Synagogue. Before long he was also involved in the creation of the American Hebrew Christian Alliance. He remained in Canada until 1919, and during that period rarely failed to communicate with Leon at least once a week. Later he was one of the founders of the International Hebrew Christian Alliance, and would be the first to rejoice when Leon, whom he loved dearly and regarded almost as 'a son in the Lord,' (although little younger than himself), was made its President. By then Rohold was back in Palestine where, at Haifa, he did magnificent work among Jews and Arabs alike, as well as for the Alliance. A man of infinite charm and rich affection, he was an enthusiast and a visionary, and to Leon a prime source of inspiration.

Leon was 'a political animal', and with all he had seen of the struggles of the poor, his enthusiasm for Lloyd George, whose reforming spirit aroused the hatred of the privileged, is not surprising. Even before the National Insurance Act of 1911 and the social measures dealing with health, housing, education, wages and employment which followed it, his sympathies were with the Welsh Wizard. Perhaps as early as the Boer War he appreciated the politician who was vilified for opposing that imperialist venture. When Lloyd George became Chancellor of the Exchequer in 1908, the humanity of the speeches in which he canvassed his budget, and the picturesque language in which they were couched, would win his immediate response. A typical example of such words comes from the famous Limehouse speech of 1909: "It is rather hard that an old workman should have to find his way to the gates of the tomb bleeding and footsore, through the brambles and thorns of poverty. We cut a new path for him, an easier one, a pleasanter one, through fields of waving corn."

Sometime in the first decade of the century Leon cast in his lot with the Liberals, and found a political haven in the Scottish Liberal Club. He would go there to read the papers (he took only *The Scotsman* and the *Evening News* at home); to play billiards; and to consort with a wide range of friends, many of whom were deeply engaged in national and civic affairs. He remained a member until in the thirties his life became too hectic to visit it.

However, he did not neglect Katie; and his absence from New College for a year could be accounted for simply by the resolve not to be overwhelmed by too many outside activities in the first two years of their marriage. The birth of children in 1909 and 1910 brought additional responsibilities, and he was also reading widely and assimilating all he had learned in the past five years. As for Katie, it is said that during her pregnancies she read the whole of Dickens!

Incidentally, in his children's infancy he accompanied Katie with the pram on Sunday afternoon excursions to Blackford Pond or the Union Canal at Craiglockhart; few fathers took part in such walks in those days. A few years later he would take them rowing on Craiglockhart Pond.

Leon 1909

He was now 28, and his appearance had changed. Prompted by Katie, he had become well groomed. The wild head of hair had been tamed and was neatly parted on the right (later, on the left). He had not yet resorted to brilliantine, but that was to come. He acquired a bowler hat, and took to wearing pince-nez, whose spring-clip was to leave almost permanent marks. His moustache was neater and his clothes and boots well brushed. His suits were well-cut and, having learned tailoring to the extent of being able to make one, he took an interest in their workmanship and texture. With a neatly rolled umbrella and a coat with velvet lapels, he was spruce without being dapper, and looked every inch a city man; this impression was enhanced indoors by his watchchain and fob and his flyaway collars. Later, when I was old enough to make the comparison, I thought that from the back view the way the bowler sat on his thick hair was distinctly Chaplinesque.

His feet were small, his gait nimble, and he bore himself well. His best feature, however, was probably his hands, tactile and beautifully formed, the fingernails cared for, the fingers not yet nicotine-stained. His mild eyes were European rather than Semitic; not black nor brown, but grey-green. His lobes were pierced, from the days in childhood when he had been compelled to wear earrings. He had an innate courtesy, and his manners were impeccable.

Katie was as tall as Leon, and smartly but quietly dressed in the fashion of the day; she wore a watch pinned above her breast, a lace-trimmed blouse, and round her throat a velvet band. Her independence of spirit was hidden behind a gentleness of manner and shyness of disposition. Although later in life she found herself serving on committees, writing articles, and exercising leadership, she did so only in the context of Leon's work. Otherwise she chose to remain in the background and to share in the lives of her family. When they were young, her children were not shut away in the nursery, and their nannie, whom they loved, was never a surrogate mother.

Though not an outstanding beauty, she was far from plain. She had wide-set grey eyes, a slightly aquiline nose, and her long brown hair was neatly rolled, Edwardian fashion, round her head (later it was gathered into a 'bun'). She had sensitive lips and a firm chin; altogether she might be described as pleasing in appearance and pleasant and gracious to meet.

Theologically, intellectually, politically, as well as in his family life and his ministry to the Jews, this was a period of growth for Leon. But one thing he had not mastered was the ability to spot a rogue. Again, in 1910, he was persuaded to lend money to a Jew to enable him to set up shop as a grocer. He also established a partnership with him and went night after night to the shop to help with the book-keeping. However, on returning from holiday he discovered that the man had been gambling over many months with the takings and was heavily in debt. Leon just had time to announce in the Edinburgh Gazette that the partnership was dissolved, and only lost the money he had put in. He should have learned his lesson, but it is doubtful whether he ever did.

John was born in May 1909, when Leon had concluded his second session at New College. Before he returned there in October 1910, Edward VII had died and the new Georgian Age had begun. Then in June 1910 an event took place in Edinburgh which was to be a landmark in Christian history — the first great World Missionary Conference, from which were to spring the International Missionary Council, the Faith and Order Movement, and the World Council of Churches. Only two Jewish Christians were there as delegates, one of them being Rohold. Whether Leon was present as an onlooker is not known; but his interest in the section on Jewish Missions is beyond doubt. Nothing would give greater encouragement to his work than these words in the Conference Report: "The Church is under special obligation to present Christ to the Jew. It is a debt to be repaid, a reparation to be fully and worthily made... The winning of this virile race with its genius for religion will be the strengthening of the Church of Christ and the enrichment of the world."

That autumn he was back at New College. On the death of Dr Marcus Dods, Dr Whyte, at the age of 73, had become Principal; but after the Missionary Conference he had had a second heart-attack, and was inactive, though only temporarily; not until eight years later did he relinquish the principalship. The evenings on which Dr Whyte entertained his students in his study are proverbial. The First Year as well as the senior men had their own evening, and the non-regular students also had an evening set aside for them each winter. His care for individual students was exemplary. He would know Leon at New College, and also at Free St George's, where he held the Senior Pastorate until 1915. The ministries of Alexander Whyte, of his colleague Hugh Black and especially of John Kelman, his colleague and successor in the charge affected Leon greatly. They were all men of ecumenical mind and catholic culture, of deep spirituality and scriptural insight, and as notable for their humanity as for their missionary zeal.

His three sessions at New College did not constitute a full course, which was then four winters, the summers being left free for other work. His missionary obligations made it wiser to confine himself to the most relevant subjects; and he continued to gain from the friendships, some of them lifelong, with fellow students such as Wales Cameron and George Troup. Another contemporary in 1910 was the saintly Donald Baillie who, like his elder brother, was to blossom into a theological teacher and thinker of the first order.

The winter term coincided with a General Election. In December Asquith was returned, as he had been in January, with only a narrow majority. However, it was enough to proceed not only with Lloyd George's Budget legislation, but also with the Parliament Act which destroyed the absolute veto of the House of Lords — "the most decisive step" wrote R.C.K Ensor, "in British constitutional development since the franchise extension of 1867" — and to press on towards the great questions of Home Rule and Welsh Disestablishment. All these topics must have engaged the lively minds of New College at a time when Election issues engendered high excitement.

In his own missionary sphere there was the commencement by the United Free Church of work among the Jews in Glasgow and the appointment of the Rev W.M. Christie as the ordained missionary. This was a take-over of two earlier missions, one of them being the Bonar Memorial Mission which Ben Rohold had led, and the other the Evangelical Mission to the Jews. In 1929 the reunited Church of Scotland was to inherit all these streams.

Leon gained splendid colleagues in Mr Christie (who had already worked in Tiberias and Safed, and was to return there in 1922) and his successor Dr Joseph Sinnreich, a former candidate for the rabbinate.

One other event in 1911 would claim his attention and that of his classmates. The Student Christian Movement gathered 600 students together at Edinburgh for a conference at which a Scottish Council was formed. "Scotland," Professor D. S. Cairns told them, "has always loved great thinking in its religion." The truth of that assertion and its combination with the movement's internationalism and missionary concern matched Leon's convictions.

Since the brothers parted at Beirut five years had passed and Nahum had not become a missionary. At some point he joined the Army and served with the Hussars in India. In 1912 he emigrated to Canada. He now knew he was called to the ministry and almost immediately crossed the border to enrol at the McCormick Seminary (now the Presbyterian Church's School of Theology) at Chicago, where he matriculated in September, 1915.

For Leon the second half of 1912 was marred by illness. He and Katie, together with Charlie Ridland and probably Charlie's brother, went on a Highland holiday during which they took long walks. On one of these, and far from home, they were caught unprepared in heavy rain. Back at their lodgings Leon gallantly said to the others, "You take the first baths," and waited without removing his clothes. The consequent chill led to a serious bout of rheumatic fever. This affected his heart, and together with his indifferent eyesight, caused him to fail a medical test when war broke out two years later.

By 1913 he was back in harness and probably well enough to meet the leader of the Persian Bahais, Abdul Baha Abbas, at Dr. Whyte's house at 7, Charlotte Square. Dr. Whyte had invited "students from the Orient, including Hindus, Moslems, Parsees and Jews." "The teaching of the Bahai leader, and the fidelity to the ideals of their faith which his followers had shown through much persecution," says G.F. Barbour, "especially to that of world brotherhood and the application of the law of love throughout all human affairs, appealed to Dr. Whyte as a significant manifestation of the Christian spirit outside the bounds of Christendom."[3] It was a tribute and a catholicity of outlook with which Leon would wholeheartedly agree.

Early in 1913 Chapman and Alexander, successors to Moody and Sankey, the great revivalists of the late 19th century, came to Edinburgh and conducted a mission in the U.F. Assembly Hall. With the backing of the churches its success was assured. Dr. Whyte, now 78, was there along with Dr. Wilson of St. Michael's, who was even more venerable. The Chapman Alexander Hymnal joined that of Sankey on Katie's piano, and it is more than likely that they themselves were there. Revivalist preaching, when it was

73

soundly biblical, and revivalist hymns, sentimental but not ranting, always appealed to them alongside the more profound and sedate Presbyterian expressions of the Gospel.

In the summer Katie was much occupied with the impending event of Kitty's wedding, which took place in October. After Katie's marriage Kitty had attended a Domestic Science College in London.

She then married John Falconer, a young lawyer from the Highlands. It was a perfect match, and when Kitty died, in 1935, at only 44, John turned for comfort to Katie and Leon. (I remember yet his grief-stricken figure at the gate.) However, John was a brave man who had won distinction and high rank in the Royal Scots through four years of war. Nine years after Kitty's death, in a unique ceremony, he knelt on the steps of the Royal Scottish Academy in Princes Street and was knighted by George the Sixth. He was then not only Lord Provost, but the instigator, with Rudolf Bing, of the Edinburgh International Festival. His daughter, Diana, still in her twenties, was the most graceful of Lady Provosts, but how he must have longed for Kitty at his side. He was also an elder in St. Andrew's Church, Juniper Green, the suburb where they lived; whereas Kitty had remained an Episcopalian. The family compromise was to worship for three Sundays in John's church and on the fourth, and at festivals, in Kitty's. It was as harmonious an inter-Church marriage as one could find.

One follow-up to 'Edinburgh 1910' was the International Jewish Missionary Conference held in Hamburg in the fateful summer of 1914; and Leon was there. A photograph taken in the Belvedere Café on the 6th of June shows him with three men, one of whom appears to be Rohold. The following month he was at home, and when the War broke out the family were on holiday.

NOTES:
1. Since demolished to make way for the Hunter Building of the Edinburgh College of Art.
2. See *King Edward the Seventh* by Philip Magnus. John Murray 1964, pp. 406ff.
3. *The Life of Alexander Whyte D.D.* By G.F. Barbour, Hodder & Stoughton 1925. 8th edn p.555

Author, Fund-raiser, Missionary, Patriot. 1914-23.

8. THE WAR YEARS

Fred remembers that holiday at Innellan on the Clyde, and how, a few days after his fourth birthday which was on August 3rd, they abruptly went home. The boys were told to retrieve their buckets and spades from under the hedge and empty the crabs and sea urchins back into their pools. "Why must we go home?" they asked. "Because there's a war on," they were told; the Germans were doing awful things and we had to fight against them. On the paddle-steamer to Wemyss Bay a disconsolate family stood apart from the rest, and Fred heard someone say, "Those are Germans."

At a time when most Britons regarded the war as a 'pushover' and said that it would end by Christmas, why was the holiday curtailed? Leon certainly did not panic, but he may have thought that Katie, being eight months pregnant, would, in the event of restrictions or upheavals, be better at home. Moreover, as a shrewd observer of world affairs he was aware of the dark forces being released. For him, as for Sir Edward Grey, "the lights were going out all over Europe" — and not only Europe. Four months before the hostilities began, Turkish officials throughout the Near East had, one of Leon's brothers informed him, received sealed orders from Constantinople and were ready for the fray. Trouble was impending in Armenia, Syria and Palestine.

On October 14th at 52 Queen Street, now known as Simpson House, Charlie Ridland married Marilyn Simpson. Since it was not a Saturday, when he would have been at the Mission, Leon was able to be there. The bride's great-uncle was the illustrious Professor of Midwifery, Sir James Simpson, who, in discovering the anaesthetic properties of chloroform, fell unconscious under the dining-room table. The wedding was conducted by Dr. Whyte in the drawing-room where he himself had been married in 1881 to Marilyn's aunt, Jane Barbour. (Church weddings were almost unknown in Scotland at that time). Leon found himself among a galaxy of Simpsons, Barbours and Barbour-Simpsons; pillars of the U.F. Church and of Free St. George's.

Katie was not there; for a few days later Miriam was born, only to die on the 27th. Mr. Kelman, their beloved minister, was in Australia recuperating from a breakdown, and the funeral was taken by the Rev. John Macrae, who was Dr. Whyte's assistant all through the war. Having ministered to the Scottish congregation at Calcutta where Leon had spent boyhood years, Mr. Macrae was neither a novice nor insular, and he and Leon had much in common.

Another in the congregation in whom he would find support and encouragement was Dr. Whyte's brother-in-law, Sir Alexander Simpson. A retired professor of midwifery, and for long on the Kirk Session, he was a supporter of the Mission. On a Sunday in 1915 he was to occupy the pulpit and speak on missions to the Jews.

As the war gathered swift momentum, many Jews enlisted or were called up, and this affected Leon's work. Later he was to recall that "Before the war I used to have a men's class in the Mission premises. This was interrupted as a result of a goodly number. . . having joined our fighting forces. Hence I began to invite Jews to my own home. . . The personal touch had a far more telling effect than I had hitherto experienced, and consequently I gave up my evenings to deal with individual Jews privately."

From then on they came. Usually it was in ones or twos; but sometimes the bench in the hall was supplemented by chairs on the landing, and occasionally by an overflow to the drawing-room upstairs. When the first caller arrived, Leon would, without demur, lay aside the book he was reading, usually a thriller by Edgar Wallace, E. Phillips Oppenheim, or William le Queux, and go to the study. From time to time he would emerge from an increasingly smoke-filled room, say a gracious good-bye, and usher in the next caller. With the last, or a solitary visitor, he was in no hurry, but spent what Katie sometimes considered an inordinate time listening to some overlong story of trouble. At the end of the evening he would either resume his light reading or unwind with a Double Wrangler, his favourite game of patience.

Like a minister at Vestry Hour he dealt with matters both spiritual and practical. I remember intruding to tell him someone had been

THE WAR YEARS

waiting long, and finding him praying; another time with an open Bible. With most missionaries he regarded any sharp distinction between *kerygma* (proclamation) and *diaconia* (service) as false. His practical compassion, no less than that, say, of Mother Teresa, sprang from spiritual roots; and proclamation and service were inextricably bound. Since there were neither Citizens' Advice Bureaux, Marriage Guidance Councils nor the provisions of the Welfare State, the appeals for practical advice and help were unceasing and compelling.

A regular visitor for many years was a Mr Bierman, a tobacconist who made his own cigarettes and was Leon's supplier. Morose and unforthcoming, he nevertheless spent hours in the study, but seemed unlikely to be discussing the finer points of theology. Nor to my knowledge, was he ever a convert; but Leon's prime concern was for people, rich and poor, wise and simple, human beings in their own right.

Katie was too fastidious to relish all his visitors. Mr H—, a Glasgow businessman, for instance, not only treated her like a long-lost sister but had the unfortunate habit of spitting into the fire! Leon made excuses for him and continued to welcome him as a genuine seeker after God.

Meanwhile the escalation of the war and of its casualties brought not disillusionment but a fresh wave of patriotism. "Your King and Country Need You" was everywhere to be seen. Leon wanted to serve; but how? In the summer of 1915 the plight of the Armenians showed him the way.

In November 1914 Turkey had entered the conflict on Germany's side, and Palestine, being within the Ottoman Empire, became enemy territory. Leon could no longer communicate with his mother. In the summer of 1915, his oldest brother, Alexander, managed to flee the country and to reach Paris, from where he sent Leon an account of the situation in Safed. He also described the hardships in Syria and Palestine of British subjects and of Christians (including Nestorian Arabs), but especially of the Armenians, of whom 800, he said, had been killed in the last 5 months.

In a 46-page pamphlet published in the same year (the first of several) entitled *How the Turk makes War*, Leon quotes freely from his brother's letter. It told how in May 1915 the sealed missives sent to all Turkish governors in the previous year had been opened. They contained instructions about new nationality and tax laws, and these, for Alexander, meant that he had to forfeit his British citizenship, become eligible for military service, or go to jail. (The other brother, Moses, seems already to have left the country).

Alexander chose prison, where the conditions were deplorable; but was released through the intervention of his mother, who told him she had paid £40 plus Stamp Duty to exempt him from military service. "Before she could lay her hands on ready cash," he wrote, "she had to sell two of our houses though, in the normal time, one alone would have brought in eight times that sum."

However, he discovered that what his mother had bought was not his exemption but naturalization papers; for she thought he could only be saved by becoming a Turkish subject. Now they were immediately informed that these papers were not in order and that a further £40 must be paid. Alexander was advised that refusal to do this was regarded as an insult to the Sultan's government, and that he should flee without delay. In fact he had only ten minutes in which to bid his wife, children and mother farewell.

In Tiberias he joined a party of British subjects. They set out on foot for Damascus and arrived there exhausted. Again, with six others, he walked on to Beirut. Here, helped by the American consul, they were shipped to Alexandria, where they joined 25,000 refugees from Palestine. At this point Alexander was incredibly lucky, for he fell in with a sympathetic English lady who assisted him to reach Marseilles.

He was familiar with Paris, for there is evidence that he had stayed there, and also visited Edinburgh, in 1909. Whether he again called on Leon in 1915 is not known. After the war he settled with his family in Toronto. From there his sons Morris and Manuel came to Glasgow University. Morris eventually settled in Israel as a lawyer and, though remaining a Jew, served the Church of Scotland as their legal agent in regard to their properties there; he was also to serve the Hebrew Christian Alliance.

When Alexander wrote of 800 Armenians being massacred, he was unaware of the full facts. On May 27th, 1915, the Turkish Government, known as the Young Turks, decided to get rid of the Armenians, who inhabited eastern Turkey and its borderlands. They accused them of disloyalty, and a decree went out that the whole population would be deported to Syria and Mesopotamia. In an act of, until then, unparalleled brutality, no less than 1,750,000 people were driven from their homes into inhospitable desert coun-

THE WAR YEARS

try. It was the precursor of Hitler's 'final solution.' Some 600,000 died of weakness and starvation or were massacred en route.

Leon's response to this atrocity was to appeal to the British public by setting up an Armenian Relief Fund, and publishing (with a Foreword by Hector MacPherson, Editor of the Edinburgh *Evening News) How the Turk Makes War.* However, by the time it appeared in 1915, he was involved in a still greater philanthropic cause. Thus even that first pamphlet describes him as 'Hon. Sec. The Russian Jews Relief Fund.'

The plight of the Russian and Polish Jews was equally heartrending. In *The Tragedy of the Jews in the European War Zone* and also in *The Jewish Problem and the World War,* both published in 1916, Leon described it movingly. Both tracts embraced an appeal for the national fund, of which he was both founder and secretary. The first words of the Appeal were these: "An area seven times the size of Belgium has been ravished five times by the Germans. Millions are homeless and starving."

It was no less than the truth. The fall of Warsaw alone precipitated the flight of 350,000 Jews to the East (Among them was Chaim Weizmann's mother). Paderewski the Polish President, is quoted as saying, "It has become necessary for the inhabitants to live off the bark of trees, and such food as can be found in the woods." There were over two million refugees, most of them women, children and old people from The Pale of Settlement, the extensive Jewish area on the Polish-German border. The Pale (the setting of *Fiddler on the Roof* and some of the novels of Singer and Malamud) was now the war zone. "The menfolk," Leon explained, "have been conscripted into the respective armies, where they fight willingly and heroically for the Russians but unwillingly and by compulsion for the Germans." Russia had recently loosened some of the restrictive laws and extended the privileges of nationality, and "the Jews fight wholeheartedly for those who have shown them kindness and given them civil and political rights." This point he reinforced by listing the decorations won by the half-million Jews who fought with the Allies.

Characteristically, Leon could not refrain from a Christian digression. He inserted a paragraph on what we owe to the Jew, reminding his readers of what nation Jesus was born. Listing the agents and agencies of mercy in the War — Red Cross nurses, hospitals, churches, chaplains, Y.M.C.A. — he declared that none of them existed in the ancient world or brought succour in ancient wars. "They all arose with the spread of the Gospel of Christ. . . Whatever view we take of His personality, it may be assumed that He alone is the supreme Founder of every humanitarian and philanthropic effort." He then pointed out that although "the accumulated cruelties of the ages have naturally had their effect on the Jews. . .they respond more quickly to the influences of philanthropy than any other civilised people." However, if the Russians had shown kindness in days of peace, their treatment of the Polish Jews in 1915-16 could hardly have made their Jewish conscripts fight wholeheartedly. For in The Pale, wrote Bishop Welldon, the Dean of Manchester, in a foreword to one of the pamphlets, "the Jews are dying, or are near to dying, of starvation." "The sufferings of the Belgians have been great," added Leon, "but how much greater those of the Jews are is shown by the fact that over two hundred cities and towns, some as large as Brussels and Antwerp, have been practically ruined, and eleven thousand villages razed to the ground."

Moreover, while this suffering was largely attributed to the Germans, the Russians could not be exonerated. *"The Jewish Problem and the World War"* contains an extract from *The Jewish Chronicle* of 23rd July, 1915. It quotes a Russian Army Order of the Day requiring the expulsion of all Jews from military zones in Galicia, Bukovnia and Poland, and indicting them for disloyalty. The result was that 200,000 people were exiled at short notice to some far-distant Eastern province. Twenty-six trains of from forty to seventy wagons were provided, into which they were crowded. The slow-moving trains were not allowed to stop at stations where food could be supplied. Before the journey ended, twenty-eight passengers had become insane and typhus had broken out. The thousands unable to get into the trains suffered equal hardship.

Examples of suffering, supported by documents and statistics, could be multiplied from Leon's pamphlets. Written in conjunction with the Russian Jews Relief Fund Appeal, they were also able to tell the British public what was being done. A committee had been set up in Britain representative of all denominations. Almost entirely Scottish in personnel, it included the Sawkinses, Mr Sawkins being a Vice-Chairman, Charlie Ridland, the Kennedys and other supporters of the Edinburgh Mission. The Chairman was the Rev. William Affleck, the Secretary Leon, the Organising Secre-

THE WAR YEARS

tary F.J. Robertson, who was to occupy 8 Albert Terrace when the Sawkinses moved out, and the Treasurer, J. Milne Henderson, a banker who was an Elder at Free St George's. There was also a Ladies Committee under Lady Gibson. A Secretary for England was also listed, and a Committee for Canada and the United States, of which Ben Rohold was the Assistant Secretary and probably, through Leon, the initiator.

Equally interesting are the Patrons. In Britain an earlier list includes Leopold de Rothschild, Claude Montefiore and Alfred Mond (later Lord Melchett) alongside thirteen clergy and thirty distinguished laymen. In a later one, two of the Jews have dropped out, leaving only Sir Alfred Mond M.P. The other Patrons included five bishops, three Moderators, seven peers, two M.P.s and five Lord Mayors and Provosts. The transatlantic committee was entirely Canadian, and there was only one American among the Patrons; but they included the Canadian Primate and Moderator and three leading Methodists.

In 1914 the United Free Church had recalled its missionary, the Rev. J. Macdonald Webster, from Budapest, and before long he was at the helm, the Jewish Committee's Secretary being in failing health. (He died in 1917 and Mr. Webster succeeded him). Mr. Webster, highly regarded as an administrator and fund-raiser (had he not, in Budapest, raised "the largest building in the world dedicated to Jewish evangelisation"?) set about raising a Special War Fund of £30,000 for Jewish relief and for reconstructing the work of the Church in Eastern Europe and Palestine.

Leon, unaware of this, enquired in July 1915 whether the Church's Jewish Committee would provide collectors for the Russian Jews Relief Fund. "It was resolved," says the subsequent minute, "to call Mr. Levison's attention to the Special Fund being promoted by this Committee, and the great desirability of keeping the two schemes distinct in the minds of members of the Church." Nevertheless in September Leon's Committee was invited to confer. Co-operation was promised but it was stated that joint public meetings were impossible because the essential Christian aspect of the Church's Fund would be impaired through Leon's Committee having entered into close relationships with certain committees of Jews.

Leon's successful approach early in the century to the Board of Guardians of the Edinburgh synagogue explains, if that be necessary, his willingness to make the Relief Fund a Christian-Jewish venture. Yet his uncompromisingly Christian references in the fund's literature put that co-operation at risk. It is most unusual for Patrons to withdraw, and it may be that Rothschild and Montefiore did so for this very reason. The marvel is that Mond remained.

Leopold de Rothschild ceased to be a Patron, but the Fund which, after all, was administered by a Jewish Committee under Baron Guinsberg, a banker, in Petrograd, retained his support.

"I shall be glad," he wrote to Leon, "if you will take an early opportunity of expressing to your Committee the sincere gratitude of us all for their noble effort to help these poor people and for the generous assistance you have secured in Scotland and also in England and Ireland." And in a later letter: "While this war lasts the only consolation one gets is just the way your Committee is endeavouring to help our people in Russia, in their whole-hearted efforts of charity and good works."

Another prominent Jew who wrote was Israel Zangwill, who said, "For any Jew to refuse you money or to refuse to be a channel for its right distribution would be tantamount to denying the Christian Church the right to help the suffering Jew."

Less sympathetic was *The Jewish Chronicle* which succeeded in suppressing a flag day on which considerable money and effort had been expended. (I remember, as a six-year-old, being taken to Charlie Ridland's office off Princes Street where collecting boxes and leaflets were stacked almost to the ceiling). The grounds of complaint could only be that this was an overtly Christian charity, and that corresponding Jewish charities had been deemed ineligible.

The Jewish Problem and the World War is a curious document. It begins with factual evidence of the plight of the Jews and ends with a passionate appeal. In between, however, there are many digressions. Ben Rohold is quoted on "Is the Jew wanted?" and Hector Macpherson in a section on "What we owe to the Jews" has several pages on the Jewish contribution to literature. Their sufferings down the ages are described by Leon, with quotations ranging from Jeremiah to Lecky. There are disquisitions on the Bible, on political rights and on Zionism, statistics of the Jewish populations, and of their enlistment in several countries and their contribution to poli-

THE WAR YEARS

tics in Britain. Amid all this is an account of the Relief Fund, with details of what Guinsberg's local committees at Odessa, Kiev, Minsk and other locations were doing: of the setting up of medical and clothing centres, workshops, soup kitchens and even a Board of Credit from which refugees could borrow in order to resume their work as artisans or small manufacturers. (The latter anticipated the self-help projects of Christian Aid and Oxfam by half a century).

Baron Guinsburg was well aware that, whether British Jewry was involved or not, the motivation was Christian. Writing before the Jewish Passover he said: "As Passover or Easter is the emblem of brotherhood between human beings, we believe that in helping the Jews on that occasion we are once again acting in the spirit of the Christian public of Great Britain. You are, of course, aware that the Jewish creed is very strict in the observance of the prescribed Passover ritual, and they will be full of deep-felt gratitude when they hear that this help comes from the Allies of a different creed from over the sea."

Hector Macpherson, like Leon, made no bones about his Christian stance. "How," he asked, "are we to explain the ferocity of Christians up till recent times?" Then having deplored the attempts to convert the Jews by force, he goes on to declare that their conversion "will be brought immeasurably nearer when they witness the life of the Master mirrored in the lives of His disciples. Antagonism is out of place when consideration is had to the sacred associations between Christianity and Judaism. The founder of Christianity was born of Jewish parents, and in Him Jews as well as Christians recognise the ideal of humanity. Christians go further and exalt Him far beyond humanitarian limits. But that does not alter the basis of agreement so far as the social side of His mission is concerned. In this as in other respects Judaism was a preparation for Christianity. The one was the seed of which the other is the flower."

Leon went still further. He seemed to forget he was writing a humanitarian tract and was not, for the time being, a missionary proclaiming the Messiah. "In Christianity the struggling ideals of Judaism find their realisation. In the Founder of Christianity, in whom the Jews refuse to recognise the fulfilment of the Messianic Hope, there is presented a conception of God in His relation to man, and of man in his relation to God, which must be accepted as absolute and final."

Whether the Fund lost the support of many Jews because of these utterances we cannot tell. In any case, together with a similar Palestine Jews Relief Fund of which Leon was also the Founder and Secretary, it raised some £200,000, which was not only an impressive, but a phenomenal sum. The equivalent purchasing power, according to the December 1988 index, is now £5,206,656.

Alternatively, for an assessment of what £200,000 meant then, one could draw a comparison with the overseas work of the United Free Church. In 1915 there were 230 principal mission stations and 1,411 out-stations, employing 4,954 missionaries, most of them teachers. The total annual revenue for all this, apart from a small amount received from fees at certain schools and colleges, was £139,512 received from the Home Church, plus £50,836 from Government Grants abroad — almost the exact equivalent of what Leon's fund raised.

It was, of course, not only Leon's fund; nevertheless, there is every indication that he was its source and inspiration. Hence when honours were awarded it was to him that they came. For instance, he received this letter, dated December 1916 (the very month of the murder of Rasputin, whose baleful influence speeded on the Revolution) from The Winter Palace, Petrograd.

"Secretary to Her Majesty the Empress Alexandra Fedorovna.

Dear Sir,
I have pleasure in informing you that Her Imperial Majesty the Empress Alexandra Fedorovna of Russia has been graciously pleased to confer upon you the enclosed order in recognition of the valued services rendered by you in connection with the Russian Flag Day Movement in England. Her Imperial Majesty has expressed her great appreciation of the energy and devotion displayed by the members of the various organising Committees in England as a result of which such marked success has been achieved.
 I have the honour to remain
 Your obedient servant
 Count J. Rosholsov."

Leon held no brief for the doomed Empress and the Tsar, the last of the Romanovs, who was to abdicate three months later. Yet he

THE WAR YEARS

treasured the silver medal jewelled with emeralds, the insignia of the Imperial Order of Russia. Six months later the Imperial family was murdered.

On March 22nd, 1917, the United States was the first foreign government to recognise the Provisional Government in Russia, and on the 23rd the First Secretary of the Imperial Russian Embassy in London, where the events in Petrograd had not yet struck home, wrote to Mr. Affleck, the Fund's Chairman as follows:-

"Dear Sir,
I beg to refer you to my letter of the 23rd January, in which I informed you that a recommendation of Mr. Levison's excellent work in raising a Fund for the relief of Russian Jews in the Eastern war zone would be directed to the proper Department in Petrograd.
I now write to say that I am desired by the Russian Government to state how much they appreciate Mr. Levison's devoted services, and fully recognise the value of the work he has been doing in alleviating the sufferings of the Russian Jews.
    I am, dear Sir,
    Yours faithfully,
    P. Sabline
    The First Secretary of the Russian Embassy."

Addressed to "Wm Affleck Esq. Russian Jews Relief Fund, 122, George Street, Edinburgh," this corrects the inaccurate title of "the Russian Flag Day Movement" in the previous letter. It also reveals that on March 23rd the Russian Embassy is still heading its notepaper "Ambassade Impériale de Russie." More importantly, the reference to 23rd January, together with the date of the first letter, suggests that the final sum, or close on it, had been transmitted by the end of 1916 and, we hope, distributed before the Revolution swept Baron Guinsberg away.

On fund-raising in general it should be added that Ben Rohold and his Canadian colleagues did well, contributing some £28,000; also that through Mr. Macdonald Webster's efforts the U.F. Church's Fund, which did not close until 1920, raised £25,600, to which must be added an almost similar sum in a special Hungarian Relief Fund. All of these were considerable results.

Before the end of 1916 an event may have taken place which, if true, adds a small grace-note to history. According to family legend, an immigrant Jew by the name of Braunstein turned up at Albert Terrace. His ship had put in at Leith on its way from Nova Scotia to Russia and his boots were worn through. Leon gave him a pair of boots and set him on his way. When he arrived in Russia (in time for the Brest-Litovsk Conference of January 1917) he resumed the name of Trotsky! The money that friends and subscribers of the magazine *Novy Mir* had collected for his fare had not been sufficient for boots; and his journey from America had been prolonged by internment in Halifax until the Provisional Government in Russia asked for his release. I can think of no other date when this episode could have occurred. There is a short story lurking in it somewhere — "Comrade Trotsky, where did you get those boots?" "If you must know, from a missionary in Scotland."

The legend, if true, provokes the question, how did a stateless Jew find his way to Albert Terrace? Had someone at Leith Docks heard of the Mission? Or had Braunstein been reading Leon's pamphlets? Anyhow, it points to the fact, confirmed in later years, that it was not only Edinburgh citizens who beat a path to Leon's door.

Other events of 1916 were the birth in March of Rosalin, and news that Nahum, having taken a B.D. degree at McCormick and been ordained in May to a small parish in Arizona, had, after the briefest of ministries, returned to Canada and enlisted. He was just too late to be thrown into the carnage of the Somme, where, in the first hour of battle on the 1st of July, 20,000 British and Commonwealth troops died.

When the Russian Revolution took place Leon lost no time in writing about it. *The Revolution in Russia; its causes and consequences* appears to have been written before the dire events of July 1917. Not only are the rise of the Bolsheviks and the royal family's assassination not mentioned, but the pamphlet is pervaded with a spirit of optimism. To Leon the Revolution was the inevitable outcome of centuries of autocratic rule, the liberation of a great people and the planting of their feet firmly on the road to democracy. In this he was soon proved wrong.

Yet his analysis of the causes is sound; and his recognition, shared by few in the West, that something more momentous than the French Revolution, more far-reaching in its consequences even

THE WAR YEARS

than the Great War, had taken place, marks him out as singularly perceptive.

As a student of Russian history he gives a clear account of the alternations between oppression and toleration in successive reigns from Ivan the Terrible and Boris Godunov to Peter the Great and the Romanov dynasty. He quotes Professor Charles Sarolea, the great Russophile whose Inaugural Lecture at Edinburgh University he had probably heard in October 1905. Sarolea had then said that the Russian people were not ready for Revolution but that pressures were building up. They certainly were. By the turn of the century Tchekov had known it. Hence the autumnal setting of his plays; and the symbol of the cherry orchard where the sound of the axes could already be heard. "All Russia," says his Trofimov, "is our orchard."

In the first Imperial Duma (or parliament) in 1906, the Russian people became articulate and there were open rumbles of criticism. By the fourth Duma in 1912 there was an abortive Revolution, and by 1917 the discontent was ready to erupt again.

"Fortunately for the success of the Revolution", wrote Leon, "Nicholas II, excellent as a man, well-intentioned, a good husband and father, was essentially a weak ruler. Like Louis XVI he lacked backbone. Nicholas II had the welfare of the country at heart, his mind luxuriated in an atmosphere of benevolent intentions, but a victim of vacillation, he stood shivering on the brink of indecision. The tragedy of it was that he was apt to be coerced into wrong decisions by artful and designing counsellors. Here, as in the case of Charles I and Louis XVI, Nicholas II was allured on the road to ruin by his wife. To her pro-German influences were to be traced indirectly, if not directly, the disasters, internal and external which befell Russia in the dark days of the War."

The thirty-page pamphlet represents some of the best of Leon's writing. It is vivid and dramatic, his vocabulary has enlarged, and there are no digressions. These further extracts convey both its style and content:-

"A colossal despotism, deeply rooted like some giant oak, protected from revolutionary blasts by superstition and militarism, in a few brief days was levelled to the dust".

"The leaders of the Revolution were thirsting not for the blood of the reactionaries, but for liberty. Content with overthrowing a hated Government, they had no desire to let loose the demon of revenge."

"The Revolution was a triumphant success. To this several causes contributed, among them being the Army and the statesman-like methods of the leaders... The remarkable feature... is its moderation. Its leaders are... animated by a noble purpose, inspired by a high ideal."

"The Revolution means... the liberation of fifty nationalities. At last the Slav race is entering into their heritage. Britain and France entered the War as champions of liberty. In a brief short day Russia has contributed more to the realisation of that ideal than the three years of fearful conflict. She has set free 175,000,000 Russian people and in the end 110,000,000 Germans will experience the beneficent influence of the events at Petrograd. Who can estimate the tremendous international results that will follow the fact that on the side of Democracy the votes of 180,000,000 free Russian citizens will be cast?... Consider what possibilities lie in... a nation loosened from the chains of theocracy and autocracy and sent careering along the democratic road."

If in Britain, as Leon maintained, interest in the Russian Revolution had been faint, he at least did something to stir it up. So too did Lloyd George who persuaded the House of Commons to send fraternal greetings to the Duma. He believed that Kerensky's provisional government would continue to support the Allied struggle — until the chaos brought about by near starvation spread to the Russian army, a power struggle ensued, and disillusionment set in.

Pamphlets and books continued to pour from Leon's pen. Already in 1916 he had produced a small-scale account of *The Jew in History*, its foreword by Dr Norman Maclean of St Cuthbert's, Edinburgh being dated 15th May. A booklet on Zionism and the least ephemeral of his writings, a life of St Paul, were also to appear in 1917.

We shall come to these presently. Meanwhile, the war had taken its toll — one only has to remember that 60,000 died on the Somme on the first whole day of battle — and Leon's Reserve group (although he was 36 in 1917) was due to be called up. He appealed for exemption on the grounds of being an author engaged in national propaganda; but this, we shall see, was not the whole reason for his deferment. The grounds for exemption, attested by a Justice of the Peace, were as follows:-

THE WAR YEARS

26 Charlotte Square
Edinburgh

24th May, 1917

"It is with my knowledge that Mr Leon Levison, 9 Albert Terrace, Edinburgh, Author, and Director of the Jewish Medical Mission, has been for nearly two years engaged on literary propaganda work in the interest of Britain and her Allies, to counteract the German publicity campaign in America and Russia, and that with official cognisance and active support. Copies of his books to the number of over 800,000 have been circulated abroad. I have further satisfied myself that, by arrangement, he is now engaged in the preparation of literary work for extensive distribution in Russia, emphasising the importance of active co-operation between the people of Russia, particularly the Jewish population, and the Allies. I observe that the recruiting authorities have been advised of the nature of Mr Levison's services.
    Joseph Dobbie J.P.
Justice of the Peace for the County of the City of Edinburgh."

Fund-raising and propaganda were not Leon's only contribution to the war effort. There were other services of which even Katie seems to have been kept in the dark.

For many years, all that the family knew was that he had been able to provide the Government with first-hand knowledge of Palestine. "I know Palestine," he would say, "like the back of my hand." It was a claim which extremely few in Britain could have made at that time. Hence, with the Allies preparing an offensive in the Near East, his services as an adviser on the terrain, its inhabitants and its politics were invaluable.

So it was that when Lloyd George and an entourage of experts paid a brief visit to Edinburgh, Leon was summoned to the North British Hotel for breakfast. Katie expected him back sometime during the day but he was there well into the night and told her they had been locked in — literally 'locked in conclave'.

He then, throughout 1917, made frequent and sometimes prolonged visits to London, ostensibly for further consultation. That is all that was known for about forty-five years. Then Fred, attending a branch meeting of Toc H in Edinburgh, was introduced to Professor Roy, formerly of the Chair of English Literature at McGill University, Montreal. "Are you by any chance," said he, "a son of Leon Levison?. . . I knew your father well. We were together in Cairo in the First War. We were working for British Intelligence." On hearing this, Katie, then in her mid-eighties, said: "He went to London often, but I never heard of him being in Cairo." (She may have forgotten.)

A visit to Israel by Fred and his wife in 1972 led to a further discovery. Nahum Ashkenazi, the son of Leon's sister Rachel, who still lives in his parental home, the farm-house at Yeshud Hamaala where Leon had stayed in 1907, told them of a strange incident. "It was in 1917," he said, "when I was twelve years old. One night I went upstairs to bed, but I couldn't sleep. Then I heard someone knocking at the front door and coming in. My mother was excited and they went on talking for about three hours. In the morning I asked her who the caller was and she said, 'You must promise not to say anything to anyone if I tell you.' She then said, 'That was your Uncle Leon, from Scotland. He came from Gaza, in a Piper aircraft, to talk to me, then flew away'."

When Leon literally dropped in out of the blue, what were his intentions? He must have convinced the authorities that his sister could help them; for Rachel was politically-minded and well-informed. She would be able to tell him of the disposition of the Turkish troops, and of reliable contacts at Jerusalem and elsewhere. She may also have provided information of the pro-Ally spy network 'Nili' organised by Aaron Aronson. Leon, for his part, may have been conveying instructions to the latter.

Whatever transpired, it was an audacious mission; even more so for the pilot, who, unless he were a Palestinian, had little chance, if challenged, of passing himself off as a native.

It was late October when Allenby began his well-prepared advance through Beersheba, Gaza and Jaffa, and the surrender of Jerusalem occurred on 9th December. By then Leon was probably at home.

That he never spoke of his work for British Intelligence can only be explained by the stringency of the Official Secrets Act. But it would be strange if he never told Katie that he had somehow obtained first-hand news of his mother.

9. THE ZIONIST DREAM

The war, and more especially the collapse of the Ottoman Empire, revivified the millenial dream of Israel's return to its Promised Land. It was a hope strongly revived before the war by the two visionaries whose names are commemorated in the modern city of Herzlia and in the many Herzlia Streets and Herzlia Hotels in Israel; and in the renowned Weizmann Institute at Rehovot.

At the age of sixteen Leon, already interested in western culture and ideas, would be aware of the first Zionist Congress to which Theodore Herzl had summoned Zionists from near and far. Herzl's death in 1904 gave further prominence to the cause. Then gradually there came to the forefront Chaim Weizmann, dedicated to Zionism since, in 1886, at the age of eleven, at Motol in The Pale, he had written to his school teacher about "Jerusalem which is our land." His letter had ended with the fervent words, "For why should we look to the Kings of Europe for compassion. . .All have decided: The Jew must die, but England will nevertheless have mercy upon us. . . To Zion, Jews, to Zion! Let us go!"

In 1907, when Leon and Nahum were re-visiting Safed, Weizmann was also in Palestine. It was his first visit, and what he saw convinced him that the political Zionism of Herzl must become more practical. For Weizmann was "a mystic schooled in the disciplines of modern science," and even under Turkish rule he envisaged ways in which more Jews could become settlers. Only ten per cent of the population was Jewish; but land could be bought in small plots and pilot factories tried out for future industry. His ideas were commensurate with those of Leon and his colleagues for the Hebrew Christians seeking a homeland nearly thirty years later.

At the Tenth Congress in 1911 the Zionist Headquarters were

transferred from Vienna to Berlin, where a new executive planned methodical research into Palestine's economic potential. Meanwhile in Manchester Weizmann, now a British citizen, was planning both a Technion at Haifa and a Hebrew University at Jerusalem, to the latter of which the aged Baron de Rothschild had promised to contribute. Moreover, the number of colonies had grown to forty-five, with a population of 15,000 Jews.

At this stage the Great War intervened. For Zionism it was initially a cruel setback. With its headquarters in Berlin, and scattered Jewry drawn into both sides of the conflict, every practical scheme came to a halt. However, the declaration of war against Turkey in November, 1914, opened up the possibility of an end to the Ottoman Empire and a new beginning for the Near East. From that moment the prospect of Palestine being delivered from an alien rule fuelled to blazing point the aspirations of the Zionists. Thus by 1915 not only Chaim Weizmann but Herbert Samuel, who had not hitherto espoused the cause, were proposing a Jewish State. Samuel, who was to become the first British High Commissioner from 1920-25, has described in his *Memoirs* the course of events which led up to the Balfour Declaration. They have often been recounted elsewhere. Yet his intimate knowledge of the parts played by Asquith, Lloyd George, Balfour, Weizmann and himself makes fascinating reading.

Leon was an admirer of Samuel, and when the latter abandoned the idea of an immediate Jewish State in favour of a British Protectorate, his own sense of justice towards all in a multi-racial community brought his agreement. As early as 1915 Samuel's second thoughts were that "the more the situation was explored, the clearer it became that the idea of a Jewish State was impracticable. At some future time, perhaps, it might come about in the course of events; but so long as the great majority of the inhabitants were Arabs it was out of the question."[1]

It was not until 1917 that Weizmann, together with Nahum Sokolov and Rabbi Gaster, began to negotiate with the Cabinet Office. On the 2nd of November that year (when Leon was probably with Allenby's army at Gaza) the Balfour Declaration was formally sent to Lord Rothschild, as President of the English Zionist Federation, and published.

"His Majesty's Government view with favour the establishment in Palestine of a National Home for the Jewish people, and will use their best endeavours to facilitate the achievement of this object; it being clearly understood that nothing should be done which may prejudice the civil and religious rights of existing non-Jewish communities in Palestine, or the rights and political status enjoyed by the Jews in any other country."

It was Lloyd George who had set the wheels in motion by commending Dr. Weizmann to Balfour, the Foreign Secretary; it was, he declared, a reward for Weizmann's contribution to the war effort — his discovery of a new process for producing acetone, an ingredient in the manufacture of cordite. Yet "if acetone had never been heard of", says Samuel, "I believe that the Balfour Declaration would have taken precisely the shape that it did, and been promulgated just when it was."

Unfortunately the legend has persisted that the Declaration was invalid from the beginning, the British Government having given a contradictory pledge to the Arabs. It was alleged that two years previously Sir Henry McMahon, the High Commissioner in Egypt had, during negotiations with the future King Hussein (then Sherif Hussein of Mecca), promised Palestine to the Arabs. Palestine and Syria were not mentioned by name in the final document, but the Arabs were assigned a large part of south-west Asia "with the exception of areas bordering on the Mediterranean." Was Palestine or part of it, then, within the Arab line? McMahon, in a letter to *The Times* in July 1937, when the matter was again debated in Parliament, said categorically: "I feel it my duty to state, and I do so definitely and emphatically, that it was not intended by me in giving this pledge to King Hussein to include Palestine in the area in which Arab independence was promised. I also had every reason to believe at the time that the fact that Palestine was not included in my pledge was well understood by King Hussein."[2]

T.E. Lawrence, although gravely dissatisfied with the treatment of the Arab people as a whole after the war, stated in a letter to Professor William Yale, "It is my deliberate opinion that the Winston Churchill settlement of 1921-1922 (in which I shared) honourably fulfils the whole of the promise we made to the Arabs in so far as the so-called British spheres are concerned."

Yet Palestine is still believed by many to be "the twice-Promised Land."

Both in his books and in his pamphlets Leon discussed the nature of the forthcoming settlement and the requirements of citizenship in a Jewish State; and almost every one of them ends on a note of hope — that the sufferings and yearnings, the homelessness and repressions of the Jewish race, would find release through a return to Zion.

However, he did not share in the mystique of a Promised Land. The Old Testament promises were within the Old Covenant which had been superseded by the New. Christ had made no promise concerning either a return to the Land or a Jewish kingdom. His kingdom was to be universal, with neither Jew nor Greek, and its centre of worship would be neither in Jerusalem nor Samaria, nor for that matter in Geneva or Rome. Nevertheless Leon recognised and rejoiced in the historic bond between the Jews and Jerusalem, and saw Palestine as the authentic Jewish homeland. For the Jewish race to find there both refuge and nationhood was a dream in which he shared.

He also held, with St Paul, that God has not abandoned Israel; and that it might well be His purpose to gather her again as a nation and to give her a new role in His universal plan, with those, like himself, who had become Christians but were still Hebrews, playing their part. That would certainly include bearing witness in the nation-to-be to *Yeshua Ha-Mashiach*. He also had a prophetic vision of a day when the Jewish nation, having found in Christ their Saviour, would, with their human warmth and adaptability and their divine capacity for religion, become the most effective missionaries to those of other faiths and of none.

The Jew in History, a book of 124 pages, was published in 1916. It is essentially a succinct history of the Jews based on a wide range of reading and detailed research. An example of the latter is the brief paragraph on modern France:

"France in like manner has profited by her tolerant treatment of the Jews, notwithstanding the disgraceful Dreyfus scandal. Her greatest living philosopher, Bergson, is a Jew. Over ten thousand Jews are in the ranks; and before the war there were in the regular army eight Hebrew generals, fourteen colonels, twenty-one lieutenant-colonels, sixty-eight majors and one hundred and seven captains. General Heymans is in charge of one army corps, and five Jews hold important positions in the Cabinet."

The book was also a contribution to the current debate; especially its final chapter, "The Future of the Jews", which Leon largely reproduced in his pamphlets of 1917 and 1918.

THE ZIONIST DREAM

The fate of the Jews, a contemporary historian and anthropologist Dr. Fishberg had said, was assimilation. According to his theory, wherever the Jew enjoyed civil and political freedom he ceased to preserve his identity. "Judaism thrives best when its faithful sons are isolated from the surrounding people, segregated in Ghettos or Pales of Settlement." Apart from this the Jews have no nationality.

In *The Jew in History* Leon repudiated this view. He analysed the elements that constituted nationality. According to Renan they were the desire to live together and the will to preserve the inheritance handed down. To Sarolea a nation was "a moral personality"; for it was bound together by common ideals, institutions, traditions, and most of all by the memories of common glories and sufferings. Dr. Fishberg would, no doubt, accept this. But his contention was that when war and persecution, the great nation-making factors, cease, the cosmopolitan takes the place of national feeling. That was not borne out by history. Ireland, given toleration and freedom, was not drawn towards assimilation with England, but against it. In Scotland and England the Roman Catholic minorities showed no desire to sink their religious individuality as Protestantism became more tolerant. Nor did Scotland, after the Union, proceed far with the process of assimilation to the English language and customs. Thanks to Burns and Scott Scottish nationality reasserted itself. "Is it conceivable," Leon asked, "that the racial temperament of a people, which has come to them from a long past, can be radically changed by social environment and political machinery?. . .If what constitutes a people a nation, is common religious ideals, common traditions, common glories and common sufferings, then, without hesitation, the Jews may justifiably lay claim to the principle of nationality. . .But for the realisation of its ideals a nation needs a local habitation and a name. . .The aim of Zionism is to realise in Palestine the national ideal."

He then turned to the question of sovereignty. How would a national homeland square with imperial rule? Germany he said, solved this problem by subjugation, the crushing of the individuality of small states; Britain, by giving her colonies all the rights and privileges of free states. He cited South Africa, where the Boers now rallied round the British flag, "a tribute to Britain in her role of a pacific, liberty-loving imperialism."

Unfortunately, as Leon did not see, all was not well under the imperial flag, and it was to take another world war to bring most of the colonies and protectorates, including Palestine, into "all the rights and privileges of free states." But if he was over-sanguine about Britain's beneficent rule, it was because he himself, as a recipient of British citizenship, had experienced its benefits; whereas under Turkish rule he had seen his family suffer. It was from the heart that he wrote the final sentence of *The Jew in History*: "Moreover, under Great Britain a Jewish state will be another testimony to the magnanimity of our imperial rule, another bright page in our glorious history, another precious gem in the royal diadem."

In 1917 he reproduced much of this chapter in *The Jewish Problem and the World War*. He added the thought that Palestine, under Britain, and thereafter, would be a buffer state restraining Turkish aspirations towards Suez, and came to this conclusion: "We believe that by the resurrection of this wonderful people the benefit to the nation and to the Church will be like life from the dead. Yes! A great future awaits the Jew."

The following year he again wrote on Zionism in a 70-page booklet, *Zionism: Racial or Sectarian?* Here he dealt with the nature of the coming state. "It is imperative that such a State should rest on a broad democratic base. It should be representative of all phases of Jewish life and thought. The Zionist State must not be the monopoly of a band of religious fanatics. It must be a haven of refuge for the sorely-tried, heavy-laden, storm-tossed sons of Israel, the shadow of a great rock in a weary land, a covert from the tempest of perpetual persecution."

What he dreaded was the creation of a sectarian state; a kind of large-scale synagogue, whose entry would be confined to those who professed the Jewish faith, and from which both secular Jews and the growing number of Christian Jews would be excluded.

To digress for a moment, to some extent this has happened. As late as 1972 I heard Mrs Meir, in an Independence Day broadcast, declare that there is no separation between religion and state, for every Israeli adheres to the Jewish faith. It may be merely the formal adherence of those who spend *Passover* and *Yom Kippur* on the beaches, but it means that they are 'in', whereas everyone else is 'out'. This is a symptom, perhaps, of the insecurity of a young nation. Now, in the 80s, the Hebrew Christian has obtained a precarious foothold but is regarded as an alien, and the Arab, like the medieval Jew, is supposed to keep to his ghetto.

A nationalistic but unsectarian Zionism also won Leon's support because its fulfilment would deliver the Jews from their alienation among the nations and reduce the pervasive threat of anti-semitism. His booklet contains a historical survey of that alienation, from the reign of Pharaoh to that of Titus; from the early Christian era to the Reformation; and in modern Europe.

"The Assyrians, the Babylonians, the Chaldeans, the Persians, the Greeks, the Romans all in turn had wreaked their vengeance," with policies of deportation and oppression, but "over those ancient empires the waves of time have swept, and buried them, while the Jewish race. . . remains rock-like in solitary and imperishable grandeur."

How had the Jews fared under Christianity? "It is a depressing fact that under Christian emperors [their] condition was infinitely worse than under Pagan emperors." Moreover, "It is a sad commentary on early Christianity that the Jews were more kindly treated under Mahommedan rule than under the Roman Catholic Church."

The horrors of the Middle Ages were succeeded by the creation, under Gregory VII, of the first ghetto — "10,000 souls in less than a square kilometre," in an area where the Tiber overflowed. Luther's attitude was "as bad as that of the Pope's." Since then, "the anti-semitism of Russia, Austria, Roumania, Germany and France remains a disgraceful chapter in Continental history."

And Britain? "As regards anti-semitic crusades of the Continental type Great Britain has a clean record, but the spirit of persecution has shown itself more than once. . . there is no geographical Pale, but there exists what might be called an industrial and social Pale."

In 1902, following a great influx of Jewish refugees, the Tory Government attempted to pass restrictive legislation. To the credit of Britain, they failed. Nevertheless, a social boycott persisted. "When a Jew reaches a certain political position," wrote Leon, "and especially when he becomes a Right Honourable and has titles added to his name, he receives all honour, but when he belongs to the rank and file the Jew finds himself, even in Britain, a stranger in a strange land."

Leon then described the Zionist movement and the attempt by Joseph Chamberlain to buy Herzl off with alternative schemes —

a settlement in the Sinai Peninsula or a plateau in East Africa. "I converted Mr. Chamberlain," wrote Israel Zangwill, "to the conception not of a plateau, but of the whole of British East Africa turned into a British Judea."

The Zionist Congress of 1905, however, turned this down. "The Zionist Organization," they said, "rejects, either as an end or a means of colonising, activities outside of Palestine and its adjacent lands."

Leon continued his survey up to the War and concluded it with an apt quotation: "In the eloquent words of Mr. Zangwill, 'Napoleon, under the spell of the forty centuries that regarded him from the Pyramids, announced his design to restore the Jews to their land. Will England, with Egypt equally at her feet, carry out the plan she foiled Napoleon in?'."

History disposed of, he had a few more trenchant points to make on the dangers of sectarianism.

"Identity of faith is not now the basis of national life. . . the policy is glaringly reactionary. It has been long exposed by the Act of Supremacy and the Test Acts against dissenters in England; by the Pilgrim Fathers whose dissent in England became a new despotic Puritanism in America; and by similar dark chapters in Scottish Church history." As for the future Jewish State, "If the Jew who changes his faith ceases to be a Jew he has no business to be in the new State at all, and the Zionism of this type, like Romanism in the day of its power, is committed to a policy of persecution and expulsion." Moreover, "In the modern world the creation of a State separated from other states by a religious barbed-wire fence is absolutely impracticable."[3]

He went on to describe how Gladstone, who had once propagated similar sectarian doctrines, had them shattered by Macaulay. (Gladstone soon abandoned them). He also elaborated on how a religious test would deprive a nation of many of its ablest citizens. His last word on the subject was: "You cannot — nay, you dare not — interfere as a state with the conscience of the individual."

In an appendix to his booklet he did not hesitate to cross swords with two leading Jewish figures in the constitutional debate, who had expressed views in conflict with his own. These were Dr. Gaster, a henchman of Weizmann's, and Dr. Claude Montefiore, the liberal Jewish scholar, who had written articles in *The Fortnightly*

Review and *The Jewish Chronicle* respectively. However, these are now "battles long ago."

Ten years later, presiding over a conference of the International Hebrew Christian Alliance, Leon was to say this: "We, as Hebrew Christians, cannot be indifferent to the great hopes and aspirations of our people. Everything that concerns the welfare of the Jewish people must concern us, and unless we identify ourselves with their hopes and their longings we are no part of them. We are essentially still, and want to remain, Jews. The only difference between other Jews and ourselves is that we have come to see that in Jesus all the hopes and aspirations, and the call of our people, have been fulfilled."

Zionist hopes were realised in 1948 with the creation of Israel. But, as Leon well knew, the Jewish-Arab tensions which were increasing in his lifetime would have to be resolved. As long as the Arabs were predominantly an illiterate peasantry the provisos of the Balfour Declaration could be fulfilled without recourse to partition or a state within a state. But from 1920-1940 a 70 per cent growth of both populations, as noted by Lord Samuel, occurred; and the standard of living of the Arabs vastly improved for, as the Peel Commission of 1937 pointed out, "they had shared to a considerable degree in the material benefits which Jewish immigration had brought."[4]

Leon saw only the beginning of these changes, nor could he foresee the magnitude of the ultimate Jewish settlement. He continued to believe that Palestine would remain a geographical entity bounded on the east by the Jordan. His attitude to the Arabs was never less than friendly, courteous and cordial even, we are told, towards one who cheated him later. He would have deplored the ruthlessness of the more intolerant successors of the Zionists and understood the Arabs' frustration when, for instance, having sought higher education abroad (the Hebrew universities making little concession to non-Hebrew-speaking students) they returned to a dearth of job opportunity and the status of second-class citizens. He, too, would be baffled by the complexity of the problem, but he would have continued to hope that Jew and Arab would live and work together, in a multi-racial Israel, in peace.

NOTES:
1. *Memoirs.* Viscount Samuel. Cresset Press, 1945, pp. 144-5.
2. *Ibid* pp. 172-3
3. It is also dangerous. Today Leon would have seen his argument reinforced. For the identification of religious beliefs with national and ethnic aspirations has spawned intolerance and violence in Northern Ireland, Lebanon and Iran as well as in Israel; and the secular faith of hard-line Communism has been no less destructive.
4. *Ibid* pp. 289-90

10. "ST. PAUL"

Towards the end of the war Leon wrote a *Life of St. Paul.* It ran into several editions and is still to be found, seventy years later, on second-hand stalls and the shelves of elderly ministers. Its frequent quotations from contemporary sources, and applications of Pauline insights to contemporary issues, have made it now obsolescent. Yet it is probably the best of his writings and must have enhanced his reputation. Above all, it is self-revelatory.

It is a brief book — only 179 pages — and has no index. However, it presents an uncluttered picture of one who has too often been obscured by the vast edifice of theology, and with whom Leon strongly identified — a high-born Jew whom Christ had constrained, like himself, to become a missionary. What Lucas Grollenberg wrote of St. Paul might equally have applied to Leon: "[His] life now had a meaning: to involve as many as possible in this newness, in this faith, in this perspective. That was what God had chosen him for even before his birth. . . That was the purpose of his life, to tell Israel that there was something else in God's heart before the Torah, and that was His Son."[1]

Paul, too, was both preacher and thinker, pioneer and leader; and was not ashamed to proclaim and interpret the Gospel to both Jew and Gentile, emperor and slave, the superstitious and hostile Ephesians and the scoffing and sceptical Athenians. His very versatility made it appropriate that a many-sided disciple should write of him. "In Paul", said Leon, "the speculative, the practical, the mystical are blended, with the result that his is a full-orbed personality. This it is which makes his life so fascinating". "And in the prisoner's dock", he wrote in describing Paul's final trial before Nero, "stood the best man the world ever possessed". He was Leon's hero of heroes, and a pervasive influence in his life.

Interspersed with a description of Paul's career there are studies of his personality, his missionary methods, his ecclesiastical statesmanship and his philosophy of religion. The quotations, often lengthy, evidence wide reading. Renan, Pfleiderer, Matthew Arnold and the Tübingen school come in for criticism, Leon rejecting their assessments and repudiating their devious explanations of Paul's conversion; whereas Stalker, Farrer, Cornford, Lyman Abbott, Ramsay, Deissman, Caird and Sabatier reinforce his arguments. He also discusses the theories of Carlyle and Buckle on human greatness, Liddon on Plato, Philo on mysticism and Hegel on the impersonality of God.

Through all this, the portrait is clear and persuasive. The inner struggle in coming to terms with a crucified Messiah culminated on the Damascus road. In assessing the reality of what happened there he says: "Accept Paul's statement as literal fact and his authority remains. Make out that Paul was the victim of hallucination, a weakling, subject to disordered nerves, and his authority is shattered. . .[Critics] theorise on the assumption that intense beliefs may produce visions. In the main that is correct, but they overlook the important fact that in his case it was not intense belief that produced the vision, but the vision that produced the intense belief". Again, on the apostle's understanding of his mission he has this to say: "Great as St. Paul is, his is not the greatness of the founder of a religion. From first to last he gives only what he has received. . . Fully conscious of his limitations, Paul yet recognised the great task which had been assigned to him by God, namely, that of breaking the bonds which threatened to bind Christianity to Judaism, and of making the gospel of good news what Christ intended it to be, the one universal, absolute religion."

The relationship between Judaism and Christianity was Leon's lifelong concern and at the crux of his own experience; and he had found in St. Paul the answers that he sought. "In his view," he wrote, "Judaism had done its work and must now retire to the background. It was the schoolmaster to bring men to Christ." However, "This great conception did not find favour in Jerusalem where the early Church. . .laid it down that Gentiles, on entering the Church, must go through the gateway of Judaism. . .To Paul this was tantamount to prolonging and extending, instead of abolishing, Judaism, and was a blow at Christianity as the universal religion... The controversy was long and bitter. The mind of James, lacking breadth and flexibility, clung to Judaism and Peter, more open-minded but vacillating, as usual played the part of a trimmer. For instance, Peter sees no harm in waiving circumcision and eating with the heathen converts, but in deference to pressure from Jerusalem he recanted and fell back upon the Judaic attitude. Paul, in his own words, withstood Peter "to the face because he was to be blamed". "Eliminate Paul," says Leon in another passage, "and Christianity, bound hand and foot to Judaism, would have been arrested at an early stage of development." Thus, while Roman Catholics talk of the supremacy of Peter, "as a matter of fact supremacy lay with Paul." Moreover, "The greatest minds in Christendom are his direct creations. It is from Paul that Augustine learns the doctrines of grace of which he is so great a master. It is from Paul that Chrysostom imbibes his vivid sense of the range and applicability of Christian morals. It is at the feet of St. Paul no less than at those of St John that Athanasius discerns what was really meant by the Incarnation of the Son of God."

Paul sees clearly that Jesus called his disciples to go and proclaim the good news not to the Jews only but to the world. Judaism, too, says Leon, from the days of Abraham was intended to be a missionary religion. Was not Abraham himself the apostle of monotheism? "But what is surprising today is to see that the Jews seem to have forgotten the essence of Judaism, and boast that they do not interfere with other people's religion." In a digression he refers to the hatred that the words 'mission' and 'missionary' arouse even in Liberal Jewry. He quotes Claude Montefiore on "those who dream of a prophetic Judaism which shall be as spiritual as the religion of Jesus and even more universal than the religion of Paul", and whose adherents are "the champions of Monotheism, herald-soldiers of a worldwide Theism which, while raising no mortal to the level of the divine, can yet proclaim the truth of man's kinship and communion with the Father of all." Yet championship of monotheism, declares Leon, "is more likely to rest with a living, energetic Mohammedanism than with an academic, paralytic form of Judaism." For Judaism, whether orthodox or liberal, is no longer missionary. "The Jews seem to think that they are perfectly happy in their religion, owing to the fact that it is the best, the purest, the richest and the loftiest religion in existence." Yet "In our day and generation, it is expected — in fact it is demanded — that the strong, the healthy, the comfortable should come down out of his comfortable surroundings and assist his weak brother. Likewise in religion. The more the Jew boasts of the wealth of his religion, the more one would expect that he should try to share that wealth... Strange to say, this has not even been thought of." As Israel Zangwill, the novelist and Liberal Jewish leader, had himself said in a letter to Leon: "It is, indeed, the defect of modern Jewry that it has no missionary department of its own, as it must have had in the days when Jesus said: 'Ye compass land and sea to make one proselyte'."

Back with St Paul, and describing his first missionary journey, Leon accentuates his lonely heroism. "Luther was upheld by German princes... Knox was the spokesman of a nation struggling to be free. In his religious conflict he could draw upon a great reserve of patriotism. Contrast this with Paul's position. He stands before us in solitary majesty. On all sides surrounded by enemies, he had to fight the battle practically single-handed. By the Jews treated as a renegade, by the Greeks as a setter-forth of strange gods, by the Romans as a sedition-monger... Add to this the chilly attitude, on his return, of the leaders of the Church at Jerusalem, and the wonder is that a depressing sense of loneliness and isolation did not tempt him to abandon in despair his missionary enterprise."

Yet instead of losing hope, Paul soon set out on a second journey the importance of which, said Leon, Professor Stalker did not exaggerate when he described it as "perhaps the most momentous recorded in the annals of the human race. In its issues, it far out-rivalled the expedition of Alexander the Great into the heart of Asia, or that of Caesar when he landed on the shores of Britain, or even the voyage of Columbus when he discovered a new world."

Leon would be transported as he worked at the book, for no subject could encourage him more in his own missionary work; and later, when he was to make exhausting journeys to the sometimes beleaguered groups of Hebrew Christians in Europe and beyond, being in the succession of St Paul would bring inspiration and hope.

In studying St Paul he touched on one other topic which should be mentioned here, for nowhere else does he reveal his attitude towards it: that of Christian unity. The fragmentation of the

"ST PAUL"

Church, he believed, sprang from its failure to apply the principles laid down by Paul and the intrusion of practices deriving more from Pharisaic Judaism than from Christianity. Quotations from the beginning and end of the book illustrate this theme.

"Out of the vision on the road to Damascus grew another vision — the vision of a Christian Church united in the bonds of love to its Head. . . Does the Church today rest on love as its one foundation? It has been made to rest on dogmatic beliefs in which there need be no ethical influence. Paul would never have made belief, for instance, in an infallible book a condition of church membership. The Old Testament was to him merely a preliminary revelation, a kind of religious primer which no longer suited the advanced stage of the Christian life. Nor would he have encouraged the manufacture of elaborate creeds which, by creating divisions in the Church, have frustrated completely Paul's great idea of Church union. The creeds, as has been well said, have been wedges to split the Church asunder, not bonds to bind it together. Thus, the Nicene Creed was framed to exclude Arians, the Heidelberg Catechism to exclude Romanists, the Westminster Confession to exclude Arminians and the Creed of Pius IV to exclude Protestants. And what would Paul have to say of our ecclesiastical rivalries and divisions? He would treat with a kind of pitying scorn all our modern talk about Papal Claims, Apostolic Succession, Erastianism, Presbyterianism, Independency, etc. To Reverend Moderators and Episcopal dignitaries he would have repeated what he wrote to the Corinthians: "Now I beseech you, brethren, through the Name of our Lord Jesus Christ, that ye all speak the same thing, and that there be no divisions among you; but that ye be perfected together in the same mind and in the same judgment."

The following passage may be added: "With the decline of Paul's influence in the early centuries began the decline of the Church during the Middle Ages. . . [and] with the renewal of Paul's influence at the Reformation began the purifying process. . . What a melancholy record is that of ecclesiasticism after the death of Paul. The Church lapsed into Roman Catholicism, which is simply a new form of the Judaism against which Paul waged life-long conflict. Like the Judaism of Paul's time, the Church of the Middle Ages became an exclusive, intolerant organisation, laying stress upon ceremonial observances and a host of burdensome details under

107

which the Pauline idea of religion and Church membership was completely crushed. . .

"Even after the Reformation, Paul's guidance was not followed in its entirety. . . In the words of Lyman Abbott. . . 'The Anglicans affirm an Apostolic succession; they recur to Judaism and propose as the bond uniting their churches a spiritualised survival of the Aaronic priesthood. The Independents abolish Church unity altogether and for a planetary system substitute a universe of wandering comets.'." and, adds Leon, "Presbyterianism is in danger of developing into another 'ism' — . . .cliqueism."

So what is the remedy? It could not be a Church based on the Bible. "The Bible could not logically be made the basis of ecclesiastical unity, for. . . when the Church was founded the Bible, as we have it, did not exist." Nor could it be based on an elaborate creed. For "if the Bible is the creation of the Church, the creed is the creation of the Bible along with Greek speculation." Paul's remedy is simply a Church loyal to Christ, " 'not to a creed about Christ, not to a sacrament in honour of Christ, not to a Church which Christ has founded, not to a Book which tells about Christ, but loyalty to Christ himself is. . . the only basis of union which Paul recognizes'."

The tendency of Protestantism, says Leon, is to make ecclesiastical organisations an end in themselves; and to justify their existence by appeals to the New Testament. However, "The true view, and the one which Paul held, was that there was no special sacredness in ecclesiastical forms."

I have quoted extensively because the book represents so clearly its author's beliefs. By many these would be regarded as somewhat naive; his cavalier dismissal of the creeds, by-passing of Biblical authority, and definition of the Church in terms only of its simple beginnings. All this would not have passed muster with those who had taught him at New College, let alone with the mainstream Churches. They would have argued that as the Church developed and extended it could only be safeguarded from heresies and brought into any semblance of unity by doctrinal agreement. What *was* "the faith once delivered to the saints?" Hence Nicea and the creeds. Nor could Church order be left to chance. Again, as the years passed, those traditions which were most historic inevitably became hallowed.

As a missionary Leon avoided controversy on such topics. His task was to bring people to Christ and to pass them on for baptism and membership to any convenient church — usually of his own denomination, but if they had friends in another one, or chose to become Baptists or Episcopalians, it would serve equally well. And should they go on to be missionaries or ministers, the training college would be the one most suited to their circumstances, ability and age, and their sponsor's purse.

Regarding the place in organised Christianity of the creeds, the sacrament, and the Bible, Leon never departed from his conviction that

"The Church's one foundation
is Jesus Christ her Lord,"

and that to demand anything else than love and loyalty to Him as essential for salvation was to distort the Gospel. Later, however, when the question of creating a Hebrew Christian Alliance and, subsequently, a Hebrew Christian Church arose, he recognised the need for a statement of faith and for institutional and sacramental order.

His aversion to credal, sacramental and Biblical imposition was partly due to his deliverance, like St Paul's, from the burden of the Law. It was also due to his attachment to Free St George's, "a church for prophets not for priests." There, at that time, no creed was said, not even at Communion. The emphasis at the Sacrament was on Christ's cross and victory, and on the common fellowship as the whole congregation gathered for the quarterly celebrations. The prayers, though not unprepared, were delivered extempore; and there was no liturgical tradition. (A liturgical revival was under way, an attempt to repair the damage wrought by the English-dominated Westminster Assembly of 1643, and to build on Knox's Liturgy; but the United Free Church was little affected until its first *Book of Common Order* appeared in 1928).

"I remember well", wrote Leon, in a symposium on *The Tradition of St George's West*[2], "my first visit to St George's, and how the preacher, the Rev. Hugh Black. . . when he entered the pulpit very reverently knelt down in prayer. . . No liturgy or prayer-book was used — just the voice of a man speaking to God with simple assurance that He was there listening to every word. That prayer, which was never to be forgotten, gripped the soul and put it into communion with the unseen."

The present generation is apt to deride this mode of prayer; and there is much to be said for common worship being participatory rather than an overhearing of the minister's monologue with God. But for Leon, as for many Scots of his generation, such prayer was a means of grace. Others entered into communion with the unseen through set forms, but this was the way for him.

For many, the recital of creeds is a means of grace; for when they are used in worship, as John Baillie says, "the element of commitment clearly takes precedence over the element of assent." But to Leon they were no more than doctrinal statements and potentially divisive, as his book indicated. Yet in their totality, and recited from a worshipful heart, others still see them as testimonies to that glorious full-orbed faith which our world of broken images so sorely needs.

The Bible occupied a central place in his life and thoughts. But though he moved in evangelical circles, where many attributed to it inerrancy and an authority akin to that of Christ Himself, his attitude was less extreme. It was, in fact, that of the Church of Scotland, whose articles of faith acknowledge "the Word of God, which is contained in the Scriptures of the Old and New Testaments, to be the supreme rule of faith and life." The Christian's task, he believed, was to discern the Word contained in the scriptures, but not to treat every word as holy writ.

The observance of the Lord's Supper meant much to St Paul and also to Leon, but neither could be called a sacramentalist. The Communion was more than an act of remembrance — Leon was no Zwinglian — and precisely what it said, a communing with Christ. The Church of Scotland minister says "Take, eat: this is My body which is broken for you," Christ's own words, in the first person, to denote that Jesus Himself is present, speaking thus to the sinner — to us all. This high doctrine, with its sense of the Real Presence, not in the elements, nor mediated through a priest, but in the whole event, both word and action, places the Church of Scotland firmly within the Catholic tradition, but its usage is more Pauline than that of the Anglicans, Romans or Orthodox. For Paul did not believe in an élite priesthood, nor, as any concordance will show, did he ever use the words 'priest', 'high priest' or 'priesthood'.

In the interests of good order, Leon recognised that the celebration of the sacraments must remain a ministerial act. However, the minister, to him, was called to be a prophet and pastor, not a priest. It was a view of the ministry which in the later 20th century has enabled the Church of Scotland more readily to accept the ordination of women than those Churches which believe in priesthood, and specifically in the male priest at the Eucharist as an *ikon* of Christ.

St Paul's theology is profound. Yet his churchmanship and discipleship were simple. To be "a man in Christ" was all that really mattered. With "men in Christ" in charge it did not matter whether the Church had bishops or elders, a hierarchic or democratic structure, liturgical or charismatic worship. None of these are of the *esse*, but let those for whom they are of the *bene esse* or *plene esse* use them if they please. And let the Church treasure and teach the Apostles' doctrine, handing it on from generation to generation, that all may learn of their debt to Judaism, of the teachings of Jesus and of Him to whom Scripture, Sacrament and Church together bear witness — the Risen Christ.

Because Leon had sat at the feet of St Paul and learned there 'the simplicity that is in Christ Jesus', his attitude to institutionalised Christianity can be summed up in words which were once used of the writer Charles Williams: "Organised and official Christendom did not displease him, but it had about as little to do with his own view of religion as has a tin of sardines to do with a dinner of freshly-caught trout."

Nahum's book was on a larger scale. In 1937 he wrote "I have just completed a book on *The Life and Teaching of St Paul*, about 340 pages, which I hope to publish before the end of this year." When he died in 1968, however, it was still unpublished, and the manuscript appears to have been thrown out by his widow. "Aunt Margaret", recalls her nephew David, "said of one bundle of papers, 'This is all too disjointed — I'll never make anything of it: it had better just go!'."

Its insights are lost. Yet in other papers we can discern some of them. Presenting Paul's beliefs on Christology, the Virgin Birth, Baptism and Resurrection, for instance, he makes these comments:-

Christology. "How comes it that this monotheist, this Pharisee, this student of Gamaliel came to use this term Son of God? . . . I maintain that St Paul had absolutely no choice, nor indeed have any modern thinkers who have had a vision of the risen and living

Christ... I myself am an unrepentant monotheist... Intellectually and spiritually, I can find no other God than the God I find in and through Jesus, and I find no other term that satisfies me than Son of God, Very God of Very God. If anyone has a better I will welcome it, always providing that he or she has had a vision of the Christ such as St Paul had... St Paul did not base his doctrine of the God of Christ on any previous teaching or saying, but... upon experience, the experience on the road to Damascus."

The Virgin Birth. "Mary was still alive when Paul wrote most of his Epistles, and he would avoid any allusion to the birth of our Lord... for such references would draw attention to her person, a thing any Christian gentleman would avoid. Nevertheless the argument from silence which many have adduced against belief in the Virgin birth is surely invalid. St Paul's own phrase is 'born of a woman'. That is strangely un-Jewish, for the Jews generally counted genetic matters from the father's side... A careful examination of all the facts leaves the strongest impression that St Paul knew and believed that Jesus was born by the power of the Holy Spirit of the Virgin Mary, but that it did not call for the formulation of a doctrine by him, and that he was satisfied with the attention the matter received in the Gospel which was about to appear from the pen of his trusted companion, the 'beloved physician'."

Baptism. "Though I belong to a denomination of the Church which practices Infant Baptism, and I believe in its expediency, I must say that so far as St Paul is concerned, there is not a shred of evidence that he favoured or ever practised Infant Baptism. 'The household' does not imply children; they may all have been grown up in the household of Stephanas, or he may be speaking of grown-up relatives, who would be included... in the usual idiom and usage of the Semite... (Paul's) teaching on Baptism justifies only three conclusions: (1) that Baptism was administered by St Paul; (2) that it was administered to those who could exercise faith; and (3) that the exercise of that faith identified the baptised person with the death and resurrection of Our Lord."

Resurrection. "Christianity has unfortunately inherited what Judaism borrowed from Zoroastrianism, viz. a doctrine of the resurrection of the body. This persists in spite of the teaching of the Old Testament, Jesus and Paul. The lower forms of Christianity have clung to the belief in a resurrection of the identical body which is laid in the grave... Jesus has made me realize that He is the resurrection, that I through faith in Him attain to an immortality, not a resurrection of the body but an unending life. . . I often wonder if people will ever come to understand the full implication of this conception in the teaching of St Paul?"

These passages all occur in articles contributed to *The Hebrew Christian Quarterly*. In a posthumous manuscript on *Biblical Theology* and in the fragment of his *Life and Teaching of St Paul* Nahum wrote with equal freshness about the apostle himself:-

"Jerome states that the family which Saul came from belonged to Gishcala (probably the modern el Jish) in North Galilee. I am disposed to accept this tradition because. . . it would hardly occur to anyone to pick on Gishcala.

"What took the family to Tarsus? I think that Saul's father was called to be ecclesiastical head, not only of Tarsus itself, but of a larger area, and as head of a larger community he was granted Roman citizenship, an honour very few Jews had conferred upon them." (Nahum would remember the similar honour bestowed on his own father, of British citizenship.)

"Saul's place in the school of Rabbin Gamaliel also points to the high place his father must have held among his people. Only the most outstanding families and the most brilliant boys would find a place in this school. . .

"The question whether he was a Sanhedrist is the most difficult to solve. But we cannot get away from Acts 26:10, 'When they were condemned to death I cast my vote against them'. To have had a vote on capital punishment, one had to belong either to the provincial Sanhedrin of 23 or the Jerusalem Sanhedrin of 71 members. . . It would seem that pure Jewish descent was one qualification for the office of a Sanhedrist; another was that he should be married and have a family. Marriage was contracted at an early age (say between eighteen and twenty) and bachelorhood was unknown among the Jews, save the Essenes. . . I have no more proof for my conclusion, that he had parents in Tarsus, for he does not mention them nor does he include the taking away of his wife and children."

Fascinating stuff! Is it not time another Hebrew Christian, also a rabbinic scholar, gave us a Life of St Paul?

It only remains to be said that Nahum's preferences in public worship were, like Leon's, in line with the simplicity which he found in St Paul. No aesthete, the beauty of Gothic and the significance of ceremonial held little attraction for him. The story is told that when he went to take the service in a ceremonious church the assistant minister explained, "You begin behind the table, then move to the prayer-desk, then to the lectern, back to the desk then to the pulpit and down again for the offering" — to which Nahum replied, "Young man, my ancestors wandered for forty years in the wilderness, so I think I'll just go to the pulpit!"

NOTES:
1. *Paul*, S.C.M. Press, 1978, p.39.
2. Free St George's had acquired its new name on the union of the United Free and Established Churches in 1929.

11. "THE MENACE OF SOCIALISM"

Immediately after the war, in a spurt of literary energy, Leon was writing several books. They were on disparate subjects, and only two of them, *The Life of St Paul* and *The Menace of Socialism*, saw the light of day. Two others, *Heroes of the Old Testament* and *Studies in the Life of Christ*, are listed in his entry in *Who's Who*, which may indicate that he assumed they would be published; but they were not. Extracts from the latter were to appear, some years later, in the *Hebrew Christian Quarterly*. These are helpful expositions, but neither distinguished nor original enough to merit publication in book form, for which they may well have been rejected. As for *Scotland's Contribution to Philosophy* and *Philosophy and Life* it seems that the publisher or Leon had second thoughts; for in 1919, on the end-paper of the book on Socialism, they are advertised as "In the press. To be published shortly. By the same Author."

Rejections may have caused him to forsake authorship; and when in 1928 *The Hebrew Christian Quarterly*, under his editorship, appeared, that, added to his other activities, absorbed all his energies. Thereafter, a small booklet, *The Passover in relation to the Lord's Supper* — the script of a lecture-demonstration which he frequently gave to church groups — and the Edinburgh portion of a booklet on Scotland's two Jewish missions were, apart from articles and editorials, his whole literary output.

The Menace of Socialism is a contentious title. However, at the end of the war Lloyd George, alarmed at the spread of militant Socialism in Europe, was already talking of the possibility of a Red Revolution in Britain, and Leon's aim was to help stem the tide. The book also reflects his political credo and that of progressive Free Trade Liberals of the time. Socialism, to them, had been given a bad name by the course of events in Russia, where the Revolution, instead of bringing the freedoms of democracy, had issued in an oppressive political system which subordinated the individual to the state and crushed all individuality and enterprise.

Had he lived long enough, he would have seen forms of Socialism far removed from those he attacked. In Norway and New Zealand, in the Germany of Brandt and the France of Mitterrand, and in the Welfare State in Britain he would have encountered compassionate expressions of Socialism of which he was unaware. Even in Russia, where the monolithic monster of Communism has long reigned, there is now in the eighties a cracking of the ice.

Leon's polemic, however, is not entirely outdated, for it is a reasoned statement containing many valuable insights. Moreover, in references to "the haves and have-nots", to profit-sharing and to proportional representation he sounds well ahead of his time.

The initial theme is poverty, and he considers the remedies offered, from the theories of Aristotle to those of Rousseau, and by various forms of voluntary Socialism from Robert Owen's to the Australian settlements, the Brook Farm community favoured by Emerson, and an experiment in Peru. All, he points out, had come to grief through selfishness, greed and indolence, endemic flaws in human nature.

Turning to Marx, he treats him with respect even while demolishing his theory of labour and wealth. There had been, he said, no degradation of labour at the hands of the capitalists as Marx had forecast. On the contrary, wages had risen, prices fallen, and people, under the organising ability of the capitalist classes, worked shorter hours, ate better food and committed fewer crimes.

What he feared was that collective ownership would lead to State control with the industrialists becoming salaried officials. This would not work. Already, during the war, he wrote, "supply and demand have been controlled by the State, under the supervision of salaried officials, and what has been the result? . . . scarcity and high prices and fearful muddling and inequality . . . At present we see the workers determined to secure the largest possible share of the national wealth regardless of the effect upon other classes in the community. Under Socialism, the same tendency would manifest itself, greatly to the disadvantage of the brain-worker."

Yet Leon was not a reactionary. He was open to new ideas and welcomed social experiments. He acknowledged that much of the

"THE MENACE OF SOCIALISM"

unrest of his time was due to the inhumanity of the capitalist system; much of it also to the maintenance of colossal standing armies in peace-time. Capital and labour, he thought, could be harmonised, and both Robert Owen and, more recently, the Cadburys of Bournville had shown the way. "Had the great capitalists of the Industrial Revolution been inspired by the spirit of Bournville," he wrote with some exaggeration, "the world would have known nothing of Socialism."

In his own work he was an individualist. He was also creative. In fact, he saw Socialism as inimical to new ideas and the taking of risks. "Officialdom as a rule is shortsighted," he wrote, "it has not an open mind for new ideas nor for the current spate of inventions. . . Great knowledge and discrimination are needed to pick the useful from the fantastic ideas. This can only be done by men who are willing to run great risks, and will certainly not be done by state-paid officials whose first and greatest interest is to remain secure in their posts. . . The private capitalist, in his eagerness to make wealth, runs great risks where Government officials have no inducement to run risks. . . The greatness of the drag of officialdom on the wheels of industry is frankly admitted by the Belgian Socialist Vandervelde, in his remarks regarding the state control of the railways. . .", where, apparently, no one could take responsibility for anything and each problem had to be passed on to a higher and again a higher authority.

How, asks Leon, is the growing competition from India, Japan and, shortly, China to be met? "Not by State control, whose inefficiency has become a byword. Competition can only be successfully met in one way — by reliance on the spirit of individualism, which in the past gave Britain its industrial and commercial supremacy."

Reform, he maintains, must come not by Socialist imposition but under the guidance of Christian influences. He also advocates the principle of worker-participation. "In many large establishments," he says, "profit-sharing has been introduced as a method of improving the relations of employer and employed; and in several cases schemes have been adopted whereby the workers hold shares in the concern, thereby in a sense becoming partners."

All this is now familiar, but in 1919 it was ahead of the general thinking of the time; this remains true even though Leon can quote

John Stuart Mill on the subject, and give an example of profit-sharing in America from as early as 1908.

In the same chapter he reveals the extent of land monopoly in Scotland, "one great obstacle across the path of industrial harmony." Half Scotland, he tells us, is held by 70 persons and two-thirds by 350 persons. A sixth is under deer forests, although the Highlands and Islands Commission had found that 1,780,000 acres in this area were suitable for small farms. It is a problem which is with us yet.

Land monopoly, he declares, is the root problem; and he goes on to ask, "How was it solved under the Jewish Constitution?" (i.e. the Mosaic dispensation). The answer is that God owned the land, and that absolute human ownership was not tolerated. "The land was distributed among the people, and if by misfortune a family had to sell its land, it could be redeemed at the end of every half century."

Another illustration of theocracy blending with democracy was in the realm of education. "It is a striking fact that universal education, which moderns have only recognised as a national necessity over half a century ago, was introduced under the Jewish Constitution." It was carried out both by parents and by the Levitical order of teachers.

"State control there certainly was in the Jewish Commonwealth; but it was prevented from . . . despotism by the fact that the rights of the individual were not at the mercy of majorities, but were specially conserved by the enactment which placed the laws of God above the laws of men, and by the wide sphere left for the three great principles which modern states have never been able to harmonise — liberty, equality and fraternity.

"In its attempt to secure equality, Socialism parts with liberty, and in legislating on the majority principle, it creates class antagonisms which are fatal to fraternity. The history of the Jews conclusively shows that the theocratic form of government established by Moses was productive of two things not usually found together, namely strong individuality and national solidarity. The lesson to be learned from the study of Jewish history is that democracy can only be preserved from shipwreck on the rock of Socialism by recognising the place and power of religion in the government of the states."

In a chapter headed "Christianity and Socialism" he carries this further. "So long as the people proved true to their Constitution, they enjoyed all the advantages of an ideal government, in which a beneficent State control was not allowed to repress individual liberty. Duties and rights, which never can be properly harmonised on purely secular lines, were satisfactorily blended by religion."

The Jews, however, forsook Moses. All the warnings of the prophets could not bring them back to allegiance, and the outcome was the destruction of the nation. Nevertheless, the religious conceptions of life which had formed the root of their constitution were not lost. "The great ideals. . . were taken over by Christianity and universalised."

Leon would not at that time have understood the term 'Christian Socialism'. "In their aims and methods," he wrote, "the two are totally distinct. According to Socialism the perfection of humanity is to be attained along the lines of the equal distribution of wealth; the economy is the determining factor in civilisation. Socialism, it will be observed, places the main stress upon environment. The keynote of Christianity, on the other hand, is regeneration of the individual."

Here, as in his wartime pamphlets, he finds the consummation of his argument in the New Testament; especially in the Sermon on the Mount and Jesus' teaching on the Kingdom of God. Jesus "adopted an ideal which entirely reversed all previous conceptions . . . [He] set Himself to form a new community whose principles were opposite to those which had hitherto ruled in the world . . . The gospel . . . was a leaven which was calculated to permeate society and result in an entirely new relation between the individual and society . . . By the Kingdom of God, Jesus meant a community resting upon affection, resulting in service, a community in which not class warfare but class co-operation is the ruling motive."

Leon was convinced that neither war, poverty, economic slavery, nor any other evil would be banished by Socialist methods nor by any other governmental contrivance, but only through the sensitivity of the Christian conscience. In this his own missionary task the application of Christianity to individuals was not a sideline but a practical engagement in the human dilemma.

Again, Socialism, with its emphasis on the rights of man and the evils of wealth, had gone astray. For although Jesus denounced those who made wealth at the expense of their souls, whose god was Mammon and who admitted no social obligations, He "could have no sympathy with schemes of wealth distribution which implied forcible taking from the haves to give to the have-nots. The Gospel did not contain a declaration of the Rights of Man, but of the Duties of Man. Between Socialism with its gospel of Rights and Christianity with its gospel of Duties there is a great gulf fixed."

Leon was not a pietist. He did not believe in "Sit down, O men of God, you cannot do a thing." The healing of nations required the Spirit of Christ, but economists, politicians and, indeed, ordinary citizens had their part to play. Hence he was grieved that ordinary citizens were not being equipped for it. The results of universal education were disappointing.

"As at present conceived, education has little connection with citizenship. In a commercial and industrial nation questions of the most complex nature are constantly arising which the inadequate education given in the schools, even in the higher schools, does not fit the youth of the nation to study with cultivated minds . . . The root error has been the neglect of political economy as a branch of education and as a potent factor in the training for citizenship. History is taught, but the economic side of history occupies a subordinate position . . . The view implanted in the popular mind is that our national greatness is due to our military and naval prowess."

Against this view, Waterloo, for instance, was only rendered possible by the economic condition of France. "Bankrupt in men and material, Napoleon's armies were quite unable to continue the struggle. Waterloo was an economic as well as a military victory." Again in the Great War "All honour to the military, but let it not be forgotten that . . . our industrial supremacy decided the issue."[1]

Neglect of the economic factor, he believed, had also given an impetus to the military spirit and fostered a spurious patriotism, which he found even in the Boy Scout movement, "in which the youthful mind, impregnated with militarism, loses its individuality and becomes an easy prey to imperialist ideals." (This did not prevent his son John from becoming an enthusiastic Scout a year or two later!)

In the industrial sphere, the neglect of economic teaching, he averred, had led to the heresy of Joseph Chamberlain's Protectionism, which served only the nation's short-term interest. However, the workers saw through the Protectionist doctrine, because for them it meant dearer food and other price increases. At the same time they fell victims to Trade Unionism which increased their wages by limiting their output to produce a scarcity; demand became greater than supply, and the worker as a consumer found his purchasing power had decreased. Furthermore, the very failure of Trade Unionism gave rise to Socialism, with its belief that better results would accrue through the State owning the instruments of production and distribution. "Such a heresy would never have taken hold of the workers had they been well grounded in economics at school."

Economics too exposed the folly of boycotting Germany and demanding a substantial war-indemnity. "If we deliberately paralyse her industries, where is the money to come from to secure an indemnity and to repair the damage in France and Belgium?"

The rising generation, he says, with its superficial thinking, has become an easy prey to any Imperialist or Socialist demagogue. Its mind is deluged with the outpourings of a crude and strident press. "John Bull is no longer the solid and phlegmatic person he used to be; he has become hysterical, a prey to sensationalism, the victim of epidemical emotionalism . . . He believes in a League of Nations which prevents war, but he will, at the same time, agree to treat Germany as a kind of leper, to be kept outside the League, thereby sowing the seeds of future wars. He believes in disarmament, but he will favour a continuance of conscription. He declares that Germany must be allowed no annexations, but Great Britain has to keep what she has got. We are suffering severely as a nation by our narrow system of education and our superficial thinking."

From education he turns to the dangers of democracy under majority rule: how, in John Stuart Mill's words, "to establish safeguards against an all-powerful, unchecked democracy." A possible check, thought Leon, might be found by adopting the scheme by which minorities would be represented; a scheme which had blossomed into Proportional Representation. P.R. has not yet come in Britain; but it is remarkable to find Leon advocating it so long ago. It would, he thought, mitigate some political evils, one of which was "the wire pulling and political manipulation [which] foists candidates on constituencies, thereby preventing the selection of men of promised individuality," for "representatives tend to become mere delegates who slavishly come to heel at the crack of the party whip. As the result, we have political demoralisation on a large scale."

A penultimate chapter on Russia powerfully reiterates much that has been said. The final one looks to the future. The optimism of the 19th century had been dispelled by the Crimean War and the revival of the old dread and hatred of Russia. Then came the Russo-Turkish War, conflicts between the Balkan States, and the Great War. "Another factor which made for war arose indirectly, strange to say, out of missionary enterprise. When Livingstone opened up Africa. . .commercial enterprise followed in his wake. A scramble took place among the Europeans for territory, and to this was due the war with the Boers. Rhodes vulgarised the work of Livingstone. Jealousy arose among the Powers, Germany demanded an outlet for her increasing population. . . By the close of the last century optimism had vanished and the minds of leading thinkers were filled with gloomy forebodings." These were realised, and Socialism given its opportunity as a remedy for the chaotic condition of the world.

"Is there then," Leon concludes, "no bright outlook for humanity?" Yes — "but it will come not from secular schemes but from religious." This in spite of the Churches, which "have weakened the influence of Christianity by binding it up with nationality. . . Instead of the clergy of all nations closing their ranks in a campaign against the evil passions which create wars, they have taken sides with the military in all countries and sent prayers for vengeance to the God whom they profess to serve. Christianity, with its doctrines of the Fatherhood of God and the brotherhood of man has not failed. It has been betrayed by ecclesiastical leaders like Harnack, who has made patriotism into a religion. The one hopeful sign of the time is that humanity is sick to death of wars. . . men in all countries are crying for peace. . .

". . . National hatreds will not die all at once at the bidding of a League of Nations, but an appreciation of the blessings of cosmopolitanism will gradually weaken the spirit of an aggressive nationalism. Gradually there will dawn upon the minds of men the vision of a universal church. . .

"Religion has been thrust into the background, treated as a purely individual affair. The world has been viewed as a kind of Vanity Fair, and the duty of the Christian has been to embark on a pilgrimage from the City of Destruction to the Celestial City. As a consequence, secular affairs have been given over to materialism. . . Make religion universal, make it overleap purely national boundaries. . . and the millenium will be in sight.

"THE MENACE OF SOCIALISM"

Material success, national supremacy, Imperial ambitions, Socialist utopias — these will never satisfy the soul of humanity. We live by admiration, hope and love, and these find their enduring inspiration only in religion. From the Pisgah height of religion, humanity, gazing far beyond the valley of the shadow, will catch a glimpse of the gleaming lights of the City of God."

It is an eloquent ending to a book which makes plain both Leon's flair and zest for politics and his conviction that politics per se is not enough; that "except the Lord build the house they labour in vain that build it."

The Menace of Socialism manifests his antipathy to bureaucracy and to the fettering of the human spirit. In his missionary work he found himself beholden to bureaucrats and did all in his power to avoid them and go his own way. Had he been lured, as he almost was, into a political career he would have chafed under any Party Whip.

The book may have drawn the attention of politicians. Not many years later he was invited not only by the Liberals but also by Ramsay MacDonald's National Government to become a parliamentary candidate. However, apart from all other considerations — and the missionary one prevailed — he was too gentle for the hurly-burly of the House of Commons.

He was, however, to modify his views on Socialism; to recognise that the spirit of individualism had taken too little account of the collective good, that the workers were not as deeply tainted with sluggishness and self-aggrandisement as he had inferred, and that the menace had proved less serious than he had anticipated.

For all its limitations, his book speaks at times with an astonishingly contemporary voice; a Christian voice not muffled by piety, but pregnant with knowledge and wisdom for the new world emerging from the smouldering ashes of a great conflagration.

NOTE:
1. That economic forces are the true source of military success in struggles for supremacy is the seminal thought of Paul Kennedy's brilliant book *The Rise and Fall of the Great Powers* (1988). Kennedy's conclusions are drawn from history; Leon's were prompted by his insight into contemporary events.

12. RE-ENTER NAHUM

On the 13th of May 1918, Nahum, on Army leave, was married before rejoining the Wiltshire Regiment, first as a sniper, then as a German interpreter in France. Margaret Nicol, a Scottish nurse whom he had met in Canada, was anxious to settle in her native land, and it was this above all that brought Nahum back to England in 1919 and to Scotland in 1922. Their romance, it is said, began in a railway station in Canada when Nahum, ever gallant, went to the help of a maiden in distress who had lost her ticket.

It was to be a devoted, but childless marriage. Margaret bore this grief well; but the added disappointment of Nahum's lack of recognition, in contrast to the honours which befell Leon, tinged her mind with an envy which she could not entirely conceal. As a minister's wife, in comparatively obscure parishes, she gave unstinting leadership, but of ministers as a whole she had a low opinion and few matched her requirement of them. Someone who, sixty years ago, was a clerkess in the church's Jewish Mission department says that she terrified her as a girl, and berated her for some ignorant observation about Jewish women.

However, although Nahum was sometimes henpecked, his composure and forbearance, like their love, never wavered. In her later years, Margaret was less waspish, and belied Washington Irving's adage that "a tart temper never mellows with age".

By the spring of 1919, they were lodging with her mother at Chatham, and Nahum found employment with the British Society for the Propagation of the Gospel among the Jews, which forthwith sent him to Mesopotamia to assess post-war conditions and the prospects for their work. A part of his report has survived and merits our attention inasmuch as it deals with matters beyond these now obsolete concerns of the Society; in fact it goes far beyond Nahum's brief.

He saw Mesopotamia (now Iraq) as ripe for colonisation. Its infant mortality, poor medical facilities, and large financial deficit displayed an urgent need for outside help, and the British could find a solution "which would work out the salvation of Mesopotamia". A part of that solution was to populate the country with either (i) the Arab-speaking people of Syria and Palestine, (ii) Indians or (iii) Jews.

Having dismissed the first of these as having no ties or sympathies with the Empire, and the second because, though good colonists, they were not acceptable to the Mesopotamians, he turned to the Jews. Mesopotamia, he thought, would solve the Jewish problem.

One would have expected him to share the Zionist vision of a Jewish homeland in Palestine. That, he says, however, "may be relegated to the sphere of Utopian dreams." Palestine had only a million acres of arable land, and had been unable to be self-supporting. "Even the Rothschild colonies, with all the money lavished on them, and the best European skill, could not be made self-supporting and with its present population of about 600,000 Palestine could not hold another 400,000. The Arab population is opposed to Jewish immigration, and the neglect to study this may lead to serious disturbances. . . I think therefore that the Government might redeem its pledge to the Jews by offering to colonise them in Mesopotamia."

He backed up this original suggestion by saying that the Hillah and Hamah Lake districts when drained would be sufficient to hold all the settlers, and that many benefits would accrue. As colonists the Jews would be progressive and inventive, and they would supply the money for improvements. They were the hardest working people in the United Kingdom; and in Palestine, Russia and Roumania had proved their worth as farmers.

Moreover, with a Jewish settlement the European holding force could be cut to 2,000 troops. At this point he went on to assess the military occupation "Going out as a civilian and being able to speak the language gave me special opportunities to discuss with the natives, who know the country and its needs.

"The only weapon the Arab possesses is the rifle. Most of the rifles are of German or Turkish make, for which there exists a very limited supply of ammunition. . . . Against this weapon the armoured car is a very effective and mobile weapon." He also advocated "(i) the employment of armoured cars to a greater extent than used so far, and (ii) the employment of Indian troops for the policing of the country". He went so far as to name the districts where such a policy should be applied. "The policing in the north and more troublesome districts might be done mainly by Indian troops."

There is more about the Indian troops. He compared them with the Egyptian officers who were creating disaffection in Palestine and antagonising the Jewish population. The Indians, by contrast, were respected as well as feared, and their presence was a guarantee of peace.

Looking into the future, he foresaw an exchange of land between Palestinian Arabs and those Jews who desired to go from Mesopotamia to Palestine. However, "the granting of any Jewish claims in Palestine at present would be to commit a wrong against the natives which may undermine our authority in the Moslem world and make Syria a hotbed of disaffection if it should become a French Protectorate." Prophetic words!

The Report breaks off before he has so much as mentioned the Society for the Propagation of the Gospel, but two of his concluding remarks about Mesopotamia should be noted. In the civil administration he advocates that the government be decentralised, and warns against the revival of Abbyssiad [sic] traditions centred around Baghdad. Then in returning to the Jewish question he again avers that "the Jews should be offered a National Home in Mesopotamia which does not necessarily mean giving up the idea of Palestine, but rather a just and satisfactory solution to all concerned."

What are we to make of all this? With hindsight, his assessment of Palestine's capacity was wide of the mark. The 'Utopian dream' became a reality. Malarial swamps were redeemed, deserts made to blossom, and there arose a densely-populated, highly industrialised nation. Yet one cannot but be impressed with his conviction that the granting of any Jewish claims in Palestine at that time would be to commit a wrong against the natives; also with his vision of a thriving Mesopotamia, his belief in the Jews as colonisers, and his foresight into disturbances to come through unwise administration.

Some twenty years later, in a booklet, *The Truth about the Jew*, which he wrote for the Church of Scotland, he returned to the subject. "Mesopotamia has a vast territory that is unoccupied, and I have been given to understand on the best of authorities, that as soon as the Arab-Jew question is settled, the door will thereby be opened in Mesopotamia for large-scale Jewish settlement. There is also the possibility of an Arab Confederacy between Syria, Lebanon, Transjordania and Palestine. Should this eventuate, the possibility of Jewish settlement would become large indeed; large enough to accommodate the bulk of the Jewish people who would have to emigrate from Central and Eastern Europe. This would make possible the vision of the prophets, who saw Israel gathered together again in the Land of Promise, stretching from the Euphrates to the Nile."

Tragically, the Arab-Jewish question has remained unresolved. It was exacerbated at the beginning, says Nahum, by the expulsion of the Emir Feisal from Damascus by the French, an act which upset the whole political balance of the Middle and Near East and led to a new Arab nationalism with which the promoters of the Balfour Declaration had to come to terms. This is a legacy which has lasted to the present day.

Nahum's political awareness was evident again in later years in his correspondence with Jacob Javits, the Republican Senator for New York City. 'Jack' Javits, described in *The Times* as "one of the most effective politicians in the senate of his time and a leading supporter of Israel," was a notable critic of the Vietnam war. He was a senator for 28 years until, in 1980, the Republican party moved to the right.

In *The Guardian* of August 11th 1970 Alistair Cooke presented him as "probably as true a spokesman for the Jews of New York as Mrs Meir is for Israel. He's technically a Republican but he is primarily a Liberal. So adroit is his appeal to all the ethnic groups of the city, from the Russians, Italians, Poles and Irish to the Puerto Ricans and the WASPs, that he is the most resounding vote-getter in the State's history."

Javits was Nahum's and Leon's cousin. His grandmother was their mother's sister. Such a relationship is highly regarded among the Jews, and hence there was a deeply rooted friendship. Only one letter from Nahum to Javits has survived, and it is of some interest, being written at a turning point in American history.

"August 15, 1968

My dear Jack, Marion and the children,

I hope you are not too disappointed by the election of Nixon as the Republican candidate for the Presidency. I think the convention made a mistake, but there it is, and I hope the party will now stand behind Nixon. Whether he can win. . . is of course another question. Many people in this country thought that Rockefeller could have done so, but let us hope Nixon will win in November. . .

I am getting sceptical about U.N.O. and the political conduct of the Western bloc. The Eastern bloc have swallowed a very bitter pill administered by the Czechs, but unfortunately the Czechs are very dependent on Russia economically, and while the Russians did not want to repeat the Budapest onslaught, they will bide their time and bring the Czechs to heel.

I heard that Nixon is intending to go to Russia soon but it will take a lot to effect any change in the Russian policies. . .

Last night Sir Robert Menzies was on the TV advocating your proposal for a common market for the English-speaking nations and he even went further; he said that in time Japan and India could join and that this combination could further the growth of the under-developed countries. He was thinking of writing a book on the subject.

I have been reading a good deal on ethics. . . and am reaching the conclusion that only an ethic based on the principle of theism can get us out of the mess in which we are. . .

I am sure that the Middle East situation must be giving you anxious moments. This area is one in which the Russians are fooled. The Arabs are not communists, they are still in the tribal era and it will take many years for them to come to some agreement among themselves, but they are not anti-Israel, and the sooner the U.N.O. realises this and takes effective measures to curb the killing of Israelis the more likely there will come peace. . .

Well, Jack, I am sure you are all very tired and I trust that you will be able to snatch a holiday between now and Labour Day.

With our joint affectionate greetings and love,
    As ever yours,
                                    Nahum."

The Senator would find food for thought in Nahum's letters.

He is also known to have spoken to Nahum about his religion. Secularised and assimilated, he had, with many others, on the birth of the State of Israel in 1948, experienced a spiritual conversion; not into Christianity but into the re-discovery of his Jewish identity and the faith of his fathers.

However, we are still at 1919 and wondering whether Nahum made any progress with the Society's requests. They had asked him to investigate where a Bible School and an Industrial Institute could best be established in Mesopotamia. The Secretary, Mr Exley, wrote, "It is especially in relation to your own future missionary station that they (the Committee) desire information. . . on the general prospect of work in Basrah, the present Government of the town, and whether any other missionary work is in being. . ." Also, whether a suitable house can be rented, and an estimate of the initial and annual cost of the projected mission "calculating for two married couples, one medical, the other evangelistic."

Nahum's reply is not known, and if the mission at Basrah was ever set up, his future did not lie there. Three years later he was still employed by the Society but about to leave it. Mr Exley wrote to him in June, 1922:

"Your letter [of resignation] does not altogether surprise me, but I am exceedingly sorry that the course you have taken appears to be necessary. If however to continue deputation work would endanger your sight, there really seems no alternative. . . it is good to feel that if you leave us it will be with the most complete feeling of friendliness on both sides, and this will make it easy for you to return to us if, as I hope will be the case, you get the better of the trouble with your eyes. Possibly later the way may be open for service for you on the Continent. . .

"It is very good of you to offer to give such occasional service as you may find possible in Scotland and we shall of course be grateful for such help. I cannot close without saying that I have been deeply touched by the spirit in which your letter is written. It seems to me to have about it the fragrance of Christ. . . May He lead you out of the present time of trial into a life enriched and glorified by the experiences through which you are passing."

Nahum was already in Edinburgh when he received this, and the previous month the General Assembly of the United Free Church had granted his petition for admission to its ministry. Five months later he was inducted to St John's U.F. Church at Johnshaven, and settled into a manse which he and Margaret found to be haunted!

13. FAMILY AFFAIRS

The war was over. The family had come through outwardly unscathed, but Nahum, a victim of mustard gas, was never again robust and his eyesight was affected. The hardest hit were those in Galilee where, as the U.F. Church's Jewish Mission Committee reported early in 1919, in launching a thank-offering appeal for the deliverance of Palestine, there had been "a veritable reign of terror, famine and pestilence." "We at home," the Appeal began, "have little comprehension of what devastation war has wrought in the Near East. . . Whole villages have been depopulated. . . There is neither wood nor oil for fuel. Nearly all the trees in the north are gone. Donkeys, mules, horses are all dead, and means of transport, save what is provided by the Relief Fund, is practically non-existent. There are thousands of homeless orphan children."

The missionaries returned to find their buildings damaged, vandalised and ransacked. All the medical equipment had to be replaced at Dr. Torrance's new hospital at Tiberias. Mr Semple, the educationalist, lost his library, valued at £1000, the books having been used as waste paper or for making cigarettes. The furniture and furnishings of every other missionary had gone.

What hardships Leon's mother endured is not known. They would be alleviated, as far as possible, by Rachel and her farmer husband. However, from then on Leon sent her money, and did so regularly to the end of her life.

At home, he was completing *The Menace of Socialism*, in which he had warned against the dangers of a hysterical patriotism and a 'Make Germany Pay' policy. He would equally deplore the 'Hang the Kaiser' campaign. Yet he was patriotic and shared in the mood of proud thanksgiving. He retrieved from the cellar a large, but by now somewhat faded, Union Jack — a fittingly muted symbol perhaps — and erected it on the balustrade under the attic window. It had last seen the light of day at the Coronation in 1911. He also took his children to the Victory Parade in Princes Street; and through the good offices of their new neighbour Bailie Robertson they secured a stance on the side steps of the saluting dais at the Royal Scottish Academy.

The changes wrought by the war were evident in the domestic as in the wider social life of the times. Housemaids, for instance, in starched caps and aprons were a diminishing band, and Katie had parted with hers. Nannie, however, now called Old Nurse, stayed on to tend the younger children until, a year or two later, she left to get married — only pausing at her friend's, Mrs Wilson the fishmonger, for a quiet cry in the back shop.

Everywhere the lights shone brightly again; and Fred, whose room faced north, found it strange at bed-time not to see the shadows of searchlights criss-crossing on the blind. Strange, too, to see butter on the table; yet, being faddy, he would not look at it for several years, so addicted had he become to margarine.

The simple diet enjoyed by the family was little altered. The Sunday roast reappeared, and so did bananas, but there was still porridge for breakfast, soup and perhaps Irish Stew or mince for lunch, and a variety of rice and custard puddings: semolina, tapioca, rhubarb, bread-and-butter pudding and the like. It was heavy fare, but all that the boys desired. Leon too enjoyed his food; and high tea, a popular six o'clock meal in Scotland, gave him time to relax before the doorbell started ringing.

It should be added that he had no shibboleths about ham or anything else. Christian freedom meant for him that he was at liberty to eat or drink, or to refrain from eating or drinking, anything whatsoever (or going anywhere or reading anything) according to the circumstances.

On Sundays, after church, there was a more leisurely meal, which often ended with Leon helping himself to fruit and nuts before drawing the cigarette holder from his waistcoat pocket. The aroma of the flat Egyptian and Turkish cigarettes which he sometimes favoured was particularly pleasing.

The boys were now too old for their Sunday rigout of sailor suits. No longer could they race down the terrace shouting "I'm Admiral Jellicoe". . . "I'm Admiral Sturdee", names acquired from *The*

Illustrated London News to which their parents subscribed during the war; from its pages they reproduced dreadnoughts, cruisers, and naval battles in their drawing books. They had also assumed less familiar characters, such as General Pershing and General Browning, culled from cigarette-cards, which they solicited from soldiers emerging in their sky-blue woollen suits and scarlet ties from Varrick House, the convalescent home at Church Hill, and from their father who collected them from his friends at the Club. Again, with their mother's now out-of-date muffs on their heads, they would become a bear-skinned Cossack or a beavered Hussar.

When John and Fred left their primary school the ritual of morning prayers came to an end. Formerly, after breakfast the bell was rung and the staff trooped in. Leon then read from one of the slim volumes of their wedding Bible, and the seven persons gathered in a circle round the fireplace knelt at their chairs while he led the prayers.

"Admiral Jellicoe" and "Admiral Sturdee"
complete with lanyards and whistles!

By 1918, the political parties were intensifying their struggle for power. Lloyd George succeeded in ditching Lord Northcliffe (Alfred Harmsworth), the Press baron and proprietor of *The Times*, who was his severest critic and implacable enemy. When Northcliffe heard that he was not to be appointed a delegate to the Peace Conference, he decided that the only recourse to power lay in complete control of the national press. To defeat him, Lloyd George, drawing on his accumulated War Fund, set up a consortium which bought *The Daily Chronicle* (later the *The News Chronicle*) for two million pounds, as well as *Lloyd's Sunday News*. He also established a controlling interest in *The Yorkshire Evening News* and the *Edinburgh Evening News*, and set up the company entitled United Newspapers.

Sir Henry Dalziel, the Member of Parliament for Kirkcaldy, headed the syndicate which carried out this coup in October 1918, and one of its members was Leon. His role may well have been confined to the *Edinburgh Evening News.* The experience was a valuable one, for a few years later he was to initiate a deal which brought two religious publishing firms and their respective weekly magazines *The Life of Faith* and *The Christian* together.

In August 1919, the Levisons were on holiday at Nairn, where incidentally, according to family lore, Leon was seen chatting amiably on the sands with none other than Lord Northcliffe. However, it was on the day of their arrival that, walking the boys to the beach he asked them: "How would you like it if your Daddy became a 'Sir'?" It was more than a possibility; the letter from Downing Street, signed by Lloyd George, was dated 2nd August. There followed the command to attend the Investiture on the 18th, and the holiday was interrupted by the parents' departure.

David, the youngest, was still an infant. Nevertheless, he recalls that in later years his mother told him that a baronetcy was first offered, but that lacking all social pretension they declined, on the grounds that they could not live up to the style demanded.

The citation reads: "Has rendered valuable work in connection with the Russian Jews Relief Fund. Public services during the war." One wonders whether the latter included not only the advisory work on Palestine, but also the recent consortium; for the Honours List included a Viscountcy for Dalziel and awards to the proprietors and editors of Lloyd George's newspapers.

In the family the knighthood made no difference that I can recall.

Nor did it distance Leon, as a 'Reverend' might, from the Jews. Some years later Rob Sutherland, a close family friend, was heard to declare that Katie was an ideal lady of title; she had the dignity, discretion and grace for the role. As for Leon, though not without vanity, he never traded on his title, but remained unpretentious, regarding every man as his equal and his friend.

The Scotsman, baffled by the award, raised astonished eyebrows and made an acid comment: "This," it said, "apparently refers to the gentleman whose name was prominently associated with the controversy in which also Bailie Robertson was concerned about the administration of an Edinburgh fund that was sharply criticised in the Press a few months ago.[1] It may seem remarkable that this should be the sequel to that controversy, but apparently such is the fact."

The Scotsman's innuendo that the knighthood might be linked to some financial chicanery can only have wounded Leon and distressed Katie. But if only for the phenomenal sums he had raised (and this without the aids of modern publicity and technology) the honour was well deserved. The scandal of Lloyd George's post-war lists with their purchased peerages and awards to sycophants can in Leon's case be discounted.

By 1919 the boys had enrolled in the Sunday School at Free St George's. Dr Kelman, who had resumed his ministry, devised quizzes and competitions from the pulpit: "Send me a postcard saying where you have found these people in the Bible." The next Sunday parents, including Leon and Katie, proudly heard their children named.

It was a marvellous church to be brought up in; and though Leon and Katie had chosen it for themselves, they must also have hoped that it would prove an attractive spiritual environment for their children. That hope was fully realised. Sons and daughter alike graduated into the flourishing youth organisations, and from 1921 they had in James Black a minister with an unrivalled appeal to youth. Even before his coming, however, it was a singularly unstuffy church. Dr Kelman, for instance, was no aloof, forbidding minister of the old school. Fred vividly remembers him blindfolded and down on his hunkers, and the assistant minister likewise, swiping at each other with batons of rolled newspaper at a Sunday School party.

The question of whether one should take one's children to the local church or to where the action is, if it is not there, is a debatable one. The enormous influence on all Leon's children and on scores of their contemporaries of such a church as Free St George's (later St George's West) suggests that his and Katie's choice was the right one.

There was less scope for the adults in such a congregation. The days of lectures were past, leaving only organ recitals and, for the women, an Association later to become a branch of the national Woman's Guild. Leon became known through his affability and the desire of the Association, as well as that of the Girls' Association, the Young Men's Guild and the other groups to hear about the Jews. However, Katie did not make friends easily and was not a great attender of meetings. Later on she responded to the approaches of two kindly ladies who called on her and asked her out; but their interests, almost exclusively in church and family affairs, soon palled, and for lack of anything wider she became increasingly lonely.

At the same time she enjoyed a happy family life, in which the annual holiday was a major event. Many Edinburgians went year after year to the same resorts, the coastal villages of Fife and those of East Lothian, such as North Berwick and Dunbar, being the most popular. The Levisons, by contrast, preferred fresh fields: one year Speyside, the next the English Lakes, Nairn or Northumberland, Eyemouth or Rothesay, a manse in Kintyre or a guest-house in Wales, Callander, Eccelfechan, Aberdour. . .

Furthermore, because 'Grandpa' and 'Grandma' Sawkins had, before the war ended, left Edinburgh for their native Devon, there were two or three holidays at Axminster or Seaton.

Leon occasionally took his sons fishing; but they failed to endure the Highland midges or to enthuse. He also, on a holiday at Dulnain Bridge, hired bicycles so that the family could regularly visit Grantown-on-Spey. One day, however, as he was passing a haycart, both handle-grips came off and he narrowly avoided an oncoming car before subsiding not too gracefully on the road. Cloth cap, tweed jacket and knickerbockers were his holiday garb.

Sport became a feature of the boys' lives. Leon, who knew nothing of cricket, would bowl and bat (less well) in the garden. He preferred, however, to set up his tripod, insert plates in the camera, dive under the cloth, and photograph them posing at the crease. He played croquet with the family, but not, as Katie did, tennis (in a foreshortened court and serving through overhanging trees). He attempted golf, but only once. His fluke drive, he said, reached the first green, but then he went to pieces and gave up for good. Katie, on the other hand, until she was in her fifties, occasionally had a round with the boys.

The Mission service being on Saturday afternoon, he rarely saw a football match. However, in the late twenties he took John and Fred to Tynecastle to watch Hearts play Rangers. It was when the "Wee Blue Devil", Alan Morton, was on the wing. Yet none of them was to know that 'Wee Johnnie' McRae, a Rangers inside forward, was, some forty years on, when a widower, to marry Rosalin. They were, by then, both handicapped, she on two sticks, he with calipers; and Katie had recently died leaving Rosalin on her own. Rosalin and John are both dead now, but they had ten very happy years of marriage.

In Fred's diary for 1931 there is on March 21st the following entry: "Morning. Took Daddy to Watsonians v Gala. Afternoon — Scotland 28, England 19, with Mary and Uncle Nahum." The rugby international at Murrayfield meant a morning kick-off for the clubs; hence Leon was free to visit Myreside. What he made of it no one knows; but he would enjoy Fred's talk of 'Ikey' Carmichael, 'Jake' Selby, 'Beefy' Mathewson, Courtney Morrison (who, 57 years on, is still seen at Myreside) and the other stalwarts.

In later years at Sunday tea-parties his conversation was wide-ranging, but Rob Sutherland, who was most frequently present, cannot recall him ever speaking of sport. Fred, however, marks one exception — his father's interest in Jack Dempsey and in the Beckett-Carpentier fight. (Fred, at the age of eleven, became so star-struck that for a time he slicked his hair and parted it down the middle like Carpentier!). To Leon, in those less critical days, boxing was still the noble art.

Nahum, who shared that Scottish victory at Murrayfield with Fred and his girl-friend, had wider sporting interests. During his Edinburgh ministry in the 1930s he would arrive at Albert Terrace on a Saturday night (when his colleagues were polishing their sermons) with *The Times* sticking out of one coat-pocket and the sports edition of *The Evening Despatch* from the other. Moreover, he was as well versed in English and even in American football as in Scottish. He had himself played in an army eleven. When he lived on the Kincardine coast, as well as going out with the fishermen, he swam in the North Sea, albeit with a kind of doggy-paddle. It was too cold for Leon who, after Galilee, never ventured in.

At home Leon mowed the lawns and, during the war, turned part of them into a potato and vegetable patch which he afterwards filled with roses. But horticulture meant less to him than agriculture, and it was Katie who tended the flowers.

Marjory Davidson Kelly, Katie's niece, came to Edinburgh as a medical student, and mirrored the new spirit of emancipation. She would arrive on the pillion of a young man's motor-bike, or from playing in a Ladies' Cricket XI. She had bobbed hair and modern fashions, smoked, and went unchaperoned to dances. Yet beneath the gaiety of the 'flapper' there was a bright intellect and dedication to her profession. Katie and Leon loved her dearly, and she took her young cousins to the old Theatre Royal to see Nellie Wallace as Widow Twankey.

Indoors, family games ranged from Ludo and Snakes-and-Ladders to Mah Jong (a craze around 1924) and Canasta, in all of which Leon joined. He also bought a three-quarter size Bagatelle table (not the Corinthian knob-pulling variety, but the real thing with cues and balls). At the Liberal Club he played Billiards and also Bridge.

Every Christmas he took the family to the Synod Hall to see Poole's Myriorama and to the Waverley Market circus, where he ate candyfloss, rode on the dodgems, and tried his luck at the sideshows. It was at the Myriorama that they saw the first 'talkie' to be shown in Scotland — a few seconds of Harry Lauder singing (I think) *I Love a Lassie*.

He was a participating father, and an indulgent one. He was no disciplinarian, and correction in the early years was left to Katie. He could possibly have said, as Lord Longford did in an interview, "I think I was a pretty wet father but well-disposed." He was too tender-hearted to raise his voice to his children. To say that his bark was worse than his bite would be misleading, for he had neither bite nor bark. He did, however, try to castigate with his tongue. "Your friend, Johnnie," he said once, referring to the boy next door, "said 'Shut-up' to his mother, and his father gave him such a hiding he won't be able to sit down for a fortnight. If either of you ever did that," he added darkly, "I would break every bone in your body." Such dire threats, though only half-believed, served to keep the boys on the right path.

Only once did he raise his hand. It was John, aged eight or nine, who was punished. Fascinated by the 'T Wood' on the Pentlands, visible from the upstairs windows, he set off after school with a companion, to explore it. When darkness fell his parents, not knowing where he was, became extremely anxious; and when he turned up Katie said he must be punished. Fred, cowering in his bedroom, heard the yells from the bathroom where his father was applying a razor-strop; but since the business end of the strop had a softly padded handle, John was less hurt than scared.

When Fred recklessly slogged a cricket ball through the study window — fortunately shattering only a small upper pane whose glass just missed his father's head as he sat in his favourite rocking chair, Leon's response was characteristic. There was no livid rage. The cricketers were only banished forthwith to the lower lawn. Again, when from there they contrived to toss croquet balls over a neighbour's wall, endangering his cucumber frame, it was their father who dealt with the policeman at the door.

Yet the children were not pampered in the way of lavish gifts or excessive pocket-money; nor were they allowed to show off before visitors, or to make scenes or interrupt conversations. It was a well-ordered home where there was much freedom, where affection, seldom stated, ran deep, and where husband and wife, as well as parents and children, were in complete harmony without being of only one opinion.

Leon's affections lay nearer the surface than Katie's. He would sometimes give her a sudden embrace from behind and kiss her neck, and she would start away saying, "Oh, no Leon, no!". (Not in front of the children?). Sometimes too he would hug one of his sons, to their very Scottish embarrassment, which Rosalin did not share. She, too, the most Jewish by nature, was voluble and openly affectionate.

At the piano Katie played hymns but little else. Leon had a violin but never touched it. It lay in its case on top of his cupboard and he let the children play with it. He had probably brought it from Safed in 1907, but why? Katie once said he had vowed never to play it again. . . but until when? Perhaps until his mother shared his faith, and the music of that relationship was fully restored.

He was musical, but his taste buds were never developed. He had a miscellaneous collection of records which he enjoyed, but there was neither Beethoven nor Mozart nor any chamber music there, and of Schubert only the 'Unfinished Symphony' and a couple of songs. The records were, in fact, not personally chosen but brought to him in batches by Captain Thorburn of the Gibson Line, who plied between Leith and Hamburg. (He was taking advantage, I suspect, of the extreme devaluation of the mark). They included, on the one hand, Caruso and Scotti, Kreisler and Paderewski, Lauritz Melchior and Frieda Hempel and, on the other, the Palm Court orchestras of Vienna and Budapest under Marek Weber and Edith Lorand. He loved Italian opera: Caruso singing Verdi, and Hempel Rossini, but he seldom, if ever, went to opera, for its high prices seemed to him an unnecessary extravagance. He did, however, take Katie to hear Joseph Hislop sing, and he enjoyed especially such ballads as 'Bonnie Wee Thing', which the great tenor included in his Scottish programmes. Among the records were some superb ones of Wagner: orchestral music from 'The Ring', Emmy Heckmann-Bettendorff singing Elisabeth's arias from 'Tannhäuser', and, with Melchior, the love duet from 'Lohengrin'. He appreciated these, but they were not so much his 'scene'.

He occasionally went to the theatre and more often to the cinema where, not surprisingly, his favourite film actor was George Arliss, whose 'Disraeli' and 'The House of Rothschild' he particularly enjoyed. The swashbuckling of Fairbanks, and Chaplin's silent slapstick also appealed to him greatly, and so, on the stage, did Harry Lauder.

He enjoyed the visual arts and etchings adorned his study walls. A sizeable print of Rembrandt's 'Light of the World' predominated, and he had a James McBey and one or two simple rural studies. Later, he turned to oriental rugs and decorated two flights of stairs with them.

Jokes about Aberdonians and Jews, or of the "An Irishman, a Scotsman and a Jew. . ." variety fed his sense of humour, which was unsubtle but relished the ridiculous. The Jews are verbose, and their humour is largely verbal. Leon chuckled over the puns and 'one-liners' that appeared daily in his evening paper. Typical of his brand of humour is a joke, heard from his minister Dr Black, which he repeated several times. A snobbish young man at a ball was delighted to hear his hostess say "Let me introduce you to the daughter of the Countess of Ayr." However, when he danced with her he found she was the daughter of the County Surveyor!

Some years earlier he had joined the Freemasons; and now after the war he became a founder-member of Lodge St Leonard's in the Newington/Pleasance, or Jewish, area of the city, and from 1921-3 its Right Worshipful Master.

The esoteric side of Freemasonry with its cabbalistic and Old Testament references and its reputed origin in King Solomon's Stables appealed to him, but its chief attraction was the opportunity to consort with men from all walks of life. Being naturally gregarious, he enjoyed their company. He liked, for instance, to catch a certain tramcar on the Morningside route, knowing that its conductor was a fellow Mason, and he would enquire solicitously after his family.

The social side, no less than the ritual and symbolism, appealed to him. He kept a notebook with the words of songs which he contributed at the soirées. They were the popular ballads of the day: "I'll sing thee songs of Araby," "Pale hands I loved," "Believe me if all those endearing young charms," "Genevieve," "My love is like a red, red rose."

He took the family to masonic picnics; at one of these I remember him taking part in the men's sprint. Jacketless and, I think, shoeless, but still in his waistcoat, he flashed off the mark and led until halfway when he tripped on the uneven ground and went full stretch — fortunately without being hurt.

Later in the century the Churches became uneasy about Freemasonry. The Church of Scotland, in 1964, asked its Panel on Doctrine to draw up a report on "Societies Involving Secret Ceremonies." The Methodists then explored the subject. In 1973 the Rev. Kenneth Leech of the Church of England, under the heading "Can a Christian be a Freemason?" raised the issue again in *The Times*, and sparked off more soul-searching and a fresh enquiry. (That this, and other important matters, e.g. children and Communion and the ordination of women, were and still are dealt with piecemeal, each denomination ignorant of the others and doing again the spadework that has already been done, is a sad comment on the Churches' disunity.)

Leon saw no incompatibility between his masonic vows and those he had professed as a Christian. And if he observed that some in the movement were finding in Freemasonry a substitute religion, he would regard such an aberration as no different from that of the idolator of sport or any other pursuit. He would fully have concurred in the findings of his own Church, accepted at the General Assembly of 1965:

"(a) If Freemasonry is a religion it must be condemned as a religion of works which is at variance with the Christian Gospel.

(b) Freemasonry itself, however, claims to be a system of morality which makes free use of allegory and symbol, and which, as a movement, deliberately stands back in neutrality so far as religion, revelation and redemption are concerned.

(c) In practice, there are individual Masons who make a religion of their Masonry and there have been a few who in print have offered an interpretation of the movement as a religion or 'super-religion'; but in the light of the official view which Freemasonry has of itself such people must be regarded as in error, even if the ritual seems to lend itself to these misconceptions."

In the 1980's the Churches again examined Freemasonry and their verdicts were more severe; but the 1965 assessment reflects Leon's beliefs accurately.

The choices Leon and Katie made for their children were, on the whole, wise. Nonetheless, it was probably a mistake to dress the boys up on Sundays in Eton suits. The alternative to school blazers was, in other families, kilts, but the Levites could claim no tartan! (John, however, was to wear a kilt in his school and university O.T.C.). Eton suits and straw boaters were *de rigueur* on Sundays at public schools such as Fettes and Loretto, but were unknown on the Morningside tramcars, where their wearers felt horribly conspicuous. In a short time, however, the parents came to their senses and the suits were abandoned.

Leon's and Katie's own schooling had been largely private. However, they had been in Scotland long enough to appreciate that there were excellent alternatives to the English public schools and their Scottish counterparts; and so, very wisely, they chose day-schools for their children and delivered them from the loneliness and heartbreak, as well as the neuroses and the sexual isolation, which so often attend boarding schools and have contributed not always advantageously to the English character.

They sent John, in 1919, to the Edinburgh Academy. It was a good school, of high academic repute, but too far from Morningside. Its playing fields were even more remote. Consequently John took a lesser part in school activities than he might have done. He was well taught and made lifelong friends. Dr Ferrard, the Rector, was a zealous classicist and tried to turn him into one. Only after crashing to a 3rd Class degree in classics did he discover that his *métier* was in accountancy.

His parents may also have chosen the Academy because it catered for a more select social range than the other day-schools. They were not snobbish, but at the Academy it seemed that their boys would have less contact with roughnecks and would acquire good manners.

A year later, however, Fred rebelled. His friends were going to George Watson's College, and besides, he added, "The Academy is a snob school!" Few parents would have listened to his plea, but Leon and Katie did; and it did the boys good, especially the younger one, to make their way along separate paths. At Watson's, where the professions mingled with trade and the curriculum catered for all and sundry, Fred's classmates included Lionel Daiches whose father, of whom we shall hear more, was Edinburgh's rabbi. His second son, the distinguished David, was two years behind, and Fred only remembers him as a violinist in the school orchestra. As I have already mentioned,[2] the Daiches brothers were precluded from much of the life of the school. They did attend 'The Merchant of Venice', but were so horrified at the misrepresentation of their race in Shylock, underlined by a ranting and whining schoolboy characterisation, that they probably failed to notice Fred as Portia. In class Fred and Lionel, aware of their fathers' antipathy, refrained from friendship, though no ill-feelings were harboured.

These were the years, prior to 1925 when Leon's life was to change course, in which he was able to spend time with his family. Afterwards, with the troubles of many on his shoulders, he would say to Nahum: "I wish I could see more of my children — but what can I do?" David, who in 1925 was only nine, says that in the following years his chief recollection of his father was that he was usually away from home.

NOTES:
1. See Chapter 14.
2. In the Introduction.

14. DISPUTATIOUS RABBI

The controversy to which *The Scotsman* referred in the autumn of 1919 in its comment on Leon's knighthood had occurred in April, when the editor of *The Jewish Chronicle and Jewish World* sharply criticised the administration of the war-time Relief Funds. He pointed out that their committee contained several members of Leon's own Mission committee, and concluded from this that the funds were "mission-related"; he went on to infer that under a cover of philanthropy Leon, together with Bailie Robertson, the Organising Secretary, had been propagating Christianity and even subsidising missions to the Jews. Leon replied vigorously that the books were available for scrutiny, that not a farthing had gone to missions, and that the late Leopold de Rothschild had recommended a Jewish distributor in Russia — Baron Guinsberg. He added that, in the four years of the Fund, he had written eight books and tracts, none of which contained Christian propaganda.

His critic returned to the attack with the allegation that money had been passed to a missionary, the Rev. John Wilkinson, whose work, it was said, would be furthered thereby. Moreover the whole enterprise had promoted the work of Leon and his like, who were only succeeding in turning bad Jews into nominal Christians.

The Scotsman, which had offered no comment on the correspondence, now seemed to take the ungenerous view that if the scheme was open to criticism it was in all probability tainted. Those who knew Leon, on the other hand, would not doubt the honour of his motives, while recognising his proneness to indiscretion. He may well have said, "When they see what we have done for their suffering brethren, some Jews may be less prejudiced against Christianity." Alternatively he may have told Mr Wilkinson, "This will, incidentally, help your work." And his books and tracts, as we have seen, though not intending to be missionary, veered as by a magnet to the Gospel.

The episode marks the beginning of a campaign of vilification. For it is evident that *The Jewish Chronicle* had an informant in Edinburgh. Who else would know that members of The Relief Fund Committee were also on that of The Edinburgh Jewish Mission? Who but Edinburgh's new rabbi, Dr Salis Daiches?

Dr Daiches, on coming to Edinburgh early in 1919, had resented the Mission with a bitterness unknown to his predecessors, who seem to have regarded it simply as the occupational hazard of living in a Christian country. Had not one of them visited the Mission to see its medical and social work? And after Dr Daiches' day, in the sixties, was it not said of Willie Marshall, the Church's Jewish Mission Secretary, that his relations with Rabbi Weinberg were such that when the latter suffered a heart attack he arranged the synagogue services for him?

But Dr Daiches was rigidly Orthodox and unwilling, or unable, even to discuss whether Christianity was an intrinsically missionary religion. The very existence of the Mission offended him, and he declared his intention to destroy it.

That same year (1919) the Right Rev. Professor W.P. Paterson, Moderator of the General Assembly of the Church of Scotland, opened the Sale of Work. He commended the Mission for both dispensing medicine and preaching the gospel; and as "an extraordinary example of moral progress . . . in comparison with the Russian pogrom or the Slavonic massacre".

Dr Daiches reacted immediately with a letter to *The Scotsman* of no less than a thousand words. The gist of it was that the Moderator had been hoodwinked; for the paid agents of the Mission only succeeded in enticing a few poor Jews by bribery to forsake their religion and indoctrinated them with another one. And these converts showed no signs of moral improvement. "In conclusion, sir," he wrote, "allow me to inform your readers that, while deeply appreciative of the kindness and goodwill towards the Jew which animates the supporters of such institutions . . . we regard the attack on the faith of the poor Jew by paid agents who try to capture his soul by relieving the pains of his body, in no more favourable light than we do the attack by the instigator of pogroms in Russia or massacres in Poland, who kills the body of his victim but is unable to reach the soul".

The Moderator expressed surprise. "I remarked," he wrote in his diary, "that it seemed to me evidence of moral progress that instead of having a pogrom *à la Russe*, we opened a dispensary. On Saturday a Jewish rabbi wrote in *The Scotsman* that he had more respect for the pogrom."[1]

Had he been less intransigent, it is possible that he and Leon would have been on amicable terms. They were of an age and had much in common: both were students of philosophy, staunch liberals and keen Masons and Zionists. And they had common ancestry, both claiming to be descendants of Rashi, the eleventh century biblical and talmudic scholar. Unfortunately, Rabbi Daiches was a recurrent thorn in Leon's flesh, and took every opportunity to attack him; and Leon, who from boyhood had been a peacemaker, could make no headway and was unable to find anything good to say of his antagonist. Had he lived to read David Daiches' account of his father, in the deservedly acclaimed *Two Worlds*, he would have regarded him more sympathetically, and the rabbi's rabid dislike of Leon would, I hope, have been modified had he lived to read this biography.

Many who appreciated *Two Worlds* would be taken aback by a virulent passage in the author's subsequent work oddly entitled *Was*. After remarking on "the futility of attempts to convert people", Professor Daiches wrote: "The Church of Scotland had its mission to the Jews and each year they reported on their activities to the General Assembly and each year his [David's] father wrote to *The Scotsman* to protest at the hypocrisies and dishonesties involved. No one in fact was ever converted in Scotland, though the egregious Sir Leon Levison, a one-time Jew of odd Levantine background who had turned Christian in foreign parts and tried to organise conversionist activities in Edinburgh, liked to make vain claims, for they gave him status. No passover knight he; he had already passed over to the majority religion whose life was easier; but the dour citizens of Edinburgh regarded him warily. . . His name had probably originally been aryeh, Lion; but now he was a lion whose prey remained elusive. The conversionists went abroad and tempted starving Jews with free soup; each one who came was chalked up as a conversion, and the same person coming several times appeared in the figures as several conversions"[3]

I wish that, as scholar to scholar, Nahum and David Daiches had met. For personal contacts often dispel prejudice and this passage is

DISPUTATIOUS RABBI

filled with the prejudices of a son who has inherited his father's hurt.

Coming from an academic, with its gratuitous and imprecise allegations, it is an extraordinary farrago. What is odd about being born in a rabbi's home in Safed? Again, to turn Christian meant passing *from*, not to, the majority religion there, and made life initially harder. No one ever converted in Scotland? Then not Leon only, but all on the Mission's committee, which scrupulously examined every candidate for baptism, must have conspired to deceive, and a succession of highly respected ministers, from Dr Hood Wilson and the Rev. George Davidson onwards, must have been hoodwinked.

By the same token those members of the committee who were also on the Russian Relief Fund Committee must have been dishonestly promoting their own ends — i.e. conversionism — under the cover of philanthropy. To Rabbi Daiches and *The Jewish Chronicle*, however, the names of Dr and Mrs Kennedy, Mr and Mrs Sawkins and the others who served on both committees, would mean nothing. To all who knew them they were honest and guileless people who undertook work for the Relief Fund only from their love of the Jews.

The tempting of starving people with free soup is an age-old allegation against missionaries. But every reputable missionary society is on guard against such dangers. I have quoted the Edinburgh Mission's early minutes on the subject; let me add this from the 1927 International Conference on the Christian Approach to the Jew:

"The reports from different countries indicate that the problem of finding means of livelihood for converted Jews is real and pressing. In many cases conversion means loss of employment, especially if, as so often happens, the convert's employer is a Jew. The missionary necessarily feels some responsibility in the matter, and various methods are attempted to secure employment.

The warning is given that no promise of employment should be made before conversion or Baptism, and in some Societies the practice is to baptise only those who have assured means of existence. There is unanimity that material assistance should only be given in exceptional circumstances".

In most of us "the futility of attempts to convert people" rings a bell. Aggressive evangelists, whether they would foist on us a new religion or a different brand of what we already have, frequently put our backs up. Rabbi Daiches' distaste for missionaries, intensified by his deep faith in Judaism, is understandable; it was in fact identical with Leon's own family's attitude towards Dr George Wilson and the mission at Safed. Young Nahum's attitude was similarly conditioned to that of Rabbi Daiches' sons: he told how he joined in stone-throwing at the Mission. It was impossible for those entrenched in Cabbalistic Judaism to appreciate or even to know the missionaries in Safed. Had they been told, for instance, that Dr Wilson was so altruistic that he would only accept a portion of the meagre salary offered to him, they would have refused to believe it.

One wants to be fair to Rabbi Daiches. He was a sensitive man, as his son has shown, and deeply hurt both by Leon's encroachments on his flock and the unfriendly tone of the Church's ripostes to his allegations. These came, for the most part, from the pen of Dr Macdonald Webster, the Jewish Committee's Secretary, a man who never minced words nor tried to mollify, and whose comments could be crushing.

Moreover, Dr Daiches' appearance and manner offered an impregnable façade to those who did not know him well, and concealed the kindliness which his son portrayed. Fred recalls seeing him once. It was at Watson's College during a morning break that a pudgy little man in a frock-coat and top hat, and wielding an umbrella, crossed the quadrangle. He had a small beard and a grim expression; his legs were short and his gait rapid. It was obviously Daiches' father, and someone, probably the headmaster, was in for it!

A report of the U.F. Church's Jewish Committee in 1924 contained this sentence from Dr Webster's pen: "In our own land, it is stated, many Jews have come under the liberating movements of the time, and although at Glasgow, where our work has its centre, the Synagogue sets its spies and tries to intimidate those who seek to hear the Christian message, activities are pressed on with evident signs of success". Dr Daiches was particularly incensed by this and wrote to *The Scotsman* repudiating the words 'spies' and 'intimidate' and launching an attack on 'activities' listing all those, in Edinburgh as well as Glasgow, which he saw as nothing but enticements.

The rabbi's attacks on missionary work were virulent, yet it has to be said that he referred courteously to those Christian ministers and scholars whose friendship he claimed. He respected the Church, he said, save for its proselytising. Churchmen, on the other hand, often found him exasperating; chiefly because he never passed up an opportunity to complain. In 1922, for instance, Dr Webster's quarterly magazine *The Jewish Register* reported that "Rabbi Salis Daiches of Edinburgh has discovered another mare's nest. This time it is the iniquitous proceeding of a Glasgow secondary school in studying, in a mixed class of Jewish and non-Jewish girls, a prose version of Chaucer's Prioress's Tale. The tale is an old-world legend that a little boy was foully murdered by Jews because, as Chaucer says, they were stirred up thereto by "the serpent Satan that hath in Jews' heart his wasp's nest". Dr Daiches demanded that the book be withdrawn from circulation; but the magazine reminded him "that English literature cannot be expurgated to suit Jewish palates any more than it can be edited to eliminate offence to any other nationality. We owe a debt to Israel, but it cannot be paid by re-writing English literature."

Leon wisely kept clear of these exchanges, leaving it to Dr Webster to respond. Six months later he did so, sharply, again in *The Jewish Register:*

"The Edinburgh Rabbi has already made himself notorious by his numerous and oft-times violent controversial letters on Jewish missionary affairs in the Scottish daily press. More and more frequently it is being said that no one in Scotland today can say 'Jew', but Rabbi Daiches must needs rush into print. By his action he is not tending to make either himself or his people beloved in the land, but unfortunately he does not see things that way."

Referring to an interview Dr Daiches had given to *The Jewish Chronicle*, Dr Webster pointed out that "over half the whole interview is devoted to the Jewish missionary work of the Scottish Presbyterian Churches. Among other things he says, 'One of my aims since I have been in Scotland has been to influence Scottish public opinion against the attempts made by the Jewish Mission Committees of the three Churches of Scotland.' So Church members will now know the purpose of the Rabbi's letters to the press — it is the endeavour to force them not to fulfil our Lord's commands. It is the old, old story over again of the Rabbinical antagonism to Jesus Christ. . . It is different with the Jewish people, who hear Him gladly."

In the interview Dr Daiches had suggested various ways of combating and undoing the work of evangelisation. "But why all this bother" asked Dr Webster, "if it be the case, as is so often contended, that Jewish Missions have no success? For the facts we refer readers to our last issue." The whole of that issue, under the title, 'The Success of Jewish Missions', was a response to the saying attributed to Luther that "It is as possible to convert the Jews as to convert the devil." It consisted of factual reports from the L.J.S., the S.P.G.J., the Hebrew Christian Testimony to Israel, the Hamburg Mission of the Irish Presbyterian Church, the Galilee Mission and Scottish centres in other fields — and most impressive it was.

To meet the constant allegations "that few Jews become Christians and that those that do are of the basest character", a previous issue of the magazine (September 1921) had said this: "The United Free Church does not require to be assured of the untruth of such statements. At present she can point to the converts who are being received into the Christian Church in Hungary by the hundred, and she can give a list of many names of Jews who by character and attainment stand in the front rank of Christian preachers and scholars, and who have been brought to the light through her Missions. The English Presbyterian Church has just added her testimony. At the recent General Assembly it was stated that out of seventy converts of The Bethnal Green Mission in London fourteen had become ministers or missionaries."

The success of the Hungarian Mission provoked Dr Daiches that same year to launch in a Hungarian newspaper a bitter attack against the Budapest Mission, in which Dr Webster himself had done notable service. Dr Daiches accused the missionaries and their fellow Christians of involvement in certain anti-semitic pogroms. "The story about pogroms in Hungary", wrote Dr Webster, "has been investigated and proved from independent sources to be untrue. Our own Government's White Book on the subject has set forth the facts, but the tale still goes the round. None is more ardent in re-asserting the untruth than the Edinburgh Rabbi, even though a fellow Jew like General Horowitz of the American army has on investigation declared the tale to be a myth." Dr Webster then related how an 81 year-old Budapest rabbi was admitted to a Protestant hospital after being refused the Jewish ones. His widow and family were deeply touched by the compassion and care he received. "Our Edinburgh Rabbi, however, will have the Scottish public believe that the delight of Hungarian Christians is to kill the Jews."

In the subsequent interviews in *The Jewish Chronicle* Dr Daiches claimed to have struck a blow against evangelisation in Budapest. "But", said Dr Webster, "the actual result of his interference was a larger enrolment in our Jewish schools than ever, and outspoken indignation on the part of Jewish people in Budapest against Dr Daiches for his attempt to cast aspersions on an institution which they regarded with affection. The Edinburgh Rabbi's attacks on Jewish Missions are really excellent advertisements."[4]

Rabbi Daiches' abrasiveness, provoked by the presence of a mission on his own doorstep, made life difficult for Leon. None the less some credence must be given to what the rabbi's son said about his father's fluent pen. "His letters on such subjects as Zionism, the activities of Christian missions among Jews, the position of the Jews in Europe and in Scotland in particular, Jewish ritual slaughter, anti-Semitism, and on any topical subject with reference to which the Jewish position required defence or explanation, became my father's best known claim to fame: they were read and admired throughout Scotland, and they did an immense amount to create a pro-Jewish public opinion in the country."[5]

These letters, his son concludes, "divorced from the context of the particular occasion that prompted them, have no special interest today". It may be so; but the conflicts some of them engendered are preserved, like bees in amber, and disclose the highly charged Jewish/Christian confrontation of those times. The inter-faith dialogues of today are eirenical and without bigotry but, in Scotland at any rate, there seem to be fewer conversions. This, however, may be due to the non-observance of the advice of that Scottish saint Andrew Bonar who, as long ago as 1839, pioneered missions to the Jews. On being asked how Israel might be won for Christ he replied, "By more tears". Both confrontation and dialogue have their place; but only love, with its silent tears, the love of Christ who wept over Jerusalem, can win the Jew. Leon knew this, and practised it.

Some time in the early Twenties he made the acquaintance of a young woman named Kate Thomson. A clerkess with Lindsay's, the Edinburgh coal merchant, she worked in the branch office which he passed on his excursions to the bank; and occasionally he called there to order coal. Now since for Leon, as William McIlvanny, the novelist, says of one of his characters, "almost any meeting was a vestigial relationship, people normally responded to his openness," he struck up a friendship and discovered that her ambition was not to sell coal but in some way to serve the Church; and as he told her of his work she became enthralled. The outcome was that after some training as a Church Sister she was appointed as his assistant, and for some twenty years served the Mission. Her designation was Lady Visitor, and her prime task to minister to the women and children, but Leon also encouraged her to take services, standing in, if need be for himself; this, however, was not often, for she was diffident about it.

Kate wore glasses, and looked through them benevolently and with humour. Her quiet Scottish voice and pleasant appearance made it easy for the Jews to welcome her, as they did. She was paid a pittance, probably less than she earned as a clerk, but she had counted that cost. (By 1934 when Leon's salary was £300 hers was £130). She was on excellent terms with Katie and a friend of the family; and in later years when Fred was a minister in Edinburgh, she would from time to time forsake her own congregation and worship in his.

Kate's elder sister — or was it her aunt? — was married to Captain Thorburn, the skipper on the Hamburg run who supplied Leon with gramophone records; which explains the origin of that ploy.

Apart from his work at the Mission, Leon continued to serve Freemasonry. Rising through all the Degrees, he was installed in 1921 as the first Right Worshipful Master of Lodge St Leonard's, Newington, of which he was a founder member. He marked the occasion by presenting an ornamental silver-gilt collar to be worn by each successive reigning Master. There followed two busy years, and when his successor was appointed in 1923, Leon was presented with the Apron, Gauntlets and Jewel of a Past-Master and his portrait in oils. A likeable though bland portrayal, it depicts him in informal dress but with starched collar and cuffs, a blue tie, a carnation in his buttonhole, and between his fingers the addictive cigarette.

His masonic interests were maintained, for it is recorded that in 1930 he displayed to the Brethren his decoration, the Grand Cross and Star of the Church of the Holy Sepulchre. He no doubt unscrewed the 3 inch cross to reveal to them, preserved in amber, the miniscule particle of wood which, according to legend, is from the True Cross. And in December 1931 it was reported that "the Past Masters, headed by Sir Leon Levison, worked a degree". But from that time onwards Freemasonry saw little of him as he became hard-pressed with a multiplicity of concerns.

In May 1921, a new minister was inducted at Free St George's, Dr Kelman having departed in 1919 to succeed Dr Jowett at Fifth Avenue Presbyterian Church, New York. Visiting the United States towards the end of the war, Kelman had pleaded for the solidarity of the English speaking peoples; then, at home, for the League of Nations, "the one means by which . . . . 'a war to end war' might be made good". Now he hoped to do more to draw the nations together in the tasks of peace. However, his health did not endure the strain and he returned in April 1924 to London, where he had a brief ministry in St Andrew's Presbyterian Church, Frognal. Leon, Katie and Fred, attending the Wembley Exhibition that year, went round to his vestry to welcome him back and be welcomed.

They responded to his Edinburgh successor in a different but no less enthusiastic way. Dr Kelman's sermons had a high literary quality, as befitted the author of *The Faith of Robert Louis Stevenson* and books on Bunyan, and great spiritual depth. They were especially appreciated by those to whom the relationship between Christianity and the culture, philosophy and ethical values of the day, and of the ages, were important.

James Black adapted the same Gospel to less cultivated minds. A wider range of young people, nurses, office-workers, apprentices as well as students, flocked to hear him.

He had a clear mind, vivid imagination, and an ability to build up a case like a skilled advocate; moreover, his personal charisma, passionate utterance and simplicity of language made him the most effective of preachers. These qualities are well illustrated in the sermons which he published under the title *An Apology for Rogues*, consisting of a re-assessment of the 'black sheep' of the Bible.

Casting about in his mind as to what to preach on at the Mission services, Leon began to find his topic in Mr Black's (he was not Dr Black until 1924) sermons. It is strictly speaking *verboten* for a preacher to reproduce, without acknowledgement, another's sermons, and Leon came close to doing so. From the mid-twenties he employed as secretary a young Jewess named Eva Lea, and it became his custom, on any Sunday when he was away, to have her take down the sermons in shorthand. Before long she was doing so even when he was at home, and I still have a cache of these typescripts. Speaking not to a church congregation but to a bustling roomful, mainly of women with toddlers at their feet and babies on their laps, Leon did not regard his exposition as more than a sermonette, and felt justified in re-presenting, extempore and by no means verbatim, the Gospel à la James Black.

Likewise he was to be seen on a Saturday morning browsing through the sermons of Reid of Eastbourne, Morrison of Wellington (Glasgow) and Jones of Bournemouth, popular preachers of the day whose books were frequently given him on his birthdays. He pencilled them heavily, and would reproduce paragraphs and phrases both in speaking and in writing.

In January 1925, along with his old friend Charlie Ridland, he was ordained to the Eldership. This, in Presbyterian churches, is a spiritual office which involves sharing with the minister (who is not a priest but a teaching and preaching elder), in the spiritual oversight and rule of the congregation. The minister alone is responsible for the ordering of worship, but the elders distribute the elements at Communion. Most importantly, it was resolved in 1648 and has been adhered to ever since, "that every elder should have certain bounds assigned to him, that he might keep himself acquainted therewith and report to the session". These reports have ceased to be formal, but when the congregational roll is revised, or catechumens admitted, the elder is able to speak for or about those in his district. He also informs the minister of pastoral needs. Many elders — though Leon was never free to do so — also represent their congregation in the higher courts of the church.

Albert Terrace was at the very centre of Leon's 'district', which covered both the Morningside and Merchiston areas. He enjoyed visiting his flock of perhaps fifteen families before each of the plenary (quarterly) Communions. Year in year out, this is for most elders a formidable assignment, cheerfully undertaken after working hours. For Leon it was an addition to the pastoral work in which he was already engaged. To give time to it, as well as to meetings of the Kirk Session and Deacons' Court, was never easy; but he was conscientious in visiting, and out of 60 Session meetings was present at 34. Some absences were due to the deputation work which took him on many a week-end to far-flung parishes. Moreover, as the Session met on Monday afternoons, a practice discarded as younger men were ordained, he was not always ready to be there.

The eldership brought new friendships both in his district and within the large Kirk Session, as well as a deepened friendship with

DISPUTATIOUS RABBI

his minister, who became, under Leon's tutelage, an expert on Jewish missions, being appointed in due course Convener of the Assembly's Jewish Mission Committee. He and Leon were delegates to an international conference on "The Christian Approach to the Jew" held first in Budapest and then in Warsaw in 1927. The chairman at both centres was the great missionary statesman, John R. Mott, whom Leon may have seen presiding over the World Missionary Conference in Edinburgh in 1910. In his address at the opening of Memorial House in 1938 (the house in Chelsea which was purchased as a memorial to Leon) Dr Black, then Moderator-elect, recalled the opening day of the Budapest Conference. "John Mott," he said, "was sitting beside me, and Sir Leon had just finished his opening speech on the situation of world Jewry and the possibilities of Christian work among his own people. At that time John Mott was fairly new to this puzzling problem, but he listened with unwavering attention to every word of the speaker, and when Sir Leon was finished Mott turned to me and said: 'That is a masterly presentation and that is a big man'. I know he was right".

Dr Mott remembered Leon. For seven months later Leon told the Mission Committee that he had received an invitation from him to visit America on a four month tour on behalf of missions to the Jews, but that he had not felt able to go. The two were to meet again on the International Missionary Council, to whose section on Jewish Missions Leon was seconded; they also met at a conference in Jerusalem in 1928, when Leon's companion was again Dr Black, and a few years later when the Nazi persecution had commenced.

This lay ahead. Meanwhile in the twenties Leon had other problems. One was indifferent health. Constantly below par, he consulted his doctor, who unfortunately accepted the current myth that, when no other source was apparent, debility derived from the teeth. A dentist was called in and concurred in this fallacy, which is now repudiated. Sepsis from the teeth does not spread throughout the body. Leon was duly dispatched to his bed, where all his teeth were extracted on successive days. For one who had enjoyed cracking nuts and gnawing bones to the marrow (which he recommended) this was a grievous blow. Furthermore, as well as being unnecessary, it could only have done harm to his system. This was equally true of other victims, from whom muscular dentists were known to remove twenty teeth at a sitting or a lying down!

To turn to happier things: there was the advent of broadcasting. The crystal-set came to Number Nine in 1923. On May 7th an entry in Fred's diary reads, "Plumber put up wireless but we could hear nothing." The plumber? I wonder if that was the overweight Ebba Eban-like Jew who got stuck in the attic window! We hauled him in and he proceeded to staple the aerial-lead down two flights of stairs, finishing by the dining-room window on the ground floor. An external lead had not yet been thought of.

Leon would lie on the floor, don headphones (there were two pairs) and twiddle about with the crystal. Meanwhile the boys searched the coal-cellar where fragments sensitive to the needle could be found. In the period that ensued I can only recall two of the programmes that appealed to him: "John 'Enery Calling", the weekly monologues of a slow-spoken, much put-upon Yorkshireman, and a recital from the Albert Hall by one hailed as the new Caruso, the young Polish tenor Jan Kiepura. That was a night to remember, for Kiepura had a glorious voice and brought the house down. Leon bought his record of the arias from *Tosca*, which Fred, inserting the strongest needle, would listen to with his ear to the sound box! Unexpectedly, after making one or two popular films, Kiepura faded out, and Leon transferred his affection to John McCormack.

A year or two later a phone was installed in the study. When Jews were being interviewed it could not be used, but not all of the boys' friends were aware of this and some made evening calls. This resulted in John, perhaps, conversing *sotto voce* at the study mantlepiece while at his back another conversation was resumed in whispers. Leon, as always, remained unperturbed and forbearing.

In the late twenties the older boys were adolescent, and one of them, beset with the problem of masturbation and overcome with guilt, decided to confess to his father. It is generally acknowledged that young people can talk more freely, especially on intimate subjects, to friends or other relations than to their parents, and it says much for Leon that he was approached. He wisely did not make much of it but, slightly embarrassed, said, "I'm glad you told me. If you ever want to talk about it again, come to me. I think that might help".

Politically this was not a happy period for the Liberals. Lloyd George not only lost the 1922 Election, but was swept from power forever. Bonar Law's victory was followed in 1923 by that of

Baldwin, who in 1924 increased the Conservative vote by 2.5 million. The Labour vote, too, was on the increase, whereas the Liberals, within ten months, had gone into a 30 per cent decline.

Leon remained faithful to Liberalism and Lloyd George. Temperament as well as conviction continued to draw him to the latter. Like himself, Lloyd George was a pragmatist who cared little for tradition but much about getting things done. He was intuitive, imaginative and buoyant, had cared for the common soldiers and withstood their generals in the War, and in peacetime had shown compassion for the common man. When Leon took his sons to hear him there in 1929 the banners across the Usher Hall proclaiming: "We can conquer Unemployment," said it all. Alone among political leaders he had the vision the nation at that time needed. "Taking the advice of many experts," says L.C.B. Seaman, "he produced plans for agriculture, for town planning, for the control of public services by public corporation, for more systematic methods of credit control, and for a large public works programme, involving road-building, railway modernization, more housing and more electric power, to absorb the unemployed and add to the nation's capital assets."[6]

Unfortunately, few believed that the Liberals could implement this programme, and many thought Lloyd George insincere and only concerned with getting back into power. Leon thought otherwise, and now, in the eighties, would no doubt have supported the same policies advocated by both the Labour and Alliance parties in face of still vaster unemployment.

He also at this time stood by the views he had expressed in *The Menace of Socialism*, and would applaud the outstanding speech made in the House of Commons in 1924 by Sir Alfred Mond, the supporter of his war-time Fund and a member of Lloyd George's Cabinet. In the course of a debate on capitalism versus socialism he spoke out eloquently in defence of private enterprise.

During the twenties Leon did all he could to support the succession of Liberal candidates who stood in his own constituency. They were less than astute politicians but shone in other fields. They included the ageing Principal Laurie of the Heriot Watt College (now University), an expert on plants, scientific warfare and Rembrandt's brushwork, and David Cleghorn Thomson who, as well as being Director of Broadcasting in Scotland, was a poet and musician. However, Morningside for twenty-three years seemed content with the stolid Sir Samuel Chapman, whose sole claim to fame seemed to be his connection with the Perthshire Prisoners of War Fund. Leon regarded him as a nonentity. "What does he do?", he would ask. "He never speaks in the House. I think he spends his time in the Library. His only use in Morningside is opening Sales of Work." As for the Morningside electorate, "You could plant a Union Jack there," he declared, "and they would vote for it!" From 1922, when Chapman was first elected, Leon with his fellow Liberals sank into political obscurity.

If Edinburgh spurned the Liberals, however, it continued to be the pride of its citizens. In February 1923, Leon framed the following certificate and hung it in his study: "Which day in Presence of William Forrest Esquire Lord Dean of Guild of the said City Sir Leon Levison, Author, 9 Albert Terrace, Compearing is made Burgess and Guild Brother of this City. . . A. Grierson. Town Clerk." This was not an honour bestowed, but a privilege available to anyone resident for three years and willing to pay a guinea. And because the Merchant Guilds banded together for charitable purposes, it brought him into touch with the business community and perhaps enabled him to share in disbursements.

Though the Sawkinses had gone south as the war ended, Leon did not abandon them, but made regular excursions to Axminster. It may be from one of these that he returned in April 1923, as Fred's diary records, "with 5/-each for John and me and a lot of silk badges, flags and pictures." However, it was the cartons of clotted Devonshire cream which came by post that were his most eagerly awaited gifts. Family holidays too were enjoyed either at Axminster or at the adjacent resorts of Seaton and Lyme Regis. On the Scottish children the warmth of the sea and the profusion of butterflies in the lush meadows made a lasting impression. Only when they accompanied the Sawkinses to the parish church did they feel alien. Leon was at home there, as he could be anywhere and so, naturally, was Katie; but Fred, for one, reacted vehemently to a service at which only the choirboys sang and prayers were intoned or, as it seemed to him, said by rote and without feeling. He found the Methodists more congenial, responding to their warmth but noticing the marked class distinction; here were no figures of the Establishment but only the humbler tradesfolk.

In years to come, Leon was to plead his cause from Anglican pulpits and Fred to appreciate Anglican worship wherever the liturgy came alive; but the fact remains that on both sides of the Border support for Leon's work and that of the Hebrew Christian Alliance came markedly from those congregations furthest removed from the Establishment, and those least obsessed with the upholding of traditions, punctiliousness in liturgy and their own preservation. It was not in England, however, but within the Established Church of Scotland that Leon was to encounter a congregation which forbade him its pulpit for, said the eminent lawyer who was its Session Clerk, the pulpit is the preserve of the ordained and to allow a layman there would be a defamatory act! The minister could have overruled this, but deferred to his Kirk Session.

Meanwhile, Nahum was both ministering to his congregation of fisherfolk, organising for the community the building of a tennis court and putting green, and becoming known as a scholar. Early in 1924, Professor James Moffat invited him to contribute some short articles to *The Expositor* on Old Testament texts.

NOTES:
1. *The Diaries of William Paterson Paterson*. Faith and Life Publications Ltd 1987. p.261.
2. *Two Worlds. An Edinburgh Jewish Childhood*. Macmillan 1957.
3. *Was*. Thames & Hudson, 1975. p.36.
4. The quotations from *The Jewish Register* of 1919-1922 are from the columns signed "Observer"; but this is patently a pseudonym for the editor, Dr Webster.
5. *Two Worlds*, p.93.
6. *Post Victorian Britain 1902-1951*, Methuen (Paperback Reprint) 1972. p.201.

The Hebrew Christians.
1924-33.

15. ISLINGTON TO HAMBURG

In 1887 Jewish Christians in Great Britain formed a national association both for their mutual support and to bear witness to the Jewish world. Similar movements sprang up in the next thirty years. In Russia, for instance, the New Israel movement started by Jaskoff Prelovku at the turn of the century was echoed by the Rev. Joseph Bibinovich in Kishinev and by Rabbi Lichtenstein in Hungary. At the outbreak of the Great War there was another movement among the Russian Jews called Seekers after God. Then in 1915 Ben Rohold, Leon's old friend, proceeded with American colleagues to form an association in the United States. (This is not a complete summary: in 1865, 1882, 1885, 1901 and 1903 there were significant comings together of Hebrew Christians both in Britain and in America). The British and American organisations chose the name of Hebrew Christian Alliance, and this title has generally been retained. Recently, however, the American Alliance has become the American Alliance of Messianic Jews.

Leon always described himself as 'a Jew by race and a Christian by grace', but he never questioned the term Hebrew Christian, which was the accepted usage in his lifetime.

Within the British and American Alliances the desire was to bring together the converted Jews of many nations, and it was from America that the initiative came. Mark John Levy crossed the Atlantic no less than seven times in order to pursue the matter, and the Rev. Samuel Schor and the Rev. Bendor Samuel, President and Secretary of the British Alliance, joined with him in the planning of an international Hebrew Christian Conference. It took place at Islington, London, in September 1925. There were less than sixty delegates but eighteen nationalities were represented, and as a result ten overseas Alliances sprang into being.

Mr Schor had been appointed Chairman of the Conference and it was known that he would almost certainly become the first President of the international body. He was well equipped by experience and reputation as well as by his outstanding ability, energy, tact and gifts as a speaker, to hold the office.

Born in Jerusalem of Hebrew Christian parents, he had started missionary work in the East End of London, and in 1889 was the first Palestinian native to be ordained in St Paul's Cathedral. At Felixstowe in 1891 he held his first Palestine Exhibition, which spawned many others, all of them stirring up a great interest not only in the Holy Land but also in Jewish missions. After a ministry at Christ Church, Blackpool, he became Director of the Barbican Mission to the Jews in London, which under him extended its work by setting up mission stations in Poland.

When, two days before the conference, Mr Schor had a stroke, it was a devastating blow. Nevertheless, it was too late for cancellation, and a daily rota of chairmen carried on. Mr Schor watched and prayed from his bed; and, although he lived for eight years and could only contribute by prayers and pen, his widow continued to be an outstanding servant of the Alliance.

On the third day of the conference the following resolution was carried:-

"That we Hebrew Christians from different parts of the world, standing for the Evangelical Faith, now met in Conference, reaffirm our living faith in the Lord Jesus Christ as our Messiah and our oneness with Him; and do hereby declare that we now form ourselves into an International Hebrew Christian Alliance."

The assembly rose and sang the Doxology, and prayers were offered. Then came two crucial tasks: the election of office-bearers and the defining of aims.

Leon had not been a member of the British Alliance. (Had he lived in London he would, presumably, have joined). However, he had been invited to Islington as a distinguished Hebrew Christian; and Mr Rohold, who was on the committee, no doubt urged him to come. When the Nomination Committee proposed him for the presidency he may have been taken aback, but his acceptance was immediate and wholehearted. And everything he said thereafter suggests that the vision of an International Alliance had already captivated him. He knew, I believe, that his hour had come; that over and above what he would continue to give to the Jews in Edinburgh, he could pour all his talents into this worldwide task.

Words of T.S. Eliot's come to mind —
"It is out of time that my decision is taken,
If you call that decision
To which my whole being gives entire consent."[1]

There is no doubt that apart from his conversion it was the turning point in his life. A larger horizon appeared, and it was as if the Lord had said: "Behold I have set before you an open door." His quick imagination would conjure up the courageous Hebrew Christians of many lands, lacking spiritual support even from the Churches of many nations, which could be less than welcoming. He would see their material needs and empathise with them in the struggle to survive and to raise their families in peace. He would see also their potential as workers in the Kingdom, and the ways in which God could use a redeemed Israel.

The summons was to something new. This, however, does not mean that his life was blown off course. Rather it was as if, in the words of that great missionary to the Moslems, Temple Gairdner, he was "seized by the scruff of the neck by an invisible angel" and set towards the goal and destiny of his existence. "Others", wrote Harcourt Samuel, the I.H.C.A.'s General Secretary, "had conceived the idea of an Alliance extending its work wherever Hebrew Christians are found; he saw how it could be done and was given the chance by being unanimously chosen as our joint leader. For eleven years he spent himself in our service, and he left an indelible impression on our work."

This book is the story of Leon, not of the Alliance. Yet the two are inextricably bound together, and there is no more revealing account of him than that contained in the reports of the triennial I.H.C.A. Conferences held in Hamburg (1928), High Leigh (1931), and Mildmay (1934). At the same time it should not be forgotten that he continued to regard the Edinburgh Jewish Mission as his prime responsibility, and that absorption in the Alliance did not preclude him from other religious, political and business activities.

The aim which the I.H.C.A. set itself was to build up national Alliances which would be linked together in a universal fellowship of Hebrew Christians. Its purposes were to inculcate the loyalty of all members to the church of their adoption — with the exception of the Roman Catholic Church, for this was a purely Protestant movement; to enable Hebrew Christians to meet for fellowship and worship; to provide in every country an annual conference to consider the welfare of Hebrew Christians; and to inspire its members to seek and win for Christ their unconverted Jewish brethren.

A fuller list would comprise the welfare of converts, including those offering themselves for the ministry; the interpreting of the spirit of the Jewish people to the Christian world and of the Gospel to the Jews; making it possible for Hebrew Christians to share in the activities of Zionism and claiming for them equal rights under the Balfour Agreement; and identifying them with the Jewish people in the defence of their just rights where these were denied them, and in protest against anti-semitism.

Anti-semitism and its consequences soon became a dominant issue, for although Hitler did not rise to power until 1932, his first irruption into the limelight was in the Putsch of 1923 when there were portents of things to come. As early as 1899 there had appeared a book, both seminal and sinister, whose influence was, over thirty years later, to cast a shadow over Leon's life and work. Entitled *Foundations of the 19th Century* and filled with anti-semitism, it glorified the German race and deeply influenced Hitler. Its author Houston Stewart Chamberlain, an English traitor, shared the anti-semitic views of his father-in-law, Richard Wagner. He was the friend of Hitler, whom he visited in Landsberg prison while the future dictator was writing *Mein Kampf.*

Membership of the Alliance was open to any Jew "who professes the Christian Faith and loves the Lord Jesus in sincerity"; and on joining a national branch he was *ipso facto* a member of the I.H.C.A. Christians not of Jewish birth were also invited to join as associate members, with equal rights and privileges, and it was emphasised that neither was a new sect being formed nor any wall of partition raised.

As for the basis of faith, Leon expressed it thus. "We believe in the inspiration of the Word of God, and we accept the Bible as the rule of our life and faith. We believe in the Virgin Birth, in the vicarious sufferings which our Lord Jesus Christ bore upon the Cross; and we believe in the Resurrection of our Lord, and not merely in the Divinity of Christ but in His Deity."

An immediate task was to inaugurate a fund for various purposes: (i) to succour Hebrew Christians in distress; (ii) relief for widows and orphans; (iii) to aid students for the ministry and mission field; (iv) if and when practicable, to establish an industrial home for the training of converts; (v) an enquirers' home; and (vi) a Colony, in Palestine or elsewhere, which would provide training in farm work.

There was also the question of literature, and in this connection a start was made by the American Alliance's decision to print a bimonthly paper called "The True Light" in both English and Yiddish.

Under Leon's leadership the I.H.C.A. (henceforth referred to as the Alliance) made rapid progress, and within two years there were twelve affiliated branches: in Britain, America (including Canada), Germany, Russia, Poland, Latvia, Sweden, Denmark, Hungary, Austria, Switzerland and Palestine. These were followed by Holland, Roumania, Yugoslavia, Australia, Danzig and Portugal, making eighteen in Leon's lifetime.

The Alliance needed much fostering; and for Leon this meant monthly executive meetings in London (where the Mildmay Mission kindly provided office accommodation), several continental journeys, and one to America, and a deluge of correspondence, for which the Alliance provided him with a secretary. That he chose a young Jewess, Eva Lea, as his secretary and befriended both her and her family was only to be expected.

The journeys to London were allowed to interfere with his Edinburgh commitments as little as possible. He took the night sleeper to Euston and, if possible, two days later caught an afternoon train home. In London he stayed at the Strand Palace Hotel, where he interviewed a variety of Hebrew Christians. As the months and years passed a routine was formed whereby he always had the same sleeping coach, whose attendant he sought out and dated for their cup of tea; and at the hotel he greeted certain waiters and porters by their Christian names. Occasionally, the Strand Palace being full, he lodged at the Regent Palace in Piccadilly; and from either he was well-placed to kill an idle hour or two, should they occur after lunch or before a night train, at a West End cinema.

More than once Katie and the boys visited London, en route for Axminster, and Leon took them — a splendid choice — to Maskelyn and Devant, the supreme purveyors of magic and mystery at the theatre. Once too, Fred took his parents to the Marble Arch cinema to see his favourite, John Barrymore, in *Beau*

Brummel — or was it *Monsieur Beaucaire*? When his father visited New York, not long afterwards, he reported that in Central Park he had seen Barrymore stop his car and address a small crowd of his fans.

Either from busyness or disinclination, however, Leon did not accompany the boys to see the youthful Olivier and James Mason in Gordon Daviot's *Queen of Scots* nor Balliol Holloway as *Richard the Third*. Nor would Noel Coward's *Bitter Sweet* have been to his taste; like Fred, he would have found it hollow.

Back in Edinburgh his postbag contained pleas for help from far and wide. It was a time of world depression and for many their hardships were augmented by their being Hebrew Christians. From Chisinau, in Bessarabia, for example, where there were twenty baptised believers and others not yet baptised, came this plea: "In addition to their spiritual battle, most of them suffer material loss by dismissal from employment, business boycott, and desertion by friends. The Orthodox Christians do not consider them Christians at all, and heap upon them even more hardships. . . For instance, a young woman educated at a French university was converted; in consequence of this she was turned out of home, but in spite of her splendid education is unable to secure employment owing to approaching blindness. Again, a brother with a wife and five children to support was converted, losing his position as a result, and, owing to the absence of factories, remaining unemployed. His fight for bare existence has lasted nearly six years. Such examples could be multiplied. . . It is not our purpose to distribute all the money in relief alone, but to invest a part wisely in the purchase of shoemakers', carpenters', ironworkers' tools, etc., to supply work for the capable ones and training for the untrained ones, that they may become self-supporting. I am delegated to draw your attention to these solemn matters, urging you not to forget us."

Leon responded with an immediate donation of £10 and a call to the Hebrew Christian community for further help. By now, however, he had realised that a vital and urgent task confronting the Alliance was that of fund-raising. It was needed not only to alleviate suffering, but for a whole range of practical projects as well. There was a colony to be founded in Palestine, a children's home in Poland, and a hostel for girls in London. In addition there were students, already some seventy in number, who needed to be educated for the ministry and for missionary work. He was, as we have seen, a consummate money-raiser able both to inspire others in a cause and to win the contributions of individuals, churches and organisations. Beginning in the South of England, the wealthiest area of the British Isles, he persuaded several devoted supporters of the Alliance to organise drawing-room meetings which he and others — but chiefly himself — addressed. These supporters were, for the most part, elderly ladies of evangelical sympathies who had been drawn to the Alliance through the pages of *The Life of Faith* and *The Christian*. They were non-Jews, they had means, and they lived in resorts such as Hove, Eastbourne and Bournemouth. They became devoted to Leon, who never exploited them but gave them genuine friendship, and it is not surprising that they left considerable legacies to the Alliance. One of these legacies was to enable the dream of a girls' hostel to be realised, and the name of its donor was perpetuated when it was designated The Logie-Pirie Hostel.

As the years passed he found patrons in other parts of the country. In Scotland one of them was Lord Kinnaird, the evangelical Perthshire landowner, who had house-parties for him from time to time at Rossie Priory.

By the end of 1927 a generous gift, again from a lady, enabled the Alliance to fulfil its project of a magazine which would be its organ. Thus in April 1928 *The Hebrew Christian Quarterly* was launched with Leon as its editor. For the rest of his life this forty-page magazine was to be a major occupation.

The tone was set in the first editorial. "We shall endeavour," he wrote, "to demonstrate to Jews and Christians alike that our deepest Christian convictions. . . do not in any way interfere with our loyalty and affection for the race to which we belong. . . We shall dare to point out the difficulties and shortcomings of Judaism, but shall do so with a delicacy. . . and if criticism will be necessary it will not be directed against the Jewish people, who are the most sensitive and lovable people on earth, but against the yokes which the synagogue has imposed upon them."

From its start the *Quarterly* interspersed a wide variety of articles on biblical and missionary themes with news reports from the branches and items from the world press. The latter included startling statistics regarding the Hebrew Christian population. It had been reported, for instance, in several papers including Jewish ones, that since the war some 40,000 Jews in Budapest had been received into the Christian Church. "Since then," wrote Leon, "Dr Macdonald Webster, the Secretary of the Jewish Committee of the U.F. Church of Scotland, who is probably the greatest living authority on matters relating to Jewish Missions, has ascertained that the number in that place. . . was not 40,000 but 97,000. Other striking figures may also be quoted. In Vienna 17,000 Jews accepted Christianity; in Poland 35,000; in Russia, 60,000; in America over 20,000, and in Great Britain 5,000. At the same time smaller groups of Hebrew Christians were found in Germany, Sweden, Denmark, and in the British Overseas Dominions."

Most interesting of all, in this first issue, are the five photographs. The Islington one has Leon in the centre, flanked by Dr Arnold Frank of Hamburg, one of the most eminent of Jewish missionaries, who at the age of 70 was to succeed him as President and to live to be 106! Another notable figure was Dr Max Reich, an American Quaker and regular contributor of devotional articles and deeply felt, if unsubtle, verse, a trimly bearded and kindly little leprechaun. The second photo is of thirty Poles at their conference in Bialystok. The third is of thirteen Russians, their Executive Committee, some bearded and all physically tough and strong. The fourth is of sixty Germans, including several uniformed Deaconesses of the Kaiserswerth Association, i.e. nursing sisters belonging to a 'mother-house'. These were on the staff of the Jerusalem Hospital in Hamburg which stood beside the Jerusalem Church, rebuilt in 1912, of which Dr Arnold Frank was one of the pastors. The fifth photo is of a hundred and twenty Americans at their conference in Baltimore. In the foreground stands a group of young men who were future leaders, among them Jacob Peltz who became a full-time servant of the Alliance.

The early numbers of the *Quarterly* inevitably contain from Leon's pen a good deal more than the editorial. His style lacks crispness and is sometimes fulsome, but the meaning is always plain. The vividness and verve of his public speaking is not captured on the printed page; and yet one feels his passionate belief, his love for Christ and longing for his fellow Jews to come to Him.

"Let us pray even with tears that God will open the eyes of our people. Till God opens men's eyes they are like those mariners who, having lost their course and been becalmed off the mouth of the Amazon, were dying of thirst, imagining there was no drop of water to drink, while all around them for hundreds of miles there was

ISLINGTON TO HAMBURG

nothing but fresh water. The Jews thirst where streams of living water flow . . . .
"Who will give this Christ to the Jews? It is our solemn duty. . . . to do so, and when they see Christ as we see Him the world will suddenly grow brighter for them, as it has for us; and they shall see their joys reflected in every face, instead of anti-semitism which they see today. This, then, is the only solution to the problem of our people."

In 1926 he attended the American Alliance's conference at Buffalo. It was the first of many gruelling overseas tours, and included engagements in Newfoundland, Toronto and Baltimore as well as Chicago, New York and other centres. Recuperation on the sea-crossings, however, made this itinerary less exhausting than the extensive journeys he was to make in Eastern Europe with Edinburgh as their starting-point.

The American tour was not only an encouragement to Hebrew Christians, but an opportunity to publicise the work of the Alliance. The Press, drawn by his title and parentage, reported him widely. Two fragments are all I have come across. He had been speaking in Toronto of a seemingly phenomenal trend in post-war Jewry towards Christianity. "The Roman Catholic Church," he declared, "is seeing the significance of this movement. They have sent out letters to their priests in Europe to show kindness to these Jews, because, 'If you can get 200,000 Hebrew Christians with their zeal and intelligence we shall win Protestantism for Rome'." At the same meeting Leon also stated that if the Mohammedans were to be won to Christianity, the Jews, humanly speaking, were the only people who might accomplish it. "But the devil," he added, "has done his utmost to shut the eyes of the Christian Church to the great possibilities in the Christian Jew in this regard."

And in an interview he spoke of the Jewish contribution to the interpretation of the Bible, and of those who, like himself, had come from the Middle East. "They lived in the country where Jesus enacted His miracles. . . They know what He talked about in a way that many people of the Western hemisphere, who do not know the customs of the East, cannot realise."

He probably illustrated this from a text on which he often preached, "Ask and ye shall receive." He used to say that these words meant more to the Easterner who had seen long rows of beggars sitting with outstretched hands. Again, he would picture a beggar wondering today whether someone will drop him enough coins

171

to feed himself and his family. The beggar knows what it means to ask. Likewise, he would illustrate "Knock, and it shall be opened" with the picture of a traveller pounding on the city gate which had just been closed for the night — rather than face the perils of the desert.

However, the chief consequence of the visit was the inspiration it brought to the American Alliance. It was at this conference that a dynamic young convert, the Rev Jacob Peltz, a worker in the Jewish Department of the Presbyterian Church, became its General Secretary, a post he held until, to Leon's delight, he crossed the Atlantic in 1933 to become General Secretary of the I.H.C.A. Writing of Leon's visit, Peltz said: "I could see the value of the Alliance as the beginning of a great Hebrew Christian movement. And when Sir Leon Levison addressed our Twelfth Annual Conference. . . my vision of the possibilities of this movement became enlarged and my enthusiasm for it knew no bounds. Sir Leon addressed the delegates again and again. He stirred our hearts as no Hebrew Christian had done heretofore. His pictures of world Jewry, bewildered and destitute and in dire need of the Gospel of God's grace; his masterful arguments showing the power of a united Hebrew Christian movement to win the Jews for Christ and to inspire the Christian Church; the example of his own love for Hebrew Christians as well as his devotion to the cause of Jewish evangelisation at large — these things stirred our imaginations and led us all to reconsecrate our lives for the promotion of a united Hebrew Christian movement."

Home again, Leon, whose designation was now Superintendent of the Edinburgh Jewish Mission, endeavoured to establish its future. He wrote to the Jewish Mission Committee of the Established Church of Scotland requesting them to consider taking over, or at least becoming partly responsible for, the Mission. The union of the Established and United Free Churches was now in sight, and it seemed wise that in the final settlement (which took place in 1929) the work among Jews in Edinburgh should have a firm foothold in the Church. In Glasgow, where the Mission had been taken over by the U.F. Church in 1910, there was no problem. Both denominations joined forces at the U.F. Church's premises in Bedford Street.

His request resulted in the formation of a Joint Board drawn from the Church's committee and that of the Mission. Among its members was Katie, for whom it was an apprenticeship in committee work and a source of confidence for the years when, without Leon to support her, she would carry on his work on the Alliance's Executive and others of its committees.

An elderly Jewess, Mrs Withers (neé Stolle), has provided a glimpse of the Mission at this time. One Saturday in 1928 her mother took her there. Annie was aged twelve and now, sixty years on, says she cannot forget that day. She was entranced by Leon, who spoke as she had never heard anyone speak before. "It wasn't like a sermon. He just stood and looked at us and explained the stories in the Bible so simply and" (with her hand on her heart) "his words seemed to come right in here. And he was so smart in his grey suit and so handsome. . ." Well, she was twelve! She added that Miss Thomson was at the piano, and that Sir Leon had told them what page the 23rd Psalm was on and had taught them to sing it. Afterwards she met him and he sent her to a chemist's to get some Vapex, which he recommended to her mother for colds. Later she was sent to Albert Terrace with a note from her mother. Lady Levison brought her in and she watched Rosalin and David playing tennis until Sir Leon came. He asked so kindly for her mother. Later again, he asked her mother if he could take Annie to an exhibition in the Music Hall, where he let her wander around while he saw some friends. And when she left school, and the headmaster said she should not go to work yet because she was bright, it was Leon who offered to buy the books she required for the secretarial college. Several years later she came home one afternoon to find Miss Thomson with her mother, who was distressed and tried to hide her tears. "What has happened?" asked Annie: "I can't believe it," said her mother, "Sir Leon has died."

Annie's most cherished memory was of that day in 1928 when her mother said, "Come with me to Nicolson Street: I want you to see someone who loves all Jewish people and helps them." And at the Mission she noticed many poor people and that Sir Leon was giving them small sums of money — say, five shillings or half-a-crown. In this, of course, he was overstepping the guidelines and giving Rabbi Daiches grounds for his allegations of bribery. Yet he never offered money as a persuasion. It was a time when extreme poverty had hit the working classes, the year of the General Strike. Britain had gone off the gold standard and the poorer Jewish families were suffering alongside their British compatriots. At home as well as at the

Mission Leon and Katie did what they could, providing not just for the next meal but for future maintenance. In this they probably erred, as Leon had done twenty years before, on the side of generosity, and were 'taken for a ride' by one or two to whom money was lent to support their businesses as small traders.

Yet though philanthropy ran hand in hand with evangelism, it was not its tool. Evangelism as practised by the mainstream Churches and missionary societies was neither predatory nor aggressive. When all the Jewish missions came together for the first time in conference in 1927, they deliberately avoided the word 'conversion' in defining their theme. It was entitled not The Conversion of the Jew, but The Christian Approach to the Jew. Nor did they think in terms of abrogating one religion for another. Jesus had come not to destroy but to fulfil, and they saw in Christianity the fulfilment of Jewish aspirations, of Moses, whose Law was not rejected but re-stated, and of the prophets. When a Jew accepted Jesus as the Messiah he forsook neither Moses nor his own heritage. He entered a larger room; but the house was still Jewish, for Jesus never ceased to be a Jew.

This is a point which Leon, as a missionary, would attempt to convey without clichés of the 'born again' or 'washed in the blood' variety. He had no religious patter, and his normal phraseology was that of a reticent Scottish Presbyterian. Only at the Keswick Convention, or in similarly evangelical circles of which there were many among the Hebrew Christians and their supporters, did he use such phrases as 'our dear Lord'. Like Paul he had learned to be all things to all men, or, as we say today, to have empathy. Confronted with friendly Jews, he would be interested in their concerns, put his feet under their table, enjoy their Yiddish phrases, their Jewish jokes and traditions, and explain quite naturally to them why he had become a missionary. His longing was certainly for their conversion, in the sense not of adopting a new religion but of becoming 'new men in Christ'. They believed already in a forgiving God, but here was the personal assurance of forgiveness; they had heard of the *chesed* or graciousness of God, but here was the amazing grace of which John Newton sang; they had striven to obey the *Torah* but here was the power to do it; they had known suffering and injustice and been baffled by *Yahweh*'s seeming impassivity, but they now heard how in Christ He carried their griefs and shared their sorrows.

To the orthodox Jew conversion means something different — the 'conning' of the gullible into an alien religion. Hence when strident young Messianic Christians in America, Britain and even Israel today, with zeal outrunning love, make a dead set at young Jews, especially in the student world, they gratuitously anger not only the Orthodox but, as in Israel, the secular Jews as well. Moreover, their aggressive proselytism has earned the rebuke of Christian leaders, among them Cardinal Hume.

We are still at the year 1926. Nahum at this time was midway through his Johnshaven years. He was seldom in Edinburgh, but remained involved in the Alliance and contributed regularly to the *Quarterly*. He also published *The Parables: Their Background and Local Setting* in 1926 and *Passiontide* in 1927. "Books on the parables are numerous", wrote Professor Peake in the *Holborn Review*, "but this has a distinctive place of its own." He gave examples of the fresh insights supplied from the author's Palestinian background and unique experience. "There is a further interest in observing how certain elements in Christianity, very familiar to ourselves, strike one who has been brought up in Judaism." Professor W.F. Howard characterised *Passiontide* also as "a fresh and devout study." "Needless to say," he added, "there is a flavour not often found in devotional addresses on that theme."

In his Preface to *Passiontide* Nahum refers to the nightly Holy Week services he had held "ever since I came here in 1922," and expresses the hope "that we of the Free Churches will forget the associations which Lent and Passiontide have had; that we will restore Christ's steps with minds disabused of all superstition." In other words, it was time the puritan backlash of the Reformation gave way to the restoration of the Christian Year; it was a process then gaining ground in the Established Church but scarcely begun in the various Free Churches in Britain.

In June of that year Leon took part in another Palestine Exhibition which visited Edinburgh and Glasgow. He was also exercising his eldership. From February 1925 to March 1927 he attended fourteen Kirk Session meetings, missing only four, two of them when he was in America. He also took his turn at policing the queues waiting for admittance to the evening services. For Dr Black's charismatic ministry was now in full flight, and the pews in such demand that only seat holders, who paid a rent, were admitted until ten minutes before the service. In his contribution to *The Tradi-*

tion of St George's West, Leon remarked on the charitable spirit of the queue, members of which he had found acknowledging the fairness of the system and realising that their stewards also had to wait in the rain; though so full was the church that the hindmost in the queue had often to sit on the wide pulpit steps. It was in 1926 that Leon first addressed the congregation's Young Men's Guild, his subject being "The Old Testament Today". A student who was there still remembers that he told them the origin of spring cleaning; probably it was the Passover injunction that "there shall be no leaven in your house" (Exodus chapters 12 and 13).

1927 was a comparatively uneventful year, much of it being taken up with planning the Alliance's second international conference. The venue chosen was Hamburg, where Dr Frank's Mission offered splendid facilities in and around the Jerusalem Kirche and its Deaconess House and Hospital. Dr. Frank's reputation in the city and among Hebrew Christians, and Mrs Frank's Irish warmth and hospitality (she had been a deaconess, as was also their daughter, of the Presbyterian Church of Ireland), made them ideal hosts. Gradually a programme was devised, papers invited on a variety of subjects, and invitations despatched. The latter included a return-ticket for a Russian delegate, provided by a lady supporter.

The fact that the international conference on *The Christian Approach to the Jew* took place in Budapest and Warsaw in April gave Leon the opportunity to visit some of the recently formed European Alliances. He spent eight days at Lodz with Pastor Peter Smoljar who was for several years on the I.H.C.A.'s Executive Committee, and became familiar with several groups in Poland. Probably it was at this time that he visited Vienna, where the Austrian Alliance was led by a distinguished advocate, Dr Foldes.

In London in September there was a follow-up to the Budapest-Warsaw Conference. Meanwhile Leon was not neglecting his work in Edinburgh. In his first report to the Church's Jewish Mission Committee he said: "Our work is not restricted to the Edinburgh Jewish population. Jews come in for interview from such places as Greenock, Dundee, Aberdeen and as far South as Newcastle, and it may interest the Church to know that amongst the former converts we had a rabbi from Greenock, his wife and family, who joined the Church by baptism." In October he reported three more baptisms.

In November, the Rev. T.B. Stewart Thomson, who was now

convener of the Committee, reported the baptism of a young Jewess in his church of St. Stephen's, this being the fifth he had performed as fruits of the Edinburgh Mission. Then on January 30th he informed them that since the Mission had been taken over by the Church of Scotland he had received eight Jews into the Church by baptism and that others were being prepared.

Meanwhile Leon had become involved, as so often before, in a dubious act of charity, the recipients being a Dr Shawkat, of Middle Eastern origin, his wife and four children. The doctor apparently needed money in order to pursue his studies while waiting for a sum promised from Egypt. Leon guaranteed that a loan would be refunded, and the Committee agreed to give not more that £50 in weekly payments. Three months later Dr Shawkat returned £13 of the £25 he had received. However, a letter of a year later addressed to Leon's friend Ernest Brown, the Liberal M.P. for Central Leith and signed by J. Locker Lampson M.P., Minister at the Foreign Office declares:

"With reference to my letter . . . of the 6th February regarding the claim of Sir Leon Levison against Ahmed Shawkat we have now received a report from the Residency, Cairo.

"The Acting High Commissioner. . . fears he can make no useful suggestions as to the course which Sir Leon Levison should pursue other than that suggested in my previous letter to you, that he should bring an action in the Court in Egypt. . . Mr Hoare doubts, however, whether in view of the facts concerning Shawkat and his family. . . Sir Leon Levison will stand to gain anything financially by pursuing the matter. There seems, unfortunately, little doubt that Shawkat is a thoroughly undesirable character." Whether this refers to the father or his repatriated son, the Shawkats seem to have embroiled Leon in a hopeless situation; it was one in which he might have been dubbed by Americans as a 'sucker' or a 'fall guy'. Once bitten, he was always ready to be bitten again, such was the softness of his heart.

We do not know how the debacle was resolved. What is certain is that in what might have seemed to him an act of penance, Leon undertook an additional commitment for the Mission. "It was resolved", says a minute, "that the monthly meetings addressed by Sir Leon Levison, be re-started on the fourth Thursday of each month, the first meeting being held on 25th October in 22, Queen Street". This was then the Church of Scotland Offices. The object of these meetings was to introduce a new clientèle, that of the Established Church, to Leon and the Mission.

As his activities expanded, so did his circle of friends. The Alliance produced many and in particular its General Secretary, the Rev. A.P. Gold-Levin, appointed with Leon at Islington. A Baptist minister, distinguished scholar, and able administrator, with a considerable presence, a finely shaped head, dark eyes, sensitive features and a pointed beard, he was a gentle companion and colleague until his early death in 1932.

The Liberal Club was also a source of friendships. Ernest Brown (of the Shawkat letter), who became an M.P. in 1927 and was in World War II to become Secretary of State for Scotland, had met Leon before Westminster claimed him. He was an engaging character, warm, friendly and very able. He was successively Minister of Health, Secretary to the Mines Department, Minister of Labour, and a Privy Councillor. However, it was the mingling of political acumen with evangelical sympathies which drew them together; for Brown was also a lay preacher, a Brotherhood worker, and Honorary Treasurer of the Baptist Missionary Society.

Another good friend at the club was Sir James Leishman, who was chairman of the Scottish Board of Health in 1928-29. A generous-hearted man, he did much for the welfare of his city, among his benefactions being a cricket pavilion in The Meadows. On one occasion he helped Leon out of what threatened to be another scandal. A Jewish picture-dealer told Leon that he had acquired some valuable pictures from an elderly lady in Glasgow, and he brought several of these, over a period of days, to Albert Terrace. Leon was not hard to convince, and encouraged his next-door neighbour, Bailie Robertson, to make a large purchase. When Leishman heard of this he offered to bring Stanley Cursiter, the distinguished Scottish artist, to evaluate them. Cursiter found that they were all fakes. A financial arrangement was made by which Robertson was, as far as possible, reimbursed, and Leishman contributed £50 to let Leon off the hook.

Leishman, being fond of Leon, wanted to meet his family, and he invited Katie and Fred (John was unavailable) to the club for lunch.

The name Cramond was often on Leon's lips. It belonged to another club member who, as a small token of his indebtedness to Leon, presented John and Fred, shortly after the War, with cricketing gear. Leon had stood by him at a time of great distress.

Mrs Cramond had died of arsenic poisoning, and when some arsenic was found in the garden shed, suspicion was aroused and her husband charged with murder. He was cleared, but not before every detail of his family life had been exposed in the Press; for it was a *cause célèbre*. Many, assuming his guilt, deserted him, but Leon never doubted his innocence.

Acquaintances at the club were wide-ranging. There was Fred's headmaster, Dr John Alison — "Ah, Alison, I know him at the club" — a disquieting remark to a schoolboy who wanted to remain inconspicuous! Later, when Fred was taken by a fellow student to Nicolson Square Methodist Church to hear Dr Alfred Whitham preach, Leon said "Ah, Whitham, I know him at the club; go round and tell him who you are." After hearing a magnificent sermon — for Whitham could outpreach anyone in Edinburgh save Dr Black but, not being of The Kirk, was generally unknown — the two young men were warmly welcomed and invited to the Methodist manse. To have met the saintly Whitham, whose *Discipline and Culture of the Christian Life* and other books were to become a spiritual standby, was a privilege, and to hear him speak warmly of Leon a delight.

Rob Sutherland, who as a student became a close friend of the family, was invited to the club by Leon in 1931. It was a thoughtful gesture, for Rob, a Caithness man, was devoted to his local laird and M.P., Sir Archibald Sinclair, and Sir Archie was a guest of honour. The occasion was a complimentary dinner to the Liberal members of the Cabinet in the new National Government — Ernest Brown, Sir Godfrey Collins and Sir Archibald.

Leon's other guest was Dr Donald Davidson, with whom Nahum, who by that time was ministering in Leith, had struck up a friendship. The two brothers and Dr Davidson were to combine in several enterprises — for instance, in bringing the Australian evangelist Lionel Fletcher to Edinburgh; and Dr Davidson was, in 1935, to become Fred's 'bishop' in South Leith Parish Church. Many years later it was he who took the funeral services of both Katie and one of her daughters-in-law.

By the mid-thirties Leon's work was so all-absorbing that he was seldom at the club, and by 1936 had left it. This, however, was not before both the Liberal and Labour parties had made overtures to him to become a parliamentary candidate.

That, though, is a later story. By 1927 he was becoming known,

and not only in Christian circles. That July the Samaritan High Priest appealed to him for help. Only one page of his letter from Nablus, the ancient Shechem, remains, but it is worth quoting:-
"Dear and Honoured Sir,
On behalf of my small but ancient Community I take the liberty to approach you. The. . .Community is small, a little over 150 souls, but. . .has suffered untold agonies during the past two thousand years.

Our lot has been a very sad one, especially during the six hundred years of Turkish rule. And now a terrible calamity has befallen. . . and being the smallest community and with no friends, and no kind of representatives in the world, we are simply helpless. . .People write books about our past history, but no one cares to know if we are able to keep our bodies alive and continue the struggle of life.

Our houses are gone and those of my people who had some little shops are all destroyed and we are literally starving. Now it's summer, we live in the open and we can exist, but winter will come and if some aid will not come. . ."

Leon must have responded for when, with Katie and Fred, he visited Samaria in 1930, they received a particularly warm welcome, as Fred's travel-diary shows: "Met Samaritans and High Priest. Took snaps — privilege, he doesn't allow photos. To synagogue and High Priest's house. Saw scroll that King Edward not allowed to see — 2000 years old, time of Maccabees — kept in cheap case, other in silver case, so that thief will steal wrong one. Priest gave us coffee. Poverty of Samaritans — want school, even under Christians as long as not under Moslems. . . Through narrow, dirty, smelly streets. . ."

Nablus is now a modern city on the West Bank, and the Samaritans have survived.

As 1928 began Charlie Ridland handed over the Mission's books before departing for California, and the Alliance donated £10 towards the hire of a room at 24, Nicolson Square, where the Mission's new headquarters were to be.

In April, Leon and Dr Black were in Jerusalem for a meeting of the International Missionary Council. In the same month he addressed the British Alliance at its conference. He then busied himself with the July number of the *Quarterly* and with final preparations for the Hamburg Conference in July.

Meanwhile word was coming in of distress in Russia. The Rev. Boris Shapiro, President of the Russian Alliance, had visited groups of Hebrew Christians in Moscow, Kiev and other places. He reported "a great revival among the Jews in several towns" but was heartbroken at the suffering he encountered. There were "almost indescribable conditions" and "the scourge of consumption taking a deadly toll." In each place he had given £8 in relief, but this was "merely a drop in the ocean". The I.H.C.A. sent £50 and appealed for more. There was also the £35 donation to enable a Russian to come to Hamburg. After the Conference a further £50 was sent to Russia and £110 to seven other countries.

The Hamburg Conference was an enormous success. There assembled 130 delegates from twelve Alliances, and representatives from others in the process of formation. 153 members and friends attended the closing Communion Service. It was the largest reunion of Hebrew Christians from many lands since the time of the Apostles. But the success was not in the numbers; it was in the unity of spirit manifested in this multi-national, multi-lingual, multi-denominational Christian assembly, most of whose members were strangers to one another. Many had arrived conscious of being 'the twice-exiled people' — as Jews from Zion and as Christians from their fellow-Jews; they returned rejoicing that they had found a new Jewish family.

In the light of history Leon's opening words at the Welcome Meeting seem ironical. When, he said, the proposal was made that the Conference should take place in Germany, "I was overjoyed at the opportunity of being able to express our thanks to Germany, the Germany that has led so many brothers of Israel to the Saviour."

Leon's contribution was vast. Not only did he preside and give the opening and closing addresses, but at every spare moment he gave himself to the delegates. Each day as he walked to the Zoo Restaurant for lunch, he arranged to have someone from a different Alliance beside him, as well as a different leader at every meal. Katie too, at her first international gathering, mingled freely. She was especially impressed with a Mr Feighin from Bessarabia, formerly a cantor in the synagogue, who had come to Christ "well advanced in years". "He stirred us to the depths", she wrote in the *Quarterly*, "by his singing unaccompanied (in Yiddish) of a hymn which translated is 'As a heart panteth after a water brook'. It was our privilege to stay in the same house . . . and his beautiful faith and trust about all the minor things of everyday life were an example to us all." Nahum added that his testimony was given "with Pauline fire and Johannine tenderness."

Among Fred's memories is an excursion by pleasure-boat on the Alster. The delegates were arriving and Leon was meeting them; but thoughtfully he arranged that Katie and Fred, who did not speak German, should have with them a Hebrew Christian girl and her German fiancé. Deeply in love, innocent and kind, they were mercifully ignorant of their doom. Yet by the time they were married and had an infant family — if that was their immediate future — their home would be shattered by Hitler's decrees. Did she end up in a death camp and he in the Army? Or, did they by a miracle, escape? And what of the children? We shall never know. The memory, tinged with sadness, of that trip on the Alster remains.

No major decisions were taken at the conference. These came later, when a strong Executive had been formed and the organisation had matured. Nevertheless kites were flown on many subjects, and there were papers on "The Training of Hebrew Christians", "An Industrial Centre in Poland?", "A Colony in Palestine?" and "The Religious Condition of the Jews in Hungary". A committee was appointed to create "an organisation for the publication of literature, presenting Christ to the Jew and interpreting the Jew to the Church." Yet another resolution pledged aid for the hiring of halls in many countries to enable the Hebrew Christians to come together and make a united witness.

Papers, scholarly, devotional and practical were given, and were published subsequently in the *Quarterly*. Several languages were employed, often the exile language of Yiddish. However, in the well-attended public meetings in the evenings it was German.

The Alliance was greatly strengthened by the appointments of Gold-Levin as Hon. General Secretary and Harcourt Samuel as Recording Secretary. Four Vice-Presidents representing the work in Europe, America, the East and Far East (including Africa), and the British Empire, were also elected; and Leon's plea that they should serve for three years, and so give him maximum help, was granted.

Gold-Levin and Samuel were a splendid duo. The former, of Russian origin, was, like Nahum, intended for the rabbinate and studied at Jerusalem. He came upon a New Testament and, for studying it, was expelled. Like Leon he came to Britain and, through the Jewish Mission of the English Presbyterian Church, received missionary training and commenced work as their Deputy. Ordained in 1910, in 1917 he transferred to the Baptists. He served the British Society for the Propagation of the Gospel to the Jews as their missionary in Liverpool. A scholar but not a recluse, he had doctorates from Athens and Serbia, and was an F.R.G.S. His was a wise and gentle influence in the Alliance, of which he became a Vice-President, and in which he was much loved.

Harcourt Samuel, a younger man, is with us still, and in his eighties has become President of the British Alliance. A Baptist minister in Essex and then in Ramsgate, of which he also became Mayor, he was awarded the O.B.E. From the I.H.C.A.'s inception Leon marked him out, and from then on they were friends and colleagues. Harcourt's contribution to the Alliance, and his support for Leon, have been immense.

During the conference Leon spoke on "The Further Consolidation of the I.H.C.A." At the close of his address all the delegates stood "as a token of their deep respect for the President, and their grateful appreciation of his labours." A resolution was then passed recording "deep gratitude to Almighty God for the blessings of health, of general mercies, for gifts of grace and intellect vouchsafed to our President, Sir Leon Levison, during the past three years." Following this, his re-election became a formality!

The assembly also expressed thanks to Katie "for her valuable co-operation with Sir Leon in all his labours", and Ben Rohold spoke "as a personal friend" of the sacrifices she had made. Katie replied impromptu: "Believing, as I do from my heart, that this movement is in the plan of God, how could I stand in the way by holding my husband back? To feel I was sharing in that plan was compensation enough for any little sacrifice I have had to make."

She was to speak again. For on the last day she was given a gold wristwatch, "a memento of the Conference", said Dr Frank, "and as an expression of our love for your husband". Leon then presented a gold pen to Mrs Frank. It was, in Germanic fashion, received by her husband, who thanked the delegates on her behalf.

The greatest token of appreciation, however, was the decision to seek a full-time secretary for the Alliance. The conference was very conscious of the burden Leon was carrying. The Treasurer, on presenting his balance-sheets, for instance, referred to the amount of work Leon had done. "Nearly all the money that the two balance-sheets represent, with the exception of the monies that have been sent to us from America, has actually been raised by the President himself through his unfailing efforts on behalf of our cause."

Mr Rohold, too, was concerned for Leon. "Our President is now in the prime of life. Does the Conference want him to become old before his time, or to break down in health?" He was moving the resolution that £1,000 be raised for the salary and office expenses of a full-time General Secretary, and a further £2,000 "to meet the various obligations pertaining to this office." It was before the next Conference, three years later, that Harcourt Samuel was appointed.

It should be said of the conference that it was not a hermetically enclosed group of Christians withdrawn in a city to which they paid no heed. Not only were the evening meetings open to the public, but on the eve of the conference Leon addressed Hamburg's English-speaking community in the British and American Seamen's Chapel; again, a rally in a public park drew some two thousand people.

To say more would be to obscure the essence of an event which was essentially inspirational. As Katie expressed it in her second utterance, "It has been a great inspiration to be here and to see you all, and I feel I shall be inspired to help my husband even more. . . for seeing is realising in a way that one could never do by letters, or by what he tells me." Finally, both she and Nahum in their written impressions, and Leon in an editorial, fastened on the closing Communion Service, whose prayers and readings were mainly in Hebrew, as the high water mark.

The Jerusalem Kirche, then, seemed the Jerusalem of Pentecost, of many tongues but one spirit, and of tongues of fire. Hence, like the disciples when on another occasion they had been with the Risen Lord, they returned to their everyday tasks with great joy, continually praising and blessing God.

NOTES:
1. *Murder in the Cathedral.* Faber and Faber, 4th Ed., p. 73.

Leon, 1928

16. HAMBURG TO HIGH LEIGH

In returning from Hamburg, Leon and Nahum were, in addition to their everyday tasks, involved in new enterprises, in Leon's case the amalgamation of two publishing firms, in Nahum's the production of another book.

Leon's intervention was triggered off by a breakdown in the relationship between *The Life of Faith* and the authorities of the Keswick Convention. The other leading evangelical magazine, *The Christian*, and its publishers also had a deep interest in the Convention and a stake in its publications. Leon had for long been concerned about this divided witness, and now grasped the opportunity of making the evangelical testimony more effective.

He bought the firm of Morgan & Scott, including *The Christian*, and amalgamated it with Marshall Brothers, including *The Life of Faith*. He then became Chairman of the Board of Directors of Marshall, Morgan and Scott Ltd. As a result, his meetings in London were extended, and he became a regular visitor to the Keswick Convention where he presided over an annual lunch on behalf of the firm. The guest-list, at the Royal Oak Hotel, included Council members, speakers, editors and publishers, and as a result Leon deepened his growing friendship with Fred and Harold Marshall, Dr Thirtle, editor of *The Christian*, for whom he gave a complimentary luncheon, and his successor, Charles Cook.

How was the merger financed? Was it with Katie's money? She was certainly well-off, but scarcely to this extent. When she died, forty years later, she left £46,000 and a modest house to her four children. She had for many years contributed generously to Hebrew Christian and Church causes but was too cautious to have reduced her capital drastically. It is likely that Leon, with his capacity for money-raising, found other sources; but there appears to have been no consortium. Anyhow the venture was successful, and the Alliance, as well as the Christian press, benefited through increased support from all the parties concerned.

During and after the negotiations the Marshall brothers came from time to time to Edinburgh, and Fred, who was reading *The Forsyte Saga*, saw in them a resemblance both to Galsworthy himself and to his Edwardian characters. Neatly dressed, impeccably mannered, clean-shaven and bald, reserved and silent, they might have been City stockbrokers; yet an occasional twinkle in the eye, or gentle smile, revealed men not only of property but of faith.

Leon was becoming more and more involved in the staunchly Protestant-Evangelical wing of British church life, and he became less enamoured of the churches of the Establishment which, in Scotland as in England, appeared somewhat formal in worship and lacking in missionary zeal. This was also the stance of the Alliance, which even in these latter more ecumenical days has little rapport with Catholic or Roman Christianity.

As for Nahum, his new venture into authorship was not a happy one. Together with his old friend and teacher, Dr James Kennedy the New College Librarian, he had written *An Aid to the Textual Amendment of the Old Testament*. Unfortunately, the abundance of Hebrew and Greek words made its printing costs so formidable that only Nahum's cousin Jacob ben Zvi, who was manager of a printing press in Jerusalem, would take it on. The results were disastrous. "Printers' errors abounded", wrote Nahum, "and made this book, which is the best scientific attempt at amending the Hebrew text, very difficult to follow save by experts in these matters." Since the pages, as they were printed, took six weeks to reach Edinburgh, the printers would not agree to send a second proof, and T. & T. Clark published a very faulty edition. Two years later, in 1929, Sir Thomas Clark wrote to Nahum, "It has come to my knowledge that a certain scholar who had been asked to review the book has been so struck with the number of glaring errors that he would have no option but to write an extremely unfavourable opinion. . . There is, I fear, a real danger that the reputations of Dr Kennedy and yourself will suffer. In this case I would commend for your serious consideration the advisability of withdrawing the book from circulation. Even withdrawal will be difficult to carry out effectively, but it may be the lesser of two evils".

The authors did not withdraw, and their reputations may well have suffered. Some years later, when Nahum failed to obtain a professorship, this may have been a contributory factor.

1928 ended quietly. In September the family attended Marjory Kelly's wedding in Glasgow, and in December Leon was able to take time off to see Fred perform as Macbeth at Watson's College. 1929 began with Nahum being inducted to a new charge at Blantyre, the mining village in Lanarkshire which was the birthplace of David Livingstone.

This was the year in which the major Presbyterian Churches in Scotland were reunited. In Scotland, and indeed in Christendom, it was a major event. Yet one wonders whether Leon was right to assume it was a topic of prime concern to the *Quarterly's* cosmopolitan readership. Certainly he did not report other religious events outside the Jewish field. Here, however, he 'went to town', printing in full two sermons which he had procured from distinguished guest preachers at Free St George's, Dr Henry Sloan Coffin and Dr J. Douglas Adam.

He also went out of his way to report the death of Dr Kelman. "We cannot let this issue go to press without referring to the Home-call of Dr John Kelman on May 3rd. Dr Kelman was Sir Leon Levison's minister. . .and was always most sympathetic and interested in [his] work amongst the Jews and, during a time of serious illness he was a most devoted pastor and a pillar of strength . . . [He] occupied a place in the affections of countless numbers which was unique, for there are scattered about the world today thousands of souls who have benefited by his ministry and. . . owe their faith in the Lord Jesus Christ to his influence and teaching."

Leon was being rather self-indulgent, for few of his readers would have heard of Kelman, but as with the formation of the united Church of Scotland, the occasion was of profound significance to himself. Moreover, both the resolving of the Keswick-*Life of Faith* impasse and the Union of the Churches were acts of reconciliation, the breaking down of walls to the greater glory of Christ, and that, in Leon's view, was a prime concern of Christianity.

The Union affected his work in that the Mission came under the jurisdiction of the General Assembly's Jewish Mission Committee and of its Secretary, the formidable Dr James Macdonald Webster.

Leon knew Dr Webster well, for the latter had been secretary of the Budapest-Warsaw Conference and of several others, and in addition had a wide reputation as an expert on Jewish missions.

The two men contrasted sharply. Macdonald Webster made a virtue of the fact that he did not, as Leon always did, suffer fools gladly. Across the mantelpiece in his office was inscribed in pokerwork, IF YOU HAVE HALF AN HOUR TO WASTE DON'T WASTE IT HERE. In contrast to Leon's leisurely evening interviews he would greet callers with an abrupt "I'll give you five minutes." His successor at the Budapest Mission quoted some Hungarians as saying "He is a good man but a *paraszt* [peasant]". He barked at people, sent scolding letters, and was feared more than loved. Few barked back. However, Principal Semple of Safed, a quick-tempered Irishman, did. When he went to see Dr Webster, their bawling matches resounded along the corridors!

With patience and tact Leon worked with him; and Dr Webster responded to the extent of sending his good wishes when the first *Quarterly* appeared. Leon also printed an address on *Christ and the Jewish World* which Dr Webster gave to the Presbyterian Alliance in 1929. Nevertheless, to work with someone who was brusque, irascible, and a Tartar for efficiency was a strain. Leon would frequently come home tired and grey after a session with his administrator.

However, any abrasiveness endured in Edinburgh was offset by positive achievements elsewhere. By now, in addition to its relief work, the Alliance was training a number of young converts: four girls for secretarial work, and three as nurses; a medical student in his final years before going to Mesopotamia as a missionary; and eight candidates for the mission field doing a three-year course at Bible Schools.

At this point came a windfall: the gift of an estate of 53 dunams (11.6 acres) a mile from the centre of Jerusalem. It seemed to be the answer to many prayers, for ever since 1925 the question had been put to Leon: "What about Palestine? Can we not do something there; set up a Hebrew Christian Institute or establish some other form of witness?" At the Budapest and Warsaw conferences in 1927 Hebrew Christians from various countries asked it. From Warsaw some of them had gone on to Bialystok. "Here", wrote Leon, "we spent three memorable days addressing crowded meetings and witnessing scenes the like of which we have never seen before, where Jews waited in queues for over an hour to hear the Gospel. . . In taking a walk in the company of the Rev. E.S. Greenbaum, President of the American Alliance, the first words he uttered were 'What about Palestine?'. . . In short, this topic occupied the minds of all of us at the Second I.H.C.A. Conference at Hamburg, and was made one of the principal subjects of prayer."

Soon afterwards, "I was addressing one of our monthly meetings in London," wrote Leon, "at the New Alliance Club, when our dear friend Mrs Petrie came up and informed me that the Committee for the Relief of Distressed Jews possessed a property in Jerusalem. . . and suggested that I might write to them to consider the possibility of their handing over this property to the I.H.C.A.. . . I addressed a letter to Miss Finn, the Acting Secretary of the above Society, of which her revered and esteemed mother was the Founder."

Miss Finn's father had, from 1845-1863, been H.M. Consul in Palestine. A devout Christian, he took a keen interest in the needs of the different peoples in the land and, according to Ben Rohold, "The Jewish people found in him a protector and friend, a guide and counsellor." Mrs Finn too, being a daughter of Dr Alexander McCaul (a renowned missionary who was offered the Anglican bishopric of Jerusalem but declined on the grounds that the first Bishop should be a Hebrew Christian)[1] was imbued with the same spirit. She devoted herself to the amelioration of the condition of impoverished Jewish immigrants. She was, said Rohold, "not only a pre-Herzl Zionist, but also a pre-Baron E. de Rothschild coloniser. Long before the Chovove Zion Society started their colonisation schemes. . . Mrs Finn already had a scheme at a place called Urtas. Later on she realised that [this] could not bring immediate relief. She therefore brought into being the Society for the Relief of Distressed Jews. . . She secured as President of that Society that great, noble Christian statesman and philanthropist, the Earl of Shaftesbury."

In 1851, Mrs Finn bought, and put in trust for the employment of poor Jews, the parcel of land known from time immemorial as Kerm el Khaleel — the Vineyard of the Friend of God, in short, Abraham's Vineyard. At that time there were no buildings outside the city walls, and a stone cottage on the estate was the first modern house erected there by Jewish hands. Later there was a large mansion-house. An interesting feature of the estate was two small mounds of earth, reputed to be the repository of ashes from the Temple sacrifices — a theory confirmed by an analyst from Vienna.

Miss Finn's Committee having resolved to hand the property to the Alliance, its Trustees consented to the appointment of Leon, Gold-Levin and Rohold to act as new Trustees along with Mrs Petrie.

The Alliance's proposals were clear, and by midsummer 1929 Leon described them thus: "We intend to adhere to the policy of the Society. . . and to give work to Jews in distress in Palestine, whether they be converted or not. Secondly, our plan will be to set up buildings where we can teach Hebrew Christians trades such as boot-making, carpentry, tailoring, printing, etc., in order that they may become self-supporting. Thirdly, in past years Jews were taught on this property to make olive oil soap. This we intend to revive. Last, but not least, we hope, in the providence of God, to build a Hebrew Christian Church. . ."

"I have decided," he added, "to go out personally to Palestine on the 17th March, 1930, in order to inspect the property and report thereon. . . Meantime we intend to start poultry farming and market gardening."

The suggestion was then made that at the same time a party might be formed to make a pilgrimage to the Holy Land. The Rev. William Burton D.D., of Everyman's Tours Ltd., was chosen as organiser, and a new friend of Leon's, the Rev. W. Erskine Blackburn, to conduct the religious services; while on the sea journey Leon would lecture on the sites to be visited, and later Rohold, long resident in Palestine, would accompany the party as guide.

In the event Mr Blackburn, on being called from Renfield Street Church in Glasgow to Egremont Presbyterian Church in Liverpool, had to withdraw. However, a few months later he was to be a guest speaker at the Third I.H.C.A. Conference. A man of great charm, and having had considerable business experience before entering the ministry, he was also a gifted communicator and was able by voice, pen and personal persuasion to do much for the Alliance.

The arrangements for the trip were all but halted by the horrendous events of August and September 1929 — the simultaneous, and therefore orchestrated, massacre of Jews in Jerusalem, Hebron, Tiberias and Safed, of which it is now generally accepted that the

CHRISTIAN AND JEW

Mufti of Jerusalem, Amin al Husseini, was the instigator. Fanatical and power-hungry, he had, at the age of thirty-five, seized the presidency of the Supreme Moslem Council, an event which would not have happened had not Sir Herbert Samuel, while Governor of Jerusalem, made the supreme mistake of his career. To appease the Arabs he gave an amnesty to some who had fled the country on being sentenced for acts of violence in 1920, and among them was both the future Mufti (who took upon himself the title *Grand* Mufti) and his henchman, the future District Officer of Hebron, both of whom found it easy to arouse to religious frenzy the illiterate fellahin. They had only to spread the infamous rumour that the Jews were going to destroy the Dome of the Rock and use its stones to rebuild their Temple.

News of the massacre aroused horror in many countries, but not everywhere. Beatrice Webb, whose husband Lord Passfield was Britain's Colonial Secretary, wondered what all the fuss was about. "As many are killed every week in London in traffic accidents, and no one pays any attention." Yet Professor Einstein, still in Berlin, wrote to the *Manchester Guardian* in sorrow at the coldness and lack of understanding shown by a section of the British press. "Arab mobs... murdered and plundered wherever no resistance was offered. In Hebron the inmates of a rabbinical college, innocent youths who had never handled weapons in their lives, were butchered in cold blood; in Safed the same fate befell aged rabbis and their wives and children... Is it not then amazing that an orgy of such primitive brutality upon a peaceful population has been utilised by a certain section of the British press for a campaign of propaganda directed not against the authors and instigators of these brutalities, but against their victims?" As for Dr Weizmann, these events marked the beginning of his struggle with the Colonial Office, in which he was to win the support of Baldwin, Smuts and Lloyd George.

With his family endangered in Safed, and friends and acquaintances murdered, Leon, though deeply upset, did not harbour anti-Arab feelings. He was fair-minded enough to isolate the elements that were responsible. In the *Quarterly* he analysed the causes, and concluded that "left alone, there is no reason whatever why the natives of Palestine and the Jews should not live happily together. Of this we have evidence in the acts which were not uncommon during the terrible days of outrage and pillage, when natives took Jews into their homes for shelter." Eight months later he made a point of telling his Church's General Assembly that on visiting Palestine and speaking to Arabs about the riots he had been confirmed in the view that it was the work of a few agitators who had incited the mob, but that the better-class Arabs had been dead against it.

In describing these events in the *Quarterly* he made the observation that "a thing was done which, to our mind, no fellah would have done under any circumstances in days gone by, namely the burning of the harvest, which was always held sacred by these Moslems as God's own gift and provision to man." He also commented that, shocked as he was, "the whole situation did not come as a surprise since we anticipated something of what has taken place as a result of the great blunder that was committed by the Palestine Administration during 1920."

Detailed accounts of the Safed massacre were given in letters from Mrs Semple at the Scots College. ". . . Troops were sent up from Tiberias, but they did not arrive until after the massacre was over, although looting was still going on in the town. . . Soldiers who did not know the town had no idea of what was happening. The one available British police officer was dropping with fatigue as he had not been in bed for five nights. . . There was no one to show the soldiers where to go but [he], as the twenty-five native police were all traitors. . . and, to make matters worse, the Commanding Officer in charge of the troops was poisoned on his way from Jerusalem at Jenin by taking a drink offered to him by a Moslem. He died and was buried here next day. This is a British officer added to the list of atrocities.

"Sir Leon's people are well and here with us, but they have lost everything, in fact they were burned out. His mother [she was then 79] was brought up from Ein Zeitoun by her daughter Rachel, grandson and his wife. There are many others; all, in fact, who are with us in the college have lost home and property and are destitute. . . Dr Torrance and another young doctor from Nazareth are now here. They were sent by the Government to attend to the wounded. We are gathering provisions wherever we can and making careful distribution amongst the helpless."

Leon lost no time in getting the Alliance to launch a Palestine Relief Fund, which Rohold was appointed to administer. He, together with his colleague in Haifa, Dr James Churcher, then toured the country assessing the most urgent needs. Rohold's first report on Safed contained this passage: "Two hundred and two houses were burned and looted and nineteen Jews were killed. The orphanage was burned and the old Rabbi — Ishmael Cohen — aged 85 years, and his wife, aged 80 years, were both killed.

"Here I had a very trying time. Safed is so far away from Jerusalem. . . thus they are away from the centre of relief. I spent a whole day there and arrived home late in the evening exhausted. It is terrible to think that in this town alone there are 270 families homeless. . . I spent £60 in Safed and I felt that it was well spent. And the gratitude of these dear people, I wish I could convey it to you."

Two months later Rohold was again in Safed accompanied by Paul Doany, an Arab Christian. They parted company and Doany later described some conversations he had with Jews. "Before they bid me 'Shalom'.", he wrote, "one old Orthodox Jew with the religious side-curls said: 'We have no doubt that the Nazarene Christ was a Jew, because we know a certain Jew who became a Christian. He was not well treated at first, and yet in this time of trouble as in all troubles, he visited the town many times and helped many of those who never wanted to shake hands with him before.' I said, 'Do you know his name?' Some of them said 'Robold', and I told them, 'That is our Superintendent, Mr Rohold', and showed them where he was to be found. Everyone began to say. . . 'We have missed him. We will have to go and shake hands with him. . .' Then the old man said 'We have seen from experience that that old man. . . has the spirit of the deliverer'. . . and an old woman said, 'God increase the number of those that love Israel.' Then I went on and found Mr Rohold still surrounded by many of those who had his sympathy and love and help. . . We slept that night with great joy because we felt we had done our duty to the relatives of Christ. . . And I remembered the word of Christ when he said: 'Whatever you do for the least of my brethren you do unto me.'."

Rohold was also asked by the Alliance to inspect Abraham's Vineyard. His report was not a good one, and must have caused some of the initial hopes and dreams to evaporate. The property was in a state of neglect, its boundary walls laid waste, the house unusable, and its sanitation destroyed. "The house suffered terribly during the war, and after the war the Government used it as a correction school for young offenders, and whatever they had then they have taken away with them."

Rohold's recommendations were: (a) that no one should be allowed to live there for "in the East if you put a man in your place you can never get him out!" (b) that any decision about repairs should be left until Leon's visit, (c) that the property was a white elephant and should be sold, and (d) that with the proceeds more suitable land should be purchased for a colony.

A few months later, however, it was reported that under the direction of the Rev A. C. Karmouche, a young Hebrew Christian working with the L.J.S. in Jerusalem, unemployed Jewish workers had cleared the grounds and set up walls. When Leon arrived in April Mr Karmouche showed him round. Pleased as he was with the progress, and finding that poultry farming had been started, beehives were being assembled, and a market garden attempted on two or three acres which seemed cultivable, he nonetheless shared Rohold's misgivings. Apart from these acres, the land was only fit for building on. Yet to put the house in order (vandals had removed even doors, window-frames and stairs), erect workshops, and purchase machinery and tools for an industrial colony, would require a capital of £8,000 — £10,000. At present £70 a month was needed to employ twenty-five Jews. To build a training school to prepare young converts for the ministry and mission field would require a further £10,000. Could these sums be raised?

Three suggestions, said Leon, had been put to him, and he offered these "in order that I may get a frank expression of opinion from our members, readers, and friends." Briefly, these were: (a) An Abraham's Vineyard Settlement on which Hebrew Christians and others would build houses. The Title Deeds would be held by the Alliance until the instalments representing the value of the land, plus five per cent, were paid. The proceeds would then go into a Trust Fund from which further settlements could be built. Sir Moses Montefiore's property, it was pointed out, had similarly expanded to six settlements, while the original Montefiore Fund had increased. (b) The property should be sold, on condition that its name was retained. Agricultural land could be bought and a colony established, each settler paying back by instalments its cost, and ultimately becoming a landowner. (c) Half the land should be retained, and the other half sold to establish a Trust Fund. Its investments would provide sufficient interest to equip the buildings as an Alliance headquarters, a meeting-place and a library and reading-room.

Meanwhile, with Hebraic shrewdness and enterprise, a stone-crushing machine was hired and 250 metres of stones crushed. "It is reckoned that it will cost us 7s. per metre and we hope to be able to sell the crushed stones at 9s. per metre. [They] are used for mixing with cement to make concrete blocks."

Improvements were carried out in the house, and a married couple was installed as wardens. They were optimistic as to the Vineyard's future, but in January 1931 Leon reported in the *Quarterly* that in the Jerusalem Development Scheme roads were scheduled to cross the property, which was also an obstacle to residential expansion. "We are being urged on all sides to sell. . . Promises are being made that the name of Consul and Mrs Finn will be perpetuated by naming the streets after them. . . and the houses will be called 'Abraham's Vineyard Settlement'. . . We are also led to understand that with the money from the sale. . . we could buy eight times as much land."

Early in 1931 the Trustees, meeting in the house of the Rev A. H. Finn, their benefactor's son, decided to sell the property, to purchase arable land, and to found a Hebrew Christian Colony. They hoped to gain £15,000 but estimated that £22,000 would be needed for the project.

The scheme met with delays. The High Court of Palestine had to grant permission, and the purchasers had to satisfy the Town Planning Commission. It was April 1932 before Leon was able to intimate that a first instalment of money had been received. It would be tedious to describe the frustrating attempts to buy land which then followed; the visits not only of Leon but of other emissaries such as Hugh Schonfield and Harcourt Samuel, the attempts to buy land at Gaza foiled by ever more restrictive land laws, the sudden inflation of land values, and the deviousness of landowners. Had Rohold not died in 1931, had Karmouche not been moved from Jerusalem to Baghdad and then Australia, had the Palestine Alliance not then collapsed in an acrimonious dispute, and had the decision to sell the property been taken earlier, something might have been achieved.

Sir Arthur Wauchope, the High Commissioner, told Leon in July 1934 that a survey was being carried out and "I have arranged for them to deal first of all with that part of the Turkman lands in which the plot that you are purchasing is situated. . . I appreciate your anxiety on behalf of the refugees. . . and I regret that these processes of survey and settlement have been so long delayed, but I am sure you will understand the necessity for the firm establishment of your title before proceeding further with your scheme."

Yet by 1936, the colony was still in abeyance. "Our own disappointments," wrote Nahum in the *Quarterly*, "have been hard to bear. For the second time we were on the point of getting land when our Alliance there, whom we asked to co-operate with us in the matter, countermanded the orders given by the Trustees in London. . . but we hope that as soon as things settle down a little we shall at last acquire the land."

Far from settling down, however, the situation became more disturbed. That June, Richard Hughes, the I.H.C.A.'s agent in Jerusalem, wrote, "Owing to the serious riots all through the country, it has been impossible to meet the owner to discuss terms. . . These riots have made the colonisation of a new area a very serious matter, and I feel discouraged. . . No negotiations can be entertained until the political question is quieter. At present it is more than anyone's life is worth to enter into land transactions of any kind."

Before 1936 ended Leon had died. By this time the scale of emigration from Europe had closed Palestine's doors to virtually all who clamoured for admission. A year later, in desperation, the Alliance turned to Ecuador as a possible alternative. However, although some Jewish organisations succeeded there, the Alliance did not, and the dream of a colony remained unfulfilled. The most that can be said is that in the post-war years a few pockets of Hebrew Christians are to be found in Israel; that the Alliance is at work in Haifa; and that missionary endeavours associated with the Alliance are succeeding, in spite of the Israeli Government's clampdown on proselytising, in making a fruitful witness up and down the land.

Now, however, we return to 1930. Before setting out for Palestine on March 9th Leon managed to have a clear fortnight at home, in the course of which the whole family and Katie's sister Annie, now widowed, saw Fred and his friend Mary Duncan perform the dream sequence from *Dear Brutus*, and also as Hamlet and Ophelia, in St George's West's *Sketches and Dialogues*. Three days later Leon and

Katie were at the outstanding war play, *Journey's End*. They also called on Nahum and Margaret in their new manse in Blantyre, and were visited by Mrs Macleod, formerly 'Old Nurse'.

Katie and Fred joined Leon's and Dr Burton's tour on March 29th. The party had called at Athens and Constantinople (where Leon visited the Scottish Mission) and at Beirut they were joined by Rohold. Katie and Fred journeyed via Port Said, and on the voyage from Marseilles she joined in the deck-billiards and read Wodehouse. Leon and Rohold, arm in arm and in ebullient form, met them at Haifa, and they rode through the streets in Rohold's open and ancient car while he greeted the passers-by, most of whom were his friends.

Of that visit to Palestine I select some highlights. Apart from the sacred sites, which were visited with the party, these are occasions concerning Leon. None was more memorable than the meeting with his mother and other members of his family. Small and frail, she greeted us affectionately outside her house, but was unwilling to have any but Leon in, either because we were Gentiles, or in the belief that ours was a grand house in Edinburgh and hers a shameful dwelling! She had no English, but Leon translated her words of delight. None of us would see her again, for she died a few months later. "It's of poignant interest," said the *Quarterly* in November, "that Sir Leon should have seen his mother so recently... and he is greatly comforted by hearing that in the last letter which she wrote to a brother she said how greatly she had been helped by his talks with her on religion, and how at last she saw everything from his point of view." For his part, he described her as "just as sweet a mother as God has given to a son."

Leon was surprised and impressed with the welcome he received in his home-town and elsewhere. "I never dreamt that I, a Hebrew Christian, and one who is looked upon by the Jews as the leader of Hebrew Christianity throughout the world, would be received, far less welcomed, by the Jews in the Holy Land... They sent deputations to me and even gave receptions in my honour, but the thing that cheered my heart most was the numerous callers who sought me in private to discuss religion."

He had spent a few days in Safed before Katie arrived, and wrote: "I had hardly any rest, since Jews kept calling on me from five o'clock in the morning until two a.m. the next morning, and no matter whether I was at meals or in my mother's house, I hardly had a moment's peace."

Those who called before sunrise explained that since he would be too busy later they wanted to catch him before his day's work began![2] "On two mornings," he wrote, "at about 5.30 a.m. I awakened to hear murmurings. . . I opened up my eyes on the first occasion to find an elderly rabbi, and. . . he greeted me with the words 'Peace be unto you'. On enquiring why he had come he at once answered that he had come to ask whether a Jew had to be converted in order to believe in the Lord Jesus Christ. I told him that we Jews who believe in the Lord Jesus Christ were not converted but completed Jews. . . He then asked whether it was true that missions to the Jews sought to proselytize the Jewish people and win them away from the Jewish race. . . I explained to him that what Jewish Missions were trying to do was to interpret the Messiah of the Old Testament as the Saviour and Redeemer of the New Testament who had fulfilled in His own life and person all the fondest hopes of Israel.

"On the second morning, about the same hour, four or five other Jews came. . . It would take too much space to give an account of this second interview, but I was amazed to find such a deep knowledge of the New Testament and especially of St Paul's Epistles. . . On each occasion after dismissing these early morning Nicodemuses I felt just full of praise to God for working so mightily in their hearts."

It was not only Jews who quizzed him. "An eminent Arab leader was discussing religion with me, and I asked him what he thought of the Bible. 'I believe', he said, 'that Mohammed is the greatest prophet of God, that Jesus is the grace of God and that Moses showed his greatness, according to my mind, when he said, A greater one than I will come and to him shall ye listen. It takes a very great mind to make such a statement.' He concluded by saying that he believed that at the end of time Jesus will come again, and while he is at present the grace of God he will then be the Messiah of God and accordingly he will be like unto God."

While Katie and Fred toured with Dr Burton, Leon was for the most part active elsewhere. "I was able to see very little of my wife and son as I was busy with Mr Rohold and alone, interviewing members of the Arab Grand Council, Orthodox Jews, Zionists, Armenian, Roman and Greek Catholics, as well as a large number of Protestant Christians." There was a conference with Hebrew

Christians and a Reception by the Zionist Movement at which a statesmanlike address was given, "And," Leon declared, "we were all surprised at the achievements which the Zionists have so far accomplished in the land."

The Zionists proudly showed them over their new Technion, or polytechnic college, at Haifa. At nearby Acre, Leon and Rohold had coffee with the former Chaplain-General to the Turkish Army, who had also been the Sultan's private chaplain. They then had an Arab lunch with the Mayor and took part in a gathering in the public gardens attended by many Arabs and their Chiefs to celebrate the anniversary of a former Mayor, at which Leon was invited to speak. At several such events and services addresses were given in Arabic, Hebrew, Yiddish, German, French and English, in all of which he was proficient.

There followed visits to the Scottish missions at Tiberias and Jaffa. Then on to Jerusalem, from which the inspection of Abraham's Vineyard took place.

Leon had now rejoined the touring party and came to Jerusalem via Nablus, where, with Katie, Fred and two others, he met the Samaritan High Priest. At Jerusalem, no sooner had they arrived at the St John's Hotel, close by the Church of the Holy Sepulchre, than his presence became known and, as he recalled, "Jews, Arabs, Zionists, and Christians of all denominations called on me and I was kept busy from early morning until late at night during our eight days' stay in the city."

There was a gathering of Hebrew Christians, and he discovered that there were as many in Jaffa as in Jerusalem; also that they were impoverished and required relief. "A plan was brought to my notice whereby with the sum of £700 to £1000 we could work up a scheme that would give permanent employment." There was an hour with the High Commissioner, of whom Leon said: "At present I am sure that the cause of Palestine cannot be in better hands than in those of Sir John Chancellor." There followed an interview with the Greek Orthodox High Priest and the Armenian High Priest's reception. Now and again he had encounters with relatives or old schoolfellows. (On a similar occasion Nahum, in Safed, met one with whom he had shared a school bench some sixty years before. "Hullo, Nahum," he was greeted, "are you still following the Nazarene?")

Before leaving Palestine, Leon, Katie and Fred had a final

excursion by taxi to the north. For once the new roads, which Leon had greatly admired, let them down. Returning from Haifa to Jaffa, they found the track uncompleted and were twice ditched in sand. Rescued the first time after fifteen minutes, they were on the second occasion bogged down for two hours. Twenty noisy Arabs were eventually recruited to haul them out.

Three days were spent in Cairo before they embarked at Alexandria. Then, surely, Leon would have revealed that he had been there during the War. When Katie denied knowledge of this she was in her eighties, and her memory probably failed her. They visited the superb Museum, and Katie and Fred perched on camels at the Pyramids, but Leon still had engagements to fulfil., He produced a nubile and richly perfumed Hebrew Christian girl to chaperone Fred, while he and Katie were at some function. Fred was taken aback when, having declined an invitation to her flat, she kissed him a passionate farewell. "We don't do that in Scotland", he said primly, and shook hands!

The voyage to Marseilles was rough and Katie was desperately seasick, but Leon kept on his feet and took part in the Sunday service. Katie and Fred arrived home on April 23rd; Leon however, visiting Hebrew Christians in Paris and London, was not back until May 1st, the very day of John's 21st birthday.

Three weeks later, when the first Report of the post-Union Church's newly-formed Jewish Committee (on which Nahum now served) was before the General Assembly, Leon was invited to speak. Before describing his time abroad, he referred to the work in Edinburgh, and included the indiscreet remark about Rabbi Daiches' threat to kill missions to the Jews.

"Since I came to Edinburgh," he went on, "we have had no less than 144 adult baptisms. From among these Hebrew Christians we have 7 ordained ministers and 6 in the mission field. If you take the average family as numbering 3 to 4, these baptisms would represent a congregation of roughly 400 souls. So the Jews abroad could not taunt the missionaries by saying that they came to bring them Christianity yet did not offer it to the Jews in their own land."

He had visited Palestine, he said, as President of an Alliance of 200,000 converts whom they sought to look after. At the same time he had visited all the Church's stations, where excellent work was being done. While he was there he had found a new generation of Jews springing up in the Holy Land who were quite different from any Jewry in the world, and who were studying the religious situation from every angle. "We are living" he declared with characteristic hyperbole, "in a day which is probably the biggest day in the history of the Jews."

Referring to the events of August, he again went out of his way to absolve all but a few Arabs. He also said that the riots had been unexpected by the British and would not have happened if they had had a well-ordered Intelligence Department. This had now been remedied.

Turning again to Scotland, he appealed to the Church for garments for women and children. "The need is great. Owing to unemployment and the depression. . . the Jewish community in our midst is passing through a time of great distress. . . [Those] who are not of British nationality are not entitled to any relief under the Government schemes."

He also told them that "many Jews have called on me wanting to know about the Union, what it means and what effect it will have on the future of the land and its people."

He ended with this peroration: "The Jews are no longer rejecting the New Testament and despising Christian missions. I ask the Assembly: are you going to be true to the trust which God has confided in you? If so, you need not be downhearted, but should go out with stout hearts to take advantage of the great and open door which the Jewish people present to you in these wonderful days. Let us remember that the future of the Jew is as bright as the promise of God."

Three days later, exhausted by the labours of the last few months, and the victim of a chill or virus, he took to his bed and remained there for three weeks. He was up on June 6th (Katie's birthday) but was unable that week to deliver his Communion cards. In less than a month, however, he had taken up the reins again, for his train from London was met on the 25th, and on the 26th he had an hour's walk with Fred, though he was not with him and Katie that night at Barrie's "Mary Rose".

On the first Saturday of his illness Miss Thomson took the mission service, Fred, with John, being otherwise engaged at the University Sports, in which John ran in the half mile and the obstacle race without disgrace. About the same time in Glasgow two hefty students, Leon's nephew Manuel and Katie's nephew Graeme, met in the putting the weight event and discovered that they had the same uncle and aunt!

Fred was by then drawn to the ministry although not yet confirmed, and at his father's bedside had a talk about it. Leon refrained from persuading him towards either, but was sure that in taking Greek, Philosophy, Moral Philosophy and English he was setting a wise course should the conviction come. When, three years later, Fred entered New College, he still had heard no supernal voice. But in reply to Principal Martin's request for a paper on *My Call to the Ministry* — a request which caused at least one student to change course — he wrote that two things had persuaded him. The first was a remark of Dr Kelman's that "faith is interpretation"; it enabled him to interpret the signposts of his past experience as pointing to the ministry. The second was a sentence of Leslie Weatherhead's that "the world's need is God's call to you." The world needed ministers at home and abroad, and, being a hopeless linguist, he would have to serve at home. Had he thought of it he might have added two other persuasions. One was Henry Drummond's reply to a student seeking a sign: "Look for no other sign than an increasing readiness to do His will." Above all however, were the examples of his father and of his minister, Dr Black.

Leon was nurturing Fred in many ways; the trips to Keswick, the pilgrimage to Palestine, the Alliance conferences, one of which he was asked to report; later came the reviewing of a book of Principal Martin's for the *Quarterly*, and, of course, the taking of services at the Mission.

John was less articulate about his convictions; nor was he eloquent enough for the pulpit; nevertheless he played his part in St George's West, becoming a deacon, not in the Anglican nor the traditional Reformation sense but in the narrower Presbyterian meaning of one who looked after the finances and fabric of the congregation. He was also President of the Young Peoples' Society, a member of the Young Men's Guild, and a teacher in the down-town Sunday School.

However, John's career was problematical. Graduating that summer with a disappointing degree in classics, what was he to do? His parents suggested a cramming school in London with a view to diplomacy; however, by November the Colonial Service had turned him down. Further efforts were unproductive, and he gradually came to see that his vocation was in a direction which had never crossed his parents' minds: that of accountancy. Yet it was not until 1936 that he sat his final Chartered Accountants (Scotland) exam and became a member of the Society of Accountants. When Leon died both his older sons were on the eve of leaving home, and John was the first to go, departing twenty-six days later for London, where he was to find his life's work in the Plastics Division of I.C.I. and, in a short time, his wife.

Leon's illness in 1930 rang alarm bells in the Alliance. It was clear to the Executive Committee that he was over-burdened, and that they must fulfil the resolve, made at Hamburg, to have a full-time General Secretary. Harcourt Samuel accepted the post and, as has already been said, they had chosen well. Leon could have had no more understanding, enthusiastic or willing colleague. Harcourt at once gave up his secular post with an insurance company and, more sacrificially, resigned the pastorate of a Baptist congregation which he himself had founded eight years before. Furthermore, in order to plan the future, he joined Leon and his family on their August holiday, which that year was in Ambleside. That same summer Dr Gold-Levin, who had held the post of Honorary Secretary, had a severe breakdown, from which he never fully recovered. Thus Samuel's appointment was not only opportune but providential.

Before Ambleside there was Keswick; and before and after Keswick Leon recuperated and enjoyed being with the family. Together they saw the Graf Zeppelin pass over Edinburgh. They entertained, having the Davidsons to lunch and the Semples to tea. They saw more Barrie — *The Professor's Love Story* — at the theatre and, the next month, Esmé Percy and the Macdona Players in Shaw, whose shafts of wit appealed to Leon.

The holiday in the Lake District was interrupted by Leon going back to London with Harcourt for two days. Then August ended with the news of his beloved mother's death and the sad impossibility of attending her funeral. On September 1st the family moved on to London and then Seaton in Devon, Leon visiting the Sawkinses at Axminster before joining them on the coast. Thereafter they both entertained and were entertained by 'Grandma' and, as he called himself, 'Grandpapa' Sawkins.

When they returned to Edinburgh it was to the final month of a splendid venture. St George's West was being renovated, and the congregation, under Dr Black's imaginative leadership, was worshipping in the Usher Hall. At first services were conducted only in the area and parts of the grand tier. Such was the power of Dr Black's preaching, however, that later for the evening services, first the gallery, and then the organ gallery, had to be opened. At a morning service, to Leon's delight, a Jewish family were baptised.

In London that same October the Alliance held the first of its bi-monthly meetings at the New Alliance Club off Oxford Street and designated the intervening months for drawing-room meetings. Most of the invitations were sent out by Mrs Sheffield, a notable supporter, who also paid all the expenses. Arrangements were being made at this time for the Third International Conference of 1931. Here too it was she who provided the £1000 which secured its location at High Leigh in Hertfordshire, and enabled many overseas delegates to attend.

Over the years Leon had won the sympathies of a group of enthusiastic women who gave generously of their time and money. Prominent among them were Miss Edmondson and Mrs Logie-Pirie, who was shortly to establish in London a hostel for girls and later for refugees, known as Logie-Pirie House. Leon was, in the best possible sense, a ladies' man, at ease with women, who responded to his kindliness and found themselves appreciated and understood. He was probably also sexually attractive. This may have been so regarding a Miss Juckes who accompanied her father to meetings where she occasionally sang solos. She certainly seemed to attach herself to him despite their physical disparity, she being large and tall; whether he encouraged her it is impossible to say. Again, Katie was once heard to refer to some flirtatious behaviour between him and Lottie Davidson at a lunch-party in a Princes Street restaurant. Dr Donald Davidson's wife was quite exceptionally beautiful and vivacious, but which of them was monopolising the other it would be hard to say. Katie was not too serious, for a year or two later we find Lottie chauffeuring Leon to Keswick.

In the remaining months of 1930 he was at home. He attended Fred's confirmation, John's graduation and a nephew's wedding, and two days after Christmas saw Hearts play Rangers at Tynecastle. He also bought two oriental rugs — a new hobby related, perhaps, to his upbringing. When Fred described to him the installation of Barrie as Chancellor of the University he wanted to know whether he had said anything about 'McConachie', for he was intrigued with Barrie's whimsical *alter ego*.

What rounded off his year and brought special delight was the conferring on him by the Patriarch of the Greek Catholic Church in Jerusalem of the Knighthood of the Grand Cross and Star of the Holy Sepulchre; he was pleased not only for the letters K.C.H.S. which he could now append, but for the recognition of any services which he may have rendered to the peoples of his native land. So we come to 1931 and the High Leigh Conference.

NOTES:
1. He was Michael Solomon Alexander, and was consecrated at Lambeth in 1841.
2. Other missionaries have suffered similar loss of sleep. Dr Peggy Martin has recalled how, at a village near Nagpur in India, she was called out of bed. Fording a river and traversing difficult terrain she arrived to find little wrong with the patient. She asked indignantly why his relative had brought her out in the middle of the night . "Well", he said, "you are much too busy during the day!" Is there a sidelight here on the story of Nicodemus?

THE YEAR OF HIGH LEIGH

The Insignia of the Order of the Knight Grand Cross and Star of the Church of the Holy Sepulchre, conferred on Sir Leon Levison by His Beatitude the Archpatriarch of the Orthodox Greek Catholic Church.
Note: The inscription on the Cross reads "In this is victory."

17. THE YEAR OF HIGH LEIGH

Several events at the beginning of 1931 had a bearing on the agenda of the July conference at High Leigh. The first of these was a supper-party, held in a restaurant in Soho, at which the guests were thirty-four Hebrew Christian girls gathered together by Mrs Rachel Schor, who had found them living in sub-standard and, in some cases, rat-infested lodgings. Leon and the Samuels (Harcourt and his father, the Rev. E. Bendor Samuel, then President of the British Alliance) as well as Hugh and Hélène Schonfield were present; also Miss Juckes, who sang. As a result of this party Mrs Schor and Mrs Schonfield together with Mrs Flecker (mother of the poet Elroy Flecker) inaugurated at High Leigh a Women's Auxiliary, one of whose objects was to care for such girls; and they made Katie its President.

The second event was the unexpected death in February of Ben Rohold. He was resting near Cairo when he developed a fatal throat infection. Not only was this a deep personal blow to Leon, but the Alliance was deprived of a trusted leader and of its expert on Palestine where, in Leon's words, "[he] was not only beloved of the Hebrew Christians and the Jews, but also the native Christians, Arabs and Druses". His vibrant personality and avuncular presence, no less than his counsel, would be sorely missed.

Thirdly, in April a conference on Jewish Missions was held in Edinburgh under the auspices of the Conference of British Missionary Societies and the International Missionary Council. The panel of speakers included the distinguished ecumenists William Paton and Ruth Rouse, the Moderator (Dr Bogle), Professor A.R.S. Kennedy and Dr Black, as well as Dr Macdonald Webster and Leon. "The Jewish people", Leon told the conference,

Ben Rohold

"stand between two worlds — the world of dogmatic authority which is dead, and the world of spiritual experience which is not yet born. Orthodox Judaism is breaking up, and in the Reformed Judaism that is taking its place heaven is missing and God a mere abstraction. The spiritually-minded Jew is out in search of someone *like* Christ." He also spoke of the fellowship the Christian should share both with the Hebrew Christian and the Jew; at the same time he deplored the American "Goodwill Movement", which soft-pedalled the Gospel. He also described the Alliance and its hope of a Palestine colony.

For Leon, however, the outstanding contribution came from Dr Paul Levertoff, a parish priest from Stepney. It was on literature for the Jews, a subject on the Alliance's agenda, and Leon applauded his plea for the Hebrew tongue, so sacred to the Jew, and for a Hebrew New Testament and commentary. Dr Levertoff became a speaker at High Leigh and a key member of the subsequent Commission on a Hebrew Christian Church, without wholly identifying himself with the Alliance.

He was a remarkable man who, at Shoreditch, drew Jews from

north and east London to Saturday morning services, held in Hebrew and with traditional Jewish music. He also edited a quarterly paper, *The Church and the Jews*, which, with his church, was supported by the Bishop of Stepney's East London Fund for Work among the Jews. Such was his reputation that he is the only Hebrew Christian apart from Bishop Alexander to be accorded a place in the *Jewish Encyclopedia*.

There it is recorded that he was born in Russia and converted at the age of 17. He studied in Russian and German universities, travelled in Europe, Palestine and Asia Minor, and became Professor of Old Testament and Rabbinics in Leipzig. After the War he came to Britain and was librarian at St Deiniol's Library at Hawarden. Then in 1922 he was appointed director of the London Diocesan Council's work among the Jews. He translated considerable parts of the Anglican Liturgy into Hebrew and, with H. Sperling, translated the *Zohar*, a central work in the literature of the Cabbala, into English. He also wrote in Hebrew, German and English on liturgical and theological subjects. The encyclopedia does not neglect to add that he was an apostate! Such a man, whose early background was not unlike Leon's, had much to contribute to the Alliance.

The conference that brought Levertoff to Edinburgh was planned by Dr Mott, who in February, with other members of the I.M.C's Jewish Committee, had been entertained to lunch by Leon. During lunch Mott invited Leon and Dr Black to a conference to be held in Atlantic City in May, on the Christian Approach to the Jew. On returning to London Dr Mott again pursued the matter. He wrote,

"Dear Sir Leon,

The more I have reflected upon it, since our last meeting in Edinburgh, the more important it seems to me that you should be with us. . . You hold an absolutely unique relationship to this great enterprise. I consider the approaching Conference to be not one whit behind those held at Budapest and Warsaw. . .It will be impossible to substitute you. I am hoping, therefore, to receive your favourable decision shortly. . .

Very cordially yours,

J.R. Mott"

Nevertheless Leon did not go (though Dr Black did). He felt that neither his work in Edinburgh nor the impending High Leigh conference would permit it. Moreover, he had other commitments. In March he was on deputation duties in Inverness, and in April was in London. He had considerable business there, for Katie, John and Fred had more than a week in Moffat during his absence.

In June Katie went to London to visit John, who had resumed his studies. In early July she had two games of golf with Fred in Edinburgh, and was at home until she went to High Leigh on the fourth day of the conference. Fred was there from the beginning, writing a day-by-day account for the autumn *Quarterly*. En route he had joined his father and John for dinner at the Strand Palace.

There assembled at High Leigh close on 200 delegates and, their genes not being Anglo-Saxon, they were quick to fraternise and extremely voluble. "The hum and noise of conversation and greeting when we sat down to our first meal," wrote Leon, "would have jarred upon the nerves of a stranger, but to me it was the sweetest music conceivable". A stranger, too, unless the conference had taken place today and he was familiar with debates in the Knesset, might have been unnerved by the free-for-alls at the plenary sessions where, in a babel of languages, delegates rose simultaneously to address both the chair and one other; sometimes the tone would become angry, for it is not only Palestine Jews to whom the term *Sabra* (cactus) belongs. It means prickly on the outside but sweet within.

Amid the shouting and gesticulating Leon remained calm, good humoured and in command. Alex King, the Scottish missionary at Budapest, who was there as a guest, still remembers his emollient presence. "I was dumb with admiration at your father's chairmanship," he told Fred. "Hebrew Christians, you know, can be difficult, and this was the rowdiest conference I have ever attended. They would be on their feet all speaking and shouting at once. The way he handled them was magnificent — almost magical. His patience must have been sorely tried but he never showed it." To a colleague Dr King said, "He was the finest chairman I have ever seen". It was not an acquired skill but a flair, the same capacities for conciliation and leadership that he had shown in his youth at Safed. Surprisingly, the clarity and decisiveness of the conference reports bear no trace of the shindy in which they were formed.

Fred's impression was that the turbulence frequently dissolved in laughter, brought about by Leon's attempts to quieten each national group in its own tongue. Aware of the comicality of his efforts at, say, Hungarian or Polish, he would press on in what might have passed for pidgin-Croat, pleased that even if what he said didn't make sense it was proving effective.

Those delegates unversed in conference protocol were not the only ones to be comically naive. The official photograph shows a little man standing out on the flank alone. He has done his best to honour the occasion, but his borrowed plumes combine an overlarge tail-coat, black bow-tie, and a bowler hat!

The previous triennial conference at Hamburg had been one of consolidation. High Leigh in contrast focused on various constructive projects: colonies in Palestine and Poland, the production of literature, and the caring for converts (with emphasis in Britain on women and girls).

The dominant concern was Poland, where converts were suffering persecution, unemployment and hunger. Leon was convinced that the missionary societies, whose work had borne fruit, should either themselves attend to these desperate needs or support the Alliance in its efforts to do so. A prime concern should be the setting up of an agricultural colony.

The societies, however, were unwilling to help; and the Rev. Henry Carpenter, himself a Hebrew Christian and a missionary in Poland, was a stumbling block. He asserted that money given for evangelistic purposes could be used for that alone. "I regret," said Leon, "having to differ from Mr Carpenter. The bogey that money is only to be used for evangelising is all wrong. We cannot get money to bring people to Christ. . . and let them die. This we must oppose. The phrase 'dedicated money' used in this manner is almost irreverent. We must remember that Christ told us to feed the poor."

Two days later Leon was even more outspoken. He said that he had invited the four societies working in Poland to a meeting in London. The B.J.S. and the L.J.S came. The Mildmay Mission wrote that they could afford neither the time nor the money to set up a colony. The Barbican Mission, having expressed their interest, failed to send anyone, and afterwards their Director gave the impression that he was unwilling to play a subordinate part. "A spirit," said Leon, "that breaks one's heart. If it came to a question such as is before us, I would rather play third or tenth fiddle than show such a spirit".

Those who met gave their approval. But after returning to their committees they wrote regretting that for financial reasons they could not participate, and Leon was moved to make an unusually caustic remark: "If money can be spent travelling about in first-class carriages and staying at first-class hotels it could be put to helping our Hebrew Christian brethren."

He never withdrew his allegation. However, feelings between himself and the Barbican Mission, whose Director was the Rev. I.E. Davidson, were strained, and a few months later he had to apologise for another remark concerning their lack of co-operation. When the Mission failed to send a delegation to High Leigh, Leon alleged that obstacles had been put in the way of certain of their staff, at home and abroad. "I did so", he confessed, "as a result of information given by one of the Mission's workers... Since then the Director has told me that my informer was utterly wrong. I therefore feel it my duty to accept my friend Mr Davidson's statement, and to say how sorry I am that this should have occurred. As Christians it is imperative that we should live at peace, and consequently we have no other desire than to extend our good wishes to Mr Davidson and his Committee and pray that God may abundantly bless their labours."

Harmony restored, the work went ahead, and by 1935 a Girl's Hostel and Children's Home were opened at Lodz, only to be swept away after a few fleeting, but halcyon years. It is with heartbreak that one looks now at photos of the children and the older girls who shared that haven.

The colony never took off. At the conference its need was so obvious that Hugh Schonfield leapt to his feet saying, "I am prepared to offer £5 towards starting the Polish Hebrew Christian Colony." Others took part and £308 was pledged on the spot. Anonymous gifts followed including £1000 from a non-Jewish supporter of the Alliance. Yet before the minimum target of £3000 could be reached events in Germany caused subscribers to turn instead to the German Relief Fund. In Poland a few families were given employment. Almost certainly it was providential that the larger scheme was aborted; for the rise of anti-semitism was swift and ruthless even before the Nazis came. Jews and Hebrew Christians, regarded as surplus citizens, were being driven out but had nowhere to go.

The tragedy of Poland is encapsulated in the memory of a

serenely beautiful Polish girl, seated at the piano at High Leigh when the day's conferring was done, and pouring out the strains of a Chopin Ballade or Barcarolle through the French windows into the summer night. Did her life end in Auschwitz or Treblinka, or was she one of the few who escaped?

From Poland the conference turned to Palestine and Abraham's Vineyard. In his account of the latter Leon said this:-

"In this scheme we must have men with vision, men who look forward to becoming farm proprietors. We must be careful that we choose the very best. . . to see that we get men and women who are not only good agriculturalists but good Christians. These settlers can become informal missionaries, and be a beacon of light to the whole country. It is of the utmost importance that they be trained first, and this is where Poland comes in. Abraham's Vineyard will be sold but I would like to see the Polish scheme start before we acquire the new property in Palestine." It was a splendid vision and the project would have been of immeasurable benefit could it have been realised.

The conference became aware of the situation in many countries. In Germany, week-long meetings had been held in Cologne, Stuttgart and Berlin, and recently fifty Hebrew Christians had gathered in Hamburg for a visit by Rohold. Berlin had had a problem. The relief work had had to be separated from the missionary work because of the reproach that they were buying the Jews; but they had engaged a third party, a clergyman, to administer relief, and every poor convert was sent to him.

Leon commented on relief work in general. He said that the I.H.C.A. had assured the I.M.C Conference at Warsaw that they would be delighted to care for all converts; and it was agreed that the missionary societies and churches would give their support. Yet none had given a penny. The societies did bring converts to the Alliance, but he alone could not raise the money for them. He therefore appealed to everyone for more sacrificial giving.

A Dutch Alliance was soon to be affiliated. The Hebrew Christians of Bessarabia had joined with other groups to form a national Roumanian Alliance. A Budapest fellowship met twice a week. The Swedes, though small in number (there being only 3,000 Jews in Stockholm and 3,000 elsewhere), had had an Alliance since 1903, and were emissaries to the Russians, transmitting funds and reporting on tribulations.

THE YEAR OF HIGH LEIGH

The Russians, though expected at High Leigh, were prevented from coming; they asked that the money sent for their fares might be given to a woman to enable her to follow her husband to Siberia, whither he had been exiled because of his evangelistic activities.

In the United States, the Alliance founded by Rohold sixteen years earlier now stretched from coast to coast; but the Wall Street crash and the ensuing slump made it difficult for them to continue to act as Europe's generous big brother.

One of their spokesmen was Jacob Peltz, later to serve the I.H.C.A. for some years as its Field Secretary and to share the deputation work with Leon and Harcourt Samuel.

Others whom Leon admired were the spokesmen for Hungary and Latvia, Dr Deszo Foldes and Pastor Peter Smoljar. The former, one of the quieter and less pungent delegates, was a leading advocate in Budapest and gave legal help freely to many a poor Jew. He also employed his forensic skills in a book on Christianity directed towards the Jews, which the I.H.C.A. helped to subsidise. He was known to share his salary with less fortunate converts, and when the Nazis dismissed him and he was reduced to penury the Alliance went to his aid.

A glance at the conference programme over the weekend may give something of its flavour. On the Saturday night, between addresses on "Causes of Israel's Sufferings" and "Hebrew Christian and Gentile Christianity — is there a Difference?" the Hebrew Christian girls of London sang the 24th Psalm in Hebrew. Someone, probably Leon, had the happy idea of a testimony meeting at which, under the theme "What I have found in Christ that I did not find in Judaism" as many as eighteen delegates spoke, fortunately with extreme brevity. This was held on the Sunday afternoon. In the morning a service according to the custom of the Free Churches was held at which Gold-Levin and Peltz officiated and Nahum preached. In the evening the rites of the Church of England were observed. On the Monday morning the business sessions were resumed after the singing of a hymn and prayers in German and English.

Leon and Nahum both contributed to the testimonies. Leon's was not biographical, but it revealed the mystical element in his nature; something which Hugh Schonfield had observed, for years later he told Fred: "Your father was something of a mystic," though he could not explain this further. In his contribution at High Leigh

Leon remarked that "We have a great experience here that we cannot have in heaven; for you cannot tell an angel that there is a thing called sweet and another called bitter, any more than you can explain a rainbow to a blind man". This mystic sense of heaven as sweetness unalloyed may not appeal to everybody; yet it is of a piece with John Donne's heavenly house "where there shall be no cloud nor sun, no darkness nor dazzling, but one equal light, no noise nor silence, but one equal music. . ."

Leon also declared: "In Judaism we had to give a sacrifice; in Christianity God is the Giver. . . To take another thing: we never heard a Jew say 'Not I, but Moses — or Hillel — in me'. . . Judaism is full of bewilderment. . . there is always something wanting in it. . . In Christianity is the solution to the mystery of the universe."

Nahum's approach was more personal. "I told you this morning [in his sermon] of Dr Anderson of Safed, and when I came to this country I found a Mr Sawkins, a very saintly man. . . When I came among those saintly men I found Christ. . . As a minister I am happy to say that I find Christ more and more in Christian people. . . I have known in Judaism some saintly men, but I have never found that tenderness and self-sacrifice that I have found in Christians."

Two days later these thoughts were echoed in an address by the Bishop of Norwich, Dr Bertram Pollock. Leon had hoped to have, as a distinguished guest, a Keswick acquaintance, Bishop Taylor Smith, the former Chaplain-General. His absence, however, was no great deprivation, for although Bishop Pollock was not given to turning somersaults — an accomplishment of which the elderly and rotund Taylor Smith still boasted — he was a more cogent speaker and gave a thoroughly relevant address, the passage which reinforced Nahum being as follows:-

"Christianity is a life dominated by a creed, and it is the life in which the outsider will take an interest, before the creed. It is the lives of Christians that the critics look at. They usually pick out the worst; I do not know why. If anybody wants to know what a strawberry is like I don't pick up the most measly strawberry in the garden, that the birds have been at, or a slug or a bug! I feel it is not Christianity that makes the poor examples what they are, but the want of true Christianity. They should look at least at the lives of the saints and judge Christianity by such as St Paul."

It would cross the minds of his listeners that Jews also are judged by their worst.

The thank-you note which Dr Pollock wrote afterwards to Leon was effusive. "How can I thank you? I had a really delightful afternoon yesterday. There was such a lovely spirit of brotherhood and it was a privilege to be welcomed into it. . . . With warm thanks for that delightful spirit of friendship."

The warmth that the Bishop encountered was a characteristic of the I.H.C.A. conferences, and distinctive in that other Christian gatherings, though rich in the joy of the Spirit, are without that super-abundance of affection, emotion and even sentimentality which is part of the Jewish make-up. Put in the simplest terms, Jews, and more especially Hebrew Christians, wear their hearts on their sleeves.

How explicit, for example, were the expressions of love and concern which surrounded Leon's re-election to a third term as President. Dr Frank was the proposer. "God", he said, "has sent us the right man. Sir Leon is possessed of the wisdom of Solomon, the patience of Job, the zeal and energy of Paul and the love of John." He then told a story of a famous painter who had produced a richer red by painting with his own blood. "That is what our President has done for us — poured out his very heart's blood. During the last six years. . . I have seen great changes in him. Sir Leon's eyesight has weakened with the work he has done and he has aged visibly."

The election being unanimous, the chairman, Dr Gold-Levin, exclaimed "Long may he live!", and when Leon had been fetched, and the ovation subsided, he addressed him as "President, beloved President" and told him, "If you had been present to hear the expressions of gratitude, of love and concern for you it would have given you encouragement in the work even more than the great love you have already shown. . . Thank you for the past, and as for the future 'The Lord bless you and keep you. . . .'."

Replying, Leon addressed his "dearly beloved brethren and sisters" and said how their love and prayers had upheld him. "Our people", he went on, "are desperately in need of Christ, and you and I can give them Christ. Our Hebrew Christians are desperately in need of fellowship and love and brotherhood in Christ and you can supply them with that. . . We will go on and on until we win our people for Christ and make ourselves worthy in the eyes of the Church, both visible and invisible. This is my desire. This I have promised you to do, and this I want you to promise me in silent prayer."

The prayer was followed by further elections, the chief of these being that of Harcourt Samuel to the new post of General Secretary.

These events took place midway through the conference and there were items before and after which need not be detailed here. A typical act of generosity, however, was the presentation, one day at breakfast, of a gold pen to Leon and an umbrella to Katie, together with a clock to Miss Rose Strachan from Aberdeenshire, who had acted as conference secretary and handled the multifarious bookings.

In presenting the umbrella Mrs Flecker made a significant remark. Katie, she said, had been friend and helper, "and had been with him in rejecting the temptations of worldly advancement that had come his way, and putting the Alliance first." To what did this refer? Later there were to be definite offers in the political sphere, but whether at this time the temptations were political or commercial is not known. Probably they were the former, for the Government was in crisis and in August Ramsay MacDonald's National Government was formed. The support of men like Leon may well have been canvassed.

Three further matters claimed Leon's attention before the conference closed. The first concerned the Alliance's attitude, and his own, towards the Roman Catholic Church. The question had not arisen in Britain or America but was acute in Poland and Hungary, where Roman Catholicism was predominant. A Polish delegate moved that since the Catholics looked after their own converts, only those baptised by the Protestant Church or by a missionary of that Church should, if denied work, be helped by the Alliance. Other delegates, however, thought that as the Alliance was inter-denominational any convert, even if he were a Catholic, should be admitted. Dr Foldes said that in Hungary they had many contacts with the Catholics; and they should avoid antagonising them. However, the teachings of that Church were alien to their spirit, and they must make this plain and build on a Protestant foundation.

Leon agreed with Dr Foldes, and did not feel the Polish motion was necessary, for the Alliance could say who was to be given work, for example in the Polish colony. He added that when a Roman

Catholic came to them they should befriend him, but if he wanted to join them he must agree to what they asked.

The Alliance, he said, must stand under its colours. A Roman Catholic might be as good a Christian as himself, and better, but they were Protestants. "I believe," he went on, "that the Roman Catholic religion is more akin to heathenism than to the New Testament. The difference between the Roman Catholic Church and ourselves is vital. We must stand where we are. We want to bring back the purity of the pristine Apostolic Church. I believe with all my heart that we are right in going straight to Christ."

Before the watershed of Vatican II Leon was probably right in upholding the Protestant tenets of the Alliance. Even so, his use of the word 'heathenism' shows a failure to appreciate how Roman Catholicism, exemplified by its best exponents, regarded itself. It was a failure to observe Bishop Paget's standard for assessing strawberries — always to judge by the best. It was unfortunate that the best of Catholics did not seem to cross Leon's path; there would be less excuse were the I.H.C.A. to be intransigent today.

Another matter of concern was that of missionary leadership and literature. Leon felt the need for "cultured Hebrew Christians of social and personal standing to command the respect of the Jews and overcome their antagonism". There was also a need of a higher standard of literature; not the customary Christian tracts, but skilled apologetics written with the insight of those who understood the spiritual needs and difficulties of the Jewish enquirer.

At the same time he found the missionary societies, and the international bodies whose conferences and committees he had attended, singularly lacking in understanding. They continued to appoint leaders and commission authors from their Gentile clientèle and bypassed the Alliance which could have recommended several skilled and knowledgeable candidates. "Hebrew Christians", he said, "participating in the work of evangelising the Jews have constantly been given subordinate positions and not been encouraged even in these. The position is tragic in the extreme. In pleading the cause of the Jewish people an advocate of these Churches and societies never fails to point out how clever the Jewish people are and the position which they occupy in every branch of knowledge. Yet it would seem that the Jew ceases to be clever as soon as he becomes a Christian, for we have been told time after time that a Hebrew Christian is only fit to occupy an inferior post, and can only work under the supervision of a Gentile Christian! The result has been that some of our ablest Hebrew Christians have been forced to enter the Church as ministers and forsake the Jewish mission field."

He might easily have accused the Christian establishment of anti-semitism. A lesser man would have done so. However, he gave them the benefit of the doubt and told himself that it was only a lack of imagination that caused them to squander their opportunities. He also knew the inherent conservatism of public bodies and their unwillingness to take risks involving people not entirely of their own kind. Yet because he looked for something better among Christians — "What do ye more than others?" — he was saddened; for the failure to meet the world's need was acute.

The modern strategy of not deploying specialist missionaries, but leaving it to local congregations to witness to and win the Jews, had already met with his disfavour. Today he would continue to say that if the Churches are serious in their desire to bring the Jewish people to their Messiah, they should seek out and commission those from a Jewish background to do so; and, if they cannot find them, should turn to the Alliance for help.

The point is a wider one. It concerns not only work among Jews but every field of missionary work. Those who can identify most with the people they serve are usually the most effective missionaries. In the past they have included such figures as Father Damien, a leper among lepers, C.F. Andrews with his Indian ashram, and Jane Haining staying on in Budapest to be martyred with the Jewish girls in her charge. Today we may think of such missionary spirits as Tilly Wilson, a Scottish girl who, as a deaconess, went back as the Church's agent to her own "travelling people" and who said: "I didn't have to build a relationship first; I know how we travellers think."

The third topic to engage Leon's attention was the need for a Hebrew Christian Church. He had heeded the strictures of the Warsaw Conference of 1927 about not forming another denomination. Nevertheless, new Hebrew Christian congregations were springing up —. there was one, for instance, at Chisenau in Bessarabia; and there were larger areas in Europe where the Hebrew Christians found no welcome in the national or independent Churches — such was the festering sore of anti-semitism, "that light sleeper" — and begged to form their own.

Rather than let congregations form willy-nilly, with disparate creeds, constitutions and liturgies, the High Leigh Conference decided to set up a Commission to produce a model constitution and guidelines for the worship and missionary objectives of such a Church. They had set themselves, said Leon, a tremendous task, and it was to occupy much of his own time and thinking during the coming years.

So the Conference ended, and he returned to Edinburgh and the Mission. His mornings were spent, as always, reading the Jewish Press and dictating letters, articles, news items and memoranda to Miss Lea; the afternoons at the Mission, in visiting, or at Macdonald Webster's office or a committee room; then on, perhaps, to relax at the Liberal Club (where Debenham's now stands, at 109 Princes Street); home to a typical Scottish high tea with the family — a compromise between tea and supper taken around six o'clock; then an interval until callers arrived — or, if there were none, he might retire to the study to memorise Masonic ceremonies.

From his return on 28th July the pressure seemed to ease. Certainly he needed a rest. In the first fortnight of August he visited the theatre with Katie, Fred and David, to see Leon M. Lion, the Jewish actor, in Galsworthy's "The Silver Box", whose theme was anti-semitism in London's clubland, and the cinema for "Resurrection" (not, I think, Tolstoy's story). He also took Donnie McIntyre to lunch with Sir James Leishman, and on the next four days "sat" in the drawing-room for Donnie to paint his portrait. It was only moderately successful, for Fred's old art teacher, who was to become Principal of Art Colleges at Leamington Spa and Worthing, was not a portraitist. Nevertheless, Leon acted on Fred's instigation and it served to cement a friendship. When Leon died Donnie was to say of him: "I don't think any man has impressed me as much with 'the Love of God in man'."

Not many months afterwards Fred persuaded his father to bring together Sir Herbert Read, who lived nearby and was for a brief spell Professor of Fine Art at Edinburgh (he was arguably the greatest critic of his day and a distinguished poet) and Donnie. Read, a shy man, came only to please Fred who, with a fellow-student had been, at the raw professor's request, showing him the ropes. The encounter did not go too well. Donnie was overawed and Read

221

silent, but Leon kept the show going and his kindliness saved the evening.

On August 20th the family holidayed at West Kilbride and then went on to Rothesay where Leon enjoyed the pierrots. Nahum and Margaret joined them there. Nahum was on the eve of leaving Blantyre after a ministry of only two years to come to St Ninian's, Leith, known as 'the Seamen's Kirk'. The brevity of his stay in the mining community would be frowned upon today. I can only surmise that he left either because Margaret was not at home there or to be in closer touch with Leon and the affairs of the Alliance. It is also true that Leith offered a larger sphere, and he was to remain there, though not in the same church building, until his retirement.

A fortnight before the holiday ended Leon was off again to London. In October, when his parents were at Nahum's induction, Fred was taking part in an evangelistic campaign with the Edinburgh Student Campaigners. This was a group created by the Rev. D.P. Thomson, a Dunfermline minister who had a far-reaching influence among students, and who was universally known as 'D.P.'. He it was who enabled many to stay in the S.C.M. rather than to join the more conservative Evangelical Union by providing the former with an evangelistic arm, thereby sabotaging the allegation that it was only a talking-shop. The Edinburgh Student Campaigners held missions, usually in small industrial towns. Their basic textbook, apart from the Bible, was *Jesus Christ is Lord*, written by Studdert-Kennedy for the Industrial Christian Fellowship, with the result that socio-political as well as theological questions featured alongside the evangelistic appeal. Round-table discussions and works' gates meetings were held as well as rallies and services.

Fred had had a previous encounter with D.P. who, with his friend Eric Liddell, fresh from the Olympics, had addressed his school assembly. The contrast between the booming, ebullient D.P. and the quiet, diffident Liddell could not have been greater.

D.P. had a profound influence on Fred, who was to become leader of a subsequent campaign, and Leon was impressed. He met D.P. and discovered that one of his ambitions was to create a small publishing firm, to be known as the Lassodie Press. (Lassodie was a Fife village where D.P. held student retreats). D.P. came to Albert Terrace to discuss the venture and Leon must have given him financial help; for he was later to write: "I owe more to Sir Leon than

I can say. He made one of my dreams possible and he helped and encouraged me again and again, as he must have done many." D.P. also came to know Nahum, and persuaded him to contribute his life-story to a Lassodie Press symposium.

As the year of High Leigh ended the January 1932 *Quarterly* was being prepared. It contained a New Year Message from Katie to the Women's Auxiliaries, and this became an annual feature for 27 years. Katie did not write it easily. She suffered much anxiety in finding fresh themes for these 'comforting words'. Nevertheless, it was a contribution of unremitting compassion.

18. DOMESTIC INTERLUDE

Leon, now in his fifties, was not wearing too well. He no longer looked youthful and slim. His cheeks were lined and pale, he was slightly paunched, and had begun to be plagued with neuritis. He would pull and crack rheumatic finger-joints.

Outwardly he put on a brave show and presented an up-to-date image. The bowler hat was exchanged for a grey homburg, the rimless glasses first for gold, then horn-rimmed ones. The starched collars and cuffs, save on formal occasions, were discarded for linen, the holiday knickerbockers for flannels.

His characteristics had not changed. Peculiarities of speech and spelling could not now be remedied. He used the long continental vowels and would call an oven an 'ohven'. Edinburgh was 'Aidenboro', Rembrandt 'Raimbrandt', and fundamental 'foundamental'. He had difficulty with the English 'w'. "Vy?" or "Ven?" he would ask, or say "She vos a vise voman". Yet one hardly noticed this, for he had none of the deliberateness of the ham-actor's "Ve vill make you talk". The English defect of failing to distinguish 'Wales' from 'whales' is culpable; but Leon's eccentricities were excusable and endearing.

A usage which lingered in the family was his word for Katie — 'Mammy', which he pronounced 'Mahmy'. Her children held to this all her lifetime except for the youngest, David, who succeeded in changing it to 'Mummy'.

Katie was, on the whole, devoid of a native accent, but listening closely one might detect Cumbria — when she said, for instance, "I'm goin' out shoppin' this mornin' ".

Even before the thirties a feature of life at Number Nine, the Sunday tea, was well established. Every Sunday, when Leon was at

The family in 1932

home, about a dozen people crowded round the large dining-room table, which was laden with home-baked scones along with McVitie's cream-buns, iced cakes, sponges, castle cakes and macaroons. At one end Katie dispensed the tea; at the other Leon dominated the conversation.

The guests included students, Dr Black's American assistants, Ollie Brackett and Gordon Conning and their successor Harold Ditzler (a former tennis coach), 'loners' collected at the morning service, and any Hebrew Christians or acquaintances who were in town. George Seth, a future Professor of Psychology, Norman Hope who became a Professor of Church History in America, and others from the Young Men's Guild were there.

A frequent attender was an Arab medical student, Ahmed Affara. His conversion through a Scottish missionary, Dr Pat Petrie of Aden, as well as the courage with which he faced persecution and death-threats, endeared him to Leon who, though subject to less physical danger, had followed the same path. Ahmed became widely known in the Scottish Churches and spoke at many a student campaign. Unfortunately, having qualified as a doctor, he died young.

The whole family brought their friends: David's from school and later, university; Rosalin's from school and nursing college; John, among others his current girl friend, Maureen, Dorothy or, especially, Eileen; and Fred, students who included his schoolfriend, George Reid, a Moderator-to-be. But the two most regularly there were Rob Sutherland who lived in digs and Mary Duncan from her students' hostel.

John's girl-friends were birds of passage, blonde and beautiful but in his brother's view somewhat dumb! Fred's relationship with Mary Duncan was, in contrast, prolonged and serious.

More should be said about Mary for, apart from her friendship with Fred, she had a close and affectionate relationship with his parents. Indeed, after she and Fred had pursued their romance for three years — all through his university course — they fully expected her to become their daughter-in-law. So indeed it might have been had not a young accountant intervened at an Art College Ball and whisked her away. She was right to go, for Fred was not only obsessed with a world to which she did not belong, that of the S.C.M. and the Student Campaigners, but he had become not a little priggish. He criticized her father for enjoying his glass of sherry, and hauled her before Dr Black to enquire whether St Paul's warning about causing one's brother to stumble did not posit total abstinence. Dr Black fudged his reply! Nevertheless, when she went, it was a blow not only to Fred but to his parents, who week after week had welcomed her and given her the freedom of their home. It says much for Mary that before leaving Edinburgh, shortly after the break, she returned to say goodbye to Katie and Leon.

All who came to the teas, it seemed, were impressed by Leon except for Fred who, going through a phase of being critical, was often embarrassed by his father's seeming egotism, his dominance of the conversation and his constant references to himself. But Leon was unpompous and without real conceit. He enjoyed entertaining and even showing off, just as he liked to display his oriental rugs or his medals, or to be bedecked in his masonic regalia. Nor did he understand that to use the personal pronoun overmuch is, to British ears, bad form. A good story was a good story, and if it entailed saying "As I told Macpherson"[1], "Maclay"[2], or "Lloyd George said to me. . .", he was not averse to name-dropping and, anyhow, that was how it was.

The teas ended abruptly with half the guests due at the Young Men's Guild, and at seven o'clock several of them met again in church. For John and Fred it had been a full day which included Dr Black's Bible Class after the morning service and teaching in the Fountainbridge Sunday School in the early afternoon. For their parents these were the best of days, filled with worship and preaching, family and friends, and the lively companionship of the young.

In 1933 Leon bought a car, a rather heavy Wolseley Tourer. The grassy slope at the side of the house was sacrificed to accommodate a garage. No longer could the children toboggan there, or race down it with an eight-foot clothes-pole to pole-vault over the rockery. As the youngest, David, was now sixteen that did not matter. The car was provided by Mr Morrison, a garage owner and fellow elder, who proceeded to give John and Fred driving lessons. He was less successful with Leon who, at best, drove precariously.

A day or two after their final lesson John and Fred took Rosalin and David to Penmaenmaur in Wales, their parents preceding them by train. Believing that Wales lay just beyond the Lake District, the motorists set off. Before Carlisle they were delayed by killing a sheep. Later John became car sick. When, after a long and scary journey, and driving in the dark for the first time, Fred brought them to their destination, an anxious father was out on the road listening for them. Three days later an entry in Fred's diary reads: "Family motored for first time — to Colwyn Bay." and the same week, "Motored to "Bets-y-Coed 25 miles each way".

After a memorable holiday, which included two concerts by the Imperial Welsh Choir as well as hill-walking and the usual beach activities, Leon was motored to Llandudno Junction en route for Axminster while the others made a leisurely journey home. First they went to Silloth to collect John who was staying with friends, and, losing their way on a rain-swept moor near Bootle, skidded down a grassy slope into a gatepost. It took an hour to get going again, and John drove them on to Keswick where bents and dents were repaired. Then, risking further mishap, they taught David to drive, and after visiting several Barneses and Baineses, and Cousin Marjorie McCracken (née Davidson Kelly) in Kelso, got safely home.

It was now September, and after collecting his father from the Caley Station, a journey that was to become routine, Fred proceeded to give his mother driving lessons. She was to drive intermittently for a few years, but after Leon's death gave it up. Thereafter David drove her more than once to London. They sought out temperance hotels for the two or three days' journey, and Katie always carried a bundle of newspapers to lay on the bedroom floors lest she should put her bare feet on a dirty carpet!

In 1934 Leon decided to motor to the Keswick Convention. He was neither confident nor competent enough to drive, so asked Lottie Davidson to be chauffeuse. (She says there was another passenger but cannot recall who it was. Dr Davidson, being a speaker, had gone on ahead). After about 120 miles Mrs Davidson was tired, and Leon offered to complete the journey. No sooner had he taken the wheel than, cornering widely, he ran into an oncoming lorry. Both vehicles being tough and heavy no one was hurt, but they were badly shaken, and the Wolseley, whose wing had taken the impact, had to be temporarily abandoned.

Seven months previously John had taken a corner too fast, and had come home the worse for wear. "John and Eileen had skid and bust up the car," says the diary. Perhaps that should have made Leon more careful. Anyhow, considering himself a menace — and the family agreed — he never drove again.

It was in 1933 that Dr Buchman and The Oxford Group Movement came to Edinburgh. (It was not called Moral Rearmament until 1938, the time of national rearmament). Leon was too busy and itinerant to become involved, but Katie was swept in. With her husband so often away from home, and her children absorbed in their own occupations, she had become increasingly lonely. Now the Group, with its instant friendships and confident spirituality, met her need. John and Fred were less enchanted, David mildly so, and Rosalin not at all. Nevertheless, they had to admit that their mother had shed some inhibitions, and become more outgoing.

Mercifully the Group did not feature her in its public meetings, at which some well-known citizens openly 'shared' their sins. Nor did she go to any conferences, though David attended a house-party in Denmark, which he failed to enjoy. She confined herself to a small circle of women, some of whom kept in touch with her in later years. She was disappointed, however, at not having the wholehearted support of her family. John lived his faith but never spoke about it, and shied away from awkward religious encounters. Fred distrusted the Group's jargon and the brashness of some of its adherents. One in particular, a young St George's West member who was privileged to speak from the pulpit of Alexander Whyte, John Kelman and James Black, a Presbyterian holy of holies, dared to appear in plus-fours and with his hands in his pockets!

Meanwhile Leon, for Katie's sake, felt that he ought to sample the

19. SUNDRY MATTERS

Hearing of the death of the Anglican Bishop in Jerusalem, Leon had hopes that his successor might be a Hebrew Christian. He wrote to the Archbishop of Canterbury and said so. The effect of such an appointment, he told him, would be far-reaching and, in both Palestine and world-wide Jewry, would accomplish more than the witness of many missions. Dr Lang replied that he would give the request very careful consideration, but would also be bearing in mind the interest of the Arab population. It was a statesman's reply and unduly cautious. Such an appointment, offensive to the Arabs, would have been no less so to the Orthodox Jews. Nevertheless it would, given time, have demonstrated to both communities, as Rohold, for instance, had clearly shown, that true Christianity transcends the divisions of race and nation. Leon invited readers of the *Quarterly* to pray about it: "While doing so," he said, "let us also intercede that if the new Bishop is not a Hebrew Christian he may yet be a man of God with a deep love and zeal for the salvation of Israel." So in fact it was; for the office went to the humble, able, and greatly respected Dr Graham Brown, whom Leon and Katie met briefly at a reception in Edinburgh. When they reached home, to Leon's great joy the Bishop was announced, and they spent an hour and a half discussing Palestine as well as the work of the Alliance.

Meanwhile Nahum's new charge was not absorbing all his energies. In 1932 he published *The Jewish Background of Christianity; A Manual of the Political, Religious, Social and Literary Life of the Jews from 586 B.C. to A.D.1*. This study of the inter-testamental period filled an educational gap and became a standard textbook in theological colleges. It is his most competent work, and was warmly welcomed by scholars. It was, however, the last of his major writings to be published. For the next thirty-six years he continued to write voluminously, but only a few articles appeared in theological journals and not a few, on a variety of topics, in the *Quarterly*, of which he became the sub-editor. There were also two short plays, *The Mystery of the Kingdom* and *The Birth of Christ*, a pamphlet, *The Truth about the Jew* and a tract, *The Case against Prayers for the Dead*.

The plays, for his church's dramatic society, are notable for their Jewish background. The first, of 50 pages, begins at Simon the Leper's supper-party and ends at the Resurrection. The second (in 1935) shows the author's lack of confidence in his dramatic ability in that its programme records that it was "adapted for the stage by Rev. Fred Levison, M.A.". However, perhaps the most striking paragraph in either is the stage-direction in *The Mystery of the Kingdom* for a scene in the Upper Room. There are two tables, a small one for the women. They are furnished as follows:-

"On the long table stands a flagon of red wine and a glass is set for each of the twelve men expected. There is also a dish, bearing a roast lamb, or sheep shank-bone representing the Paschal victim. Another plate contains a boiled egg representing the daily sacrifice in the Temple. There are also three dishes of mixed lettuce and parsley standing in salt water; and three dishes of *charosheth* — grated apple with nuts, sprinkled with cinnamon and made into a paste with vinegar. In the centre of the table stands a brass tray with three loaves of unleavened bread wrapped in a white napkin and another tray with a number of unleavened loaves. The smaller table is furnished with lettuce, parsley and *charosheth*. . . Cushions are provided for everybody. . . Upstage there stands a jar of water, a basin and towels."

How this recalls the times, at Albert Terrace, when Leon and Katie together used to prepare the ingredients for his lecture on *The Passover in relation to the Lord's Supper* — especially the making into a paste, with pestle and bowl, of the elements of the *charosheth*! As a pamphlet, Leon's lecture sold widely in Scotland, and it was also printed in the *Quarterly*. He must have demonstrated it to church groups hundreds of times.

Nahum's tract on prayers for the dead merits explanation. Less than a month after his arrival in Leith, the minister of the High Kirk of St Giles, Dr Charles Warr, caused offence by praying for the dead at the city's Armistice Day Service. Having given thanks for the fallen he said, "To Thee we commend each one of them. Evermore

DOMESTIC INTERLUDE

movement, and in London went to a rally in the Albert Hall. He came away disappointed. He had not heard the name of Jesus Christ, and it seemed to him that the central tenets of Christianity were missing. It was not until 1936, however, that Dr Buchman made the gaffe which would have outraged him: "I thank heaven for a man like Adolf Hitler".

Katie's renewal engendered in Leon a more sympathetic attitude towards the Group; but one doubts whether its own simple message — change people and you will change the world — which left out of account the need for both economic reform and political action, would ever have satisfied his acute perception.

Fred was now a divinity student and Leon watched his progress at New College with a fatherly eye. He was quite unperturbed when his son failed miserably in Hebrew and had to re-sit the exam; for, said Leon, while a good grounding in theology mattered, he did not place an undue value on his native tongue. Unless a man was going to be a scholar, or to work among the Jews, he could minister effectively with but a smattering of Hebrew and Greek. Apologetics, however, the defence of Christianity — that was another matter, and quite essential.

Fred, still apt to criticise his father, found him evasive as to where he himself stood theologically; nor could he understand his ability to be 'all things to all men' to the extent of consorting with cranks. For Leon would address meetings of sects ranging from the Seventh Day Adventists and other Millenarians to the British Israelites, who believed the British were the Lost Tribe and drew messages from the Pyramids. Leon's patient reply never varied. These people, he said, may have some queer notions, but they love the Jews. He never went along with their beliefs, but simply said he had not time to study them. However, anyone who loved the Jews and prayed for them, and supported the Alliance in its works of Christian charity, was on the side of the angels.

The Student Christian Movement widened Fred's horizons and introduced him to some of the great Christian leaders: William Temple, J.H. Oldham, Charles Raven, Dom Bernard Clements and Hans Lilje and among the young, Visser 't Hooft and Leslie Newbigin. Under these influences he found Keswick, with its emphasis on holiness, its avoidance of ecumenical and contemporary issues, and its theological conservatism, too restrictive. Reading reports of the Anglican Evangelical Group Movement's con-

229

ventions at Cromer, he knew that that was where he would be more at home. Again, when his father brought to Albert Terrace such Keswick stalwarts as Drs Scroggie, Main and McBeath, he felt an outsider. Their spiritual power was evident, and in John McBeath's case there were imagination and literary grace, but they still seemed to wear theological blinkers, and were unlikely to express doubts or to ask anyone to think for themselves.

As Fred mellowed, he was to acknowledge more fully the contribution of these take-it-or-leave-it exponents of the Gospel. Half the population, after all, are neither struggling with doubts nor grappling with, or even aware of, the ethical, prophetic or political implications of the Faith; and, as Billy Graham was to show, the one-eyed evangelist can meet the hunger of millions for God. But in the thirties Fred did not appreciate that his father's limitation of outlook was a deliberate constraint; that only by concentrating on the evangelical essence of Christianity could he, or the Alliance, bring Jews to Christ. Nor did he realise that his father's neglect of theology, and indulgence only in popular religious books and the lightest of literature, were due to the enormous burdens he carried. Both of necessity and from the heart, Leon was constrained to say with St Paul: "This one thing I do".

NOTES:
1. President of the University Liberal Association in Leon's time. Secretary of State for War 1916-19. He became Lord Strathcarron in 1933.
2. Sir Joseph Maclay was in the War Cabinet, and became a baronet in 1922. He was a prominent Scottish churchman.

look upon them in the fulness of Thy tender love and mercy." This seemingly innocuous petition was enough to make the Moderator of the Free Church of Scotland (the 'Wee Frees') reach for his pen. Such a prayer, he said, deeply wounded the Protestant sentiments of many Scottish people, and would make it impossible for them to take part in future ceremonies at the Stone of Remembrance.

The controversy was compounded by another eminent minister, Dr Norman Maclean of St Cuthbert's, who had been accused of Popery for a similar offence. Then when Dr Warr stated his views more fully at a meeting of the Church Service Society, and the Press publicised them, the heather was set well and truly on fire.

"The problem. . . brought me more trouble than any other," wrote Dr Maclean. "Attacks in the form of pamphlets issued from the Press. . . One of the best of these came from Levison, a son of the Rabbi of Safed."[1]

Nahum's tract has a foreword by his Leith neighbour, Dr Donald Davidson, and, interestingly, was published in Edinburgh by Marshall, Morgan & Scott who now had a branch at 99, George Street. (Later they were to have a bookshop in Stafford Street whose manager Leon and Katie befriended.)

In his reasoned contribution Nahum begins at the time of the Maccabees (c. 170 B.C.). He recalls how, having had to slay their fellow-countrymen for apostasy they "then betook themselves unto prayer, and besought Him that the sin committed might wholly be put out of remembrance." This, says Nahum, is one of the Roman Church's meagre sources, along with her belief in Purgatory, for prayers for the dead. But it comes from the Apocrypha and is therefore not of divine authority. Moreover the Westminster Confession, to which the Church of Scotland adheres, enjoins that prayers for the dead shall not be made. An even stronger argument is the silence of Scripture: our Lord did not advocate such prayers.

At this point however, Nahum enters upon dubious ground. He takes the parable of Dives and Lazarus as definitive teaching on the subject. That story, he says, contradicts any belief that the living can help the dead; or that there is progression in the future life. There is fixity there, and no passing from one stage to another. Christ has finished His redeeming work, and in the beyond there is no second chance. To say that His work is somehow incomplete and in the life to come it will be completed is "a view that every evangelical Christian must repudiate."

Aware of the severity of what he has written, he acknowledges that many are cut off in the midst of life; which is why in the wake of the Great War this question and speculation about the future state had emerged. Many have had no opportunity to live the Christ-like life. But we must not argue what God must do, or judge Him by our standards; we can only leave it in His hands.

That is surely an evasion of the issue. If there is fixity in heaven, then God's hands are impotent!

Nahum's thoughts turn to his mother: "She was brought up in the Jewish faith, and she lived her life without reproach according to her light. Faith said, when the news of her passing reached us, 'She has gone into the presence of a just and loving Father, and that is enough.' Was not faith right? Would it not be a bitter agony to think that this departed loved one now depended on my prayers?" He also asks, "What of those who die friendless? They can have no chance of betterment, for they have none to help them by their prayers."

All this is true. The dead do not *depend* on our prayers. Yet prayer is more than petition. When we pray for our loved ones, whether on earth or in heaven, we are not necessarily making specific requests for them; we are simply loving them *sub specie aeternitatis* and through Christ our Saviour, an aspect which the debate omits.

Nahum's conclusion is that the legitimacy of prayers for the dead "is a harsh and bitter doctrine that must also be stamped as false and pernicious teaching." It is he himself who, for all his personal qualities of tenderness and grace, is harsh in his theology, not uninfluenced perhaps by the stern logic and biblical pedantry that led to Calvin's predestinarianism.

Leon's comments are not known; but it is likely that his would have been a more liberal view; and he would have gone further in his appraisal of their mother, whom he believed to have died believing.

In the spring the brothers interviewed the Archbishop of York who was visiting Edinburgh. They sought his views on the setting up of a Hebrew Christian Church and told him of the projected colonies and other work abroad. Dr Temple, said Leon, "evinced a keen interest. . . and promised to do all he could to help us."

In May the other Archbishop was in Edinburgh to address the Assembly and seek an open discussion on inter-communion, a matter which was viewed on the Scottish side with deep suspicion. It may have been then that Leon requested an interview at Lambeth and a date was fixed in July. This time he went alone. The interview lasted for over an hour. Dr. Lang asked many questions, and promised, wrote Leon in the *Quarterly*, "to consider the whole situation and to write to me at a future time."

It was in a mood of optimism that he had approached the Archbishops. It was, he said, "in view of the wonderful happenings abroad" as well as the work of the Alliance's special commission that he took the opportunity. Yet while there were reports of many Jews turning towards Christianity and studying Klausner's, the Jewish scholar's, *Jesus of Nazareth*, the only other good news from abroad was the formation of an Alliance in Yugoslavia. More significant was the bad news of the rise of the Nazis. In the 1932 German elections they won two out of every three votes, and the march of tyranny and fanaticism began. Had Leon gone to Lambeth only a few months later he would have had forebodings to share; but whether the Anglican hierarchy, any more than the Government, would at that time have had ears to hear is more than doubtful. Of the latter it might be said that they did not awaken to the horror of Hitler's policy of genocide until the 'Kristalnacht' of November, 1938.

The promises of support which Leon received from the Archbishops and other church leaders were not fulfilled; and several were apathetic. This brought from him the reflection that certain natures are made lukewarm by high office; and he was saddened that some who in private had been enthusiastic should find it necessary, because of their public commitments, to draw in the reins and exchange idealism for diplomacy. To arouse people and summon them to action was his constant aim. Dr Black in a posthumous tribute referred to his "constructive, leading and energising personality". Yet often in his life he had to say with his Master: "How often have I. . . but you would not."

The Jewish Mission Committee of the Church of Scotland was not apathetic; but its concern took an ominous turn. That May, at the General Assembly, it asked that a Special Commission be appointed "to conduct a survey of the whole Jewish field in Scotland. . . to consider all aspects of the problem as it affects our own land." This could only mean that change was in the air, and that the work centred on the Edinburgh Mission might not continue as before. In 1935 the Report of this Commission resulted in all the work in Scotland being taken away from the Jewish Committee and put into the hands of the Home Mission Committee (later, the Home Board). This meant, initially, that it was transferred to the hands of those less expert in the Jewish field and less aware that work among Jews is not the same as that among non-Jews in the community. This was how Leon saw it. He continued to be disquieted as the Church moved towards the 'parish approach' — i.e. to withdrawing its institutional missions and transferring their responsibilities to the parishes.

Fortunately, the plan was not put into effect in his lifetime and he was able, under God, to increase the total number of baptisms in Edinburgh during the life of the Mission from 144 in 1930 to 155 in 1933 and 167 in 1935. Subsequently, under the new policies, the decline in baptisms has been very evident. The parish minister and his flock, not unreasonably, cannot give the time to befriending the Jews in their neighbourhood and leading them to Christ that a well-trained and knowledgeable staff could supply.

In 1932 Leon and Macdonald Webster had attended an International Missionary Council conference at Welwyn where the whole Jewish situation was reviewed. However, said Leon, the Council lacked courage and insight. Its resolution on anti-semitism "would not have been worth the paper it was written on were it not for the splendid stand and attitude of Mr Maclennan.[2]" (Probably an oral appeal for action). Again he found the Council advocating the very policy which in Scotland he now feared, that of the parish approach. "The opinion of the Committee was that if this could be accomplished there would be no need of special missions to the Jews, especially in Protestant countries."

While he endorsed the endeavour to get ministers interested in their Jewish neighbours, Leon reiterated his disagreement. "Men with special qualifications and a keen insight into the Jewish character are needed if the Jews are to be won for Christ. . . there is no shadow of doubt that ninety per cent of the success. . . has been due to the special missions. . . and the Hebrew Christians who were employed as missionaries to their own people." He went on to point out that the American Alliance had now withdrawn from the I.M.C. on this very issue; for the closing down of missions there, and the fact that the rest were staffed almost entirely by Gentiles, had had a detrimental effect. "I find that the results are very meagre, and few, if any, of the Jewish people are led to confess Christ."

SUNDRY MATTERS

The American Alliance approached the Executive Committee of the I.H.C.A. who then associated itself with their protest. The ensuing break from the I.M.C. was unfortunate in that it removed the Alliance's voice from that international forum; but Leon formed a close tie with Dr Conrad Hoffman Jr., who became the very able Director of the I.M.C.'s Committee on the Christian Approach to the Jew, and they continued to work together. "We who have been associated with Sir Leon," began Dr Hoffman's later eulogy; and he went on to praise "his splendid spirit, his great ability and his good judgement."

Leon's activities in 1932 continued to be manifold. In Bournemouth he addressed the Easter Bible School of the British Alliance. In London there were now three monthly meetings; in Edinburgh he spoke at the St George's West Young Men's Guild, and throughout the country to scores of groups and congregations. In addition there was the Mission and Keswick, as well as negotiations with Mr Abrahamson, the Commissioner of Land in Palestine, and two Arab landowners who seemed willing to sell. The Commission on a Hebrew Christian Church was drawing up Articles of Faith, and he submitted these to the scrutiny of his former professor, Dr Hugh Mackintosh, who was now the Assembly's Moderator. On November 4th he received this reply:-

"Dear Mr [sic] Levison,

Principal Martin and I have carefully studied the draft confession. . .and have ventured to make a few suggestions. . . Will you consider them, and when you have done so, ring me up, and let me know your general opinion. . . We can at the same time arrange for your meeting with Principal Martin and myself for further consultation, if you judge this to be necessary.

We are most anxious to be helpful, and should like to congratulate you, if we may on the real success of your efforts.

With every good wish and kind regards.

Yours sincerely,

H.R. Mackintosh"

The advice and encouragement of so distinguished a theologian were invaluable, for the Commission did not find its task easy. The difficulties, however, were more in the areas of the Church's constitution and its liturgy than in that of doctrine. Should there be

237

bishops or a governing board incorporating an eldership? How liturgical and how synagogue-related were the services to be?

The form of worship was deferred until after the Mildmay Conference of 1934. However, by dint of hard work the Commission succeeded in drawing up a Basis of Faith and a Constitution by the end of 1932.

The prior questions for the Commission related to the extent and distribution of Hebrew Christians and the necessity or otherwise of a Church. They felt unable to deal with the first of these and said they would accept an outline given by Leon and based on his extensive knowledge. Meanwhile they could only instance the position in Germany. "Very few would have been willing to suggest that there were more than, say, ten thousand Hebrew Christians in that country, whereas the lowest estimate now is about 200,000. We believe that the number of Hebrew Christians (world-wide) amounts to more than a million souls."

The Report stated that "(a) Many Hebrew Christians have been Gentilised to such an extent that they either do not know or else are ashamed of their origin; and (b) not a few who believe in the Lord Jesus as Messiah are not ready to profess their faith in Him because they do not believe that in the existing branches of the Church they would find a home and spiritual fellowship."

Further reasons for creating a Church were given: (i) The desire for it in places where there is persecution and anti-semitism. Centres had already been formed at Bialystock, Budapest, Hamburg, Kishinev and Lodz. (ii) It would attract the best type of Jew to Christ. (iii) There is an Apostolic precedent. (iv) A body of Hebrew Christians in Spain and Portugal could be brought in. (v) In Germany an attempt was being made to eliminate the Old Testament; in some schools in Britain it was no longer used. This Church would restore the balance and preserve the Bible intact.

The Commission would therefore urge the Mildmay Conference in 1933 to accept the need for a Church and proceed on it.

The Report also stated (i) that in the articles of Faith they had sought to emphasise the unity of the Old and New Testaments, (ii) that the Constitution should be Presbyterian-Episcopal, a majority believing that this came nearest the Apostolic Church and the practical needs of today — i.e. effective supervision and wide freedom, and (iii) that different modes of Baptism be allowed.

The proposed Principles of Faith contain eleven articles of

considerable interest which are set out in Appendix A (p.349). Their characteristic is the Judaistic phrasing — e.g. 'the covenant God, the Holy one of Israel', 'of the Virgin Mary, who was of the family of David', 'that Jesus the Messiah is in very truth the Shekinah', 'the Church of the Messiah... the Sanctuary of the redeemed in which God dwells'.

Some points of interest from the twelve-page Constitution are (i) "The minister shall be required to know Hebrew and Jewish lore and history." (ii) "An Elder" (on the Board of Elders) "shall hold office for a period of five years, but shall be eligible for re-election." (iii) "Elders shall be ordained by the laying on of hands of the Minister and all other Elders present." (iv) "One of the Elders shall preside at meetings of the Board of Deacons... for a period of three years." (v) "The Deacons shall have full control of all monies... full charge of all properties." (vi) "Every country shall have a Presbytery — groups of countries shall be recognized as Synods... It is desirable that each of these shall have a Bishop (religious assessor)." (vii) "An Executive Committee shall have power to deal with any urgent matter... its decisions may be altered, on appeal, by the General Assembly. It shall deal with all matters remitted by the General Assembly and have oversight of all congregations. It shall be the Business Committee of the Assembly, which shall meet for 7-10 days."

The duties of Moderator, Bishop, Elders and Assemblies were spelled out in great detail in what purported to be a definitive document.

The vision of a Church and its careful planning did not divert Leon from the ceaseless priority of caring for Hebrew Christians everywhere. How could it have done? For he lived at the heart of a hurricane. He himself put it like this: "In view of the fact that the I.H.C.A. Executive Committee is in close contact with over twenty different countries, and that most of the correspondence ensuing is addressed to me in Edinburgh, I find myself in the position of the captain of a ship in distress, who has to send out wireless messages stating her precise position on the ocean of suffering, and transmitting a call for help. And it is my hope that this call will reach an ever increasing circle of Christian friends who have their receivers tuned to the transmitter."

Unable to go abroad himself he, with the Executive Committee, sent one of its members, the Rev. D.J. Newgewirtz, to eastern

Europe. Leon intimated his coming, asking the Alliances to detail their plans and needs that he might bring home a full report. This he achieved, visiting groups in Rotterdam, Hamburg, Berlin, Danzig, Warsaw, Bialystok, Vilna, Lodz, Lemburg, Budapest, Prague, Vienna, Frankfurt, Cologne, Brussels and Ostend. It was a formidable itinerary, but deputies of the Alliance never did anything by halves. When Jacob Peltz became its Field Secretary, for instance, and visited Glasgow and Belfast, he is recorded as having undertaken over a dozen engagements in each city.

Before 1932 ended the Alliance, not for the first time, received a windfall, when Mrs Logie-Pirie, one of its most faithful supporters, gave £2,000 for the provision of a girls' hostel in London, A house was bought at 102, Tyrwhitt Road in Brockley and an appeal issued for furniture. Before long the hostel was full and supervised by a Hebrew Christian, Miss Rayner, a motherly warden who was there for many years. The house was named Logie-Pirie House. For Leon, who had been sowing the seed for two years, it was a dream come true; and he prayed that it might become a home where girls would find again in some measure the affection they had lost by leaving home to follow Christ. He himself took the good tidings to some of them. One girl had her brother, a free-thinker, with her, and when Leon described Mrs Logie-Pirie's motives he said, "Whatever I have thought about Jesus, from what you have told my sister I believe he is the supreme teacher of righteousness. And I will say from now on that there are capitalistic saints just as there can be communistic devils! Will you kindly let me have a New Testament — I want to study the life and teachings of Jesus Christ."

The *Quarterly* from time to time published Mrs Logie-Pirie's poems, and had made known a volume of them entitled *Songs in the Night*. This came into the hands of the German-English Speaking Pickwick Club whose members were so impressed that they elected not only the poet but also Leon Honorary Life Members! The poems were mainly religious and included the theme of the conversion of the Jews; so that Leon's serious response was not inappropriate. "In thanking the members of the Club. . . I wish to assure them that I shall be delighted at any time to render them every service which may lead them nearer to Christ and to the Cause which is dear to all our hearts."

A similarly surprising honour came to Leon and Katie when they each received a scroll from the Paris Academy of Dentistry and

SUNDRY MATTERS

Radiology announcing that they had been awarded a diploma and made *honoris causa* "Docteur en Electroradiologie Dentaire"; but why, or for what, I have no idea! In France there was not yet an Alliance, but news of the I.H.C.A. may have led to its President being honoured; or perhaps it is just that honours snowball. That may also account for the fact that in 1930 Leon had been awarded the Ordre du Saint-Sépulcre Orthodoxe, and in 1934 was made an Honorary Corresponding Member of the Institut Littéraire et Artistique de France. When these scrolls arrived by post the recipients may have told their children of them; thereafter they lay in a drawer unsung, and little store was set by them.

Also in 1933, Leon sat for a portrait bust. The sculptor was George Henry Paulin R.S.A. and the sittings took place in London. It was an excellent likeness and to an amateur eye a choice piece of work. But in 1933, to Paulin's great disappointment, Burlington House rejected it. Leon wrote him a comforting letter and kept the reply. It reads:-

Studio
38 Marlborough Hill
St John's Wood NW8

8/6/33

My dear Sir Leon,

When Muriel told me this morning that you are to be in town today I was overcome with shame because I have not answered your most gracious and encouraging letter. . . I know, of course, that you are not the man to condemn a bloke for not answering such a letter on the spot. We were very greatly comforted by it, as the disappointment at the R.A.'s rejection was so acute that we have felt depressed in spite of ourselves ever since. I really don't understand why the bust was not accepted. It is in the studio now looking simply fine and, I think, impressive. I am naturally extremely pleased and proud to know that its reception in Edinburgh has been so good; especially I value Lady Levison's appreciation.

I hope to see you and perhaps play a rubber before you return north.

Kindest regards,
Yours very sincerely,   Harry Paulin.

At any rate, Leon had made another friend. The rubber at bridge reminds us, too, that he could relax. He was overworked but he was not a workaholic. In 1930 a new cinema had opened near the Mission (The New Victoria, now The Odeon) and he unwound there occasionally at the end of a busy week and straight from his Saturday afternoon service and mission tea. Once, and probably more often, he took with him a Jewish student who had found his way to the Mission. The films he saw were the early talkies and *Disraeli* was shown in the autumn of 1930. I also remember him saying he had enjoyed Noel Coward's *Cavalcade*.

The bust was presented to the Alliance, who still retain it; a better fate than befell Donnie McIntyre's portrait, which went missing when Katie put her furniture in store, and only surfaced recently in a New York saleroom.

The family spent that August on holiday at Grantown-on-Spey and during their stay Leon paid a hurried visit to London at the behest, it seems, of Ramsay MacDonald, Prime Minister of the National Government. A political career was on offer, but he rejected it. Before or after this an incident occured which throws some light. Rob Sutherland was in Albert Terrace when a man emerged from Number Nine and passed him. "Did you see that man?" asked Leon as he greeted Rob at the door. "He was a messenger from Ramsay MacDonald offering me a peerage and leadership in the House of Lords. I declined, on the grounds that I am a Liberal and will remain a Liberal." If this was before the London visit MacDonald must have believed that Leon was still open to persuasion; if after it, that having declined in London he should be approached again in Edinburgh.

Fifty years later Fred expressed to Rob Sutherland his surprise that his father should have chosen to confide to a 29-year-old friend of his sons; to which Rob replied "The words I quoted were your father's actual words which I have never disclosed to anybody till now."

Why the House of Lords? In September Philip Snowden was to resign the post of Lord Privy Seal and retire in ill-health, and MacDonald probably had wind of this. The Simonites (Conservatives) had defeated the Samuelites (Liberals) in the Lords and this, together with Snowden's absence, would weaken the Coalition Government; therefore a younger working peer as an ally for Lord Samuel seemed a good idea.

David was then sixteen, and he has a distinct impression that during that holiday his father was tempted, and that it was his mother who dissuaded him. The temptation would be twofold: the attraction of politics, and a position of power and influence in which he could serve the Alliance. The fact that his work in Edinburgh was in the next few years to suffer change, and even to decline, would also make the time seem propitious.

He would not have been drawn had he seen any inconsistency between being a missionary and being a politician. However, like Dr George MacLeod and the Iona Community which he was soon to found, Leon believed in the wholeness of life and that no occupation need be secular. He would have gone along with these words of George MacLeod's: "Jesus commanded his disciples to be in on everything. When he told them to go out into all the world, they asked him 'What shall we do?' Jesus replied: 'Feed the hungry, clothe the naked and release the people in bondage.' This means nothing if it does not mean 'get into politics, politics, politics'."[3]

In the end, however, Leon realised that a conscientious politician cannot give other commitments priority, and decided that his political interests were peripheral to his vocation as a missionary.

NOTES:
1. See *The Years of Fulfilment* by Norman Maclean, Hodder & Stoughton, 1953, pp. 204-5: also the account in Charles Warr's *The Glimmering Landscape*, ibid. 1960, pp. 172-5
2. Secretary of the Conference of Missionary Societies in Great Britain and Ireland
3. The exact reference is lost; but Dr MacLeod said this repeatedly.

20. FOREBODINGS

As 1933 began the storm clouds thickened over Germany. The National Socialists succeeded in dissolving the Central Party and in destroying all other parties, and the anti-semitic attack which followed was reinforced by the promulgation by Alfred Rosenberg of a debased form of Christianity. His followers, the new 'German Christians', declared that Christianity had been corrupted by the Jews, and that it should be purged of its Jewish elements, including the Old Testament. Many nominal or weak-minded Christians went along with this, but there was no way in which the Hebrew Christians could do so, and their opposition to this debased Christianity helped to seal their doom.

Leon, his spirit burdened, became disillusioned with the efficacy of conferences to meet the situation. Even the International Missionary Council, he declared, was only a talking-shop, whereas what was needed was practical relief on a massive scale. He vowed never again to waste his time listening to the Churches lamenting evil, but to do what he could through the Alliance to combat it; and where it could not be combated, to rescue its victims.

But everyone seemed indifferent. Jewish refugees were cared for by their fellow Jews, but it was only when Leon's life was near its end that the cause of persecuted Christians, both Jewish and Gentile, found a champion. He was George Bell, the saintly and practical Bishop of Chichester; the same Bishop Bell who was to incur the wrath and censure of politicians by his condemnation of saturation bombing and of the destruction of Dresden.

Early in 1933 Leon was also preparing the April *Quarterly*, which had to be completed ahead of schedule since he was leaving for Palestine in March. 1800 dunams of land had been found near

FOREBODINGS

Acre, and he intended to buy them, to fulfil the purposes newly expressed on the cover of the *Quarterly* in the logogram of a Menorah, or holy candelabrum, "a fitting symbol of our endeavour to light a candlestick of witness to Christ within the Jewish nation."

The journey took him to many parts of Europe as well as the Near East. It was, more than ever, an apostolic undertaking similar in many ways to the missionary expeditions of St Paul, and not least in its many unplanned 'meetings by the way'.

On train or ship he always succeeded in making friends. Between Paris and Trieste his fellow-traveller was a Soviet government official who had been on a mission to South Africa. "I was able to speak to him," wrote Leon, "of the saving grace of our Lord and Saviour Jesus Christ, and of the love of God as revealed in Him. He seemed to be very much impressed, and. . .he asked for and received a New Testament, which he promised he would read daily and keep as a souvenir of the very happy time which we had had together.

"At Trieste I met a number of Jews staying in the same hotel for the night, and soon made friends with them. They seemed to show a keen interest in the object of my journey. . .and the following morning we all boarded the *Martha Washington*. I found that we had 1200 Jews on board, all bound for Palestine. . . On the first day. . .the Captain showed me round the ship. At this, my Jewish fellow-passengers began to wonder who I was, and to make enquiries. . .and began to come to me in twos and threes for interviews. Ere long. . .deputations were sent from various groups, and so a work of witness began, and continued daily from early morning to late at night, culminating in a general request. . .that I should deliver an address or two on my faith and my work. . . I was able to deliver three addresses on the Saturday and Sunday, after which many came to discuss with me the Person of Christ and His claims, and I made many friends."

He was met at Haifa by his sister Rachel and one of her daughters, and proceeded to Acre. There he discovered, after two days of bargaining, that the owner of the land was so deeply in debt that, had they bought it, both land and money might have been lost to creditors. With Mr Karmouche of the Palestine Alliance, therefore, he inspected several other tracts, and eventually began to negotiate with the Mayor of Gaza for the purchase of 2000 dunams (some 500 acres). A contract was signed and Leon left Palestine in the belief that his prayers had been answered and that the legalities could safely be left to the lawyers. However, as we have seen, it was not to be; and the elaborate plans which Leon, the I.H.C.A. Executive and the Mildmay Conference formed, in a state bordering on euphoria, came to nothing. It took years of effort by Maurice Levison, Leon's nephew, who was a clever lawyer in Tel-Aviv, to recover the deposit they had paid to the devious Fami Bey. "It was a disappointment at the time," wrote Harcourt Samuel later, "but in retrospect we can see that a Hebrew Christian colony in Israel would be frowned upon by the State, and in any case would be out of place in the Gaza Strip."

Nevertheless, the days spent in Palestine were not futile. As well as his family he was able to see his old friends Mrs Rohold and Dr Christie; to spend Easter with Bishop and Mrs Graham Brown; to lunch with the High Commissioner, even to visit the Grand Mufti, who seemed glad to hear about the prospective colony. He also attended a two-day conference of the Palestine Alliance held at Ain Karem, a beauty-spot and the birthplace of John the Baptist. There, from his headquarters in an adjacent monastery, the Russian Orthodox Patriarch called on them. He knew nothing of the I.H.C.A. and professed himself amazed. In a private conversation he gave Leon the names of a number of Hebrew Christians and Jewish enquirers, and promised to encourage the Greek Orthodox Christians at Gaza to befriend the colonists.

An event which was to bear fruit was the approach made to Leon while he was in Jerusalem by a deputation from the Marano Jewish Christians of Portugal. These were descendants of the half-a-million Iberian Jews who had been compelled by force to accept the Christian faith during the Inquisition, but who had continued to intermarry and to preserve Jewish customs throughout the centuries that followed. *Maranos* is actually the name given to Jews who are nominally Roman Catholic, but who secretly practise the Jewish faith. When freedom was eventually restored world Jewry built them a synagogue and induced 40,000 of them to leave their churches. But there were among them genuine Christians, most of whom refused to repudiate Christ; and many of these were now attending neither church nor synagogue. Leon was told that of the nine Jewish missionaries who had tried to convert the Maranos back to Judaism, four had become Christians and the others had given up the task as hopeless. It was suggested that the Alliance might be the means of providing for those Maranos who had no

FOREBODINGS

spiritual home.
This seemed to Leon an open door. However, like everything else, it required money. "If only the societies. . .and the British Churches, as well as individuals," he wrote, "would assist us a little financially we could do one of the most magnificent pieces of work for the Kingdom that I know of. . . Some of these Marano Jews," he added, "are very keen to come and work on the land in Palestine."

The money did not materialise, but a year later a meeting was held by Pastor Eduardo Moreira in his house in Lisbon, at which an Alliance was formed. "It may interest you to know," wrote its Overseas Secretary to Leon, "that the membership of our Alliance comprises, amongst others, four evangelical pastors, one engineer, a lecturer of the University of Oporto and three medical men", all of whom were eager to take the Gospel to their "brethren according to the flesh," the Maranos. Four months later the new Alliance was welcomed at the Mildmay Conference.

At the end of April Leon left Jerusalem and travelled by land to Constantinople. There was no Alliance in Turkey but he met several Hebrew Christians, some of whom were about to be replaced at their work, according to new laws, by Turkish subjects. They escorted Leon to his train and, he recounts, "we had a short session of prayer on the platform when each of them prayed for two or three minutes asking God to bless me and guide and use me."

At Sophia he spent some time with men and women students at the Institute of the Bible Lands Missions Aid Society who were being trained to be evangelists in the Balkan States.

At Bucharest he was heartened by the loyalty and independence of the Hebrew Christians. "Everyone aimed at finding employment, so that they should not require assistance and stand in the way of their less fortunate brothers and sisters."

At Kishinev he took part in a ceremony at the grave of Joseph Rabbinovitch (1837-99), who was the founder of the Hebrew Christian movement in Bessarabia. On his tomb, in Hebrew and Russian, was inscribed, at his own request,

>Joseph Rabbinovitch
>A Jewish man, believer in the Lord
>and servant of Jesus the Messiah.

Rabbinovitch was converted during a visit to Palestine in 1882. He

247

returned to face the derision of his former friends, but gradually won them over. His reputation as a missionary grew until he was known far beyond Tsarist Russia and even in Scotland. Scottish friends built him a large hall in which he conducted services in Yiddish and Hebrew.

It was doubly fitting then that a Hebrew Christian from Scotland, should pay tribute at his grave. Moreover, Leon would relish the originality of his teaching, for instance, his famous parable of the wheel. In it he described some travellers who discovered that their cart had lost one of its four wheels. One man jumped down and ran on asking everyone he met, "Have you found a wheel?" Eventually someone told him "You are looking in the wrong direction; instead of running ahead of the cart you should search for the wheel behind it." "This is exactly the mistake that our Jewish brothers have been making for centuries," said Rabbinovitch. "The four wheels of Jewish history are Abraham, Moses, David and Jesus. Unfortunately our people lost the fourth wheel, and because they kept looking into the future instead of considering the past, they did not find it. But, thanks be to God, we have found our Brother Yeshua [Jesus]!"

The Bessarabians were a lively crowd, and Leon heard their orchestra of balalaikas and guitars and talked, probably in Yiddish, to a large open-air Sunday School. He also saw the site of the church they were about to build, and addressed a crowded meeting from which many had to be turned away. It lasted four hours, until after midnight, and it was 2 a.m. before he could leave. At 3 a.m. he had the latest supper of his life!

At Novi Sad in Yugoslavia he rested at the home of Miss Weinmann, a devoted Hebrew Christian, and others began to gather there. "They were so full of gladness at my coming," he said, "that they did not know exactly what to do with me; and I spent another delightful day giving them the love of my heart and conscious that I was carrying the love of their hearts away with me."

Then came Budapest, where he spent a day trying to get the Hebrew Christians to unite; for the Baptists, Congregationalists, Methodists and Plymouth Brethren, struggling for existence alongside the dominant Catholic and Reformed Churches, stressed denominational loyalty to such an extent that when, say, a Baptist congregation offered their church for a meeting of Hebrew Christians the others prevented their members from attending.

FOREBODINGS

Polish Alliance, Warsaw, April 1933 (Leon seated centre)

Leon suggested that if a hall were rented the Alliance would find money to meet the expenses; and that in a few years the local group would be able to shoulder the burden. After further consultations they managed to arrange a united meeting, "the like of which," said Leon, "I believe has never been held in the city of Budapest before." He left after two days, wishing he could have had four or five more.

He travelled on to Vienna, Warsaw and Bialystok where he was eagerly awaited — the staff work in London had been immaculate. Finally he came to Berlin and Rotterdam.

His original plan had been to spend some days in Germany and to visit Hamburg, Cologne and Frankfurt as well as Berlin; but his family and colleagues considered this imprudent. Hitler was on the rampage, and the Oxford Union Society's vote in February not to fight for King and Country had given him a green light to ignore any protests from humane and civilised countries. It was certainly no time for a highly vocal Jew to visit Germany. So to relieve everyone's anxiety Leon cancelled his visit. He did, however, stop off at Berlin for four hours.

He was met there by a new acquaintance, a Jew with whom he had shared a railway carriage to Bucharest. They had talked of Christ, and Leon's companion had come to accept that there was no hope for a disrupted world but the reconciling love of Jesus. "I let him see," said Leon, "that it is either this or the law of the jungle. . . and making rules that suited me and others which I imposed on other people — and the poor Jew is always the scapegoat." Deeply impressed, this Jewish merchant, a man of means who employed 10,000 workers and claimed to know them all by name, arranged to meet Leon with his car and took him to meet, as Leon put it, "eminent men of different stations" who alerted him fully on the German situation.

Before they boarded the car Leon was warned that the chauffeur was a Nazi and was spying on his employer, although for nine years he had been treated almost as one of the family. Privately, the merchant confided that his life was being made a misery and he would have to emigrate. He was one of the lucky ones who did so, and Leon later tried to help his son get a post in America.

What he learned in Berlin caused Leon, as soon as he came home, to set up a Relief Fund many months before the League of Nations made its response by setting up a Commission on Refugees.

His final stopping-place was Rotterdam, and here there was a different problem. The Dutch were well-disposed towards the Jews and both on a governmental and personal level had shown them much kindness. In such a country it was not surprising to find a strong band of Hebrew Christians. What *was* surprising was that although their Alliance had almost as long a history as the International body, they had never joined it. Indeed they were suspicious of the I.H.C.A., believing that its religious foundations might not be as firm as their own, their Biblical Calvinism finding expression in stringent standards of belief and conduct.

Leon was able to convince them that the I.H.C.A. was a soundly evangelical movement, and that they should affiliate with their Hebrew Christian brethren throughout the world. Accordingly, at their annual conference in October they unanimously decided to do so. Their presence the following year at Mildmay, and their cooperation in the years before the Netherlands were overrun, were valuable indeed. Leon was to visit them again, briefly, in January 1934, when he addressed a crowded meeting in the English Church at Amsterdam. He also met a number of refugees from Germany, and was taken to a Salvation Army Colony where a Hebrew Christian family was being trained with a view to being settled in Gaza. Though the seas from the Hook were stormy, he slept soundly on board and was well satisfied with his visit.

He was especially pleased that the Dutch, alone among the Alliances, were sending substantial sums to Russia, where the Hebrew Christians' plight was then no better than in Germany.

It was on May 19th that he returned from this 1933 tour, and he began to feel the effects. He had pushed himself hard, travelling too often by night and speaking many a time at three or four gatherings per day, and was physically and mentally exhausted. Small wonder that when he addressed his first meeting at home and emerged into the cold air he contracted severe neuralgia. For the next nine months he struggled on, fulfilling numerous engagements until the acuteness of the pains drove him to his doctor. He was then told that he must either take a five-weeks rest or face a complete breakdown and a year or two of idleness. There being nothing else for it, he complied.

During those nine months he was unable to fulfil all his engagements. At St Margaret's Church, Juniper Green and Newmilns Church in Ayrshire, as well as twice at the Mission, Fred had to stand in for him. Nevertheless, meetings proliferated. For he was taking every opportunity to plead the cause of German relief, and it was uphill work. Ever since Britain had come off the Gold Standard in September 1931, and the pound had fallen to two thirds of its previous value, nervous donors, waiting for the market to recover, had withheld their subscriptions.

"To try and advance a great cause under such circumstances," wrote Leon, "is no easy thing. It fell to your President to try and address very many more meetings than he would otherwise have had to do. When things go nicely and I go into the West End and address a drawing-room meeting, I can sometimes come away with a collection of £50 to £100, but when the financial position of the country was altered I had to address twenty meetings to get £100."

Nor were matters helped by the unsolicited call to the pastorate of Cavendish Baptist Church, Ramsgate, late in 1933, of Leon's only full-time colleague, Harcourt Samuel. When he relinquished the post of paid Secretary of the I.H.C.A. Harcourt agreed to carry on as Honorary Secretary and a member of the Executive Committee; but while he was to serve magnificently in these posts for another fifty years, he was unable to share the promotional and fund-raising meetings as before. And although it was recognised at the Mildmay Conference that there should be a full-time Field Secretary, there was a long hiatus until Jacob Peltz was appointed. Meanwhile Leon's burden was increased.

Despite these difficulties money began to come in for the German Relief Fund. The quarterly lists indicate that contributions began in June 1933, a month after Leon's visit to Berlin. They predominated in the following quarter and were soon arriving at the rate of thirty per week in sums ranging from five shillings to £10 or £20. Interspersed with these were only a few contributions towards education, the hostel, the Palestine Colony and General Relief. The Polish Colony, after some sporadic donations in March, dropped out of the picture.

The disburser of relief in Germany was Dr Arnold Frank. Stationed at Hamburg, he was also able to see refugees safely aboard ships bound for whatever country would admit them. Dr Frank, aided by the fact that the Hamburg Jewish Mission belonged not to any German Church but to the Presbyterian Church of Ireland, retained his post for several years of the régime. At the end of 1936 the Nazis suppressed his magazine, *Zions Freund,* and the

FOREBODINGS

Mission was threatened. It was spared for a time through the intervention of the British Foreign Secretary, Anthony Eden. However, in September 1937, the very year in which at the age of 78 he had succeeded Leon as President of the I.H.C.A., Dr Frank was arrested. The Foreign Office again intervened but, freed from prison, he was placed under house-arrest. Finally, on receipt of an anonymous warning, he fled via Denmark to London, where he continued to work among refugees until, with the War, their internment began. Then, aged 80, he retired to Belfast. In 1947, at 88, he relinquished the presidency; and in 1953, at 94, he was able to revisit Hamburg for the dedication of his restored church. This venerable 'father of the Alliance', who had seemed, like Pope John XXIII, to be only a stop-gap leader, also turned out to be a remarkable one.

In 1933 Leon and the Alliance were not only sending money to Dr Frank. They were also caring for individual refugees — for instance Fred was asked by his father if he could find anyone among his student friends to tutor a young exile; while Nahum and Margaret, from then on, were giving hospitality to other displaced Hebrew Christians. At the same time the Alliance was participating in every public endeavour to move the heart, if not of Hitler, at any rate of the German Church which had accepted the notorious Aryan Clause, an acceptance which meant that no one of Jewish blood (which meant, having one Jewish grandparent) could remain a minister, church office-bearer, or even an enrolled member. As a result of pressure from the British and American Churches — and Leon had written to the Bishop of Chichester (Dr. George Bell) Chairman of the Universal Christian Council for Life and Work, as well as to the leaders of all British Churches — the Aryan Clause was removed from the Church, albeit reluctantly, by Reichsbischof Müller. The protests made by the Churches outside Germany may also have fortified those Christians in Germany who, a few months later, drew up the Barmen Declaration and bravely opposed the oath of loyalty to the Führer required of all ministers. Finally, when, in 1938, the Confessing Church convened a Kirchentag in Berlin it deplored not only the mounting persecution and the interference with Christian education, but also the measures taken against Christians of Jewish blood.

Leon was quick to acknowledge that what happened within the State Church to a comparatively small number of individuals was not the major concern. After all, it was possible for those deprived of the Church to continue worshipping Christ and God. It was what was happening under the anti-semitic economic laws, where Jews and Hebrew Christians alike, and many who had never even known they were non-Aryans, were driven to starvation, that was the greater devilment.

It was becoming known that the Jews were being persecuted. Yet there was a reluctance to do anything about it. The prevalent British mood was described by Compton Mackenzie. A character in one of his novels says: "The ordinary Englishman has no ill-will toward the German. He respects him for having given him a run for his money in the last war . . . . The ordinary Englishman has been a little shocked by the knocking-about of the Jews, but says to himself that he mustn't judge the German too harshly because after all the German is a lower breed than himself and can't help being a cad and a bully. It is up to himself to show an example of gentlemanly behaviour and try to teach the Germans to follow it."[1]

Leon, however, saw that refraining from ill-will and showing an example was altogether too supine an attitude. Silence in the face of oppression was cowardly, and the lack of any real response to the European tragedy hurt him deeply. He was especially dismayed at the failure to see the dilemma of the Hebrew Christians, or even that they existed. For they were being crushed, as he often said, "between the upper and the nether millstone." World Jewry, when the crash came, sprang to the rescue and raised large sums for relief — but not for Christian Jews. The Churches supported and contributed to the Jewish relief funds, but seemed unaware that some Jews, the Christian ones, were excluded from them.

He tried in vain to alter this. Yet the response, he found, only came from individual Christians. "It was all very well", he wrote sadly, "the Churches saying 'we are all one in Jesus Christ', but when it came to practical effort they were not. Church Councils said 'We will see you'. . . but the meetings never came off." He appealed to the League of Nations Commission, but nothing was done. The Federal Council of the American Churches collected half-a-million dollars to give to the Jews; but, Leon remarked, "they did not seem to believe in *Christian* Jews". Finally he appealed to the Jewish Missionary Societies in London, but they too gave him nothing.[2] "However", he told the Mildmay Conference, "I did not wish to quarrel; I believe rather in going ahead to see what I can do." That he and the Alliance achieved much is revealed by this sentence from a review of the year 1934: "Countless expressions of gratitude to God and thanks to the donors have come to us from the 2,800 people we have been able to assist."

In some quarters help was not lacking. A number of refugees were academics, and appeals were made to various seats of learning to help them find their feet. "I must pay a tribute," wrote Nahum, "to our Scottish universities and college authorities: They have been splendid; they have done and are doing everything in their power to help our unfortunate brethren."

At some point Leon had a meeting with President Masaryk of Czechoslovakia, who strongly disapproved of Germany's treatment of the Jews. His country among others was willingly offering asylum and had received 60,000 of them. But he had to point out that they were a problem; and that other countries could not be expected to go on bearing a burden which was due to the policy of one single country. No less willing was Palestine, to which 5,000 had been allowed entrance in 1933; but the immigration laws were to become harsh there very soon. As for America, President Roosevelt had been petitioned to revise the restrictions, "but we are afraid", said Leon, "that in the prevailing distressing economic conditions. . . [he] will hardly be able to comply with this request."

For someone with Leon's prescience the outlook was black indeed; and he could only see it ending in war. Early in 1933, after his visit to Berlin, he wrote this: "In reasoning closely with the Germans one begins to realise the real situation, and to discover that the Jew is merely used as a scapegoat to cover a far bigger issue, which has in it implications of a far-reaching and disastrous nature. . . for the world at large. An attempt is being made, and very successfully, to educate two generations into a spirit of war. . . Germany is once again attempting to create a superman in a super-country. This attempt was made prior to 1914 and led to a world war, and I have no hesitation in saying that the present attempt will lead Germany to another world war."

Had Leon chosen a political career he would, along with Churchill, have been excoriated by Parliament and the Press for being a scaremonger!

NOTES:
1. *The North Wind of Love*. Book Two, Chatto & Windus, 1945. pp.4-5.
2. The B.J.S. had, however, previously donated £50, and the Irish Presbyterians had been generous.

21. FROM TANGIER TO MILDMAY

The year that had passed had not all been doom and gloom. As it began Leon was helping Nahum and Donald Davidson to plan and publicize the Edinburgh campaign of Lionel B. Fletcher, the Australian evangelist. The Usher Hall was booked for a week or more in May, and two of Leon's London friends, Dr Thomas Cochrane of the World Dominion Movement and Dr F.W. Norwood of the City Temple, were roped in as supplementary speakers. The hall was well filled, and Fletcher, a manly, down-to-earth Australian, neither sanctimonious nor sentimental, and free from mannerisms, found the Scots reponsive. He did not invite people to come forward to signify their commitment to Christ, but asked them to stand during prayer; and Fred was one who did so. Leon missed the campaign, being abroad, but afterwards entertained the evangelist at Albert Terrace and at Keswick. He also took the opportunity to publish two excellent little books of Fletcher's, one being autobiographical and the other on the Christian life.

In April Abraham's Vineyard had been formed into a Limited Company to facilitate its sale and the prospects seemed bright. The directors appointed were Leon, The Rev. I.E. Davidson, Nahum, Harcourt Samuel, Hugh Schonfield and a Glasgow business man often to be seen at Albert Terrace, Adolph Hillson.

Logie-Pirie House had been opened in June. Leon chaired the ceremony and a letter from Katie was read. Another generous donor, Mrs Edmondson, had provided further comforts, and along with Mrs Logie-Pirie continued to care for the girls. The latter arranged a summer coach-trip to her estate, where a picnic was spread, and the former laid on a New Year party in the hostel at which Leon and other friends were guests. As well as being a home for the girls, the house became the long desired London headquarters for the Alliance. It was even announced that the fourth International Conference would be held there, Jerusalem and America having been rejected as too costly; but this scheme, which would have entailed taking over every adjacent boarding house, was found to be impracticable.

The fact that the suggestion was made, and that the conference was reduced to some fifty delegates, reflects the stringency of the times. "The financial situation", wrote Leon at the end of 1933, "makes it necessary for us to invite only a strictly limited representation from each affiliated Alliance; we had indeed seriously considered postponing the Conference, but the very urgent matters that confront us just now in Palestine and in Germany and Poland, and in connection with the proposed Hebrew Christian Church, make it imperative for us to meet without delay." The problem was solved through the generosity of the Barbican Mission and its director, Isaac Emmanuel Davidson, Vice-President of the Alliance, who made available their conference centre at Mildmay in the Newington Green area of north London.

If the planning, travelling, negotiating, writing and missionary work of 1933 were intensive, this was offset for Leon by various family ploys. It was the year of the car, of the holiday in Wales and the family's visit to Axminster. There was his silver wedding to celebrate in June; and the same month he took Katie, Fred and Miss Thomson to the theatre to see an Edgar Wallace thriller, *The Case of the Frightened Lady*. He also relaxed at Christmas-time and went with Katie and Fred to an undistinguished film entitled *The Rebel*, in which the female lead was played by Vilma Bancky, one of the screen sirens of the day. It was a thin time in the cinema. He would much have preferred the derring-do of Fairbanks (*Robin Hood, The Mark of Zorro*), or the melodrama of Valentino (*The Four Horsemen of the Apocalypse, Blood and Sand*), but it was now ten years since their heyday. There was still Charlie Chaplin, however, Laurel and Hardy, and, on the stage, Harry Lauder, to minister to his taste for comedy.

Early in 1934, with plans for Mildmay well advanced, the time had come to obey his doctor's orders and take a five week break. To escape the prolonged British winter he chose Tangier. He set out alone late in March on the eve of his 53rd birthday.

In Tangier, as it happened, a Hebrew Christian from Berlin had taken refuge. Dr Winter, who had had a large specialist practice, had heard of the I.H.C.A. and its relief work. On learning that Leon was in the city he was anxious to help him and gave him a course of treatment. As a result, when he returned home on May 3rd Leon declared that ninety-five per cent of his pains had gone. And for his part, he arranged for Dr Winter, whose visa to Morocco was to expire in August, to come to Edinburgh to train as a medical missionary and serve in either Africa or India; but whether this was all achieved is not known.

The Barkeys, a Hebrew Christian family, also heard of his arrival and called on him. There was a large Jewish population and Mr Barkey, according to Leon, was doing a magnificent work among them as a missionary. He too was grateful to the Alliance for, three years earlier, his eldest son Jack had been able, through the generosity of one of its members, to enrol at the South Wales Bible Training Institute at Porth. The Barkeys ensured that Leon's stay was a happy one. They introduced him to some of their converts and to two prominent expatriates, Lady Maclean and Lady Scott who, Leon wrote, "never fail to support any worthy cause and are prepared to open their beautiful houses and gardens in order to assist such as are engaged in the service of their Master and their fellow-man." He also paid tribute to the work of the North Africa Mission among the Arab population.

Jack Barkey was about to return to work with his father. Before he did so, however, Leon had him, with his brother, to dinner in London. As a consequence Jack became a member not only of the Alliance but, before long, of its Executive Committee. The contact in Tangier also led to his sister Rena becoming a nurse in Edinburgh and Rosalin's friend; she later married a Dunfermline policeman.

Unfortunately when Leon arrived back in London he had a streaming cold — all his colds were streamers! — caught in the Bay of Biscay. He was just in time to preside over a four-hour committee meeting. Next day the cold was worse, and he had to cancel an engagement in London and three in Bristol. Nobly, Dr Donald Davidson went from Leith to Bristol — where the local Press mistook him for Leon!

As Leon resumed his efforts to gain support from the Churches and missionary societies, he had an eager ally in his brother. In 1933, when Leon was in Palestine, Nahum and Harcourt had represented the Alliance at a conference on the Christian Approach to the Jew. "I was horrified", said Nahum, "at their attitude... Sir Leon had written to the Conference asking it to do something. The Conference appointed a committee. This committee... brought in a resolution asking so many questions and offering not a farthing. We could have answered most of the questions... but were told that these questions would be sent on to Sir Leon."

On June 6th 1934 Leon was unable to attend a meeting of the International Committee on The Christian Approach to the Jew. "I have never so deeply regretted being unable to attend any meeting" he told them in a comprehensive 1700 word letter, "... as I see that the question of aid for Hebrew Christian refugees from Germany is to be dealt with. It seems to me that none of our members realise the deep and tremendous implications of this subject, otherwise there would have been concerted action."

He pointed out that while stricken Jews had, through Jewish relief committees, "at least got someone to whom they can appeal and an address where they can go and have interviews", Hebrew Christians, unless they had heard of the Alliance, "had nowhere to go, and did not know to whom to appeal."

The Alliance, he said, had tried to get Mr Malcolm MacDonald, the High Commissioner for Refugees, to elect a Hebrew Christian on to the Advisory Committee of the Commission, and it had seemed that this would be considered favourably. However, on returning from Tangier he had found that the C.M.S. Secretary who had been appointed to meet Mr MacDonald had been inadequately briefed, and had assented to other co-options, which made the Commission deem that of a Hebrew Christian unnecessary.

Leon then stated the Hebrew Christian case. He drew attention to the fact that Jewish leaders, while anxious for the support of the Churches in their protests, were pursuing a policy of persecution against Hebrew Christians. They held "Christian" Germany responsible for anti-semitism, and despised those who had allied themselves with the Christian faith. Thus when Hebrew Christians appealed to Jewish committees for relief they were left waiting from 9 till 5 and then told they were no longer Jews and should go to the Christians. As a result many had abjured or concealed their faith rather than see their families starve. Some of these committees, it is true, had provided the Alliance's address, but the Alliance could not cope alone. Furthermore, in Britain the Jewish Committees had so won over the sympathies of University and College authorities that applications for places could only be made through themselves or the local rabbi; and the rabbi would simply say his business was to recommend his own people.

No fewer than eleven Jewish societies, Leon pointed out, had representatives on the Advisory Council, whose secretary was Norman Bentwich, a well-known Jew. Five Christian bodies were also represented, but their knowledge of the Hebrew Christians and of the Jewish attitude to them was minimal.

More positively, there was a glorious opportunity to show all Christians of Jewish descent the sympathetic understanding of Christian people, and to let them realise that the Jewish Missions and those interested in them were not indifferent. "Otherwise I am sorry to say", wrote Leon, "that we are going to lose as many Hebrew Christians from the Christian Church within the course of a year or two as all the converts we have been able to make in the history of the Jewish Mission."

This may have been an overstatement, but he felt that only strong words could be effective; nor did he forbear to pitch in at the Jews: "[They] still nurse a spirit of Hitler towards us similar to that which Hitler has to people of Jewish origin.[1] They do not want us; they do not want us to intermarry with their co-religionists; they look upon us as an infectious disease... and will get all the benefits they can for the Jewish refugees and not even tolerate a single Hebrew Christian if they can help it."

He concluded on a less vehement note. "It is as plain as daylight to me that we must have a Hebrew Christian who knows the inner workings of the Jewish mind, who will have tact and statesmanship to counteract these, as a representative of the Advisory Council of the League, and if the Committee thinks that I am perhaps too severe, I would agree that a person like our beloved Director, Dr Conrad Hoffman[2]... should be on The Commission... I have understated the case rather than exaggerated, and I sincerely hope that... something is done to enable our Hebrew Christian brethren to feel that at least they can go before someone who understands them, and who will not knock them from pillar to post and make them feel degraded."

About the time this letter was written Nahum was appealing in similar terms to the Church of Scotland's General Assembly. The

Church that had called Jews into the fellowship of Jesus Christ, he declared, should give them its support. Over 230,000 Hebrew Christians were suffering in Germany, and of the 60,000 citizens who had either been expelled or had fled, some 6,000 were Hebrew Christians.

Illustrating the difficulties facing refugees, he said he had written to a hospital in Belfast asking them to receive a Hebrew Christian doctor. (It may have been Doctor Winter.) The answer was that he must apply to the Belfast rabbi for that opportunity; but after further correspondence arrangements had been made. Otherwise, he said, he had received every help from the Royal College of Surgeons and other public bodies; but there had been no expression of help from the Church.

Dr Macdonald Webster, supporting Nahum, said that many members of the Church had been contributing generously to the Jewish funds on the understanding that Hebrew Christians would get certain benefits; but they got none whatsoever.

The Assembly expressed deep sympathy. However, the Convener of the Home Mission Committee, the formidable Dr John White, said he was unable to accept Nahum's suggestion that an appeal fund should immediately be set up. The correct procedure was to remit the matter to the Jewish Committee, who would be asked to give it the most careful consideration, and to inform the whole Church of the situation.

Something was gained, but not much. The original Deliverance, while it deplored the ill treatment of the Jews and offered them "heartfelt sympathy. . . in these almost intolerable wrongs", had no reference to Hebrew Christians, and this was now remedied, the following addendum being carried:-

"The General Assembly remit to the Jewish Committee to bring to the attention of the Church the plight of the Jewish Christian refugees and the Hebrew Christians in Germany and elsewhere and commend their needs to the generosity of its faithful people."

But fair words butter no parsnips! A Scottish saint, Struthers of Greenock, once remarked that it would do the Church more good than anything else if Christians would sometimes do a *bonnie* thing. By this he meant some generous, unexpected, sacrificial act like the widow's when she gave her only coin, the good Samaritan's when he turned aside to help a Jew, or Mary of Bethany's with her costly perfume. If Dr White had set aside protocol and led the Church to make an immediate response to an urgent need, that would have been a bonnie thing. But the ecclesiastical wisdom of one of Scotland's greatest churchmen prevailed, and while men, women and children starved or could not find the wherewithal to escape or to start a new life, the matter would in time be carefully considered by the appropriate committee. Nor, thereafter, was there any specific appeal; nothing beyond the vague exhortation to be generous.

At the same General Assembly a young Polish Hebrew Christian named Bernard Fink sought permission to enter New College without a prior degree, in order to train as a missionary to the Jews. Because he had spent 14 years training for the rabbinate his petition was granted, but with the proviso that he could not, at any time, accept a call to the parish ministry without reference to the Assembly. Dr Stewart Thomson, on this occasion, informed the Assembly that Mr Fink was the 17th Jew whom he had baptised in his Edinburgh church in the past four years; a record which would seem incredible today.

Nahum's sympathies were not confined to the deprived of his own race or faith. He made a further intervention at the Assembly on behalf of those known as "the black-coated unemployed". The occasion was a motion which welcomed the Government's promise to restore unemployment benefit to the full. This, as Nahum saw, did not go far enough. He wanted the Assembly to deplore, or at least regret, the omission of any reference to those for whom there would still be no dole. His addendum was carried, but in a less critical form. "The General Assembly", it read, "trust the Government will take steps to mitigate the sufferings of the professional and administrative class of men and women by the inclusion of them in the National Health and Unemployment Scheme of Insurance."

It was a further evidence, if any were needed, that Nahum like Leon was, in the poet Yevtushenko's phrase, "an advocate for the poor".

At Mildmay in July they again sought to serve the impoverished and persecuted Hebrew Christians. That, after all, was the purpose of the Palestine colony, of the projects in Poland, and of the relief work in Germany. But as we have examined these topics already their discussion at the Conference may be taken as read. The other major concerns were education and the Hebrew Christian Church.

Leon was more than Chairman. His Presidential Address, his review of three years' work (spoken from a single sheet of notes) and his introduction to and summing up of every important issue were major contributions.

"It is with unspeakable joy that I rise to welcome you" were his opening words, and his overflowing affection for them, and of the delegates for one another, was the hallmark of the conference. He spoke also with sorrow. "We are meeting under tragic circumstances", he said, and referred to the evil spirit prevailing in so much of Europe. "As we look upon these countries it seems as if the very name of Christ will be wiped out from the minds of these people.

"But let us not forget the power of Christianity. ·. . to rise from the dust in which it is sometimes buried as in the grave. The power of Christ is capable of endless resurrection — 'He shall see of the travail of his soul and be satisfied'. We know that Christ can still the storm; that He shares our troubles that we may share His victory."

He spoke also of his continuing vision, even then, of a redeemed Israel fulfilling its purpose in the world. "I can see Jewry one day taking her place in the world, not through any influence in finance, nor through the cabinets of governments in different countries but. . . acting as light-bearers — becoming the instruments of Christ for a renewed world. . . Our Jewish people have a genius for religion which, when it is won for Christ and baptised by the Holy Spirit, may be the means of harmonising the differences between all the Protestant denominations and leading them to be united in one great Protestant Church of Christ. I would even dare to go further and to say that from the position which our people occupy in being scattered throughout every country in Christendom, God, through them, may bring about a union of all the branches of the Christian Church, including the Greek and Roman Catholic Churches into one great, undivided Body of Christ."

The note of thanksgiving was heard throughout the Conference; for progress at Gaza, and in Poland; for the church in Roumania and the Girls' Hostel in London; for the Maranos, the Dutch, and, at Danzig, a third new Alliance. "I am advised", said Leon, "that an Alliance in Danzig Free State will be enabled to speak more freely and do things our brethren in Germany cannot do." Then there was a delegate from France who told them of a Committee for the Relief of Distressed Christians in Russia, with headquarters at Berne, which had agreed to help Hebrew Christians. There was, too, Hélène Schonfield's report on the Women's Auxiliaries. In it she told of their Prayer Union, which had now extended into Europe where it wanted to have its own missionary.

Thanksgiving there was, too, in the field of education. Since the last Conference 23 young people had been trained for missionary work. "The educational task", said Leon, "is one of the most glorious things we are attempting to do." However, more resources could be found if missionary societies had the courage to close schools that had outlived their necessity. "Now every country has systems of education which are infinitely superior and better equipped. . . If they gave up these [mission] schools they would have no more deficit; and secondly they would have the money to look after the men and women they are baptising. . . to do as we are doing and enable them to become missionaries."

One of the first schools to go had been the Scots College at Safed which, only three weeks before, had closed its doors. Its numbers had once risen to ninety, but only a third were Jews; and as the roll declined, in a period notorious for Arab-Jewish riots, and the school became increasingly uneconomic, the Church wisely decided to concentrate on its medical and evangelistic work. Leon, who might have been expected to favour the retention of the college and of his old friends, Principal and Mrs Semple, saw the wisdom of its closure. Thereafter, with increased resources, the hospital at Tiberias was able to employ some refugees. There was, for instance, Dr Sacki, a German who worked at the Jewish hospital and came under the influence of the Mission. Dismissed and ill-treated, he and his wife had to seek refuge on the Mission premises. They were baptised there in February 1936 and he became an honoured colleague of Dr Torrance. At the same time Dr Lilly Wreschner, the daughter of a Jewish professor in Switzerland, was being trained at the Women's Missionary College and also at New College in Edinburgh, for work at Tiberias as an evangelist. At Tiberias, to establish rapport with the Jews, she added Hebrew to the six or seven languages she already spoke.

There was also, in Safed, Miss Asseo a convert of the Church's Constantinople Mission, which had been wound up in 1930 when the teaching of the New Testament had become forbidden. She worked as an evangelist but had to be moved to Jaffa when unrest in Safed became too threatening.

Hebrew Christians, then, were being both educated and employed. Forty-two students, it was intimated, had now been trained since the inception of the Alliance, and this was indeed cause for thanksgiving. Nevertheless, Leon was not complacent. The Alliance, he saw, had its weaknesses, one of which was intolerance. Abroad and in Britain he had observed a censorious attitude towards the many Jews who believed in Christ but lacked the courage either to be baptised or to join the movement. Ever tolerant, he accepted and wooed these fringe believers. He saw that it was the coldness of many Churches towards them, especially on the Continent, that held them back.

"I have heard it said", he wrote after his journey in 1933, "that these Christ-believing Jews number from 15 to 50 thousand, and various views about their attitude and faith have been put before me. . . It was therefore both a privilege and a great joy for me to come into contact with some of these people. . . My heart was filled to overflowing with praises to God for the wonderful testimonies to which I listened.

"In one capital that I visited some of our brethren took me to task and desired me to set myself up as a judge. They maintained that because these Christ-believing Jews were not members of Churches, therefore they could not be counted as Christians. Yet in listening to the statements which they made to me, I felt that none of us dare set ourselves up in judgement, nor are any of us competent to do so because God alone in Jesus Christ shall judge them."

He gave two examples of Christ-believing Jews. The first, questioned about baptism and the Church, said that his eighty year-old mother came from a very pious home and the shock of his baptism might kill her. He also found anti-semitic feeling in the Churches, and Christians who wanted him to give up his affection for his race. However, if there were a Hebrew Christian Church he would be able to join it and even to be baptised. The other man recounted how the minister he approached had said: "I will accept you if, to prove your honesty, you will have a meal of pork with me." His Jewish upbringing and feelings, he said, were not accepted and he did not find the love and affection which should always prevail in the House of God.

Leon was reinforced by such encounters in his conviction that the only means of reconciling the Jewish people with their Messiah would be through the creation of a Hebrew Christian Church.

At Mildmay a few months later, in his Review of the Year, he returned to the subject in a passage which reveals clearly his own methods as a missionary. "Many of our members have felt that we should have little to do with these people, but I am convinced that this is a great mistake, and would again urge an attitude of friendship. . . Christ our Lord carried no key to the human heart but the key of loving friendship. . . His power was in the fact that He had not a key. His way was, and is, to knock at the door of a man's heart with such an appeal of truth and love that men are at last won to unbar the door. . . However strong love's persuasion, it is always persuasion, never compulsion. Christ's method is the love that knocks, and waits, and knocks again. . ."

But there were some Christ-professing Jews whom he found less genuine. Not all his geese were swans, and he was discriminating enough not to give wholesale approval. "I met", he says, "with a group of Hebrew Christians who thought themselves too clever to join our movement. . . and to these had to point out that while we thanked God for cleverness and capacity when we had them, our principal duty was then to forget them, for the power to serve God's kingdom is not in brains nor cleverness but just the capacity to love. It is love that makes Him real to others, it is love which translates the Gospel, and love is His gift."

He also referred to the antagonisms and conflicts which he had found between Hebrew Christians of different denominations and within the missionary societies. "In trying to make up some of these differences", he said, "I have been conscious that the thing which stands in the way of real fellowship in most cases is just pride. . . the unwillingness to forgive and ask forgiveness. . .

"I feel that in order to overcome these things we must live more constantly in the presence of our Master. . . All real healings begin there. No problem of wrong relationships can be solved in any other way than that of putting God first, confessing our common needs, and together seeking to do His will."

At the Mildmay Conference he spoke in this vein. He also pleaded for more support, for he was feeling the burden of leadership. "You can give me", he said, "a little encouragement in my heavy task — you can give me, above all, your prayers. Sometimes it saddens me, my friends, when I pour out my life and love on your behalf for Christ's sake and the love of my people, that I either hear nothing at all, or just grumbling and complaining. Still, I never take much notice of these things, because if I did, then I would not be fit for a task such as ours. It is a glorious task — I love it. Whether you agree with it or not, love it. The Alliance has brought joy into the hearts of people hitherto hopelessly lonely, to hearts of Hebrew Christians persecuted and looked down upon by their friends. . . It has also enabled us to do things together we could not do single-handed. . . has raised our status and respect in all the Churches; is making the Jewish people look on us in a new light; they are granting there are Hebrew Christians who gave up everything. . . who chose to be messengers of hope, seeking to bring about better understanding between Christians and Jews in a way no Jew could do unless he is a child of Christ."

But if only there were a Hebrew Christian Church, he thought, all these objectives would be achieved more fully. Whether to go ahead in the light of the Special Commission's Report on this was the supreme decision of the Conference.

A whole day was given over to the crucial discussion. The adoption of the Report was moved by its Chairman, the Rev. E. Bendor Samuel (Harcourt's father). He said that there could be no doubt that in some places such a Church was needed, but it must not be a sect. It would be part of the existing Church which had a Jewish foundation. According to Scriptures there was no Church but the Jewish Church. The Gentiles, as Paul said, were like branches grafted into an olive tree, brought in along with the Jews.

Nahum seconded, and pointed out that the members of the Commission were loyal members of their own denominations; but uppermost in their minds was how to meet the European situation and the care of their brethren. He himself was a convert of the missions, but missions could no longer do what ought to be done. The problem was both national and international and faced the whole Church. In India, for instance, for lack of an indigenous Church, people were asking: Which is the true Church?

The Hebrew Christians wanted the inalienable right to go into the Church as members of the Jewish race. Unless they showed the Jews that they were not ashamed of their Judaism the Jew would never come into their Church. By creating a Hebrew Christian Church they would show they were not ashamed of their heritage.

But could anyone be a member of two Churches? That question was posed in the discussion, and Leon gave his answer. "In Edinburgh", he said, "I am a member of the Presbyterian Church;

but if some time hence, I were to reside in Palestine I would join the Hebrew Christian Church. The two do not clash."

Would Gentiles be admitted? Leon replied that all who loved the Hebrew Christians would be admitted. The questioner wondered if eventually it would become a Gentile Church with only a few Jewish members. Leon said that as they intended to preserve Jewish forms of devotion this would be unlikely.

A Hungarian was assured that while remaining an active elder in his own Church, he would be able to give help to a Hebrew Christian congregation.

Having persuaded various delegates to withdraw unhelpful amendments, Leon then called on each national delegation to voice its opinion, and it became evident that there was not complete unanimity. Some of the German and Austrian delegates, in particular, expressed doubts. "I have lost my office in Germany," said one, "because the Church there let herself be led by national principles. These principles are not of Him in whom there is neither bond nor free." He did not want them to do the same thing as Archbishop Müller and the Reich Christians. Many brethren feared that the institution of a Hebrew Christian Church was against the practice of the apostles. It would also invite anti-semitism, and would keep the missions from pursuing their work for they would say, "Let the Church do it."

But they were not, replied a Belgian delegate, going to found a national Church; it would be not only international but supra-national.

Dr Frank said that he was not against the principle that such a Church should arise, say in Palestine and Poland. But it was out of the question in Germany — there it was suggested only by opponents, and no-one would go to it just because it was a Hebrew Christian Church. He also doubted its success elsewhere. The experiments of Mr Rabinovitch in Poland and Dr Levertoff in London, he thought, had failed. And if many Aryans came in with the Hebrew Christian families, could it remain a Hebrew Christian Church?

Against this, Pastor Smoljar of Latvia pointed out that his friend Pastor Rosenberg, working in Russia, had started churches which, but for the Revolution and the Great War, would be doing immense good.

Another German wanted to drop the word "Church". Would not

a *Gemeinschaft* (fellowship meeting) fulfil the purpose? Hugh Schonfield also thought the name "Church" an unhappy one. "The only type of building and worship which a Jew would understand would be that of a Jewish-Christian *Synagogue.*"

Dr Foldes thought they should give a free constitution to whatever they constituted and avoid dogmatic principles. They should merely press the Bible into the hands of their brethren and let them have access to any desire that could be supported by Scripture. . . It was not what the other Churches would think, but what the Jews would think that mattered. For the sake of the Jews he was in favour.

So also were two speakers from Yugoslavia. They had started evangelising and the Government had asked them: "Are you wanting to start a new sect?" "No", they said, "our wish is simply to preach Christ crucified to the Jews." They would greet the day when the Church was a recognised fact and would witness to the Gentiles.

A Palestine delegate said that Ezekiel's vision of the dry bones coming together was being fulfilled: Jewish nationalism was returning from exile. And the remnant was called upon to return too, in the Hebrew Christian Church.

A Pole said the existing Churches were like vehicles whose owners drove them down the road, and the Hebrew Christian was a poor pedestrian who had to crave a lift. As long as he was travelling on the same road why should he not have his own vehicle?

Finally, the opinion was expressed that the creation of a Church should happen naturally and not be forced. The Rev. Harry Ellison, a missionary in Roumania who, with Hugh Schonfield and Harcourt Samuel — all twenty years younger than Leon — was one of the rising stars of the Alliance, voiced this view. "I think", he said, "Pastor Forrell was right in attributing a certain amount of nationalism to the proposal. I know my brethren in Bucharest would have me say, 'Let it grow by itself.' This scheme is a different thing and if it is carried out I think many members will leave the Roumanian Alliance. A Church, certainly! But let it grow up naturally."

At this point Leon intervened. He said that most of the Christians referred to in Bucharest were strict Brethren and this explained their attitude to the creation of a Church.

The discussion was brought to a close and Leon then spoke. He began by saying that they should not bring Germany too much into consideration. They should only consider, first, whether they had a right to establish a Church and, second, whether it was needed.

To meet the situation in Jewry, he declared, they must be bold and venturesome, people of vision. They had the same right as Luther, Calvin, Wesley, Fox and Knox who had faced a similar situation. And they should show equal boldness and trust in God.

Those who had done so in the past had enriched the Church Universal. The result was the beautiful liturgy of the Episcopalian Church; the social passion of the Methodists; the moral vigour of Congregationalism; the fine democracy of the Baptists; the spiritual insight and courage of the Society of Friends; and the missionary vision and intellectual vigour of Presbyterianism.

They had an equal contribution to make. They would have the advantage of being able to gather all that was best in the Protestant Churches. And they would bring back the fire and imagination of the prophets of Israel, and by the infusion of new blood add to the life of the Body of Christ.

Through such an institution Christ would alter the relationship between the Christian people and the Jewish race; and in a joint contribution what might they not be able to achieve?

The Church, he said, had lost her vision, and of late had taken short views; hence her apathy towards Jewish missions. He believed that through a Hebrew Christian Church that apathy could be removed. There had been a lack of enterprise in work among the Jews, a stunted imagination and a want of adventure. Missionary societies had always thought of locked doors, and the Church had labelled the Jewish people as hopeless, forgetting all the time that God was standing at these very doors awaiting entrance.

Moreover, the Church had never learned to accept the Jews as they were. The root of many of the frictions, ill-feelings and misunderstandings was often their desire to conform them to their own kind of pattern... Only the Hebrew Christians could accept their own people as they were; could bear with what was irksome in them, and refuse to let differences stand in the way of their love for them in order to lead them to Christ.

Before sitting down he laid aside his notes and referred directly to the discussion. "We have failed", he said, "to forget ourselves. We did not realise that it is not *my* connection with a Church and *my* view of worship that matters; but the salvation of Jewry and, through that, the salvation of the world." They had quoted texts, but forgotten that Paul stood out against Judaising the Gentiles; and now they had to plead against Gentilising the Jews. They must have seen the need, and they had to meet it. The Jewish people needed love, they needed friendship, and a Hebrew Christian Church could give it them.

As he concluded he opened his heart and shared with them his belief that his prayers had been answered and the Church he had longed for was already born. "I have something to tell you", he said. "I had been considering the whole matter carefully at Keswick, and I discussed it with a friend. Whereupon this friend" — he did not reveal that it was Miss Edmondson, a devoted supporter of the Alliance — "promised £2,000 to build the first Hebrew Christian Church in the Palestine Colony! We exchanged cards as a token and on mine I wrote. "The Hebrew Christian Church — Keswick, 18 July, 1934. Born in love, with praises to God, and with gratitude and thanks to His Holy Name."

That, he said, was the answer he got to his prayers. They had every right to establish a Church. They could still alter the proposed Constitution and anything else. But the question was, had they the right and was it necessary? "God has guided us to this Conference and led us to consider this great subject, and it is now a question between our souls and consciences and Him."

When the vote was taken by ballot the result, a majority in favour by 24 votes to 6, indicated a clear call to go ahead. Everyone rose and sang the Doxology and the session closed with prayer.

No other matter so dominated the Conference. It is of interest, however, that it was decided to approach the British and Foreign Bible Society regarding the crying need, especially in Poland, for a New Testament in Yiddish. Until the Second World War and the revival of Hebrew, Yiddish was the common tongue of some two thirds of world Jewry. It has been spoken longer than modern German or English, and since Jewish women were not taught Hebrew it became known as *Mamaloshen* ("mother-language"). It originated in the Rhineland and is an adaptation of the local vernacular which the Jews wrote phonetically in Hebrew lettering. Once a despised jargon, over the centuries it acquired a culture, rich and romantic, pious and sentimental — the culture of the *shtetle*, that area movingly depicted in *Fiddler on the Roof*, the musical based on the stories of Shalom Aleichem. And it was through Yiddish that Leon established rapport with many immigrant Jews in Edinburgh.

Any other missionary to the Jews would find it advantageous; and if that missionary were himself a Jew it would be an asset he might already have.

Leon having been elected President for a fourth term, that is, until the next Conference, urged the delegates to go back to their task and see the glory and the thrill of it; and to go in the spirit of the saints of old who were experts in forlorn hopes; the spirit in which there was nothing they could not do.

However, events were closing in. What they could not do was fulfil his dreams. The Church, like the Colony, was never achieved. When the fifth International Conference took place at Budapest in 1937, without him, the following resolution was passed: "That this Conference requests its Executive to take no further steps for the founding of a Hebrew Christian Church, but that it extend its full and wholehearted sympathy and encouragement to all Hebrew Christian Churches now in existence or that shall later be formed in which the Gospel of Jesus Christ is preached in a manner consistent with the doctrinal basis of the Alliance, and where all things are done decently and in order to the glory of God." Although five members expressed their dissent, this outcome was inevitable; for the survival of such a Church anywhere in Europe had become less than a forlorn hope, and Gaza, too, was slipping from their hands. Another resolution had been carried in the terms "that if circumstances should entirely prevent the establishment of a colony in Palestine, then the Conference would welcome the establishment of a colony in Lebanon."

The incalcitrant fact was that the world was moving into what O'Casey's "Captain" Boyle called "a state o'chassis", and the most they could do was to see that where some courageous band of believers set up a place of worship they did so "decently and in order".

NOTES
1. It should be remembered that Hitler had not yet declared his "final solution" of extermination.
2. Of the International Committee on the Christian Approach to the Jew.

Advocate for the Oppressed.
1934-36.

22. 1934—35

In the same year, 1934, Nahum applied for a professorship. His friend Norman Porteous, on being appointed to the Old Testament Chair at New College, was about to vacate the corresponding one at St Mary's College, St Andrews, and he encouraged Nahum to put his name forward. Nahum did so with thoroughness, furnishing a printed *curriculum vitae*, testimonials from eminent scholars including C.R. North, Stanley Cook and W.O.E. Oesterley, and from as far afield as his Chicago seminary, together with quotations from the reviews of all his books.

For technical reasons concerning the Edinburgh Chair, Professor Porteous's installation suffered a lengthy delay and the St Andrews appointment an equal postponement. During this time Nahum had second thoughts, and in June 1935 withdrew. Why he took this step remains a mystery. Perhaps, having left Blantyre after only two years there, to abandon St Ninian's, Leith, after but another four seemed reprehensible. Alternatively the congregation may have prevailed on him to stay. Or did he, for the sake of Leon and the Alliance and the worsening Jewish situation, remain where he could give most help? He may, of course, have discovered that his chance was remote, and dimmed perhaps by the débâcle of his *Textual Amendment of the Old Testament*.

Whatever the reason, his aspirations remained; and in April 1937 he had no reservations in trying again. This time it was for the Chair of Old Testament Language, Literature, and Theology in New College (Professor Porteous having had a further move to a University chair), and he was turned down. Rumour has it that Dr George Gunn, a forceful church leader, had a decisive hand in the appointment, strongly promoting Oliver Rankin's candidature and assuring his colleagues that they need look no further.

That Nahum became neither professor nor lecturer is a cause for regret. He had so much to give, and would have profoundly influenced the young. He had also volunteered to lecture in rabbinics, a subject in which Oxford and Cambridge had instituted lectureships but which the other universities then lacked. Relieved of a parish, he would have made a larger scholastic contribution.

He did, however, become a *guru* to whom students turned for advice. Among them was a young professor-to-be, Tom Torrance, afterwards the most distinguished Scottish (and possibly British) theologian of his generation. The unpointed Hebrew text of the Talmud presented no difficulties to Nahum who explicated it to him.

From his letters of application for the two Chairs further knowledge of Nahum's activities can be gleaned. He remarks, for instance, that during the last three years he had lectured to over thirty groups of Sunday School teachers on Old Testament subjects. Again, in 1937 he says "I have just completed a book on *The Life and Teaching of St Paul*, about 340 pages, which I hope to publish before the end of this year." He also lists his work for the Alliance: "adviser on all theological matters. . . responsible for drawing up the constitution for the polity of the proposed Hebrew Christian Church. . . joint editor of the. . . *Quarterly*, and secretary of the fund to aid German refugees."

He was playing an increasingly important part in the Alliance, and having been made Vice-President to the aged Dr Frank after the Budapest Conference of 1937, he went to Palestine with Harcourt Samuel to try to retrieve the initial deposit not yet repaid by the rascally Fami Bey for the land at Gaza. Nahum's congregation was very forbearing, for a few months later he was abroad again, fulfilling the American tour that Leon had planned to make.

At the end of that year (1938), immediately after the 'Kristalnacht' pogrom, he went to Berlin to offer help to a Lutheran pastor who was a friend of Dr Frank's and who had opened the Büro Pfarrer Grüber to succour non-Aryan Christians. Later, in a pamphlet about the bureau, Pastor Heinrich Grüber wrote: "The Rev. Nahum Levison came to Berlin at that time to offer help from his Church and from the Hebrew Christian Alliance. In answer to his question whether the bureau needed money and if so how much,

1934 – 35

Grüber named a five-figure sum, which was immediately made available to him." "The Rev. Nahum Levison of Edinburgh," he added, "devoted himself tirelessly to those who emigrated to Great Britain."[1]

However, in 1934-35 Leon was still very much alive and, indeed, rather rashly taking on new assignments. In February 1934, for instance, he took part in a public meeting on the question of Sunday trading. An attempt to liberalise the laws had been countered in Parliament by a Scottish M.P., Mr. D.M. Mason, whose Shops (Sunday Trading Restriction) (Scotland) Bill had been widely discussed by, among other bodies, the Presbyteries of the Church of Scotland. With their wholehearted support Mr Mason was invited to address a rally, held under the Church's auspices, in the Usher Hall. It was also arranged that the Moderator of the Presbytery of Edinburgh, Dr. Millar Patrick, would move a resolution welcoming the Bill and asking all Scottish M.P.s to support it. The rally took place three weeks before the Bill's second reading, and there was a large audience.

Instead of asking another presbyter to second Dr Patrick, the organisers chose Leon, thereby signifying that he was sufficiently well-known both in the church and in public life to carry weight.

Much of what he said was predictable. He saw in the Scottish moral character the tremendous influence of Sunday and what it stood for; and he testified to the feelings of gratitude and affection they had toward those who were championing the cause in the House of Commons. However, he struck a fresh note concerning Jewish tradesmen who supported the Bill. Most of them, he maintained, already opened on Saturdays and he saw no reason why they need open on Sundays as well. Even the Communists, he added, were asking for a weekly day of rest.

His championing of Sunday was endorsed by his minister. For Dr Black at that time was castigating from his pulpit those Christian town councillors who "sat there like stuffed rabbits" while their less committed colleagues permitted the opening of a Sunday cinema. (At least one councillor was in the congregation!). The zeal with which many of them fought for the preservation of Sunday has not been emulated by laxer post-war generations.

Other undertakings were the chairmanship of the London Council of the Bulgarian Bible School, whose field-work he had encountered at Samokov in the Balkans, and the Vice-Presidency of the Pocket Testament League, at whose meetings he became a regular speaker. These added to his quota of committee meetings; but none more so than a third commitment undertaken at the beginning of 1936, the chairmanship of the Moody Centenary Council. This entailed the setting up of both a London and a Scottish Council, and the stimulating of local committees in many parts of Britain; for Leon mainly in Scotland. The outcome of all this was to be widespread and simultaneous evangelistic rallies in February 1937, the centenary of the great evangelist's birth.

His acceptance of such appointments shows his sense of obligation to evangelical Christianity as a whole. As a public figure and a titled layman he was aware that his name could enhance a cause. Yet he was never content to be a figurehead and always gave more than moral support.

Nevertheless, it is more than doubtful whether he should have taken on these extra tasks. The wearing neuralgic headaches and the fibrositis in his shoulders, which found brief remission in Tangier, had returned to plague him. Others, it is true, shared the Alliance's burdens: Hugh Schonfield went out to Palestine in the autumn of 1934, Harcourt Samuel gave every possible moment in the first year of his pastorate at Ramsgate, and Nahum took major responsibility for the refugees. Of Nahum's contribution Leon wrote: "He not only had to communicate with each individual and advise them about ways and means of entering this country, but also had to meet them at port or station; to find suitable lodgings; to interview the authorities at the universities; to arrange for posts at hospitals; and to plead with various missionary societies for those who felt a call to the foreign mission field. And, last but not least, to take my place at a large number of meetings which I was unable to address owing to my state of health".

Katie's health was also worrying him. He accompanied her that summer to Harrogate, where they took the waters and she was treated for rheumatism. She was to return there two or three times in the next few years, after which her rheumatism subsided.

Of Nahum it should also be said that from as early as 1931 he was befriending refugees. For instance, he and Margaret gave hospitality to a German girl, taught her English, and then, when she reached the age of admission, asked the matron of Leith Hospital to employ her, along with another from Austria, as trainee nurses. A third Hebrew Christian girl was accepted by the same hospital; and

Rudolf Ehrlich, whose first British home was the Logie-Pirie Hostel, became a student at New College and eventually a minister in the adjacent parish to his mentor, Nahum.[2]

Something should now be said about the three young henchmen, Samuel, Schonfield and Peltz, all twenty years younger than Leon, without whom he could not have carried on.

Harcourt Samuel, now the I.H.C.A.'s elder statesman, worked in close harness with Leon through all the years of his leadership. A second generation Hebrew Christian, he sat loose, as did Leon, to most of the feasts, fasts and traditions of Israel, being content to look forward rather than to the past. At the same time they joined with those groups of Hebrew Christians who find inspiration in Sederim parties in each other's homes at Pesach or Easter, prayer meetings at Yom Kippur, and celebrations at Sukkoth and Chanukkah. His mildness of manner and ready friendliness conceal both a spiritual depth and business acumen which, along with the willingness to carry a heavy workload, have made him a prime asset to the Alliance.

It was in the early twenties that Hugh Schonfield appeared on the scene. An exceedingly clever young man, he was studying Semitic and Oriental Languages at Glasgow University when he was put in touch with Leon. They took to each other at once and Hugh became Leon's protégé. He came often to Albert Terrace and was treated as one of the family. Sixty years later Fred asked him (now eighty-six and about to go on an archaeological expedition to Malaysia!) what he remembered of those days. "I remember your sister Rosie" (as she was then called) "saying, 'You're daft Hugh, you're daft!'." He also remembered Leon, then and afterwards, as "something of a mystic but always a realist as well."

He was a first generation Hebrew Christian and retained a great love for the traditions of his youth. His family were well-known London Jews, his father, Major Schonfield, being a founder-member of Allenby's Jewish Brigade.

Small, dark and olive-skinned, his youthful appearance and unlined features belied his enormous erudition. In the photograph of the High Leigh Conference Hugh and Hélène, more casually dressed than anyone else and with their toddler at their feet, add gaiety to the scene, and through all his days in the Alliance they were buoyant spirits. Yet Hugh was something more. Turn up any copy of the *Quarterly* in Leon's lifetime and you will find a contribution from his pen; a major one was in serial form, his *Short History of Jewish Christianity*. As literary editor he did most of the reviewing and, at the same time, he was editing another quarterly called *Search*. He published over thirty books, many of them the fruit of his original research on the origins of Christianity. *The Speech that Moved the World*, a study of the Sermon on the Mount by "Hegesippus" (a 2nd Century Hebrew Christian) was his first scholarly work; then followed *An Old Hebrew Text of Matthew* and *A study in Messianic folk-lore*. Other volumes included subjects as diverse as *Bibliomania in the Middle Ages*, *Letters to Frederick Tennyson*, *A New Hebrew Typography* (which he had designed), *Richard Burton* (the explorer), *Versailles, Italy and Suez*, and studies of world citizenship, U.S. Presidents, Zionism, and the Dead Sea Scrolls.

As a New Testament scholar he had the disadvantage of having no academic training in theology, attending only some courses at the Bible Training Institute, an ultra-conservative college in Glasgow. Whether it was over-reaction to this which made him susceptible to some of the extra-canonical traditions regarding Jesus it is hard to say; but he became increasingly heretical, and shortly after Leon's death was forced to leave the Alliance, whose trinitarian tenets he could not accept.

Leon, who had brought him into the Alliance, and with whom he worked closely for two years as its General Secretary and for many more on the Executive, the Abraham's Vineyard Board and the Church Commission, would have been aghast at his expulsion and would, Hugh believed, have succeeded in keeping him in, on the grounds that he accepted the Messiahship of Jesus, though not his Godhead. And had he then been able to share his thinking with Leon, he might not later (in 1965) have published *The Passover Plot* (which won him both fame and notoriety, and sold over three million copies worldwide), in which he advanced the astounding proposition that Jesus plotted with Joseph of Arimathea to have himself drugged on the Cross and taken down alive; a plot which went wrong when, on being removed from the tomb, it was found that he was too far gone to recover. "His corpse" says Hugh, in a sentence also found in his *Jesus: a Biography* as early as 1939, "was hastily buried in a new grave whose whereabouts, like that of Moses, was never subsequently revealed."

In *Those Incredible Christians*, *The Pentecost Revolution* and other works he sought to substantiate his theory and to study its implications in the composition of the gospels, of which he considered the fourth to have been faked, or compiled by the Early Church. However questionable his judgement, he provided so many fresh insights that he has been praised, at least for these, by Dr William Barclay and other New Testament scholars.

Without Leon's influence, however, it is certain that, his mind moving more and more along heretical lines, Hugh would have had sooner or later to part from the Alliance.

The manner of his going was unfortunate. The Secretary of the British Alliance, Mr Yoelson-Taffen, laid an accusation against him, and the Business Committee of the I.H.C.A. decided that, since he was unable to accept the wording of the Article defining the Alliance's doctrinal position, he could not remain a member. Hugh, however, appealed; and a Judicial Committee set up at the Budapest Conference in 1937 upheld him. They felt that, although he was unwilling to use a phrase which he regarded as unscriptural, his views were not really in conflict with those of the Alliance. Nahum, however, was not satisfied. The Committee, he said, had not fully understood the position. Moreover, because there might be others who did not believe in the full Deity of Jesus, Jacob Peltz and he put forward a motion that required from every delegate an affirmation of faith, in terms of Article 9 of the Bye-Laws, viz:-

"Persons eligible for membership must be Hebrew Christians who a) have made public confession of their faith; b) have accepted Jesus as their personal Saviour; c) believe in the Atonement and vicarious suffering which He has wrought on the Cross at Calvary; d) believe in His Deity and Resurrection; and e) declare their adherence to the Scriptures of the Old and New Testaments as the supreme rule of faith and life."

One by one the delegates rose to affirm this, the only exceptions being the Schonfields, who were then declared to be excluded. "We are more sorry than we can say" reads the report in the *Quarterly*, "that we have lost (their) services. . . (they) are loved by us all. Nevertheless we could do no other. One piece of solid satisfaction has come out of what was a most disagreeable necessity, and that is that it has been established beyond doubt that the Alliance and all its members stand without compromise of any sort for the absolute Deity of our Lord Jesus Christ and the great doctrines of the evangelical faith."

Leon was less uncompromising than Nahum. He would have

Hugh Schonfield

Jacob Peltz

Harcourt Samuel

regarded Hugh's heterodoxy as a temporary aberration and been content to disregard Article 9. After all, the Alliance was not a denomination. Its tenets were patently Christian, for this was its *raison d'être*, but need its members have to subscribe to a credal statement? Should there not be room as in, say, the Student Christian Movement or Toc H, for fellow-travellers who, though as yet unable to articulate all it stands for, wish to ally themselves with what is clearly a Christian movement? The importance of this is evident when one considers the large number of both Hebrew Christians and Jesus-loving Jews who reckon the Alliance is not for them. A less inflexible fellowship would have had more difficulty in persuading the cautious Dutch to join. Yet it might — who knows? — not only have gathered in Anglicans such as Paul Levertoff, Hugh Montefiore and Paul Oestreicher, but also have reached out towards such Jewish literati as Singer and Bellow, F.R. Leavis and Isaiah Berlin, and some of those illustrious in music, politics and science, and shown them the possibility of Christian belief.

Hugh Schonfield, alas, still bears the marks of his rejection. He remembers Nahum's intervention with bitterness, and has found no settled home in church or synagogue. His maverick career has included the Vice-Presidency of the Spiritualist Association as well as the Presidency of the Commonwealth of World Citizens and of the International Arbitration League. His nomination for the Nobel Peace Prize in 1959 and his publications should at least have found him a place in "Who's Who", but that register of the great and the good is strangely silent. Some would say of him, with a sadness akin to St Paul's, "Demas has forsaken us". Leon might simply have chided him gently for his proneness to accept the most implausible first century traditions — perhaps in those words from Rosie's childhood, "You're daft, Hugh, you're daft!"[3]

The third member of the triumvirate, Jacob Peltz, was born in Russia. When he was twelve his family emigrated to Baltimore. In Russia he had been brought up to hate the Christians, who despised their Jewish neighbours, and to have contempt for the Church which, with its ikons and pageantry, was to a Jew idolatrous. In Baltimore, however, he met a lady who promised to give him English lessons. "How amazing it was to me", he wrote, "that this educated lady would sit with this immigrant Jew and grapple with him over the English grammar night after night. And she did it gratis, in the name of Christ. It was no wonder that I became curious about this new kind of Christians in America."

When Jacob eventually became a Christian he lost his home, relatives and friends, and was persecuted; but Christians supported and educated him and he gained degrees in both Divinity and Philosophy. As a student he became Missionary of the Chicago Hebrew Mission, and knew what it was to be knocked unconscious (twice) by hoodlums or pelted with rotten eggs. After a brief ministry in the Presbyterian Church he became its Field Representative for the Department of Jewish Evangelisation; and in 1926 General Secretary of the Hebrew Christian Alliance of America.

That was the year of Leon's visit, by which Jacob was overwhelmed. From then on he did magnificent work for the Alliance, creating local branches in eleven major cities, organising Bible and Missionary Conferences, and addressing meetings throughout the United States and Canada.

In 1933 he resigned in order to promote a remarkable work in Chicago. In an area of 70,000 Jews the Presbyterian Church had a Community Centre which, after twelve years, produced about two hundred Christians of Jewish parentage. Their leader, the Rev. David Bronstein, was himself a convert along with his wife, who was Peltz's older sister. These conversions came about under the influence not primarily of Peltz but of the remarkable woman he married. Referring to his own conversion he wrote: "But the greatest force in my life, the one to whom I owe more than to anyone else for my conversion and the development of my Christian character, is Miss Ruby Gaither, who. . . became my wife."

The work of the Bronsteins, the Peltzes, and their colleagues was to result, in a few years time, in a Hebrew Christian congregation being formed. Meanwhile, however, Jacob with his wife and fourteen year-old son had come to London to be General Secretary of the I.H.C.A. It was a new era in his life and in that of the Alliance, to whose prayers he proved to be the answer.

Adaptability is a characteristic of the Jew, and in no time he adapted himself to the British way of life. It was in February 1935 that he came, and in March Leon set out again for Palestine leaving him to address a string of meetings and to get established in London. The Peltzes wisely set up home in Logie-Pirie House. There he had not only an office but a small community of Hebrew Christians, from overseas as well as London, from whom they learned much. Before long he was able to visit Europe, including

Germany, where, with a lower profile than Leon's, he could travel more freely. He wrote movingly of his experiences in the *Quarterly*, and he also introduced a feature, "From the Secretary's Desk", in which he reviewed events affecting both Hebrew Christians and Jews throughout the world.

He was a very personable young man and, in spite of his energy and drive, entirely tranquil. Leon and he were in complete accord and formed both a dynamic and a deeply affectionate partnership. Jacob was General Secretary until the outbreak of the Second World War. He then returned to Chicago where he continued to serve the Alliance in the role of an International Vice-President. In 1967, on a visit to Britain, he called on Fred in Edinburgh and, hearing that Rosalin lived nearby, said he would like to visit her. Fred left him with her, not without trepidation, for she was a compulsive talker and inclined to overwhelm visitors with excess of warmth and hospitality. However, Jacob returned delighted. "She's a typical 'Yiddisher Momma'!", he declared, "I know so many in America." To imagine that Jacob Peltz would not form an immediate rapport with anyone was, at any rate, absurd.

Such were Leon's lieutenants. Perhaps too, we should mention one other who shared less in the leadership but stood out by virtue of his gifts. Harry Ellison, who had entertained Leon in Bucharest, had adopted his mother's name — his father's being Zackhausen. His English accent, especially when he was leading the worship at Mildmay, was a pleasure to hear, and his fluency in other tongues made him a valued interpreter. Like Hugh Schonfield he was a prolific author, and he was reputed as an Old Testament scholar. He wrote on Exodus, Ezekiel and Job, on the Prophets and on Israel, on the Messianic Idea, the Church, and many other topics. But like Hugh he ran into trouble; this time it was not with the Alliance but with ultra-conservative Baptists. A paper entitled "Some Thoughts on Inspiration" which he wrote for the *Evangelical Quarterly* in 1954 resulted in his being charged with "Barthianism" — surely not a heinous error! — and made to resign from a teaching post which, according to Profesor F.E. Bruce, his colleague in the production of a standard Bible Commentary, he had filled to the great profit of his students. This was followed by a public attack from a senior evangelical leader which brought him quite unjustifiably into serious disrepute. He was deeply wounded; but he lived long enough to be presented, on his eightieth birthday in 1984, with a symposium, *Torah and Other Essays*, by his admirers. It is sad, however, to be reminded of churchmen whose attitude resembles that of those Highlanders in Assynt of whom it was said that while others went to church to hear the gospel preached, they went to hear if it was preached or not!

In 1935 when Leon and Nahum asked their friend Dr Donald Davidson whether he might take Fred on as his junior assistant, they found the young divinity student to be over-judgmental. He was drawn to Dr Davidson and no-one could have treated him more warmly. Furthermore, the gospel was preached in South Leith Church and the Bible expounded winsomely and with power. But there seemed to be no radical social edge, no grappling with the problems of the day, no forum, such as a Young Men's Guild, for discussion. Nor did Fred's "bishop" seem interested in ecumenism or theology, or the affairs of Presbytery and Assembly.

Fred's father and his uncle, however, told him that in their opinion Dr Davidson, like Mary of Bethany, had chosen the better part. He had deliberately turned aside from the many things that could have distracted him and concentrated on the one thing needful for his vast congregation and largely depressed parish — the cure of souls. Fred came to see that this was true. Some great preachers — Fosdick in America, Temple and MacLeod in Britain, addressed themselves to the world as they found it, and gave a Christian critique of capitalism, communism and the secular society; others, like Quick and Farmer, P.T. Forsyth and Donald Baillie, expounded creed and doctrine and spoke to the student mind; but others again, like A.J. Gossip, J.D. Jones, James Stewart — yes, and Donald Davidson, — simply preached the love of Jesus and the word of the Cross as the power of God for personal salvation; and who in his senses would criticise them for that? Fred's own faith differed from that of his father or Dr Davidson, but as time went on he appreciated them more. Single-minded and determined in their calling, they said with Thoreau, "If we are alive let us go about our business", and with St Paul "This one thing I do", and went on and did it.

For Leon that one thing was to witness, along with his fellow Hebrew Christians, to the Jews. But this had many facets and in the mid-thirties it was increasingly complicated by Hitler's machinations. It was, for instance, due to Hitler and the influx of 60,000 more of his victims in 1935, that land values in Palestine had escalated that year by 300 — 400 per cent making fruitless Leon's final attempt to set up the Colony.

He left England on the 21st of March, again with Dr Burton's tour; the party of twelve including one old friend of himself and the Alliance, Mrs Edmondson, and one new one, Dr John MacBeath the distinguished minister of Hillhead Baptist Church in Glasgow. Dr MacBeath was later to say: "I shall never forget the trip, when his presence was such a boon to the whole company." He added, "Many of us wondered at his versatility and his mental grasp of such a variety of subjects." It was probably at Leon's instigation that Mrs Edmondson went, for a few months earlier she had suffered the harrowing loss of her daughter who had fallen from a motor launch and received injuries from the propeller from which she died a fortnight later. At Cairo, Leon and Mrs Edmondson left the party, which was bound for Luxor, and proceeded to Jerusalem. There she was involved with Leon in the business of the Colony, for it was she who had donated £2,000 for its projected church. She also accompanied him to a conference of the Palestine Alliance and to dinner with the High Commissioner, General Sir Arthur Wauchope. Later, when they rejoined the party, and had visited Damascus and Baalbek and embarked at Beirut, he tells us that "we again had some few Jews on board, and once again Mrs Edmondson and I had wonderful opportunities for quiet talks of witness with them."

Meanwhile, at home, Fred had taken ill and spent a fortnight in bed. Leon heard of it in Jerusalem and sent a postcard which, together with a letter from London three months later, forms the only family correspondence still preserved. Nothing reveals his affectionate and devout spirit more clearly than these, which are transcribed here without altering the wayward spelling. The postcard reads:-

"My dear Fred,
I was ever so much upset to hear of your illness, but was cheered to hear from Mamy's next letter that you where better. Do take care of yourself dear you know how much we love you. I am praying for you & hope by the time this reaches you you will be your dear self again in perfect health. With love to all. Your affect Daddy"

The occasion of the letter was Fred's engagement to Eleanor Holland. Its reference to David is to the fact that during his last year at school he underwent the removal of infected tonsils, and had laughed so immoderately at a visitor's joke that he burst the stitches and had a relapse!

> "Strand Palace Hotel
> Thursday 4th July, 1935
>
> My own dear Fred,
> I cannot tell you how glad I was to get your dear letter. Of course I got a shock to hear about David, & realised how it would afect Mammy. But was glad to know that Dr E Martain asured her that all will be well.
> You must tell David that for Mother's sake and mine, as well as for his own good, he must control himself & so give himself the chance of getting better soon.
> Do let me know how he & Mammy are progressing as I am worried about there health.
> Now for the good & joyful news. I want to congratulat you & Eleanor from the depth of my father heart. I know she is the ideal person for you & cannot wish for a better. I feel sure that you will both do your best to be worthy of each other, & sincerely pray that our Dear God may bless you both and make you a blessing to others in your future lives and work for Him & your fellow men. I shall feel it a joy to have her as a daughter & love her as such. God bless you both & keep you in His everlasting love.
> With infinit love
> I am
> alway your
> Daddy."

He was always thoughtful and kind towards his children's friends; and when Eleanor's terms at college ended and she headed south he sometimes said, slipping Fred some money, "Here, take this and get Eleanor something to read on the train."

Eleanor's father, Archdeacon H. St B. Holland, had just been consecrated as Bishop-elect of Wellington, New Zealand. The family were to sail before Christmas and Eleanor would not return to marry Fred until March 1937. In the circumstances the Hollands felt they should meet the Levisons without delay; and being of those enlightened English to whom Argyllshire rather than anywhere abroad is the true paradise, they suggested that on their way north for some final days of bliss they should call at Albert Terrace.

Eleanor came to stay and her parents were to pick her up. An hour before their arrival, however, Katie took to her bed and declared she could not meet them; and only Leon's loving entreaties could persuade her otherwise. Shyness is too simple an explanation. She was, I believe, making a psychosomatic response to a situation which brought home the impending loss of her son. She had been on holiday with him twice that year while Leon and John were both away. Then followed his convalescence at Peebles and, following Kitty's untimely death in August, a week at Rothbury. She was not unnaturally somewhat possessive, as well as suffering the stress of Kitty's loss.

She was able to pull herself together; but Mrs Holland being even more shy than herself — she was the sweetest of women but with no self-confidence — their meeting in the drawing-room was something of an ordeal. Leon and the bishop, however, smoking together on the balcony, were entirely at ease.

It was the last time he was to see his daughter-in-law to be; his only meeting with her parents.

Some time that summer there was a brief family holiday at Grange-over-Sands. Leon, no longer able for strenuous exercise (although only 54), spent the mornings at the swimming pool watching his offspring; in the afternoons he went for a drive or strolled with Katie in the park, a novel under his arm. The following year the annual holiday was at Prestwick, where he again sat and smoked at the pool. Katie, worried by his lack of exercise and interests, persuaded him to go and join in at the public bowling green. This he attempted but soon abandoned, either from breathlessness or disinterest. What he did do, however, was to make himself known to the Church's Seaside Missioners and to speak from their soap-box on the beach.

He rarely, if ever, said no to an invitation to speak. In 1934 he had again been at the Young Men's Guild, the New College Missionary Society, and a Nurses' Christian Fellowship. From time to time he was asked to address the Evangelical Union, but never the other student body, the S.C.M. This underlines the appallingly divisive nature of Christianity prior to the last quarter of this century. Only now is any real attempt being made to lower and cross the barriers between different brands of the faith, different denominations, different types of Christians, low and high, narrow and broad, liturgical and free, confessional and ecumenical. Leon was one of the few who could cross these barriers with ease; but like all who are conspicuous in the religious world, he was labelled by partisans as belonging "to them and not to us".

His diary being over-full, he did not spend time worrying about those who ignored him, but continued to address the Advent Testimony League, the Ebenezer Evangelical Church in Leith, and Christian groups as far afield as Newcastle. A news-cutting of 1936 records that "Sir Leon Levison, who is to preach the third of the "May" sermons tonight at Westmoreland Road Presbyterian Church, Newcastle, is now a well-know personality in Newcastle. This will be his third visit within recent years, though it is his first preacher's engagement."

However, the travelling, the strange beds and unintentionally exhausting hosts were an increasing strain. When it was at the Waverley Station that his train arrived, he had to be met to save the steep exit which left him breathless; and at home he would collapse into a chair asking Katie to massage his shoulders and neck. His rheumatism and her own had led her more than once to take him to Harrogate, but she must have been no less anxious about the state of his heart. On seeing the impossibility of his ever slowing down, as his doctor constantly advised, she decided that as his work could not be curtailed she could only be utterly supportive. This she achieved, becoming *au fait* with all his problems and his world-wide interests, reacting to his ideas, helping in his literary shortcomings, sharing his hopes and griefs.

His anxieties were not confined to Germany. "The cries for help," he wrote, "from Russia, Poland, Roumania and Palestine in particular have been heartrending, and we would appeal to our readers once more not to forget these brethren." There was anxiety, too, about the future of the Mission, for the Home Mission Committee had begun to consider a new strategy involving the phasing out of Leon's role and that of the premises in Buccleuch Street. He himself would probably be transferred to Glasgow, where there were 30-40,000 Jews: in Edinburgh there were only 4,000.

The new policy was to be that of the "parish approach", each parish church being asked to take account of the Jews within its bounds and to offer them Christian friendship. Leon, as we have seen, had observed this strategy in America and found it wanting. In England too Peltz had noted that, "In most cases the clergy. . . have no sense of responsibility for the spiritual welfare of their Jewish parishioners, and where the obligation is realised there is a confession of utter helplessness in the method to be pursued."

Despite these warnings this has been the accepted policy of the Church of Scotland in the forty years that have passed since the closure of the Edinburgh Mission; and the results, so far as they can be known, are somewhat negative. It seems to be through intermarriage rather than by any Christian approach that a trickle of Jews continues to come into the Church.

Missions have also been replaced by dialogue and the formation of the Council of Christians and Jews (C.C.J.). Leon would have approved such efforts but he would not have regarded them as a substitute for missionary work, for they tend to soft-pedal the Gospel. As Harry Ellison writes in *Understanding a Jew*[4], "some. . . are so committed to dialogue, which involves those who take part in it meeting as equals in every sense, that they abandon every claim to uniqueness and finality in Christianity. . . Dialogue can be fully meaningful only when one sits down with others, regarding them with respect and as one's equals, but yet believing that one has something unique to share with them. . . True dialogue must not assume that all faiths are variants of the one truth, but that the other has so experienced truth that it has profoundly transformed him, and so I may have something to learn from him that may enrich me. Where dialogue has been carried on in this spirit, though no change in religious allegiance may have taken place, both sides have profited and have probably come to a deeper understanding of their own faith."

Leon, however, whose whole life was a dialogue with Jews and Judaism, would have chafed at the self-imposed restrictions of these organised get-togethers. The Council of Christians and Jews, for example, has more than once felt compelled to dissociate itself from any attempt to evangelise. It has affirmed that "true dialogue involves mutual respect and precludes any attempt to entice or pressurise the partners to convert from one religion to the other". "I hope", said Archbishop Coggan, once its Chairman, "that our Jewish friends recognise that this proselytism is not done with the approval of the majority of Christians in the mainstream

Churches." Cardinal Hume has said much the same. In a letter in *The Times* in 1985 the severest protest of all was made by the Sisters of Sion (a Roman Catholic Study Centre for Christian Jewish Relations): — "The recent growth in missionary activity among the Jews. . . seriously undermines the good will and friendship engendered by the dialogue between Jews and Christians. . . In the work of this study centre there is no place whatsoever for conversionist activity, which is to be rejected utterly and unequivocally." The letter concludes with this quotation from an article in the *Journal of Ecumenical Studies*:

"Dialogue and conversion are mutually exclusive. According to Martin Buber each participant in a sincere dialogue should confirm the other in his or her specific existence. Each becomes aware of the elements which unite them, accepting honestly those components of their faith which divide them and which each respects. No partners in dialogue should try to persuade the others of the exclusive truth of their own position."

I have dwelt on this matter because it highlights Leon's attitude. If I read his mind and heart aright he would have responded like this:- "I appreciate your alarm", he would have said, "at the kinds of missionary methods you have seen. Some of the 'Jews for Jesus' movements are aggressive where they should be gentle, tactless where they should be sensitive, jealous where they should be loving. They also tell the Jew that if he is to be a Christian he must forget he is a Jew, and that is quite wrong. But if Christ died for us all, surely we can say so. As for Buber, should not someone have said to him, as Paul did to Agrippa, 'I would to God that you were as I am'? And it is not the *exclusive* but the *inclusive* truth I would proclaim."

In a discerning article in *The Times* (17.8.87) Clifford Longley discussed the dilemmas posed in a multi-faith society. "In place of the campaign of missionary conversion", he wrote, "the mainstream Churches have put their emphasis on the fostering of good community relations. . . The largest element in this attitude has been genuine theological uncertainty whether conversion was right in the circumstances. . . If the Roman Catholics can go to heaven, perhaps Muslims can, too; perhaps, even, it does not matter what they are as long as they believe it sincerely and follow it faithfully. . ."

He went on to say that if these various communities are to share this small island "the primary and essential lubricant is tolerance";

for Britain, which can handle a high level of political rivalry and disagreement, cannot handle intense religious rivalry. "Religious antagonism is much more of a threat to the unity of the nation than political antagonism. The paradoxical result is that everyone has to pretend that one religion is as good as another, and by implication that religion does not really matter." But since the new communities of faiths in Britain do regard religion as important, and their own religion as true, they must be puzzled by the attitude of the Churches. "Perhaps they no longer believe what they say they believe; perhaps they have merits they are not prepared to share with. . . outsiders. Perhaps. . . they are too pre-occupied with their own internal problems. . . to think clearly about the challenge on their doorstep."

For Leon there was always that challenge. For all its success in improving understanding and combating prejudice, this is invariably the missing factor in Christian/Jewish dialogue. At more than forty annual conferences the C.C.J. has achieved much, not least in the realm of scholarship and the interchange of religious ideas. Yet for Leon there had to be more. Again he stood with St Paul who could not help but preach the Gospel: "If I did it of my own choice, I should be earning my pay; but since I do it apart from my own choice, I am simply discharging a trust." (I Cor.9.17).

In 1936 there was little dialogue; nor would it have been appropriate in the down-town Jewish areas such as Whitechapel. But many London Jews now lived in the more prosperous northern suburbs such as Golders Green and Hampstead. One clergyman who had 2,000 of them in his parish of 6,000 was the Rev. G. Harding Wood, Vicar of Holy Trinity Church, Hampstead. He took the unprecedented step of inviting Jacob Peltz to give five lectures under the title "The Truth about the Jews Today", with the two-fold object of attracting Jews and informing his own people. The topics were i.) "The Modern Jew and his Survival", ii.) ". . . and his Persecutors", iii.) ". . . and his Religion", iv.) ". . . and his attitude towards Christianity", v.) ". . . and his Messiah". In March 1936 Peltz gave three of these lectures and Schonfield two. Afterwards the vicar wrote, "It was a great joy to see so many Jews — sometimes as many as twenty or thirty — coming to such meetings in our church hall. Another thing that was a joy was the frank and open way in which the Jews asked their questions, and, if I may say so, the tactful way in which both you and Mr Schonfield answered them."

Heartened by this experiment, Leon expressed the hope that other clergymen would follow suit. "These Jewish people in residential parishes", he said, "are a challenge to the Christian Church, and it behoves us to do our best to approach them with the Christian message." No word here of holding back on the Gospel during the give-and-take of discussion. Even so, he knew that any Christian-Jewish dialogues would only draw participants who were well-educated and articulate. Many of those he sought to win were neither, and such encounters would pass them by. So he continued to pursue his own line, listening patiently to Jewish men and women in their individual circumstances and predicaments, and quietly testifying, as had St Paul, that "the life which I now live. . . is lived by faith in the Son of God, who loved me and gave himself for me." (Gal 2.20).

NOTES
1. *An der Stechbahn*, pp.15 and 22.
2. Dr Ehrlich was later Convener of The General Assembly's Panel on Doctrine and Moderator of Edinburgh Presbytery.
3. Hugh Schonfield has since died. An obituary in the *Daily Telegraph* (21.8.88) says "Theologically he inhabited a sort of no man's land between Judaism and Christianity for, while claiming to be a Jew, he adored Christ, though with reservations. Christ, he believed, was the Lord's anointed and divinely inspired, but not The Son of God."
4. An Olive Press Paperback 1972, reprinted 1978. Page 50.

23. "A DRAWING-DOWN OF BLINDS"

In July 1935 the I.M.C. held another conference on The Christian Approach to the Jew; it took place at Beaconsfield in Buckinghamshire. Dr Mott was again in the chair, and Leon was invited to prepare a paper on the Hebrew Christian Church. Unfortunately he had not time to do so, and the paper was given by Principal Garvie. But Leon spoke, and afterwards wrote down what he had said. "I am not pleading", was his final word, "for a Church which we are going to found. Churches are already in existence. We already have Hebrew Christian congregations, and we must consider now whether it is wise for each of these different groups to go different ways; or whether it is not wiser to take a step in advance by binding them together." He had reiterated the value of an indigenous Church to Hebrew Christians in danger of losing their Jewish identity through assimilation, and its importance as a witness to the Jewish world.

However, after a lengthy discussion the conference approved a motion commending the establishment of Hebrew Christian churches, but not of a Hebrew Christian Church. The participants agreed that there was a need for such churches and that the I.H.C.A. had every right to encourage their growth, guide them in their worship and see that they adhered to the fundamental doctrines of the faith. This was an advance on the Budapest-Warsaw Conference of 1927, which had discouraged such congregations; and it was precisely the line that the I.H.C.A. itself, on a motion of Harry Ellison's, would take at Budapest in 1937. Nevertheless, Leon, ever optimistic, went on hoping for something more. Although in the October 1935 *Quarterly* he reported the Beaconsfield findings accurately, in the following issue he said that

295

at Beaconsfield " the question of the establishment of a Hebrew Christian Church was carefully considered. . . and a decision was arrived at unanimously that such a Church is. . . needed." Was he subconsciously seeking to endorse his own convictions? Or was it that, like Huckelberry Finn "there was things which he stretched but mainly he told the truth"?

One thing is clear: that in spite of every setback he held tenaciously to the twin concepts of Church and Colony. In July 1936 he was still looking for land in Palestine. Had he found it, there were scores of families beleaguered in Europe who were set on going there, and who, the bright vision having been set before them by both Leon and Peltz, were asking how they could train to become colonists. On that land there would be built a church; and it would provide the inspiration and the pattern for what would become a world-wide Hebrew Christian Church. When the prophet Joel said "Your young men shall see visions and your old men will dream dreams", he did not mean anything as banal as the young looking forward and the old back. *Both* were to look forward to a new day of the Lord. For his part, Leon never ceased to do so, or to believe in the fulfilment of his hopes.

By 1935, however, the times were awry. That September at Nuremberg a decree was promulgated excluding all Jews from German citizenship. In October Mussolini invaded Abyssinia; and in December Sir Samuel Hoare and the French Foreign Secretary, Pierre Laval, came to an infamous agreement to seek peace on the basis of surrendering large tracts of Abyssinian territory to Italy. The era of appeasement had begun. (Readers of Dr Norman Maclean's *The Years of Fulfilment* may remember his vivid account of how the attempted sequestration of the Abyssinian Embassy in Jerusalem was foiled.) Hitler, in defiance of the Treaty of Versailles, and in the knowledge that Britain and France would seek peace at any price and America be isolationist, introduced conscription. Churchill had given solemn warning that we were entering "a corridor of deepening and darkening danger along which we should be forced to move, perhaps for months, perhaps for years"; but few heeded him. It was an era when Wilfred Owen's title, *An Anthem for Doomed Youth*, took on fresh meaning, and when his line "And each slow dusk a drawing-down of blinds" again became poignantly prophetic.

On January 20th, 1936, George V died. The miracle of wireless had engendered a warmth of affection for the King, whose Christmas broadcasts were heard in every home; and his subjects saw in him, as his biographer says, "what they cherished as their own individual ideals: faith, duty, honesty, courage, common sense, tolerance, decency and truth." Whether these ideals would be perpetuated in Edward VIII, however, who, though likeable and unstuffy, had a playboy image, was uncertain.

Meanwhile the Levisons gathered round their crystal set to hear Sir John Reith repeat in grave tones: "The King's life is moving peacefully to its close"; and, on the 26th, for the service from Westminster Abbey when the Archbishop spoke Milton's fitting words, "Nothing is here for tears. . . .". Later the Archbishop commented (did Nahum notice this, I wonder?): "It was significant to hear Prayers for the Dead read with full unction by a Moderator of the Kirk."

Leon paid tribute to the late King in the *Quarterly*. Letters, he said, had come from all the Alliances regretting his passing and desiring to join in the thanksgiving for his life. He wrote of how the King's capacity to serve sprang from his unswerving faith in God, his regular attendance at church and his custom of daily Bible-reading. There followed an American Hebrew Christian's tribute in somewhat artless verse.

All was not well in Britain, however. The politicians were failing to confront Hitler; Baldwin was following public opinion and afraid to give a lead on rearmament. *The Spectator* warned Eden not to approach Hitler "in a spirit of sceptical mistrust that will make agreement hopeless", and only belatedly opposed aggression; worst of all, in Leon's eyes — *et tu, Brute!* — was the defection of Lloyd George.

In Parliament Lloyd George was a spent force, but abroad his reputation still stood high. In September 1936 Hitler gave a large tea-party in his honour at Berchtesgaden. A.J. Sylvester was there and took shorthand notes of the conversation which was through an interpreter. Referring to the Great War, Hitler said, "It was you who rallied the people and gave them the determination for victory. . . If I, instead of being one of many millions of German private soldiers, had been in the position of leader, I am convinced I could have prevented Germany's downfall." Then L.G. said "In our country the one desire of the people is a better understanding and a closer co-operation between our two nations." "I am deeply interested in that," said Hitler, "as a proof of my desire, I am sending as ambassador to London my best man — Herr von Ribbentrop."

Leon had no knowledge of that conversation; but he would have been hurt and scandalised that his former political idol had even deigned to meet the Führer, whose actions against dissidents and Jews had shown him to be not only a thug but possessed by a spirit of evil.

The timidity of the politicians was not the only moral blemish in Britain. There was an ominous growth of anti-semitism. That summer Mosley and his followers were on the rampage in London's East End and the movement appeared to be spreading. The accusations hurled against the Jews were similar to those that Leon had heard from Germans whom he met in 1935 on his way to Palestine. These Germans were professing Christians, but they believed Hitler to be the saviour of their country and his Jewish policy to be justifiable. Most of the Jews, they said, were uneducated immigrants who undermined their standards of living and of civilisation. They also claimed that while only one per cent of the population were Jews, they held posts in the professions out of all proportion to their numbers. "It will be obvious to our readers", wrote Leon, "what an extraordinary mentality these Germans possess because, according to their argument, when the poor Jew is not sufficiently educated he must be got rid of, and when he is educated and shows his cleverness they consider him to be a danger because he works his way to the top of every profession; so that in either case they feel they must get rid of the Jews."

"When we touched on the economic and commercial situation I found that there was nothing but sheer jealousy because of the Jewish ability to hold their own in these departments of life."

Isaac Bashevis Singer witnessed the same anti-semitism in Poland. There is a scene in his novel *Shosha* where, because he asks for a shave on Yom Kippur, a Jew is assumed to be a Gentile; and the barber gives vent to his venom. "They've taken over all Poland. The cities are lousy with them. . . they swarm like vermin everywhere. . . there's one consolation — Hitler will smoke them out like bedbugs. . .

"Those that shave and dress modern are the real dangers. They sit in our Sejm and make treaties with our worst enemies. . . Every one of them is a secret Communist and a Soviet spy. . . their millionaires have a secret pact with Hitler. The Rothschilds finance him and Roosevelt is the middleman. His real name isn't Roosevelt but Rosenveld, a converted Jew. . . But Hitler will clear them out. . . It's too bad that he'll attack our country, but since we haven't had the guts to sweep away this filth ourselves, we have to let the enemy do it for us."[1]

At home Leon could do little to counter this kind of prejudice. He relied on the good sense of the British people and, sure enough, Mosley overreached himself and was repudiated. Meanwhile Leon continued to raise money to ameliorate the lot of Hebrew Christians everywhere in their distress.

It was an uphill task, and he was not alone in finding it so. As early as 1933 the League of Nations was compelled to set up a High Commission for Refugees with Professor Norman Bentwich of the Hebrew University in Jerusalem as its Director. It was Mrs Bentwich, Secretary of the German Refugees Hospitality Committee, who raised the matter of non-Aryans, that is those who might be Christians or anything else, but had Jewish blood in their ancestry. She pleaded for action by the Churches and by "the complacent millions in England." But that plea, although it was taken up by Bishop Bell who instigated a Christmas Appeal signed by English Church leaders, had a poor response. Again, James McDonald, the League's High Commissioner, admitted that "at no stage, despite repeated appeals. . . have substantial sums been supplied from Christian sources." "Of the Christian bodies", said Professor Bentwich, in June 1934, "the Friends alone have made a continuous and sustained effort."

Bell spoke out at the Church Assembly in 1935. In January 1936 he became Chairman of the International Churches Committee for Refugees, and launched an Appeal which he broadcast on radio that September. The response of only £11,000 was disheartening and pitifully inadequate, and an attempt to secure government aid was unsuccessful. Meanwhile the Jewish organisations had, in three years, raised £2,000,000 and were striving to raise another three million.

By 1938-39 the Churches had begun to respond. That, however, was not until Bell had twice visited Germany, at considerable risk. After the war, in gratitude for his great work, the I.H.C.A. made him an honorary member "as a token of the esteem in which you are held by Hebrew Christians throughout the world." Nahum, writing as Vice-President, told him, "The see of Chichester has become a centre to which the needy and suffering turn naturally, knowing that they will not be turned away empty either in spiritual or material things."[2]

The Bishop's initial efforts, unsuccessful though they were, were a gleam of light in Leon's closing years. He was also heartened by the continual vigilance of the Church of Scotland against anti-semitism, and the vigour of its support for that part of the German Evangelical Church to which racism and fascism were equally repugnant. Yet his life was continually clouded by the reports from abroad of Jew-baiting in ever more violent forms, some of which Victor Gollancz had tried to bring to public notice as early as 1933 in his *Brown Book of the Hitler Terror*. One can only be glad that he did not live to witness the even greater horrors that were to accompany the attempted genocide of the Jewish race. At the same time he did not for a moment believe that such an outcome was incredible. It would, on a vaster scale, be a repetition of something he had seen in 1915 in the genocide of the Armenians by the Turks.

The outbreak of the Spanish Civil War in July 1936 and the execution by the Fascists of Federico Lorca in August indicated a sharpening in the conflict between Fascism and Democracy, with the democrats on the defensive and, to Leon, who was prescient, a further clouding of the European horizon. There was also disquieting news from Palestine of racial riots. But Leon continued to hammer at the doors of Whitehall seeking help for the helpless. He addressed no less than forty-seven meetings that October, mostly for the work of the Alliance. At the same time he was organising the Moody Centenary and engaged on the liturgy of the Hebrew Christian Church.

In a last despairing effort to raise funds for relief he let an advertisement appear in much of the religious press which, above a photograph of himself, stated in heavy print: "This prolonged agony in Germany is breaking my heart." To bring himself into the picture, and to speak so personally seemed to some, including Fred, to go too far. The situation was heartbreaking, yes, but if this one man's heart was broken, who cared? Was he so special that the world should share his grief? Or was he an egoist?

The answer is that he was desperate. Multitudes seemed to care little, and someone might be moved simply by seeing how much he cared. To weep for himself would have been a private matter; but his tears were for the Jews. As Jesus wept openly for His people at the

"A DRAWING-DOWN OF BLINDS"

impending doom of Jerusalem, he was not ashamed to weep openly in another day of doom. Perhaps he himself did not like the advertisement. Maybe he should have expressed his agony only to God. Who can judge?

A few days after his death the caption was again to appear. Under it was written: "These poignant words were spoken by the late Sir Leon Levison... They are a cry from the heart of one whose life had been spent in the service of his Master, and whose thoughts were ever with those of his own race who were suffering persecution for their Christian Faith."

It was a solace to turn to the Moody Centenary and to appoint friends to its Council was a congenial task. Having been approached by Dr Houghton, Principal of the Moody Bible Institute in Chicago, to see whether he might plan for Britain what the Evangelical Churches were engaged in in America — setting up prayer meetings and subsequently rallies at which the revival message preached by Moody would be proclaimed — he thought prayerfully before accepting. His conclusion was that "the young people of our land are more deeply religious than at any time within recent years. I do not say that they are more Christian, but there is certainly a real spirit of enquiry which should be taken advantage of by all the Churches, and no opportunity which presents itself should be lost."

He secured as President the Marquess of Aberdeen. He himself was Chairman, and then came a bevy of admirals, generals and clerics, all well-known in evangelical circles. Lindsay Glegg, the Vice-Chairman, was for many years a moving spirit at Keswick, where he could be seen leading the youth rallies and speaking in the town square. The Treasurer was Commander Studd D.S.O. and Sir Kynaston Studd was a Vice-President, as were also Leon's friends Bishop Taylor Smith and Ernest Brown M.P. Among the Counsellors were Admiral Sir George King-Hall (whose son Stephen was then a widely-known broadcaster), Sir Edgar Plummer, Dr Graham Scroggie, Fred Marshall, Hugh Redwood, Mrs Edmondson, Gipsy Smith, Dr Cochrane of the World Dominion Press and the Rev. C.T. Cook of *The Christian*.

In Scotland the Moderators, and representatives from the other Churches, the Y.M.C.A., Y.W.C.A., Evangelical Association and Salvation Army were included. Committees were also formed in

301

twenty mainland cities, and in Dublin and Belfast, where series of meetings running for a week or a fortnight were to be held. These would be preceded by prayer meetings which would begin in the autumn.

This formidable programme also included the recruitment of speakers. "We hope", said Leon, "to have the most eminent evangelical men from all the Churches." There would also be an exchange with preachers from America.

Leon did not live to see these events; and it is impossible now to assess how successful they were. They were more so, no doubt, in some places than in others. But Fred, who in 1937 marked the Centenary in the first weeks of his parish ministry, can vouch that on that first Sunday in February in parishes up and down the land, and on the wireless where Principal D.S. Cairns paid tribute and Sankey's hymns were sung, D.L. Moody was commemorated with gratitude, and his indelible influence on the Christian life of Britain fittingly celebrated.

A continuing concern was the Hebrew Christian Church. Its Constitution and Articles of Faith had been established, and now Formulae were drawn up for the Consecration of Bishops and the Ordination of Ministers, Elders and Deacons in what was referred to as a Presbyterian-Episcopal form of government. However, the Commission found the question of liturgy fraught with difficulties which, after several years, were never fully resolved. A contributing factor was the diverse denominational loyalties and prejudices of its members. As Hugh Schonfield wrote to Leon, "A hybrid worship compounded of features of all our Christian denominations. . . would satisfy no-one." He went on: "What with Nahum obsessed with the Church of Scotland and [I.E.] Davidson with the Church of England, that Presbyterian-Episcopal polity, not to mention the Baptists, made an extraordinary mixture. And instead of the members only holding before their eyes what would be the best thing to win over our unconverted brethren, all that they were thinking of was what would pass muster with the dignitaries of their own denominations." Whatever truth was in this, when the Budapest Conference departed from the scheme the Commission was dissolved and its findings were shelved.

Anyone who pursues the matter of a distinctive Hebrew Christian worship, however, is confronted with many questions.

"A DRAWING-DOWN OF BLINDS"

Could that tradition of the earliest Christian Church be revived which brought together the Exodus narrative, the saving act of Christ and the Jewish Passover? Even if the Last Supper was not a Passover it had elements drawn from Passover usage: could these be given greater emphasis? Should some items of public worship be in Hebrew, or in Aramaic? Should the conduct of the services be shared with the laity as in the Synagogue, or be the prerogative of the clergy as in the Temple? Should the services of ordination have a sacramental laying-on of hands or should the latter, like the *shemichah*, 'the placing' (of hands), confer nothing, but be only a recognition by one's peers? Must there always be Psalms? Should there be three Lessons or two, and who should read them? Would the Aaronic Blessing be retained? Would there be a liturgy on parallel pages, Hebrew on one a modern language on the other? Were the hymns to be the same as in other Churches or to what extent could traditional Hebrew melodies, chants and prayers be incorporated?

One member of the Commission sent Leon a draft of a suitable service. He prefaced it by saying that there must be an atmosphere in which a Jew would feel at home; and he recalled "all the homely delight and sweetness of synagogue worship, the old hallowed words, the dear tunes of praise which stir the Jewish soul in all lands."

These must not be lost, he said, in a "Gentilised" form of worship. Nor must anyone accuse the Alliance of "Judaising". "Such talk is wholly irrelevant, and what does matter is evangelising both Jew and Gentile but each in his own order and psychology." He also pointed out that it was not the formation of a new sect that was the problem, but "that of forming an advanced sect of Jews, to carry our people on from Liberal Judaism to Christian Judaism."

Leon did not view the Church in these terms. For him it was more than an instrument of evangelism; nor was it a new type of synagogue, but a manifestation of the Church Universal. A parallel today would be that of the resurgent Chinese Church, indigenous but at one with the whole Church Militant and Triumphant. It used to be said, "One Christian more, one Chinese less"; but not now, in a Church that is distinctively Chinese. To devise a Church reflective of Jewish culture and tradition was Leon's and the Alliance's aim.

The draft service sent to Leon had apparently been discussed with him, but it was only one of many. Other converts have attempted to produce a *Siddur* or standard prayer book for Hebrew

Christian worship; and there are congregations which have their own. Even so, this particular outline has features worth noticing.

It suggests that the *Aron Kodesh* (The Tabernacle) be retained and the Scriptures be kept there along with the Communion vessels. After the opening prayers and hymn the Tabernacle is opened and the Minister takes the Bible to the Lectern. He then calls (by name) on three members of the congregation to read from the Pentateuch, the Prophets and the New Testament. After the Lessons the 145th Psalm is sung, and the Bible returned to the Tabernacle. Before its doors are closed the Minister recites the first eight verses of the *Benedictus* (St Luke 1: 68-75). The psalm for the first day of the week, the *Mah Tober* (Psalm 24) is then sung, and the sermon preached. The prayers include some venerated in Jewish worship: a special form of the *Amidah*, for example ("The Eighteen Blessings"), and the following *Kadish*: Minister: Magnified and sanctified be His great name in the world which He hath created according to His will. May he establish His kingdom during your life and during your days, and during the life of the whole household of God, even speedily at a near time, and say ye, Amen. Congregation: Let His great name be blessed for ever and to all eternity.

Other features illustrate the same points; that the worship should have a Jewish flavour; that there should be an emphasis on the continuing validity of the Old Testament; and that there should be an ever-present awareness of the majesty of God.

Especially in the last of these does Hebrew Christianity have a contribution to make. For so often in worship this is a conspicuous weakness. Indeed when Nahum, on his retirement, was asked whether he missed anything in the Christian tradition which was precious in his Hebrew upbringing he replied: "Yes, the sense of the majesty of God." It was a surprising answer, in view of the solemnity associated with Scottish Presbyterianism. Yet the Hebrew response to the Almighty is more than solemnity; it is a deeply emotional and even mystical awe. Protestantism, in its endeavours to make God real to those who worship and to communicate the Good News in modern terms often needs the corrective of the numinous retained by Judaism, and especially Chasidic Judaism where "The fear of the Lord is the beginning of wisdom."

To discuss these matters is not irrelevant. For the vision of a Hebrew Christian Church was more than a passing whim of the Alliance or obsession of Leon's. Like anti-semitism it is "a light sleeper" and becomes persistently alive. I find it, for instance, in the Rev. David McDougall's excellent chronicle of the Church of Scotland's Jewish Missionary work written to mark its centenary in 1941, *In Search of Israel*. In his closing pages he looks beyond the War and concludes that two things will be necessary. First, a policy of *itinerancy*, for the Jew "is once more the Wandering Jew"; and this means — "a smaller dependence upon buildings and a larger dependence on personal contact and the use of suitable literature"; and "another thing will certainly be necessary, and that will be the forming and fostering of a Hebrew Christian Church. This had been a weakness all along, that generally when a Jew is baptised he is passed on somewhere else to avoid the resentment of his own people, or if he stays he is absorbed into some Gentile congregation and in a generation or two is lost to sight. The result of this is that nowhere do you get any large body of converts who witness to the success of Jewish missions, and by showing that a man can be both a Christian and a Jew, make it easier for others to declare their faith in Christ. . . We must ask them to stand their ground where their witness will be most telling; and to make that possible a Hebrew Christian Church will be necessary."

Yes, and most of all, perhaps, where Leon foresaw it — though the way is not yet open there — in Israel.

Meanwhile the tragedy of Germany intensified. In 1935 Leon wrote of the effects of the new Nuremberg laws. "Both the Jew and the Hebrew Christian have been classed as untouchables. . . A code of laws has been issued which denies the Jew the right to participate in any economic, financial or industrial spheres of life, and this has led to a wholesale dismissal of all Jews, non-Aryans and Hebrew Christians alike, from every avenue of livelihood. For the Hebrew Christian the outlook is perilous in the extreme."

However, action was beginning to be taken. Two meetings of representatives of all denominations took place at Edinburgh House in London, and an appeal for at least a quarter of a million pounds was made. The League of Nations Refugee Commission and other bodies were involved, and it was reckoned that the British Churches might raise £100,000, the American Churches a similar amount, and that £50,000 be raised in, respectively, Denmark, Norway, Sweden, Holland and Switzerland. Already, however, pending the formation of a National Committee in Britain, the Alliance was faced with "an ever-increasing number of sufferers who are appealing to us daily and whose letters make our burdens almost unbearable."

In April 1936 Leon described three significant meetings held in Britain. The first included delegates from the Scandinavian Churches as well as those of Holland, Switzerland and France. There it was decided to settle in Colombia and Brazil such refugees as had left Germany by 31st December, 1935. It was hoped that at least 2,500 non-Aryan Christians would be among them.

The second meeting was to consider how to raise funds. An administrative committee was set up in London and it was hoped that the Archbishop of Canterbury would issue a National Appeal. (As we have seen, the appeal was made by Bishop Bell, but with disappointing results.)

A third meeting then took place, at which, wrote Leon, "those who are advising His Grace met with me in order to discuss the best way in which the I.H.C.A. can co-operate in the Archbishop's scheme. It was decided that the Colony in Palestine should be included in the forthcoming appeal. It will take the sum of £70 to settle a person in Colombia or Brazil, and a promise was made to assist us with the sum of £40 for every settler. . ., the I.H.C.A. providing the rest of the capital outlay necessary to enable a colonist in Palestine to earn his livelihood.

"It will be observed", he adds, "that the above schemes are only touching the refugees who are outside Germany. . . comparatively speaking a handful as compared with the million and a quarter of non-Aryan Christians who are still in Germany and are day by day finding themselves nearer and nearer the point of starvation. . . Numerous letters are reaching us asking whether it is possible for Christian people in this country either to adopt boys and girls, varying in age from 4 to 18, or to assist in bringing them over to this country and giving them an opportunity of being educated. Lawyers, doctors, professors, business men and artisans are all appealing to us to enable them to come out of Germany. Many of these people are actually going mad through their sorrows, and suicides are taking place daily all over the country."

He himself approached Miss Lee, the Head Mistress of St Trinnean's Girls School, a fellow-member of St George's West, who welcomed as pupils four young refugees. One girl, it is remembered, managed to bring her violin.

On Leon the strain was telling. He became fifty-five in March,

1936, but he looked, and felt, more than his years. He was increasingly breathless and the doctor had prescribed pills for his heart. Coming home before the evening meal, he would relapse into his armchair, take off his glasses and rub his eyes, a picture of weariness until he pulled himself together. When he went on holiday that summer he was no longer the life and soul of the boarding house, but was strangely withdrawn.

From Russia and Poland tales of distress, and from Roumania and Palestine of trouble, flowed in. In October 1936 the Church's Jewish Mission Committee had distressing letters from the Rev. George Sloan, their missionary at Tiberias. Jews had been murdered there and "the situation in Safed is much disturbed." Dr Herbert Torrance of Tiberias in his annual report had stated that in 1935 there had been an immigration of around 60,000 and that "the centre of rabbinism before the war was Poland, now it is Palestine." It was this massive influx which stirred up Arab-Jewish conflict, and the tension was fostered by Italy and Germany, who were attempting to undermine the British in the Middle East. All this brought to a standstill the negotiations for a colony. Leon could only write: "We are hopeful that as soon as things quieten down we shall have good news to impart." However, they were not to quieten down. Arab nationalists organised a general strike, and a revolt developed which it needed the dispatch of two divisions of British troops to quell.

That November the British Government set up the Peel Commission on the future of Palestine. Leon heard with interest of its first meetings in Jerusalem, but knew that it would be hampered by the Mufti's refusal to participate. In the October *Quarterly* he had expressed his own convictions. "The Commission", he said, "will have to aim at producing a scheme which will create a common patriotism... There is no reason why the future of the Arabs should not be safeguarded equally with that of the Jews by guaranteeing them the inalienability of areas large enough for all present requirements, and, with improved cultivation, for a steady expansion of their numbers... As for the political outlook, the Commission may have to consider the same principle of equality... This is the only basis upon which peace can be obtained in the inter-community relationship of a country like Palestine.

"The constitutional development must be based on equality of representation or voting power between Jews and Arabs, so that neither community should attempt to legislate with the intention of injuring the other, and such equality should be guaranteed by the Mandatory power to both communities for all time, irrespective of their numbers. It is only in this way that we can allay the fears of either side."

Leon did not live to hear the findings of the Peel Commission, which in any case did not solve the problem. Palestine was to be partitioned — until this was found to be impractical and the policy rescinded. There followed two more years of unrest, and then the War. Slowly the National Home was established and firally, with unexpected speed, the State of Israel. However, being a young state, and intensely nationalistic, it was not ready to welcome colonists who, in Israeli eyes, were renegade Jews; which is why the Colony is in abeyance to this day.

Then there was Poland. Early in November Colonel Joseph Beck, the Polish Foreign Minister, visited London. He spoke, among other things, about the Jews. Most of them, he said, were small traders, now unemployed, and emigration was the only way out; therefore he was very interested in the future development of Palestine, which he had discussed with Lord Melchett and the Zionist leaders.

These half-truths, however, veiled the fact that the Jews were looked on as surplus citizens whom the Polish government intended to drive out. They were prevented because the Jews had nowhere to go, but a few years later Hitler, much as the Poles disliked him, had, as Isaac Singer's barber had forecast, solved their problem.

Before Colonel Beck's visit Leon had written of this. "The Polish Foreign Office", he said, "has issued another important statement devoted expressly to the question of Jewish emigration. This statement has strengthened the hands of the anti-semitics, who are jubilant. . . The document puts the number of Jews who must emigrate at 100,000 per annum, and the Polish Foreign Office is now working out a definite project for that purpose. . . This has added fuel to the anti-Jewish fire, and the hostile press is indulging in an unprecedented campaign."

Colonel Beck also failed to mention the outbreaks of anti-semitism which were occurring in the universities, where Jewish students were being ostracised. A fortnight after his London visit

"A DRAWING-DOWN OF BLINDS"

they were being brutally attacked in Warsaw and Cracow. There were similar scenes in Roumania. On November 8th 300,000 demonstrators had massed in Bucharest shouting "Death to the Jews!"

At this time of adversity Leon was heartened to learn that there was a growing response to the gospel and that a Hebrew Christian church had been built at Bialystok in Poland. This was the Webb-Peploe Memorial Mission Church, funded by a British legacy. Again at Chisenau the Roumanian Alliance had purchased land on which another church was to be raised. Such actions were reminiscent of the faith of Jeremiah in his purchase of a field while Jerusalem was under siege!

In the midst of the growing strife the Alliance was planning its next Conference, which to Leon was like lighting a beacon. "It had been our earnest hope", he wrote, to have held the Fifth Conference in Palestine, but God has willed it otherwise. . . we sought Divine guidance as we studied the present condition of the countries of Europe, in most of which anti-semitism is rampant. . . As a result we felt that Budapest is the most suitable centre. . . as Hungary, with the exception of Holland, is the continental country where freedom and security best prevail." He saw the Jews of Europe stirred by disappointment and grief and clamouring for something which would fortify them with hope and sustain them through life and eternity. "Our great burden. . . will have to be how best we can win our people for Christ and thus give them the surest and most priceless gift which we possess, and which the world can neither give nor take from them. Our next problem will be that of over a million and a quarter Hebrew Christians who are not wanted in the Churches of Europe. How can we organise them into a body of witnesses and help to strengthen their hands and build up their faith amidst the terror and the unspeakably sad experience through which they have been passing?"

More than ever he wanted to call his sorely afflicted people to Him who said: "In this world you will have trouble. But take heart! I have overcome the world." (John 16:33)

NOTES:
1. Penguin 1979, reprinted 1980, pp.150-151
2. Another distinguished Anglican on whom honorary membership was bestowed was George Appleton, the former Archbishop in Jerusalem.

24. "IN ALL THEIR AFFLICTIONS..."

In the summer and autumn of 1936 Leon saw his family well established. John, now 27, passed his final Chartered Accountants (Scotland) exam in June. In July he became a member of the Society of Accountants in Edinburgh and was about to take up a post in London. Fred, at 26 and in his second year at South Leith, was looking for a parish. Rosalin, at 20, was now a nurse. Finally, David, at 19, was at Edinburgh University and hoping to become a minister. Katie was still finding spiritual fulfilment in the Oxford Group, who in November revisited Edinburgh.

Leon also found comfort in his church. Dr Black was at the height of his powers and the Sunday services (to both of which he went when he could) were deeply inspiring. The General Assembly, too, by its forthright concern for both Jews and Hebrew Christians in their plight, was an ally in his struggles. That May its pronouncement was as uncompromising as ever:-

"The General Assembly learn with profound regret that the past year has brought no alleviation of the sufferings caused to the Jewish people by the inhuman political, social and economic persecution prevalent in Central and Eastern Europe. They protest against the religious intolerance, the narrow nationalism and race-pride on which anti-semitic hatreds are based... The General Assembly again commend to the liberality of their faithful people appeals made on behalf of refugee Jews from Germany and other lands, especially remembering the Christians of Jewish race who are involved in the terrors of persecution."

As he read *The Scotsman* that November he would observe that not all its news was gloomy. The new King, for instance, accompanied by Leon's friend Ernest Brown, spent two days in the

"IN ALL THEIR AFFLICTION. . ."

distressed areas of Wales. He was moved by what he saw and said "Something must be done," and his concern stimulated the efforts of many in Parliament who were, then as now, debating measures to assist the special areas. The King had also increased confidence by intimating at the Opening of Parliament that after the Coronation in May he intended to visit India as his father had done in 1911.

There was a stiffening attitude among the people. In parliament the defence debate was becoming more urgent, Vansittart and Churchill were gaining supporters, and it seemed that Britain might, after all, rebuild her arms and be able to speak from a position of strength. Counter to this were a rapid increase in the German Navy and the claiming of their right to rearm by Austria and Hungary. Then on the fifteenth of November came Hitler's final denunciation of the Versailles Treaty and his reclaiming of the Rhineland.

From Spain too there was grim news. All through November the battle raged for Madrid. On the nineteenth, a hundred tons of bombs were dropped there by German and Italian planes, and the threat of a European show-down increased.

Yet there were other less warlike anticipations of things to come. Charlie Chaplin's "Modern Times", which Leon probably saw, although it depicted the social problems of a new mechanical age and of the little man battling with mass production, was a satire on expanding industrial achievement. On November 2nd the BBC proudly inaugurated its television service, but only for two separate hours in the day and at a high cost.

Leon would also read in the correspondence columns letters on the proposed Forth Road Bridge, which the Government had stated was too expensive an undertaking in these perilous times, and which was to remain on the drawing board for almost another thirty years. More immediately promising were the railways, where, on November 16th, a new record of 5 hours and 53 minutes was achieved on the London-Glasgow line. It is a reminder to us that his own incessant journeyings had consumed many more hours then than they would now, to say nothing of the boon that air-travel would have been to him.

He would also notice that his old friend Hector McPherson, the former editor of the *Evening News*, who had given him such support twenty years ago, was still on the warpath, protesting vigorously about the move towards compulsory physical education at the universities as savouring of Fascism and a betrayal of liberal education and democratic principles. (His home was a hundred yards from 9, Albert Terrace and Leon would sometimes join him as he passed the gate — a dishevelled, kindly man with tousled hair and a bulbous nose, Chestertonian in stamp if not in girth.)

Foolish men were still whitewashing Hitler. Lord Londonderry, the Secretary of State for Air, reported on "the very friendly character of Germany's feelings towards Great Britain. Herr Hitler is thoroughly opposed to Communism and Bolshevism and in these two things he saw a tremendous danger to the world." However, whenever Germany's feelings were mentioned Leon could only think of those refugees whose pitiful plight he and Peltz were recording in heartrending detail in the *Quarterly*. Under the heading LIKE HUNTED ANIMALS Peltz summed up the experience of many of them:-

"Every policeman inspires him with fear. No landlord may receive him, because he has to report this fact to the police. Even in the home of the Salvation Army regular search after refugees takes place. So those poor people are hunted from one country to another. . . If they compel him to be brought to the frontier, his fate is a terrible one. The officer knows where there is no officer on the other side at a certain time and puts the man to flight at this place. If the refugee is fortunate he gets into the other country until it is ascertained that he has no permission to reside in this country either and the same tragedy begins again. . . The officer puts him to flight at a place where he believes the frontier is not watched, again into the same country out of which he has been driven. There are refugees who have been thus hunted fourteen times from one country into another."

Many of the refugees were women and children, or the families of professional and business men who had enjoyed a comfortable livelihood. Others were penniless, begging from door to door, some of the women even having to become prostitutes or give their young children away to some sympathiser in the hope of being saved. In such cases the hearts of Leon and his friends were ravaged. They drew some comfort from the hospitality they were able to give in the hostel at Brockley, where some who had crossed to England on temporary visas were given Christian affection. "I cannot describe", wrote Leon, "how deeply and constantly I have been touched by speaking to these victims and listening to their expressions of

"IN ALL THEIR AFFLICTION. . ."

gratitude as they were telling me how much they have been strengthened and made happy during their sojourn in our hostel." He would discuss with them the possibilities of finding more permanent refuge; but, sadly, these were very few.

On the Saturday after Leon's death, at a memorial service at the Mission, Dr Stewart Thomson said this: "In the 63rd chapter of Isaiah we find words prophetic of Christ, the Suffering Servant, which say: 'In all their afflictions he was afflicted'; and with due reverence we might well apply the words to Leon Levison." These words are on his tombstone, below the statement that he was a mis-

Leon: the last snapshot

sionary to the Jews. They do not lack reverence, for no words could be more fitting. It was Katie, who had long associated them with Leon, who was inspired to put them there.

To relieve his anguish he was working desperately hard, but he also tried to retain his balance by the normality of recreation. He continued to hang oriental rugs on the stairs, and he began to research his family tree and to devise a coat of arms. Both the tree, which he believed he might trace back to the Davidic line, the Levisons belonging to the tribe of Judah rather than of Levi, and the coat of arms are lost. Unable to frequent concerts, unless perhaps the Glasgow Orpheus Choir, whose visits to Edinburgh Katie enjoyed, he spoke of Kreisler and listened to him on the gramophone; and of John McCormack, who gave him equal delight on the radio.

That November was marked by an event that dazzled Edinburgh: the première of Barrie's *The Boy David*. After weeks of speculation and anticipation C.B. Cochran and the Austrian refugee actress, Elisabeth Bergner, arrived on the 18th. "This", said Cochran, "is the most important event of my career", while Miss Bergner went one better and declared "It is written by God."

The scintillating cast and Augustus John's costumes and décor whetted expectations, and the Levisons, who were also half-convinced that David was their ancestor, thought it a chance not to be missed. "Let's all go", said Leon, and dispatched Fred to buy the tickets. They were for Friday the 27th.

The first performance, on the 21st, was received with great acclamation. It was only in London that the critics' eyes were open to the flaws, the chief of which was that Miss Bergner was too fawnlike, fey, and as she herself said, *gamine* for the part; also that Barrie, now 76, had failed to provide a dramatic climax.

By Monday the 23rd Leon was far from well, and the family expedition was in jeopardy. To miss the play would, as it turned out, have been a very minor deprivation, for when it was finally killed by the Abdication and its own defects it disappeared from the scene; and all the *Oxford Companion to Literature* says of it today is that it "failed to capture attention." For all that, to be deprived of what was a rare, and maybe a final outing with the entire family, soon about to disperse, would be more grievous.

Leon had been poorly for some weeks. October was arduous, with his elder's district to visit and journeys to Liverpool, Manchester,

London, Glasgow and Bristol following one another in rapid succession. By the end of the month he was sleeping badly and had a heavy cold. On the 17th of November Katie sent for the doctor, who examined him, prescribed a tonic, and advised rest. Nothing daunted, he insisted on going the next day to the Dundee Council for the Moody Centenary, being driven to and from Waverley.

Nevertheless there seemed no diminution of his powers at the opening of the Jewish Mission Week in Dumfries. "He appeared to be remarkably fit," said the chairman. "Of the wonderful effect which his address produced. . . I have had much testimony." About the same time, at an Advent Testimony meeting in Leith, a friend observed that his voice seemed weaker: "He ascended the stairs to the pulpit so quietly, and he reminded me of a light that shines and makes no noise. . . [but] he was just the same lovable, kind saint as he was in days gone by."

At his last Edinburgh meeting Fred went to fetch him and noticed the relief with which he came forward, explaining that he had escaped from the minister who had been pressing him to make a date for a return visit.

Over the next few days he was very tired and had pains in various parts of his body. Wanting air and exercise, however, he walked a considerable distance on the Friday. At a friend's house he had to sit with closed eyes before he could talk; but he walked home, arriving in a state of collapse. He reluctantly agreed to rest during the weekend, and Fred took the Mission service. On Sunday he did not go to church, but enjoyed the usual tea-party of young people.

On Monday he worked and walked. But when David asked him for a stamp he said, "There's one in my waistcoat pocket if you'll help me reach it." There was a numbness in his left arm and a pain in his side which were mistakenly attributed to neuralgia. (Leon may have known better, but was not saying so.)

That evening Fred heard that he had become sole nominee for a parish in Perthshire. His parents were delighted. When Kate Thomson phoned on the Tuesday morning Leon's first words were of this. He was overjoyed, she said. He had never pressed Fred to become a minister but now it was a dream fulfilled; one, at least, that was not frustrated. He hoped he could attend the Ordination and Induction, which would be in January if all went well.

He still felt poorly and Katie encouraged him to spend the morning in bed. He was determined to attend a sub-committee in the afternoon, for it was concerned with the future of the Mission. Some who sat with him at the Church Offices said that he looked grey and ill. When he came out he was holding his side, and said to Nahum who was to go home with him, "I can hardly breathe — I need air — let's walk." But at Tollcross, having covered a good half mile, he gave in and they boarded a tram. Meanwhile, said Nahum, "though we had been dealing with a problem in which his life's work had been concerned, he passed that by with two sentences. . . . others concerned him, and though he mentioned about twelve cases, not a single name was passed over without its particulars being clearly before his mind."

They also discussed the work of the Alliance's Executive Committee, which was due to meet the following week. "The situation in Poland is becoming terrible," said Leon, "can we do anything — even any little thing? Would the Colonial Secretary allow some of them to settle in one of the Colonies? Would he? And will Palestine be closed to our brethren?"

As soon as they arrived home Harold Marshall called. He was in Edinburgh briefly on business. Noticing, perhaps, Leon's condition he only stayed half an hour. However, when he asked after Leon's health he received a cheerful reply: "I took a little walk, and I feel much better for it."

The evening was spent quietly. Rosalin and a fellow-nurse were in and he chatted with them until they had to leave for the Sick Children's Hospital. His sons were all out and he and Katie sat by the fire. He was in good spirits and told her they should be thinking of a wedding gift for a friend of the boys.

Fred had been correcting the editorial for the January *Quarterly* and the manuscript was on the mantelpiece. Katie finished the correction and Leon said, "Read it to me." When she came to the final sentence he said he would like to alter it. He had given his readers what he called a string of pearls (the "I am's" of Jesus) for the New Year, the last of which were "I am with you always" and "It is I, be not afraid". Now he dictated: "And as you make this string of pearls your own, may God grant you to be able to say, 'I am Thine and Thou art mine, therefore I shall not be afraid.'." It was a message for the threatened and afflicted Hebrew Christians but also, Katie thought later, for herself and her future without him.

They went early to bed. Sometime after one o'clock Katie woke Fred, who slept in the next room. "Daddy is very ill", she said, "we

"IN ALL THEIR AFFLICTION..."

must get the doctor."

He was sitting up, obviously in pain and gasping for breath. He could not speak and we held his hands. Dr Carmichael, the family's doctor for thirty years, gave him an injection. "It will relieve the pain", he said, "and he may just fall asleep." There was nothing more anyone could do, so the elderly doctor was sent home to get some rest, and would return. John and David were awakened and were with their father when his breathing finally ceased. And so he died, in his own bed and surrounded by his family and not, as Dr Carmichael had feared, in a strange house or at a public meeting; for his angina, as the doctor knew and had told him, was acute.

Fred gave his room to his mother and went to the attic. When he came down he found her weeping quietly while she brushed her hair. It was the only time she was seen to shed tears and through the trauma of bereavement she remained utterly composed; she was controlled, as she said in other words, by the love of Christ.

Nahum knelt for a long time by the bed. Then Dr Black came, and Fred and John made the mistake of thinking they should let their mother see him alone. However, when he had seen her he, not unnaturally, did not suggest praying again with the boys. Fred, for one, longed for a prayer, and later in his ministry made a point of inviting those in a bereaved family circle to stay should any propose to leave. Dr Black, however, paused to share his own grief before he left.

Leon was more of a public figure than his family realised. The evening paper, listing its major stories, had "Sir Leon Levison Dies", and its newsbills said "Edinburgh Philanthropist Dies." David, seeing this, wondered, "What is a philanthropist, and can that be my father?"

"Philanthropist" was misleading, for in normal usage it suggests someone who, out of his largesse, contributes to worthy causes. It was from the generosity of those whose hearts he moved that Leon was able to help others; and his charity went far beyond material relief. Yet in its precise meaning "philanthropist" is the *mot juste*. "Lover of mankind" says the dictionary, "one who exerts himself for the well-being of his fellow men."

Yet it is not the word he would have chosen; for first and foremost he saw himself as a missionary. "Missionary's Death . . . Service to the Church — Missionary and Propagandist — Jewish

Refugees' Friend" — these later headlines would have pleased him more. A sub-heading, "Convert to Christianity," both marked the turning-point in his destiny and pointed to his deepest desire, to testify to the Messiah as his Saviour.

The news was given in Scotland in the evening radio bulletin. The next day a friend saw it in the *New York Times*, and soon cables were arriving from many parts of the world. To quote at any length from the tributes would lead to over-statement, for these could only be highly laudatory. However, they included some from unexpected quarters — students and nurses who had heard him speak, individuals to whom he had written when they told him of some problem, and many on whom a brief contact had left a lasting impression. For, as Mrs Peltz wrote, "I have never met one who could so completely meet the needs of father, brother, friend." Again, a tribute from a Baptist minister is revealing when it refers to "his numerous friends at Torquay and at the above church. We have learned to love him and to welcome his visits." Yet that was only in remote Torquay, (close enough to Axminster, it may be said, to make journeys there doubly worthwhile).

A few correspondents suggested that he had died of a broken heart. That could not be. For his faith was akin to St Paul's, so well expressed in the Scottish Paraphrase, (a version of Romans 8),

"Let troubles rise, and terrors frown,

And days of darkness fall;

Through him all dangers we'll defy,

And more than conquer all".

At the other extreme was the theory that excessive smoking was the cause. However, while it is now recognised as a health risk, smoking was only a contributory factor. The reality is that he drove himself too hard; and with a heart weakened from the time of his serious illness in 1912, the strain proved fatal. To say that he wore himself out as, like his Master, he went about doing good is no less than the truth.

The service in St George's West on Friday the 27th culminated not in the Funeral March but in the Hallelujah Chorus. In the pulpit with Dr Black was Jacob Peltz, who had come post haste, interrupting a series of meetings in Belfast, Dublin and Cork. In the large congregation there were Jews from the Mission; but whether it was one of them who placed a solitary red rose on the coffin as it left the church was never known. Afterwards, at the West End of Princes

Street, a tram conductor was heard to ask, "Who are these people and why are they weeping?" They were from the Mission, and they had their own service there the next day with the family and other friends, and Kate Thomson as usual at the piano.

When the coffin was lowered at Morningside Cemetery Katie held the first cord. The other pall-bearers were her sons and Nahum, John Falconer, Nevill Davidson Kelly and Harcourt Samuel.

Thomas Kinneally ends *Schindler's Ark*, the story of the "righteous Gentile" who saved many Jewish lives during World War Two, with the memorable words, "He was mourned on every continent." By the Hebrew Christians whom God had given him as a charge to keep, Leon was mourned in many, many lands. As one of them said, "He was the father of us all."

In a few years' time much of his work was destroyed, and some of his dearest friends perished in Treblinka and Auschwitz; and when that is added to the broken dreams of a Hebrew Church and Colony what did he achieve? He did as much as any missionary to bring men and women to Christ; he alleviated the sufferings of more than anyone else I know; and he more than any other, — though he would insist it was teamwork — laid the foundations of world-wide Hebrew Christianity so well that it survived even the Holocaust and is strong today. Furthermore, he was one of those with the perspicacity to see that neither pacifism nor appeasement would stop Hitler. Evil had to be resisted and the sooner the better. Every attempt in the early thirties to move public opinion in this direction was surely worthwhile.

What he did may become known to future generations. What he was they will never, in this life, know. A biographer can merely hint at his qualities of kindness and concern, of tolerance and love, of equanimity and patience, of leadership, charisma and persuasion. The mainspring of it all is to be found in his favourite hymn (which was also a favourite of Spurgeon's). It was Mrs Cousin's adaptation of some of the *Sayings* of Samuel Rutherford, the 17th century Scottish mystic — "The sands of time are sinking." For thirty years Leon had loved to sing,

"O, I am my Beloved's,
And my Beloved is mine;
He brings a poor vile sinner
Into His house of wine."

319

These words may have been in his subconscious mind when Katie took down his last message, "I am Thine and Thou art mine. . ." This verse has now been expunged, for we no longer express Christian devotion in the language of *The Song of Solomon*; but it spoke to Leon's heart. The same is true of the other verses which were sung at his funeral, and again in the London memorial service at Kingsgate Chapel:

> "O Christ! He is the fountain,
> The deep, sweet well of love;
> The streams on earth I've tasted,
> More deep I'll drink above.
>
> With mercy and with judgement
> My web of time he wove,
> And aye the dews of sorrow
> Were lustred by His love;
>
> I'll bless the hand that guided,
> I'll bless the heart that planned,
> When throned where glory dwelleth
> In Immanuel's land."

The Victorian tune "Rutherford" is sentimental and charged with emotion. Leon, too, was sentimental and expressed his emotions freely. Warmth and love were of the essence of his nature and went out from him to others, enabling him to lead without any of that ruthlessness which effective leadership is said to require, and making him, even unconsciously, a true missionary.

It was said of Dr David Torrance of Tiberias, the beloved "Galilee Doctor", that the supreme lesson of his long experience was that only love would bring the Jews to Christ. That, too, could be said of the rabbi's son from Safed whom Torrance knew, and who himself had been brought into the Kingdom through the love of Torrance's young colleague George Wilson. His own loving nature, like theirs, was permeated with the "deep, sweet well of love" which they had found in Jesus Christ.

Today, as Rabbi Lionel Blue, speaking for many open-minded Jews, observes, "Christian groups try to love Jews more rather than to convert them." Leon did not have to try to love them, nor even to convert them. The converting was the natural consequence of the loving.

25. THE AFTER YEARS: Katie, Nahum and the Alliance

When sudden death in mid-career "slits the thin-spun life" it leaves many untied strands. Was the Mission closed, and did the Alliance survive the Holocaust? Did Katie find a new role or preserve the remnants of her life amid the memories of the past?

Did Nahum, after the War, confine himself to scholarship and the tasks of his parish?

A week after Leon's death the Alliance opened a memorial fund. The Church of Scotland, however, declined to participate on the grounds that it, too, would be considering a memorial. The obvious site for it would be at the Mission. But the Mission's future was so uncertain that the matter was deferred. A year passed. Then, in February 1938, the Home Board stated that there was by no means any assurance that work in the present premises was being given up. However, the proposal was again shelved and, perhaps by default, dropped.

None the less the Mission continued for several years, with the devoted Kate Thomson as its sheet-anchor. In 1941 Dr Heinz Golzen, formerly a judge in Berlin, a friend of Pastor Niemoeller and a member of his congregation at Dahlem, briefly became its Superintendent. He wrote to Jewish families, drawing some to the Mission, and also gave lectures in Yiddish. Unable, however, to communicate well in English, his desire to enter the Church of Scotland ministry was unfulfilled and he returned to Germany. A nearby parish minister, the Rev. Magnus Nicolson, also served as Superintendent, with the assistance of three probationers whose priority was with Jewish students. He was succeeded by the Rev. William Ross until, in 1944, it was announced to the General Assembly that "present institutional methods are being discontinued."

321

The opening of Memorial House.

Back row l. to r.: H Samuel, Dr Frank, Dr Black, Nahum, J Peltz.
Front row: Dr G MacKenzie (C of S), Katie, H Carpenter (C.M.J.).

The absence of a memorial in Edinburgh was amply atoned for in London. In April 1938 a house, designated Memorial House, was purchased and furnished at 19, Draycott Place, Chelsea. At Katie's suggestion the architect appointed to adapt the house was Percy Sawkins, the nephew of Leon's 'guardian angels'. Thus were two of Leon's desires fulfilled: the provision of a house, other than the Girl's Hostel,[1] for Hebrew Christian refugees, and an independent headquarters for the I.H.C.A. Leon, wrote Peltz, "was in full sympathy with this crying need, and less than a month before his death promised to give from his private means a sum of money to help defray the expenses of leasing such a property until, by God's help, we could acquire our own." The house was opened with a service of dedication at which Dr Black, who a few weeks later became Moderator of the Church's General Assembly, gave a dedicatory address. In the entrance hall stood the bust by Harry Paulin and a granite tablet bore this inscription which Katie had composed, and which she unveiled:

THE AFTER YEARS: KATIE, NAHUM AND THE ALLIANCE

IN GRATITUDE TO GOD AND IN MEMORY OF
SIR LEON LEVISON, K.C.S.H.
FIRST PRESIDENT OF THE I.H.C.A.
THIS HOUSE IS DEDICATED.
For 34 years he laboured to bring the knowledge of Christ to the Jews in Edinburgh, and from 1925 when the I.H.C.A. was formed until his death in 1936 he gave whole-hearted service to Hebrew Christianity throughout the world. His life was a witness that having left all for Christ's sake he had returned to him one hundred-fold.

Thirty-four years? In reality it was thirty-two since his appointment to the Mission, but Katie knew that he looked on himself as a missionary from the time when, in stumbling English, he gave voluntary help to David Sandler. She had already inscribed "For 34 years missionary to the Jews in this city" on his gravestone, and this she believed. She also believed implicitly in the words "he had returned to him one hundred-fold". In St Matthew's Gospel the rewards are, as the context indicates, entirely in the age to come; but Mark and Luke say "in this present time" and Katie took that literally. She cannot have been blind to the tribulations and martyrdom which were the lot of many faithful Christians. Yet Leon's deliverance from poverty and persecution and the honours that befell him were, as she saw it, a divine reward, here and now, for one of God's chosen ones. Most of us would say, however, that the "houses, brothers and sisters, mothers and children, and land" of St Mark are symbolic of the new personal relationships to be found in the fellowship of the Church (or, for some, in the Alliance), and these together with riches of eternal life were, indeed, Leon's reward.

For over forty years Memorial House fulfilled its purpose. However, when the flow of refugees had at last ceased, expense become prohibitive and staffing a problem, the Alliance moved its centre to Ramsgate, where Harcourt Samuel set up an office and where it also had for some years a rest house and eventide home.

Not only did the Alliance survive the war, but the branches pruned by persecution have been replaced by fresh growth. In the new *Diaspora* (Dispersal), Alliances have been born in Argentina and Uruguay, in Australia and (it is now hoped) New Zealand, as well as in South Africa. Once again there is a branch in Germany (in the Federal Republic) but not in Poland, Austria, Hungary, Czechoslovakia or Roumania. Others are in Britain, U.S.A., Canada, France, Holland and Switzerland; and there are representatives from Israel and Scandinavia. Many young people calling themselves Messianic Jews have come in, and Leon would rejoice in this sign of hope and believe even more fervently in the fulfilment of his — and St Paul's — ultimate dream that all Israel will be saved. Meanwhile the Alliance continued to find new objectives. At various periods it had centres in Haifa and Tiberias and an office in Jerusalem, and it initiated as a co-operative venture the Ebenezer Home for the elderly at Haifa. It has also pioneered successfully in Latin America, and most recently in Brazil. The support of converts and training of students continues. There is its impressive *HAGADAH for a Christian Seder*,[2] a bridge for many from the soul of Judaism to the heart of Christianity. In addition, it has achieved, in all, seventeen quadrennial conferences including the longed-for Jerusalem one in its Jubilee year of 1975.

At Jerusalem it was fitting that the Alliance should declare: "We rejoice in the founding of the State of Israel", and affirm its belief in the Divine providence. "Convinced of the eternal link between the Jewish people and the Land, and of Israel's unique place in God's plan of salvation, we urge Christians everywhere to study the theological significance of the continuance of the Jewish people and of the rebirth of the State of Israel, to see there God's faithfulness to His promises, and by prayer and effort support it." They also called on Hebrew Christians "to pray that the nation and its leaders may ever be guided by the spirit of God, and that those in their midst who confess Jesus as Messiah may be ready to give account of the hope that is in them with gentleness and reverence. Peace be upon Israel".

A man of great stature, Dr Arnold Frank, became at the age of 78 the Alliance's second President. At 80 he retired from the active ministry but continued to lead the I.H.C.A. until 1947 when he was 88. When, in 1954, a home for aged survivors of the Nazi terror was opened in West Berlin a room bore his name, and his photograph was hung over the entrance. When he died in Belfast at 5 o'clock on the evening of March 19th 1965, at the age of 106, the deaconess who attended him said, "The vesper bells will now be ringing in Hamburg."

Distinguished leaders followed him, his immediate successor being a theologian of repute, Dr Jakob Jocz, later Professor of

THE AFTER YEARS: KATIE, NAHUM AND THE ALLIANCE

Systematic Theology in the University of Toronto. Harcourt Samuel edited the *Quarterly* for many years. Under the Rev. Ronald Lewis, a minister of the United Reformed Church, it now has a circulation of some 2,000 in Britain and 4,000 overseas, largely through the efforts of Jacob Peltz in America. Harcourt holds an unrivalled place in the affections of the Alliance, as was shown in 1987 when, invited to describe the movement's history to an audience of 1000 Hebrew Christians in Pennsylvania, he received a standing ovation. The British Alliance currently has a membership of 500, including associates.

Harcourt Samuel: elder statesman

And Katie? She lost no time in telling the Alliance that she wanted to serve it still more; and that she was particularly interested in the German Relief Fund, a work in which she had shared with Leon and the correspondence of which she had attended to in his absences. She was immediately co-opted onto the Executive Committee. About the same time, in writing to the American Alliance, she said, "Let us not mourn overmuch, but let us strive to accomplish with God's help the dream which our dear one had of seeing his own people a great missionary nation."

325

She and David attended the Budapest Conference and thereafter she moved to London. There she was adrift for a period in private hotels in Finchley, Purley and Welwyn Garden City. It was not only the Alliance that drew her there. "You and Fred are settled on your course", she told David, "but John is not and in London he might slip from the church, so I want to be near him." John did not lapse but became a church Treasurer, and before long he married and settled in Welwyn Garden City. Katie, perhaps foolishly, settled there too. The proximity was less gratifying than she had hoped. She had an uneasy relationship with her daughter-in-law who, like herself, did not readily make friends nor adapt to other people's ways. And although there was a grandson Charles, of whom she was fond, she seldom crossed John's threshold. He, however, crossed hers daily on his way home from work.

Katie: the Middle Years

THE AFTER YEARS: KATIE, NAHUM AND THE ALLIANCE

Truth to tell, she was becoming difficult. Her zeal for the Alliance was not matched by a zest for living. Deprived not only of Leon, but of the warmth, light and life of Albert Terrace and, shortly, of her beloved sister Annie, and realising that her children no longer needed her, it is not surprising that she was sometimes self-pitying and desolate and had lost her sense of fun. She was no longer the laughing, loving Katie whom her niece Kitty adored; who had played the vocal line when Leon practised his songs; who had enjoyed golf and the cinema, and learning to drive, and holidaying all over Britain with her children. The curtains were drawn and she never fully opened them again. None of her three daughters-in-law saw her at her best and they all found her trying.

At Christmas 1945, when Fred was still serving as a padre abroad, Eleanor invited her to the Perthshire manse. She came and, as usual, was generous with gifts; but she could not give herself. "She isn't particularly keen on Christmas", wrote Eleanor, "which will make the day a huge effort for me." Again, "It's an awful strain with the children with Grandma being so critical of John." John, at 3½, was exuberant and not easily quietened. Sensing Grandma's disfavour and probably attributing his mother's tension to her, he caused her great alarm by chasing her round the kitchen table brandishing a bread-knife and yelling "I'll kill you!"

Eleanor, worn down by the war and with her parents abroad, longed for affection but found Katie devoid of sentiment and full of inhibitions. Could she not put her arms round her, just once, or show some warmth, or say anything loving? But that was not Katie's way. She also seemed harsh in her judgements, and pernickety in her habits.

Her loneliness was somewhat assuaged by Rosalin, who now nursed in London and shared her home; by David also, who took a year of his theological course at Cambridge, and in the Blitz drove a cinema van round the London firefighting units; and later by his wedding in 1942 to Cecilia, an ideal partner, and her visits to them and her grandchildren in their manses. Then too, there was the Alliance, its girls, its refugees and its devoted women; and at one point a Hebrew Christian actually proposed to her, but was turned down.

There were times when her spirits rose: when her sons visited her; when she worshipped, often with John, in the local Free Church; or when her younger niece Ann Davidson Kelly, or the minister, or a

327

friendly neighbour called. (Ann, whom she invited to live with her, for good reasons could not comply.) Yet without Leon her interests narrowed and she became more ascetic, spending nothing on herself, and strait-laced, condemning, for instance, ballerinas who appeared on television for "showing far too much leg"!

She did not return to Edinburgh until 1964, in her 84th year. At 80 she had resigned from her committees, and as Fred had been widowed, she decided to be near him. Accordingly he bought a house for her and Rosalin in the next street to his own. She was happy to be back, especially when Nahum and Margaret, or her older niece, Marjory, came to see her. It also gave her great joy to become a member of Fred's congregation, where she succeeded in making some friends. When Fred re-married in September 1965 she was at the wedding in a wheel-chair. Four months later she had a stroke and died. Her last Christmas was a happy one, and when her new daughter-in-law played carols for her she was aglow; "the loveliest evening I've had for years", she said.

At her funeral there was no note of mourning, only gratitude for the past and for her quiet going. Leon's hymn, which was also hers, was sung, about that place she had long desired, that new life in Christ and with Leon. . . "Where glory, glory dwelleth in Immanuel's land."

And Nahum? The beloved brother who was Leon's confidant, who shared in his memories of Safed and in all his work; who also was an advocate for the poor, and broken-hearted when his blood brothers were engulfed in a sea of suffering; and whose life in the constant shadow of Leon's has made this book almost a double biography. How devastating Leon's death was to him! Like Katie he saw that his response could only be a greater commitment to all that Leon stood for; and so it was.

Even so, he did not neglect his parish. It may not have been the ideal parish for him — the Church of Scotland not having canonries nor any system whereby scholars can pursue their theological work in quiet charges. (With the constant uniting and linking of parishes these can rarely be found.)

His energy never flagged; and he was able to be a devoted minister, a popular visitor to a local school, a scholar, a tireless refugee worker and much more besides. In the war years, when thousands of servicemen passed through the port of Leith, he was

Nahum and Margaret, 1939

the moving spirit in providing for them the Leith Churches' Canteen, an enormously successful venture. When it closed in 1945 some 280,000 breakfasts, 200,000 dinners, 480,000 teas, 392,000 snacks and 480,000 hot drinks had been served.

By 1944 he was chairman of the Edinburgh Branch of the British-Soviet Unity Council. That October he organised an exhibition which enabled Edinburgians "to see something of the heroism of the people of Leningrad and the devastation of their ancient capital." In November he wrote to every hospital in the area asking for a contribution of some specific medical or surgical appliance for the hospitals of Leningrad. (This was the brainchild of Lord Provost Will Y. Darling, the Council's President.) In 1946 he corresponded with Alastair Dunnett, the Public Relations Officer at St Andrew's House, regarding the mounting of another Russian Exhibition in Rossleigh's Motor Showrooms, and was advised to seek help from the skilled window-display department at Jenners.

During 1957 he was negotiating with Professor John Bowman and the Department of Semitics at Leeds University regarding a possible "dig" at Safed. The discovery of the Dead Sea Scrolls had set Nahum's mind working and he recalled that underneath his father's synagogue there was a *Genizah*, or sacred burial cave, in which some extremely ancient manuscripts were stored. Professor Bowman went to Safed and thought he had located the spot near, rather than directly below, the synagogue. Bowman then approached Professor Yavin, Director of the Department of Antiquities in Israel. "Yavin", he told Nahum, "is a bit afraid that the religious authorities might be hostile to the idea of opening a *Genizah*. However, after discussion with some colleagues and with the President (Ben Zvi) he is willing to issue a digging permit." Yavin made it clear that such a dig could not be undertaken by an individual, and that the University of Leeds, with his own Department supervising and assisting, could alone undertake it.

"In the last resort", Bowman wrote to Nahum, "it all depends on you. . . I for my part am very anxious to proceed. . . if, as I hope, it meets with your approval." Six months later the Israeli Ambassador wrote to Nahum, "I am afraid I am in no position to advise you. . . I hope you will not mind my writing personally to Dr Yavin, sending him a copy of your letter and asking him what he can do further in the matter." It looks as if the project then ran into difficulties, probably with the religious authorities, and it went into abeyance.

Nevertheless, when the Dead Sea Scrolls came to Edinburgh Nahum, then old and frail, would not make the effort to see them (although it was arranged that he should avoid the queue). "There are probably as good under the synagogue at Safed," he declared!

Further light on his post-war activities is thrown by the few letters which have survived. In December 1948 the Deaconess House in Hamburg wrote: "Two days ago we got the marvellous gift of 70 parcels which you ordered for us to be sent from Denmark [where Nahum had been]. . . Schw. Caroline will help us by distributing them amongst the hungry Hebrew Christians in Hamburg." The letter also mentions some wooden huts, referred to as the Barracks, which Mr Johansen of the Alliance was about to despatch from Denmark. In November 1950 a further letter from the Matron describes the Children's Home in Bevensen which was established in these huts: "In Bevensen all is well. All beds are used and the children are very happy. Probst Grüber sends us again two children from Berlin.

"I still have a great wish, dear Mr Levison. We would like to have a picture from you which could be hung up in the Kinderheim so that

THE AFTER YEARS: KATIE, NAHUM AND THE ALLIANCE

the children always know to whom they owe this home and their recovery. For all in the home has been personally selected and sent from you and Mrs Levison, and we shall always be thankful to you. I hope that you will pay us a visit next summer after you have been in Sweden."

In 1957 Nahum retired. Two years later he agreed to take charge for ten months of a Centre which the Alliance had opened in Haifa. This venture, with its reading-room and meetings for Hebrew Christians, was in crisis with the sudden departure of its Warden to Brazil. Nahum and Margaret, during a successful stay, also made contact with his Israeli cousins who, twelve years later, welcomed Fred and Mary with a warmth engendered by Nahum's visit. They expressed boundless admiration and affection for him.

When Nahum served on the Bishop of Chichester's Refugee Committee the two men formed a lasting friendship and for at least fifteen years corresponded. The Bishop's letters are brief, and some merely convey Christmas greetings or arrange a meeting; but Nahum kept them. Several times his friend chided him for being over-complimentary. "I was much touched by your very kind letter. You are, as always, far too generous in what you say about my poor self. I am ashamed at the smallness of my efforts when I think of all that you have done and are so tirelessly doing all these years."

When Nahum reported an interview he had had with Dr William Paton and other missionary leaders, Bell responded: "It does seem to me, as you say, that there are outstanding differences in the approach to the whole of the Jewish problem. There are those who minimise the difference between the Jew and the Christian, and as you rightly point out it is one of the paradoxes of the Jewish problem that it needs to be protected against its friends as well as its foes." (24.12.41).

In December 1942 the bishop is glad to hear about "the special committee appointed by your General Assembly in connection with post-war European Jewry;" but "What tragic news it is that comes from Europe; the murder of the President of the Roumanian H.C.A. must have come home to you in a special way. I am interested in your reaction to Mr Eden's declaration. I too feel that it is action to rescue the unhappy victims that is vitally important now, and I cannot somehow bring myself to lay such enormous stress on retribution afterwards, when all the harm and murder is done.

"What you say about the wish to get out of this 'cursed Continent' is very striking. Do you think that there will be a general desire, not by Jews only, to get away from Europe if they can after the war? I hope that your recommendation about the long-term commission will bear fruit."

In 1944 he wrote "You are always the imparter of encouragement and I greatly value what you say. . . I rejoice in the way in which money comes in to I.H.C.A. funds: I have no doubt of your ability and wisdom in making the best use of them."

In a reference to the great blow of William Temple's death, he said, "But now they say that had he recovered he would not have ever got right and resignation would have been inevitable."

When Nahum went to Denmark in 1946 to organise relief he carried an introduction from Bell to the Bishop of Copenhagen: —
"This is to introduce my friend. . . with whom I have worked in different ways on behalf of refugees. . . for some years. He is now in Denmark with a view to purchasing a large amount of food for distribution to Hebrew Christians in Europe."

In 1948 he wrote: "I am very glad to hear of the development of the Alliance's activities. I don't really know what these children — and indeed their elders — would do without the Alliance and your own most self-sacrificing and energetic work. I am glad that the parcels reached Berlin and will almost certainly get through in time for Christmas distribution. I congratulate you most warmly both on those gifts and on the house for the aged. . . But I am very sorry to hear that your health is not better."

Early in 1949 Nahum had an abdominal operation — not the only one. Bell wrote to Margaret: "I am so glad he is getting over the first painful stage and that the surgeon is satisfied. I shall continue to think of him."

By May 1949 their minds have been able to turn beyond the Jewish problem. "I am much interested in what you tell me about the 1st Commandment and the addition of the Greek word for 'mind'. . . I should strongly encourage you to aim at producing a small book setting the legacies of Israel and Greece alongside one another and showing how Christianity is the synthesis. . . Please be careful of yourself after so serious an operation."

In January, 1950: — "I was delighted to get your friendly and kind letter. . . I do greatly appreciate your friendship, and this fresh mark of it. . .

"I am very much interested to read of your cousin's [Jacob

Javits's] interview with the Pope... and action with Ben Gurion... also in what you say about the World Council of Churches and its relation to this particular problem concerning the internationalisation of Jerusalem — and indeed its place in world affairs... I shall be eager to hear about your plans for the journey to Israel in March."

Nahum wrote of what he had seen in Israel, and Bell commented. "What extraordinary generosity the U.S.A. Jews are showing to their unhappy brethren in other parts of the world. I can imagine something of what this tremendous inflow must mean for such a small country as Israel... What you say about the secret believers is very interesting too." (4.5.50).

A fortnight later Bell replied to Nahum's thoughts on China. "What you say about China is extremely important. I am asking Dr Mackie who is in charge of the Inter Church Aid Department... to look into the possibilities of the World Council being or providing such an agency. It is probably a matter in which the World Council would have to consult the Missionary Council and the National Christian Council of China."

Nahum also had ideas about a Biblical Institute in Jerusalem; and Bell raised the matter at a W.C.C. Executive Committee meeting at Toronto. He also discussed it with Mr Ransom (Secretary of the I.M.C.), Dr Goodall of Edinburgh House, Dr John Baillie and others. The idea was welcome but it was felt that the interested parties, which were the I.H.C.A., the Church of Scotland and the Church of Sweden, should get together and formulate a plan. "Something was also said about the uncertainty of the present position while the inter-governmental status of Jerusalem is unsettled. I am afraid you may be disappointed with this. Dr Goodall has promised to keep me in touch with any further enquiries he makes. I stressed the importance of the angle being of biblical study and research, and not a Christian approach to the Jews." (22.7.50).

Was it this initiative of Nahum's, one wonders, which eventually led to the foundation of the Ecumenical Institute for such a purpose at Tantur on the Jerusalem-Bethlehem road?

Three months later Bell wrote: "I shall be deeply interested to hear how the plan goes. I am very glad you are in touch with Principal Baillie. But I am terribly sorry to hear that you are to have a rather large operation this week. I do trust and pray that all may go well. You are a most precious servant of Christ and humanity as well as minister of the Church, with a great care for your fellow human beings and for the victims of persecution which the Church and humanity both need so terribly at the present time. Do please ask your wife to let me know how you are. May God bless you and keep you and all the heavenly powers watch over you."

In May, 1951, the Bishop was heavily engaged in the Festival of Britain and apologised for a brief note in which he said, "I am very sorry to hear of the realisation of your fears about the rising of a Judaising sect in Israel."

In January, 1952: "I am delighted that you are continuing with your book. . . it will mean a lot to scholars and divines, as well as to the ordinary person interested in the Greek and Hebrew contributions to Christianity. What you tell me about the Scandinavian "Cultic School" is news to me. . .

"You ask me about the Cross and its meaning. I agree with you that the Cross itself seems a repudiation of impassibility. I am much taken by your suggestion as to its meaning. For myself, I find the Cross a fact which remains a mystery; and I am very reserved in what I say about it. Scholastic theories and detailed assessments do not find much harbour in my own heart and mind. But your exposition, provided it is taken as symbolic, and leaving the mystery untouched, is something which has, as it seems to me, so much truth in it as ought to find a place in the full account which one day we shall be given."

Nine months pass and the discussion continues: "It was very nice to hear from you and to hear more of your theological studies, and also to read what you say about the atonement." He was also interested in what Nahum told him about reparation discussions, and the possibility of non-Aryan Christians getting some compensation; but was unable to accept a place on the *ad hoc* committee — "I am not good at financial matters anyhow, and if you are on a Finance Committee you cannot really be a sleeping partner."

The final letter is dated 26th June, 1954. After thanking Nahum for "your all too kind words about my Silver Jubilee," Bell expresses interest "in what you tell me both about your writing and about the Arab refugee problem. I fear that political questions do, as you say, only too often enter in here and stop the Arab States doing what they should do." And he adds as a postscript, "If I get a chance of a word

THE AFTER YEARS: KATIE, NAHUM AND THE ALLIANCE

about the Christian Institution for Study I'll remember your words."

Much of Nahum's writing remained unpublished, but he produced several articles for the theological journals. When the decision to publish one on "*Theocracy, Hierocracy, and Early Jewish Sects*" in the Transactions of the Glasgow University Oriental Society was conveyed to him, the Secretary wrote, "The *viva voce* delivery of your paper without reference to your notes received much favourable comment."

Another article on *Lutron* (Ransom) brought a note of thanks from Professor George Knight: "I want to thank you for emphasising the very necessary point that ethically 'God must share responsibility with me, for He gave me the freedom to sin'. . . . That is why I am thanking you. . . since I believe that Christian Theology should not be afraid of Patripassianism[3] even though it cannot subscribe to it in full."

Through his availability to students at whose Hebrew classes he gave part-time tuition, as well as in his writings, Nahum continued to exert an influence; and when his own minister, Henry Young, visited America he found that he was known and respected there.

Nahum at 72

335

"In 1960 when I gave a series of addresses at the Princeton Summer School of Theology, young ministers were eager to know if I had acquaintance with 'Rabbi' Levison, from whom they had learned much whilst in Edinburgh. The same thing happened at a ministers' conference in Monterey in California."

In his seventies Nahum retained his capacity for fresh thinking. In 1960, aged 72 and newly returned from Haifa, he made a strong plea at the General Assembly that a Christian centre should be established in one of Israel's new towns — a plea which has gone unheeded. The principal Churches and Societies, he pointed out, were still concentrated in Jerusalem, Jaffa, Tel Aviv, Tiberias and, in one instance, Haifa. But the development of natural resources had led to new industrial communities. "I can think of one new township", he told an interviewer, "which already has a population of 75,000. In a few years it will be one of the most important centres in Israel. . . The Church of Scotland should send into one of these new townships an ordained minister. . . who would cater to the Christians who are coming in as well as the Jews. . . It would be a real step towards establishing common ground between Christian and Jew." It was a progressive idea; but if the only way to achieve it were by relinquishing the Tiberias Hospice, where mission is allied to a Christian tourist centre, Nahum was asking for the seemingly impossible — or was his the larger vision?

In 1963 the debate on the admission of women to the ministry was galvanised in Scotland by Mary Lusk's appeal to the General Assembly for ordination. Nahum did not meet Mary until, two years later, she married Fred, but there was no doubt where his sympathies lay. Like her he was concerned neither with feminism nor with undue reverence for tradition but only with theological truth. Her appeal was based on the grounds of her baptism. In Christ there is neither male nor female. Those baptised into Him, men and women, are equally vehicles of His spirit, and thus able to dispense the sacraments — it is as simple as that. Nahum when he met Mary made it plain that he agreed. He was unhampered by tradition, having seen its stultifying effect in rabbinic Judaism, and for him God was free to call whom he would — and had He not in the past called Deborah and Miriam, Esther, and Philip's prophetess daughters? He would have welcomed both the women rabbis of the Reformed Synagogue and women in the ministry and the priesthood. He did not live to see Mary's ordination, but his appreciation was apparent when she broadcast a *Thought for the Day*. She had scarcely returned from the studio when a deep voice came on the phone saying, "I do not know whether it was the Archangel Gab-ri-el or the Angel Mich-a-el who told me to switch on my wireless today. . . ."

In his eightieth year he sat at his typewriter completing his *Outline of Biblical Theology*. He also read and corresponded widely; and one of the books that pleased him most was *The Table Talk of A.N. Whitehead*. Professor Whitehead was a polymath whose mind roamed over civilisations, philosophies, mathematics, science, and history both ancient and modern. Nahum, who also, as was said of Milton, "took all knowledge for his province", met in him a kindred spirit.

It is typical too that when he went into hospital in his final illness he took with him not the light bedside reading of ordinary mortals but the first volumes of Gibbon's *Decline and Fall of the Roman Empire* to re-read!

"Like the seer after whom he was named", wrote Harcourt Samuel in the *Quarterly*, "Nahum Levison could well be called a minor prophet, but his ministry was very different; he was not called to declare God's vengeance but God's grace; this he did — not only by lip, but by his gentleness and kindness. Once when he was asked advice upon modes of communicating the Gospel he replied, 'Tell them about your own experience of God in Jesus Christ.' From the time he left home and country in search of Jesus Christ he gave Him love, loyalty and unflagging service."

For him, the words from Daniel seem singularly apt: "Those who are wise will shine like the brightness of the heavens, and those who lead many to righteousness like the stars for ever and ever."

NOTES:
1. The Logie-Pirie Hostel was sold and the girls transferred to Memorial House which could accommodate sixteen people; and an inscription to Mrs Logie-Pirie was placed therein.
2. See Appendix B.
3. The belief that God the Father suffered in His Son.

26. LEON

This is Leon's biography; and it is with him that it must end.

In retrospect we must ask whether his dreams of a colony and of a Church have any permanent value. Or were they only a quest for Utopia, now to be forgotten; over fifty years on, a dead letter?

The word 'colony' belongs to the past; but the need for a refuge for the poor and the persecuted, while mercifully in abeyance, is never irrelevant: and the need for a living witness at the heart of Jewry remains. The Christian presence, chiefly in Jerusalem, of numerous Churches and sects is so familiar that it is largely ignored. A Hebrew Christian presence, as Leon saw, would offer a sharper challenge. Today, perhaps, this would be best achieved not by a colony but by the Messianic Jews in Israel coming together to rebuild a stronger Alliance; its fellowship fostered by Christian forms of Jewish traditions, of Kaddesh, Chanukkah and, above all, the Haggadah as envisaged by the I.H.C.A. (see Appendix B).

His vision of a Church has a renewed topicality. For, especially in the United States, there has been a rapid growth of Messianic Jewish congregations. Fifty-eight (and it is said there are many more) have formed a Union; while in London, at Golders Green, there is a British one. Its pastor is a Messianic Rabbi, ordained in San Francisco. He has announced that he hopes "to teach prophecy and fulfilment as we approach the end of days", a form of adventist belief to which not all Christians subscribe. Does this not indicate the need for that doctrinal foundation, so fundamental to Leon and Nahum, which is encapsulated in the Articles of Faith for a Hebrew Christian Church? (Appendix A). Perhaps the embryonic worldwide Messianic Jewish Church could be saved from sectarianism and set on a true course by the blueprint drawn up in the 1930's.

Leon would still be a visionary; not only for the Hebrew Christians but for his trouble-torn native land. For Jew and Arab, whom he would see living together in partnership, not in opposition. Even now, when their separate political existence seems inevitable, his dream would be of tolerance, forgiveness and love. Would this be crying for the moon? But the Prophets did that when they dared to dream of the lion lying down with the lamb and men studying war no more. And their dream was not futile, but remains a beacon for mankind.

Leon knew the failings of both Jew and Arab. Both were capable of perfidy, intolerance and fanaticism. When a Jew loses his faith, he more than once remarked, he can sink low. But, as in the analogy of the strawberries, he judged both by their best. And he would have welcomed such movements as *Neve Shalom*, the peace project in which a French Dominican, Father Bruno Hussar, has brought together, at Latrun, Christians, Moslems and Jews in a kind of Middle Eastern Corrymeela. (At Corrymeela, in Northern Ireland, a community of Protestants and Catholics work and pray together for understanding, reconciliation and peace.) Leon would, however, declare that one thing above all can provide a lasting solution for this as for every form of racial conflict — the reconciling power of the spirit of Christ.

This was St Paul's way of looking at things, and in many ways he was a modern St Paul. He did not have the apostle's theological capacity — that goes without saying — but he had something of his missionary zeal and universal vision. Again, he too made journeys to far-flung coteries of Jews, despised and rejected for becoming Christians, greeting them, thanking God for their steadfast faith and building them up.

The Pauline analogy cannot be pressed. Would St Paul, were he alive today be, for instance, an enthusiastic Freemason, enjoy a smoke and a game of bridge, or even have had Leon's political leanings? He would certainly have been a clubbable man, rejoicing in his friends and caring for his converts, as Leon cared for the Hebrew Christians "in minute particulars" — the only way, as Blake saw, to do good to another. It was typical of Leon that, at his last meeting of the Alliance's Executive Committee, he read in full a long letter from a young medical missionary whom the Alliance had sponsored and who had newly arrived at a Baptist outpost in the Belgian Congo (now Zaire).

Another small incident is both typical and Pauline. A Hebrew Christian, now 87, has a cherished memory of how he greeted her on the several occasions when they met. "It was always with the Aaronic blessing pronounced with the most beautiful Hebrew intonation."

It was this concern for the individual combined with the love of Christ that made him the missionary he was.

Yet behind it all lay that which the Jew finds it hard to understand: what it is that can turn a Jew into a Christian, and what makes a Hebrew Christian "tick". A life such as Leon's may help some to see it. There is also an explanation where a Christian would look for it — in the sayings of Jesus. In two short parables, for instance: of the pearl merchant who could only acquire a supreme pearl by sacrificing the lesser ones; and the farmer who found treasure in a field and "for sheer joy went and sold everything he had, and bought that field." If following Jesus meant the loss of many dearly prized blessings which a Jewish upbringing had bestowed, or even total loss, the prize far outweighed the cost. And if the cost was also hostility and abuse, to bear these for Christ brought His comfort: "How blest are you, when you suffer insults and persecution and every kind of calumny for my sake. Accept it with gladness and exultation."

That Leon was a true Christian cannot be denied. But was he a renegade Jew? The title of this book will be anathema to many Jews who hold that "Christian and Jew" is an impossible combination. An agnostic Jew may maintain his Jewish identity, but the Christian Jew, they say, is no longer a Jew. He has joined another race, has become indistinguishable from his non-Jewish neighbours and is lost in an alien culture.

Furthermore, to many of Leon's fellow Jews his chief affront was that he married a *goy*, or Gentile, and became racially impure. This fact would disturb no-one outside a highly tribal community; for is not the blood of millions an amalgam from the immemorial racial melting-pot? Only to a stateless Jew, or to a modern Israeli with a more than normal passion to belong, to create an exclusive identity expressed in pride of country, tradition, and language, would this appear a selling of the pass.

Leon was right to marry Katie, for they were perfectly matched. No one could have supported him as she did. Certainly there was no other course; there was not at that time or place any Hebrew Christian girl with whom he might have fallen in love. Daniel Barenboim's mixed marriage was resolved by his bride, Jacqueline du Pré, accepting the Jewish faith, as did the actress Felicity Kendall. That option was not open to Leon and Katie, but because the faith they shared was not that of Judaism he was sometimes vilified. This would not have worried him, nor would the fact that assimilation was inevitable. For he saw that in the last resort neither race nor nationality was paramount. To be a "new man in Christ" was all that mattered. The communion of saints is raceless, classless, and without the differentiations of colour and nationhood that distinguish earthly kingdoms. "In Christ" as St Paul saw "there is neither Jew nor Greek". When Leon came to Scotland he said, like Ruth, another emigrant who assimilated (but *into* Judah), "Your people shall be my people, and your God my God." At the same time, the land of his birth never ceased to be precious to him nor his heritage dear. But he did not impose these things on his children. He set them free to cherish the people and country they treasured most, and to transcend all divisive distinctions as he had done.

Nor were his children greatly deprived thereby. In life's busier years they could hardly be expected to enter fully into a double inheritance, and it was natural that they should neglect their Jewish one. It is also natural if, as they grow older, they turn back to it and are grateful. In any case those who assimilate cannot entirely rid themselves of the past. Siegfried Sassoon, like Leon's children a Hebrew Christian of the second generation, maintained that in his subconscious mind he remained Jewish; that he had racial memories; and that to his patriarchal forebears he almost certainly owed his love of music, his poetic gift and his idealism. We who are of Hebrew blood but of a Christian family may also, though seeing it less clearly, be similarly endowed.

That our inheritance is peculiarly missionary was one of Leon's convictions. He saw the Jews as a mobile, adaptable, eloquent and potentially missionary people — none more so than those who had been freed from the exclusiveness of Judaism, from the dangers of crude nationalism and from every form of religious narrowness. These through their religious nature and their historic path are moulded and equipped to be missionaries both to their fellow Jews and to all mankind.

His vocation as missionary was, to him, the greatest of vocations, and he expected the Churches to give missionary work high priority. His own Church was, in his lifetime, more missionary-centred than it is today. (Were not St Paul's words "to the Jew first", interpreted by many as a missionary imperative?) Even so, he wanted more. Why, he would ask, is the Moderator never a product of the mission field? There are able Indian and African Christians, whose witness would be tremendous if the Church would thus honour them. Any church lawyer could raise formidable obstacles to such a proposal; nor could it be resurrected today, when overseas Christians belong to their own indigenous churches. Yet it was a visionary and radical suggestion, denoting the kind of opportunity conventional Churches often miss.

Today the missionary, especially if he is an evangelist, is looked on in many quarters as an unwelcome intruder. "All that most Jews really ask from Christians" wrote Clifford Longley in *The Times* (7.1.89), "is to be left alone; they have no incentive to enquire what Christians really believe." In the Anglican Church, according to Mr Longley, those who promote missionary activity among the Jews "are generally seen as a slightly batty fringe by the other much larger bodies of opinion." Leon, however, was an unapologetic missionary. To him what Christians believe was so glorious it must be shared. Like the apostle Andrew he wanted to introduce his brother Jew to Jesus. It was as straightforward as that. All religions may be pathways to God, but in Jesus alone are His mind and heart, His grace and joy, and His companionship fully given. Knowing this he could not understand why any Christian should demur or any Jew take umbrage.

He himself was equipped as a missionary not only by the largeness of his outlook but by those gifts of the Spirit listed by St Paul: "love, joy, peace, patience, kindness, goodness, fidelity, gentleness and self-control." In Katie's eyes he was, if not a saint, at least a paragon. But either word is to be used warily. He was not patently holy nor disciplined in prayer, but he was whole and, as we have seen, had a holistic vision, and a profound faith. Nor was he without the ordinary faults and foibles; he could be ingratiating, flattering people more than they deserved; sometimes he stretched the truth; he was often blind to other people's failings; and, less reprehensibly, often untidy in his habits, scattering cigarette-ash and papers around him, his study a shambles.

He had, too, the limitations of his time. He remained, for instance, intransigently anti-Roman Catholic; but theirs, before Vatican II, was an intransigent Church. We were strangers, not fellow-pilgrims. Today, when it is acknowledged on both sides that in the great Reformation debate on justification and salvation there were misunderstandings; when Protestant-Catholic dialogue includes the formerly *tabu* subject of the place of Mary, whose devotion is being shorn of its more unacceptable accretions; when there is joint Bible study and both a Catholic-Jewish and a W.C.C.-Jewish dialogue (the latter declaring that the Church can learn from the Jewish Exodus theology), Leon would have been open-minded and ecumenical. Especially would he have welcomed the news of Hebrew Christian priests (one of whom, Father Elias Friedman of Haifa, has written on spirituality) and of the Association of Hebrew Catholics to whom he would have been eager to make an approach. That there is still much in Rome that he would have found unacceptable would not have deterred him. We must wait and see whether it will deter the Alliance.

He was fallible and had limitations; but the phrase "secular saint" cannot be ruled out. It depends what you mean. Someone said that the saints were those who "were cheerful when it was difficult to be cheerful, and patient when it was difficult to be patient; and pushed on when they wanted to stand still, and kept silent when they wanted to talk, and were agreeable when they wanted to be disagreeable." He could have had Leon in mind.

And the words with which Archbishop Söderblom of Uppsala concluded his Gifford Lectures in 1931 are also near the mark:

"When God's rule has penetrated a man's heart and life, so that the divine love and righteousness become the main factor, we speak of a saint. But the idea of saints is too great a thing and too much neglected in Evangelical-Catholic Christendom to be handled here. . . Here I give only my definition: a saint is he who reveals God's might. Saints are such as show clearly and plainly in their lives and deeds and in their very being that God lives."

In these terms many, many saints, fallible and human, have crossed the pages of this book; and the prince of them was Leon.

When he died Hugh Schonfield's tribute was a poem. It makes a fitting conclusion.

"Lion you were,
and we, who mourn your passing,
salute the courage in you
which withstood
oppression and the slanderous word.

> Statesman you were,
> and we of lesser vision
> salute the builder in you
> who planned
> sanely and with practical hand.

Jew you were,
and we in race your brothers
salute the mystic in you
which, by grace,
saw Messiah with unveiled face.

> Friend you were,
> and we, whose hearts you captured,
> cherish the loving life in you,
> again made known,
> even by laying down your own."

CHRISTIAN AND JEW

'And I have come so far; and the sights and thoughts of my youth pursue me; and I see like a vision the youth of my father, and of his father, and the whole stream of lives flowing down. . . with the sound of laughter and tears, to cast me out in the end, as by a sudden freshet, on these ultimate islands. And I admire and bow my head before the romance of destiny.'

R.L. Stevenson

Appendices.

Appendix A

Proposed Principles of Faith for the suggested Hebrew Christian Church.

Hear, O Israel, the Lord our God is one Lord and thou shalt love the Lord thy God with all thine heart and with all thy soul and all thy might, and thy neighbour as thyself.

Article 1. I BELIEVE in God, the Source of all being, the Covenant God, the Holy One of Israel, our Heavenly Father.

Article 2. I BELIEVE that God Who spake at sundry times and divers manners in time past to the fathers through the prophets, promised to redeem the world from sin and death, in and through His Anointed, Who should be a light to lighten the Gentiles and the glory of His people Israel.

Article 3. I BELIEVE that in the fulness of time God fulfilled His promise and sent forth His Son, His eternal Word, Jesus, the Messiah, Who was born by the power of the Holy Spirit, of the Virgin Mary, who was of the family of David, so that in Him the Word was made flesh and dwelt among us full of grace and truth.

Article 4. I BELIEVE that Jesus the Messiah is in very truth the Shekinah, the brightness of the Father's glory, the very impress of His Person, that He was made unto us wisdom from God, and righteousness and sanctification, and that by His Life, Death on the Cross and glorious Resurrection, He has accomplished our Reconciliation with the Father.

Article 5. I BELIEVE that the Father sealed all that the Son was, did, and taught, by raising Him through the Holy Spirit from the dead, and that the Risen and Glorified Lord appeared to many and communed with them, and then Ascended to be our Mediator with the Father and to reign with Him, One God.

Article 6. I BELIEVE that the Holy Spirit, the Paraclete, Who proceeds from the Father and the Son, was sent to be with us, to give us assurance of the forgiveness of sin and to lead us into the fulness of truth and the more abundant life.

Article 7. I BELIEVE that the Holy Spirit, Who beareth witness with our spirits that we are the sons of God, will quicken us in the resurrection when we shall be clothed with the body which it shall please the Father to give us.

Article 8. I BELIEVE that the Church of the Messiah is the family of God in Heaven and on Earth, the Sanctuary of the redeemed in which God dwells and of which the Messiah Jesus is the only Head.

Article 9. I BELIEVE that the Old and New Testaments as written are the divinely inspired records of God's revelation to Israel and the World, and are the only rule of faith and life.

Article 10. I BELIEVE that it is the Will of God, Who has graciously brought us into the new Covenant, that we should strive to be His witnesses, making the teaching and life of the Messiah our standard and example, till He comes again to reign in power and glory.

Article 11. I BELIEVE that the Church visible maintains unbroken continuity with the Church in Heaven by partaking of the same blessed Sacraments of Baptism and of Holy Communion and by confessing the same Father, Son and Holy Spirit, One Godhead.

Appendix B

HAGADAR FOR A CHRISTIAN SEDER

"Passover", wrote Leon, "is above everything the Commemoration of a great Deliverance — a deliverance which transformed a horde of slaves into a people. No other festival brings a Jew into such close touch with his people's past. He is one, for the moment, with his ransomed fathers; he shares with them the proud consciousness of the free."

He described it as "the only joyful feast in the Jewish Calendar," and as expressing the equality of all humanity "in God." "On this night there is no servant and master. Every Jew on this night is considered to be a priest and a prince unto God, and every Jewess a priestess and a princess."

He believed that this greatest of Jewish feasts was in Jesus' mind and that the feast he instituted had a Pascal character. "It was meant to commemorate the sacrifice of the Lamb of God upon the Cross of which the sacrifices of the Lamb year by year at Passover time [now discontinued] were but the faint types and shadows." And he saw that when a Jew became a Christian the feast which had meant so much to him would not become empty but take on new meaning.

Instead of abandoning it, Hebrew Christians could rejoice in their Jewish heritage and in the recital (*hagadar*) of the seminal and divine events of their national life.

When, with his colleagues on the Hebrew Christian Church Commission, he examined the question of a liturgy, some form of a Hebrew Christian Passover celebration must have been mooted. Yet the seed did not bear fruit for another 35 years. It was in 1969 that the Alliance published, first in English and later in Hebrew and English, a *HAGADAR for a Christian Seder*. It is not the only attempt to combine Passover and Eucharist. E.P. Lipson, a President of the I.H.C.A., also produced a *Christian Hagadah*; and David Bronstein, a Secretary of the American Alliance, a *Siddur* (Prayer Book) which is widely used by the Messianic Congregations of the U.S.A. Congregations of the U.S.A.

The Alliance's version has for some twenty years found considerable acceptance.[1] In it the declaration of the mighty acts of God is extended to include the fulfilment of the type of the Passover in the death and resurrection of Jesus Christ, and yet it does not necessarily include a celebration of the Sacrament.

The opening words are: "As Hebrew Christians we gladly join with our people in joyful remembrance of the redemption from Egypt. We remember, too, with deep gratitude our redemption from sin through our Lord and Saviour Jesus Christ."

When the removal of leaven in the days of preparation is recalled, St Paul's words about celebrating with the *matzah* (unleavened bread) of sincerity and truth is quoted (I Cor. 5:7).

Only twice, during the rest of the Seder, are there any Christian addenda. After the Thanksgivings, culminating in "fed us with the manna and gave us the Sabbath and brought us to Sinai and gave us His Word", is added "and sent the Messiah as a reconciliation and atonement for all our sins". And in the prayers that follow the Hallel (Psalms 114-116 of which a shortened version is provided in responsive form) there is "Worthy is the Lamb that was slain and has redeemed us. . . ."

In footnotes, however, there are several relevant Christian comments, none more so than at the closing words, "Next year in Jerusalem", where a wider context is given by recalling "The holy city, new Jerusalem, coming down out of heaven from God (Rev. 22:2)."

What will be found most moving, perhaps, are words spoken with the Third Cup — the cup after supper, chosen by Jesus as symbol of the new life which would be given through His death: "On this night of the Seder we remember with reverence and love the six million of our people of the European exile who perished at the hands of a tyrant more wicked than the Pharoah who enslaved our fathers in Egypt. . . On the first day of Passover the remnants in the Ghetto of Warsaw rose up against the adversary, even as in the days of Judas the Maccabee. They were lovely and pleasant in their lives, and in their death they were not divided, and they brought redemption to the name of Israel through all the world. And from the depths of their affliction many lifted their voices in a song of faith in the coming of the Messiah, when justice and brotherhood will reign among men."

NOTES:
1. It can be obtained from the I.H.C.A. Office, "Shalom", Brockenhurst Road, Ramsgate, Kent, CT11 8ED.